THE
ANATOMY OF
FASCISM

THE ANATOMY OF FASCISM

ROBERT O. PAXTON

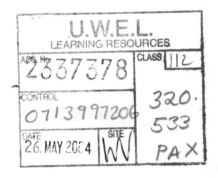

ALLEN LANE
an imprint of
PENGUIN BOOKS

ALLEN LANE

Published by the Penguin Group
Penguin Books Ltd, 80 Strand, London WC2R 0RL, England
Penguin Group (USA) Inc., 375 Hudson Street, New York, New York 10014, USA
Penguin Books Australia Ltd, 250 Camberwell Road,
Camberwell, Victoria 3124, Australia
Penguin Books Canada Ltd, 10 Alcorn Avenue, Toronto, Ontario, Canada M4V 3B2
Penguin Books India (P) Ltd, 11 Community Centre,
Panchsheel Park, New Delhi – 110 017, India
Penguin Group (NZ), Cnr Airborne and Rosedale Roads,
Albany, Auckland 1310, New Zealand
Penguin Books (South Africa) (Pty) Ltd, 24 Sturdee Avenue,
Rosebank 2196, South Africa

Penguin Books Ltd, Registered Offices: 80 Strand, London WC2R 0RL, England

www.penguin.com

First published in the United States of America by Alfred A. Knopf 2004
Published simultaneously in Great Britain by Allen Lane 2004

Printed in Great Britain by Clays Ltd, St Ives plc

A CIP catalogue record for this book is available from the British Library

ISBN 0–713–99720–6

To Sarah

CONTENTS

Preface   *xi*

CHAPTER 1   Introduction   3
             The Invention of Fascism   3
             Images of Fascism   9
             Strategies   15
             Where Do We Go from Here?   20

CHAPTER 2   Creating Fascist Movements   24
             The Immediate Background   28
             Intellectual, Cultural, and Emotional Roots   32
             Long-Term Preconditions   42
             Precursors   44
             Recruitment   49
             Understanding Fascism by Its Origins   52

CHAPTER 3   Taking Root   55
             Successful Fascisms   55
             (1) The Po Valley, Italy, 1920–22   58
             (2) Schleswig-Holstein, Germany, 1928–33   64
             An Unsuccessful Fascism: France, 1924–40   68
             Some Other Unsuccessful Fascisms   73
             Comparisons and Conclusions   76

Contents

CHAPTER 4   Getting Power   87

Mussolini and the "March on Rome"   87

Hitler and the "Backstairs Conspiracy"   91

What Did Not Happen: Election, Coup d'Etat,
Solo Triumph   96

Forming Alliances   98

What Fascists Offered the Establishment   102

The Prefascist Crisis   105

Revolutions after Power: Germany and Italy   106

Comparisons and Alternatives   110

CHAPTER 5   Exercising Power   119

The Nature of Fascist Rule: "Dual State"
and Dynamic Shapelessness   119

The Tug-of-War between Fascists and Conservatives   128

The Tug-of-War between Leader and Party   131

The Tug-of-War between Party and State   133

Accommodation, Enthusiasm, Terror   135

The Fascist "Revolution"   141

CHAPTER 6   The Long Term: Radicalization or Entropy?   148

What Drives Radicalization?   153

Trying to Account for the Holocaust   158

Italian Radicalization: Internal Order, Ethiopia, Salò   164

Final Thoughts   169

CHAPTER 7   Other Times, Other Places   172

Is Fascism Still Possible?   172

Western Europe since 1945   175

Post-Soviet Eastern Europe   188

Fascism Outside Europe   191

Contents

CHAPTER 8   What Is Fascism?   206

Conflicting Interpretations   207

Boundaries   215

What Is Fascism?   218

Bibliographical Essay   221

Notes   251

Index   309

PREFACE

For many years I taught a university course on fascism, sometimes as a graduate seminar, sometimes as an undergraduate seminar. The more I read about fascism and the more I discussed it with students, the more perplexed I grew. While an abundance of brilliant monographs dealt illuminatingly with particular aspects of Mussolini's Italy, Hitler's Germany, and their like, books about fascism as a generic phenomenon often seemed to me, in comparison with the monographs, abstract, stereotyped, and bloodless.

This book is an attempt to draw the monographic literature more closely into a discussion of fascism in general, and to present fascism in a way that takes into account its variations and complexity. It seeks to find out how fascism worked. That is why it focuses more closely on the actions of fascists than on their words, contrary to usual practice. It also spends more time than usual on the allies and accomplices of fascism, and on the ways fascist regimes interacted with the larger societies they sought to transform.

This is an essay, not an encyclopedia. Many readers may find their favorite subject treated here more cursorily than they would like. I hope that what I have written will tempt them to read further. That is the purpose of the endnotes and the extensive critical bibliographical essay.

Having worked on this subject off and on for many years, I have incurred more than the usual number of intellectual and personal debts. The Rockefeller Foundation enabled me to rough out the chapters at the Villa Serbelloni, just across Lake Como from where Partisans killed Mussolini in April 1945. The École des Hautes Études en Sciences Sociales in Paris, the Istituto Universitario Europeo in Florence, and a number of American universities let me try out some of these ideas in the seminar room and lecture hall. A generation of Columbia students challenged my interpretations.

Philippe Burrin, Paul Corner, Patrizia Dogliani, and Henry Ashby

Turner, Jr., generously reviewed an earlier version of this work. Carol Gluck, Herbert S. Klein, and Ken Ruoff read portions of the manuscript. All saved me from embarrassing errors, and I accepted most of their suggestions. If I had accepted them all, this would probably be a better book. I am also grateful for various kinds of help to Drue Heinz, Stuart J. Woolf, Stuart Proffitt, Bruce Lawder, Carlo Moos, Fred Wakeman, Jeffrey Bale, Joel Colton, Stanley Hoffmann, Juan Linz, and the reference staff of the Columbia University libraries. The errors that remain are the fault of the author alone.

Above all, Sarah Plimpton was steadfast in encouragement and wise and discerning as a critical reader.

New York, February 2003

THE
ANATOMY OF
FASCISM

CHAPTER 1

Introduction

The Invention of Fascism

Fascism was the major political innovation of the twentieth century, and the source of much of its pain. The other major currents of modern Western political culture—conservatism, liberalism, socialism—all reached mature form between the late eighteenth century and the mid-nineteenth century. Fascism, however, was still unimagined as late as the 1890s. Friedrich Engels, writing a preface in 1895 for his new edition of Karl Marx's *The Class Struggles in France*, clearly believed that wider suffrage would inexorably deliver more votes to the Left. Both time and numbers, Engels was certain, were on the socialists' side. "If it [the growing socialist vote] continues in this fashion, by the end of this [nineteenth] century we [socialists] shall conquer the major part of the middle strata of society, petty bourgeois and peasants, and grow into the decisive power in the land." Conservatives, Engels wrote, had noticed that legality was working against them. By contrast, "we [socialists], under this legality, get firm muscles and rosy cheeks and look like life eternal. There is nothing for them [the conservatives] to do but break through this legality themselves."[1] While Engels thus expected that the Left's enemies would launch a preemptive attack, he could not imagine in 1895 that this might win mass approval. Dictatorship against the Left amidst popular enthusiasm— that was the unexpected combination that fascism would manage to put together one short generation later.

There were only a few glimmers of premonition. One came from an inquisitive young French aristocrat, Alexis de Tocqueville. Although Tocqueville found much to admire on his visit to the United States in 1831, he was troubled by the majority's power in a democracy to impose

3

conformity by social pressure, in the absence of an independent social elite.

> The kind of oppression with which democratic peoples are threatened will resemble nothing that had preceded it in the world; our contemporaries would not find its image in their memories. I myself seek in vain an expression that exactly reproduces the idea that I form of it for myself and that contains it; the old words despotism and tyranny are not suitable. The thing is new, therefore I must try to define it, since I can not name it.[2]

Another premonition came at the eleventh hour from a French engineer turned social commentator, Georges Sorel. In 1908 Sorel criticized Marx for failing to notice that "a revolution accomplished in times of decadence" could "take a return to the past or even social conservation as its ideal."[3]

The word *fascism*[4] has its root in the Italian *fascio*, literally a bundle or sheaf. More remotely, the word recalled the Latin *fasces*, an axe encased in a bundle of rods that was carried before the magistrates in Roman public processions to signify the authority and unity of the state. Before 1914, the symbolism of the Roman *fasces* was usually appropriated by the Left. Marianne, symbol of the French Republic, was often portrayed in the nineteenth century carrying the *fasces* to represent the force of Republican solidarity against her aristocratic and clerical enemies.[5] *Fasces* are prominently displayed on Christopher Wren's Sheldonian Theater (1664–69) at Oxford University. They appeared on the Lincoln Memorial in Washington (1922) and on the United States quarter minted in 1932.[6]

Italian revolutionaries used the term *fascio* in the late nineteenth century to evoke the solidarity of committed militants. The peasants who rose against their landlords in Sicily in 1893–94 called themselves the Fasci Siciliani. When in late 1914 a group of left-wing nationalists, soon joined by the socialist outcast Benito Mussolini,[7] sought to bring Italy into World War I on the Allied side, they chose a name designed to communicate both the fervor and the solidarity of their campaign: the Fascio Rivoluzionario d'Azione Interventista (Revolutionary League for Interventionist Action).[8] At the end of World War I, Mussolini coined the term *fascismo* to describe the mood of the little band of nationalist ex-soldiers and pro-war syndicalist[9] revolutionaries that he was gathering around himself. Even then, he had no monopoly on the word *fascio*, which remained in general use for activist groups of various political hues.[10]

Officially, Fascism was born in Milan on Sunday, March 23, 1919. That morning, somewhat more than a hundred persons,[11] including war veterans, syndicalists who had supported the war, and Futurist[12] intellectuals, plus some reporters and the merely curious, gathered in the meeting room of the Milan Industrial and Commercial Alliance, overlooking the Piazza San Sepolcro, to "declare war against socialism . . . because it has opposed nationalism."[13] Now Mussolini called his movement the Fasci di Combattimento, which means, very approximately, "fraternities of combat."

The Fascist program, issued two months later, was a curious mixture of veterans' patriotism and radical social experiment, a kind of "national socialism." On the national side, it called for fulfilling Italian expansionist aims in the Balkans and around the Mediterranean that had just been frustrated a few months before at the Paris Peace Conference. On the radical side, it proposed women's suffrage and the vote at eighteen, abolition of the upper house, convocation of a constituent assembly to draft a new constitution for Italy (presumably without the monarchy), the eight-hour workday, worker participation in "the technical management of industry," the "partial expropriation of all kinds of wealth" by a heavy and progressive tax on capital, the seizure of certain Church properties, and the confiscation of 85 percent of war profits.[14]

Mussolini's movement was not limited to nationalism and assaults on property. It boiled with the readiness for violent action, anti-intellectualism, rejection of compromise, and contempt for established society that marked the three groups who made up the bulk of his first followers—demobilized war veterans, pro-war syndicalists, and Futurist intellectuals.

Mussolini—himself an ex-soldier who boasted of his forty wounds[15]—hoped to make his political comeback as a veterans' leader. A solid core of his followers came from the Arditi—select commando units hardened by front-line experience who felt entitled to rule the country they had saved.

The pro-war syndicalists had been Mussolini's closest associates during the struggle to bring Italy into the war in May 1915. Syndicalism was the main working-class rival to parliamentary socialism in Europe before World War I. While most socialists by 1914 were organized in electoral parties that competed for parliamentary seats, syndicalists were rooted in trade unions ("syndicates"). Whereas parliamentary socialists worked for piecemeal reforms while awaiting the historical development that Marxists predicted would make capitalism obsolete, syndicalists, scornful of the compromises required by parliamentary action and of most socialists' commitment to gradual evolution, believed they could overthrow capitalism by the force of their will. By concentrating on their ultimate revolutionary goal rather than on each trade's petty workplace concerns, they could form "one big union" and bring down capitalism all at once in one momentous general strike. After capitalism's collapse, workers organized within their "syndicates" would remain as the sole functioning units of production and exchange in a free collectivist society.[16] By May 1915, while all Italian parliamentary socialists and most Italian syndicalists adamantly opposed Italian entry into World War I, a few ardent spirits around Mussolini concluded that warfare would drive Italy further toward social revolution than would remaining neutral. They had become "national syndicalists."[17]

The third component of Mussolini's first Fascists were young antibourgeois intellectuals and aesthetes such as the Futurists. The Futurists were a loose association of artists and writers who espoused Filippo Tommaso Marinetti's "Futurist Manifestos," the first of which had been published in Paris in 1909. Marinetti's followers dismissed the cultural legacy of the past collected in museums and libraries and praised the liberating and vitalizing qualities of speed and violence. "A racing automobile . . . is more beautiful than the Victory of Samothrace."[18] They had been eager for the adventure of war in 1914, and they continued to follow Mussolini in 1919.

Another intellectual current that provided recruits for Mussolini consisted of critics of the tawdry compromises of Italian parliamentarism who dreamed of a "second Risorgimento."[19] The first Risorgimento, in their view, had left Italy in the hands of a narrow oligarchy whose soulless political games were inappropriate for Italian cultural prestige and Great Power ambitions. It was time to complete the "national revolution" and give Italy a "new state" capable of summoning up the energetic leadership, motivated citizenry, and united national community that Italy deserved. Many of these advocates of a "second Risorgimento" wrote for the Florentine cultural review La Voce, to which the young Mussolini subscribed and with whose editor, Giovanni Prezzolini, he corresponded. After the war, their approval gave respectability to the rising Fascist movement and spread acceptance of a radical "national revolution" among middle-class nationalists.[20]

On April 15, 1919, soon after Fascism's founding meeting at the Piazza

Introduction

San Sepolcro, a band of Mussolini's friends including Marinetti and the chief of the Arditi, Ferruccio Vecchi, invaded the Milan offices of the socialist daily newspaper *Avanti*, of which Mussolini himself had been editor from 1912 to 1914. They smashed its presses and equipment. Four people were killed, including one soldier, and thirty-nine were injured.[21] Italian Fascism thus burst into history with an act of violence against both socialism and bourgeois legality, in the name of a claimed higher national good.

Fascism received its name and took its first steps in Italy. Mussolini was no solitary adventurer, however. Similar movements were springing up in postwar Europe independently of Mussolini's Fascism but expressing the same mixture of nationalism, anti-capitalism, voluntarism, and active violence against both bourgeois and socialist enemies. (I will deal more fully with the wide array of early fascisms in chapter 2.)

A little more than three years after the Piazza San Sepolcro meeting, Mussolini's Fascist Party was in power in Italy. Eleven years after that, another fascist party took power in Germany.[22] Soon Europe and even other parts of the world were resounding with aspiring dictators and marching squads who thought they were on the same path to power as Mussolini and Hitler. In another six years Hitler had plunged Europe into a war that ultimately engulfed much of the world. Before it was over, mankind had suffered not only the habitual barbarities of war, raised to unprecedented scale by technology and passion, but also an effort to extinguish by industrialized slaughter an entire people, their culture, and their very memory.

Contemplating Mussolini, ex-schoolteacher, bohemian minor novelist, and erstwhile socialist orator and editor, and Hitler, former corporal and failed art student, along with their shirted ruffians, in charge of European Great Powers, many educated and sensitive people supposed simply that "a horde of barbarians . . . have pitched their tents within the nation."[23] The novelist Thomas Mann noted in his diary on March 27, 1933, two months after Hitler had become German chancellor, that he had witnessed a revolution of a kind never seen before, "without underlying ideas, against ideas, against everything nobler, better, decent, against freedom, truth and justice." The "common scum" had taken power, "accompanied by vast rejoicing on the part of the masses."[24]

In internal exile in Naples, the eminent liberal Italian philosopher-historian Benedetto Croce observed disdainfully that Mussolini had added a fourth type of misgovernment—"onagrocracy," government by braying asses—to Aristotle's famous three: tyranny, oligarchy, and democracy.[25] Croce later concluded that Fascism was only a "parenthesis" in Italian history, the temporary result of moral decline magnified by the dislocations of World War I. The liberal German historian Friedrich Meinecke judged, similarly, after Hitler had brought Germany to catastrophe, that Nazism had emerged from a moral degeneration in which ignorant and shallow technicians, *Machtmenschen*, supported by a mass society thirsty for excitement, had triumphed over balanced and rational humanitarians, *Kulturmenschen*.[26] The way out, both men thought, was to restore a society where "the best" ruled.

Other observers knew, from the beginning, that something deeper was at stake than the happenstance ascent of thugs, and something more precise than the decay of the old moral order. Marxists, fascism's first victims, were accustomed to thinking of history as the grand unfolding of deep processes through the clash of economic systems. Even before Mussolini had fully consolidated his power, they were ready with a definition of fascism as "the instrument of the big bourgeoisie for fighting the proletariat when the legal means available to the state proved insufficient to subdue them."[27] In Stalin's day, this hardened into an iron-bound formula that became communist orthodoxy for half a century: "Fascism is the open, terroristic dictatorship of the most reactionary, most chauvinist and most imperialist elements of finance capital."[28]

Though many more interpretations and definitions were to be proposed over the years, even now, more than eighty years after the San Sepolcro meeting, none of them has obtained universal assent as a completely satisfactory account of a phenomenon that seemed to come from nowhere, took on multiple and varied forms, exalted hatred and violence in the name of national prowess, and yet managed to appeal to prestigious and well-educated statesmen, entrepreneurs, professionals, artists, and intellectuals. I will reconsider those many interpretations in chapter 8, after we have fuller knowledge of our subject.

Fascist movements varied so conspicuously from one national setting to another, moreover, that some even doubt that the term *fascism* has any meaning other than as a smear word. The epithet has been so loosely used that practically everyone who either holds or shakes authority has been someone's fascist. Perhaps, the doubters suggest, it would be better just to scrap the term.[29]

It is the purpose of this book to propose a fresh way of looking at fascism that may rescue the concept for meaningful use and account more fully for its attractiveness, its complex historical path, and its ultimate horror.

Images of Fascism

Everyone is sure they know what fascism is. The most self-consciously visual of all political forms, fascism presents itself to us in vivid primary images: a chauvinist demagogue haranguing an ecstatic crowd; disciplined ranks of marching youths; colored-shirted militants beating up members of some demonized minority; surprise invasions at dawn; and fit soldiers parading through a captured city.

Examined more closely, however, some of these familiar images induce facile errors. The image of the all-powerful dictator personalizes fascism, and creates the false impression that we can understand it fully by scrutinizing the leader alone. This image, whose power lingers today, is the last triumph of fascist propagandists. It offers an alibi to nations that approved or tolerated fascist leaders, and diverts attention from the persons, groups, and institutions who helped him. We need a subtler model of fascism that explores the interaction between Leader and Nation, and between Party and civil society.

The image of chanting crowds feeds the assumption that some European peoples were by nature predisposed to fascism, and responded enthusiastically to it because of national character. The corollary of this image is a condescending belief that the defective history of certain nations spawned fascism.[30] This turns easily into an alibi for onlooker nations: It couldn't happen here. Beyond these familiar images, on closer inspection, fascist reality becomes more complicated still. For example, the regime that invented the word *fascism*—Mussolini's Italy—showed few signs of anti-Semitism until sixteen years after coming to power. Indeed, Mussolini had Jewish backers among the industrialists and big landowners who helped finance him at the beginning.[31] He had close Jewish cronies such as the Fascist Party militant Aldo Finzi, and a Jewish mistress, the writer Margherita Sarfatti, author of his first authorized biography.[32] About two hundred Jews took part in the March on Rome.[33] By contrast, Marshal Pétain's collaborationist French government at Vichy (1940–44) was aggressively anti-Semitic, while on other scores it is better considered authoritarian[34] than fascist, as we will see in chapter 8. So it becomes problematical to consider an exacerbated anti-Semitism the essence of fascism.[35]

Another supposed essential character of fascism is its anticapitalist, antibourgeois animus. Early fascist movements flaunted their contempt for bourgeois values and for those who wanted only "to earn money, money, filthy money."[36] They attacked "international finance capitalism" almost as loudly as they attacked socialists. They even promised to expropriate department-store owners in favor of patriotic artisans, and large landowners in favor of peasants.[37]

Whenever fascist parties acquired power, however, they did nothing to carry out these anticapitalist threats. By contrast, they enforced with the utmost violence and thoroughness their threats against socialism. Street fights over turf with young communists were among their most powerful propaganda images.[38] Once in power, fascist regimes banned strikes, dissolved independent labor unions, lowered wage earners' purchasing power, and showered money on armaments industries, to the immense satisfaction of employers. Faced with these conflicts between words and actions concerning capitalism, scholars have drawn opposite conclusions. Some, taking the words literally, consider fascism a form of radical anticapitalism.[39] Others, and not only Marxists, take the diametrically opposite position that fascists came to the aid of capitalism in trouble, and propped up by emergency means the existing system of property distribution and social hierarchy.

This book takes the position that what fascists *did* tells us at least as much as what they *said*. What they said cannot be ignored, of course, for it helps explain their appeal. Even at its most radical, however, fascists' anticapitalist rhetoric was selective. While they denounced speculative international finance (along with all other forms of internationalism, cosmopolitanism, or globalization—capitalist as well as socialist), they respected the property of national producers, who were to form the social base of the reinvigorated nation.[40] When they denounced the bourgeoisie, it was for being too flabby and individualistic to make a nation strong, not for robbing workers of the value they added. What they criticized in capitalism was not its exploitation but its materialism, its indifference to the nation, its inability to stir souls.[41] More deeply, fascists rejected the notion that economic forces are the prime movers of history. For fascists, the dysfunctional capitalism of the interwar period did not need fundamental reordering; its ills could be cured simply by applying sufficient political will to the creation of full employment and productivity.[42] Once in power, fascist regimes confiscated property only from political opponents, foreigners, or Jews. None altered the social hierarchy, except to catapult a few adventurers into high places. At most, they replaced market forces with state economic management, but, in the trough of the Great Depression, most businessmen initially approved of that. If fascism was "revolutionary," it was so in a special sense, far removed from the word's meaning as usually understood from 1789 to 1917, as a profound overturning of the social order and the redistribution of social, political, and economic power.

Yet fascism in power did carry out some changes profound enough to be called "revolutionary," if we are willing to give that word a different meaning. At its fullest development, fascism redrew the frontiers between private and public, sharply diminishing what had once been untouchably private. It changed the practice of citizenship from the enjoyment of constitutional rights and duties to participation in mass ceremonies of affirmation and conformity. It reconfigured relations between the individual and the collectivity, so that an individual had no rights outside community interest. It expanded the powers of the executive—party and state—in a bid for total control. Finally, it unleashed aggressive emotions hitherto known in Europe only during war or social revolution. These transformations often set fascists into conflict with conservatives rooted in families, churches, social rank, and property. We will see below[43] when we examine more fully the complex relationship of complicity, accommodation, and occasional opposition that linked capitalists with fascists in power, that one cannot consider fascism simply a more muscular form of conservatism, even if it maintained the existing regime of property and social hierarchy.

It becomes hard to locate fascism on the familiar Right-Left political map. Did the fascist leaders themselves know, at the beginning? When Mussolini called his friends together at the Piazza San Sepolcro in March 1919, it was not entirely clear whether he was trying to compete with his former colleagues in the Italian Socialist Party on the Left or to attack them frontally from the Right. Where on the Italian political spectrum would what he still sometimes called "national syndicalism" find its place?[44] Indeed, fascism always retained that ambiguity.

Fascists were clear about one thing, however: they were not in the middle. Fascist contempt for the soft, complacent, compromising center was absolute (though fascist parties actively seeking power would need to make common cause with centrist elites, against their common enemies on the Left). Their scorn for liberal parliamentarianism and for slack bourgeois individualism, and the radical tone of their remedies for national weakness and disunity, always jarred with their readiness to conclude practical alliances with national conservatives against the internationalist Left. The ultimate fascist response to the Right-Left political map was to claim that they had made it obsolete by being "neither Right nor Left," transcending such outdated divisions and uniting the nation.

Another contradiction between fascist rhetoric and fascist practice concerns modernization: the shift from rural to urban, from handwork to industry, the division of labor, secular societies, and technological rationalization. Fascists often cursed faceless cities and materialist secularism, and exalted an agrarian utopia free from the rootlessness, conflict, and immorality of urban life.[45] Yet fascist leaders adored their fast cars[46] and planes,[47] and spread their message by dazzlingly up-to-date techniques of propaganda and stagecraft. Once in power, they forced the industrial pace in order to rearm. Thus it becomes difficult to posit the essence of fascism solely in either antimodernist reaction[48] or in modernizing dictatorship.[49]

The solution is best found not in setting up binary opposites but in following the relationship between modernity and fascism through its complex historical course. That relationship differed dramatically at different stages. Early fascist movements exploited the protests of the victims of rapid industrialization and globalization—modernization's losers, using, to be sure, the most modern styles and techniques of propaganda.[50] At the same time, an astonishing number of "modernist" intellectuals found fascism's combination of a high-tech "look" with attacks upon modern society, along with its scorn for conventional bourgeois taste, pleasing aesthetically and emotionally.[51] Later, in power, fascist regimes chose resolutely the path of industrial concentration and productivity, superhighways[52] and weaponry. The urge to rearm and wage expansive war quickly swept aside the dream of a paradise for the struggling artisans and peasants who had formed the early movements' first mass base, leaving only a few thatched youth hostels, Hitler's weekend *Lederhosen*, and photographs of Mussolini bare-chested for the grain harvest as tokens of the initial rural nostalgia.[53]

It is only in following the entire fascist itinerary that we can resolve the ambiguous relationship between fascism and modernity that so troubles the seekers for a single fascist essence. Some individuals followed the itinerary in their own careers. Albert Speer joined the party in January 1931 as the disciple of Heinrich Tessenow at the Berlin-Charlottenburg Institute of Technology, who was "not modern but in a certain sense more modern than the others" in his belief in simple, organic architecture.[54] Speer went on after 1933 to become the designer of monumental cityscapes for Hitler, and wound up in 1942–45 marshalling German economic might as minister of armaments. But it was an alternative modernity that Fascist regimes sought: a technically advanced society in which modernity's strains and divisions had been smothered by fascism's powers of integration and control.[55]

Many have seen in fascism's ultimate wartime radicalization—the murder of the Jews—a denial of modern rationality and a return to barbarism.[56] But it is plausible to perceive it as fascism's alternate modernity run amok. Nazi "racial cleansing" built upon the purifying impulses of twentieth-century medicine and public health, the eugenicists' eagerness to weed out the unfit and the unclean,[57] an aesthetic of the perfect body, and a scientific rationality that rejected moral criteria as irrelevant.[58] It has been suggested that old-fashioned pogroms would have taken two hundred years to complete what advanced technology wrought in three years of Holocaust.[59]

The complex relationship between fascism and modernity cannot be resolved all at once, and with a simple yes or no. It has to be developed in the unfolding story of fascism's acquisition and exercise of power.[60] The most satisfactory work on this matter shows how antimodernizing resentments were channeled and neutralized, step by step, in specific legislation, by more powerful pragmatic and intellectual forces working in the service of an alternate modernity.[61] We need to study the whole fascist itinerary—how fascism worked out its practice in action—before we can understand it clearly.

A further problem with conventional images of fascism is that they focus on moments of high drama in the fascist itinerary—the March on Rome, the Reichstag fire, *Kristallnacht*—and omit the solid texture of everyday experience and the complicity of ordinary people in the establishment and functioning of fascist regimes. Fascist movements could never grow without the help of ordinary people, even conventionally good people. Fascists could never attain power without the acquiescence or even active assent of the traditional elites—heads of state, party leaders, high government officials—many of whom felt a fastidious distaste for the crudities of fascist militants. The excesses of fascism in power also required wide complicity among members of the establishment: magistrates, police officials, army officers, businessmen. To understand fully how fascist regimes worked, we must dig down to the level of ordinary people and examine the banal choices they made in their daily routines. Making such choices meant accepting an apparent lesser evil or averting the eyes from some excesses that seemed not too damaging in the short term, even acceptable piecemeal, but which cumulatively added up to monstrous end results.

For example, consider the reactions of ordinary Germans to the events of *Kristallnacht* (Night of Broken Glass). During the night of November 9, 1938, incited by an incendiary speech to party leaders by the Nazi propaganda minister Joseph Goebbels, and in reaction to the murder of a German diplomat in Paris by a young Polish Jew enraged by the recent expulsion of his immigrant parents from Germany, Nazi Party militants rampaged through the Jewish communities of Germany. They burned hundreds of synagogues, smashed more than seven thousand Jewish shops, deported about twenty thousand Jews to concentration camps, and killed ninety-one Jews outright. A fine of a billion marks was imposed collectively on the Jews of Germany, and their insurance reimbursements were confiscated by the German state, in order to compensate for incidental damage done to non-Jewish property. It is clear now that many ordinary Germans were offended by the brutalities carried out under their windows.[62] Yet their widespread distaste was transitory and without lasting effect. Why were there no lawsuits or judicial or administrative enquiries, for example? If we can understand the failure of the judicial system, or of religious or civilian authorities, or of citizen opposition to put any brakes on Hitler in November 1938, we have begun to understand the wider circles of individual and institutional acquiescence within which a militant minority was able to free itself sufficiently from constraints to be able to carry out genocide in a heretofore sophisticated and civilized country.

These are difficult questions to answer, and they take us a long way beyond simple images of a solitary leader and cheering crowds. They also reveal some of the difficulties raised by the search for a single essence, the famous "fascist minimum," which is supposed to allow us to formulate a neat general definition of fascism.

Definitions are inherently limiting. They frame a static picture of something that is better perceived in movement, and they portray as "frozen 'statuary' "[63] something that is better understood as a process. They succumb all too often to the intellectual's temptation to take programmatic statements as constitutive, and to identify fascism more with what it said than with what it did. The quest for the perfect definition, by reducing fascism to one ever more finely honed phrase, seems to shut off questions about the origins and course of fascist development rather than open them up. It is a bit like observing Madame Tussaud's waxworks instead of living people, or birds mounted in a glass case instead of alive in their habitat.

Of course, fascism should not be discussed without reaching, at some point in the debate, an agreed concept of what it is. This book proposes to arrive at such a concept at the end of its quest, rather than to start with one. I propose to set aside for now the imperative of definition, and examine in action a core set of movements and regimes generally accepted as fascist (with Italy and Germany predominant in our sample). I will examine their historical trajectory as a series of processes working themselves out over time, instead of as the expression of some fixed essence.[64] We start with a strategy instead of a definition.

Strategies

Disagreements about how to interpret fascism turn upon profoundly different intellectual strategies. Just what parts of the elephant should we examine? Where in modern European or American experience should we look in order to find the first seeds of fascism and see them germinate? In what kinds of circumstances did fascism grow most rankly? And just what parts of the fascist experience—its origins? its growth? its behavior once in power?—expose most clearly the nature of this complex phenomenon?

If asked what manner of beast fascism is, most people would answer, without hesitation, "fascism is an ideology."[65] The fascist leaders themselves never stopped saying that they were prophets of an idea, unlike the materialist liberals and socialists. Hitler talked ceaselessly of *Weltanschauung*, or "worldview," an uncomely word he successfully forced on the attention of the whole world. Mussolini vaunted the power of the Fascist creed.[66] A fascist, by this approach, is someone who espouses fascist ideology—an ideology being more than just ideas, but a total system of thought harnessed to a world-shaping project.[67] It has become almost automatic to focus a book about fascism on the thinkers who first put together the attitudes and patterns of thought that we now call fascist.

It would seem to follow that we should "start by examining the programs, doctrines, and propaganda in some of the main fascist movements and then proceed to the actual policies and performance of the only two noteworthy fascist regimes."[68] Putting programs first rests on the unstated assumption that fascism was an "ism" like the other great political systems of the modern world: conservatism, liberalism, socialism. Usually taken for granted, that assumption is worth scrutinizing.

The other "isms" were created in an era when politics was a gentleman's business, conducted through protracted and learned parliamentary debate among educated men who appealed to each other's reasons as well as their sentiments. The classical "isms" rested upon coherent philosophical systems laid out in the works of systematic thinkers. It seems only natural to explain them by examining their programs and the philosophy that underpinned them.

Fascism, by contrast, was a new invention created afresh for the era of mass politics. It sought to appeal mainly to the emotions by the use of ritual, carefully stage-managed ceremonies, and intensely charged rhetoric. The role programs and doctrine play in it is, on closer inspection, fundamentally unlike the role they play in conservatism, liberalism, and socialism. Fascism does not rest explicitly upon an elaborated philosophical system, but rather upon popular feelings about master races, their unjust lot, and their rightful predominance over inferior peoples. It has not been given intellectual underpinnings by any system builder, like Marx, or by any major critical intelligence, like Mill, Burke, or Tocqueville.[69]

In a way utterly unlike the classical "isms," the rightness of fascism does not depend on the truth of any of the propositions advanced in its name. Fascism is "true" insofar as it helps fulfill the destiny of a chosen race or people or blood, locked with other peoples in a Darwinian struggle, and not in the light of some abstract and universal reason. The first fascists were entirely frank about this.

> We [Fascists] don't think ideology is a problem that is resolved in such a way that truth is seated on a throne. But, in that case, does fighting for an ideology mean fighting for mere appearances? No doubt, unless one considers it according to its unique and efficacious psychological-historical value. The truth of an ideology lies in its capacity to set in motion our capacity for ideals and action. Its truth is absolute insofar as, living within us, it suffices to exhaust those capacities.[70]

The truth was whatever permitted the new fascist man (and woman) to dominate others, and whatever made the chosen people triumph.

Fascism rested not upon the truth of its doctrine but upon the leader's mystical union with the historic destiny of his people, a notion related to romanticist ideas of national historic flowering and of individual artistic or spiritual genius, though fascism otherwise denied romanticism's exaltation of unfettered personal creativity.[71] The fascist leader wanted to bring his people into a higher realm of politics that they would experience sensually: the warmth of belonging to a race now fully aware of its identity, historic destiny, and power; the excitement of participating in a vast collective enterprise; the gratification of submerging oneself in a wave of shared feelings, and of sacrificing one's petty concerns for the group's good; and the thrill of domination. Fascism's deliberate replacement of reasoned debate with immediate sensual experience transformed politics, as the exiled German cultural critic Walter Benjamin was the first to point out, into aesthetics. And the ultimate fascist aesthetic experience, Benjamin warned in 1936, was war.[72]

Fascist leaders made no secret of having no program. Mussolini exulted in that absence. "The Fasci di Combattimento," Mussolini wrote in the "Postulates of the Fascist Program" of May 1920, ". . . do not feel tied to any particular doctrinal form."[73] A few months before he became prime minister of Italy, he replied truculently to a critic who demanded to know what his program was: "The democrats of *Il Mondo* want to know our program? It is to break the bones of the democrats of *Il Mondo*. And the sooner the better."[74] "The fist," asserted a Fascist militant in 1920, "is the synthesis of our theory."[75] Mussolini liked to declare that he himself was the definition of Fascism. The will and leadership of a *Duce* was what a modern people needed, not a doctrine. Only in 1932, after he had been in power for ten years, and when he wanted to "normalize" his regime, did Mussolini expound Fascist doctrine, in an article (partly ghostwritten by the philosopher Giovanni Gentile) for the new *Enciclopedia italiana*.[76] Power came first, then doctrine. Hannah Arendt observed that Mussolini "was probably the first party leader who consciously rejected a formal program and replaced it with inspired leadership and action alone."[77]

Hitler did present a program (the 25 Points of February 1920), but he pronounced it immutable while ignoring many of its provisions. Though its anniversaries were celebrated, it was less a guide to action than a signal that debate had ceased within the party. In his first public address as chancellor, Hitler ridiculed those who say "show us the details of your program. I have refused ever to step before this *Volk* and make cheap promises."[78]

Several consequences flowed from fascism's special relationship to doctrine. It was the unquestioning zeal of the faithful that counted, more than his or her reasoned assent.[79] Programs were casually fluid. The relationship between intellectuals and a movement that despised thought was even more awkward than the notoriously prickly relationship of intellectual fellow travelers with communism. Many intellectuals associated with fascism's early days dropped away or even went into opposition as successful fascist movements made the compromises necessary to gain allies and power, or, alternatively, revealed its brutal anti-intellectualism. We will meet some of these intellectual dropouts as we go along.

Fascism's radical instrumentalization of truth explains why fascists never bothered to write any casuistical literature when they changed their program, as they did often and without compunction. Stalin was forever writing to prove that his policies accorded somehow with the principles of Marx and Lenin; Hitler and Mussolini never bothered with any such theoretical justification. *Das Blut* or *la razza* would determine who was right. That does not mean, however, that the ideological roots of the early fascist movements are not important. We need to establish just what the intellectual and cultural history of the founders can contribute to understanding fascism, and what it cannot.

The intellectuals of the early days had several kinds of major impact. First, they helped create a space for fascist movements by weakening the elite's attachment to Enlightenment values, until then very widely accepted and applied in concrete form in constitutional government and liberal society. Intellectuals then made it possible to imagine fascism. What Roger Chartier had to say about cultural preparation as the "cause" of the French Revolution is exactly right for the history of fascism as well: "attributing 'cultural origins' to the French Revolution does not by any means establish the Revolution's causes; rather, it pinpoints certain of the conditions that made it possible because it was conceivable."[80] Finally, intellectuals helped operate a seismic emotional shift in which the Left was no longer the only recourse for the angry, and for those inebriated by dreams of change.

Fascism's ideological underpinnings became central again in the final stages, as the accompaniment and guide of wartime radicalization. As the fascist hard core acquired independence from their conservative allies at the battlefront or in occupied enemy territory, their racial hatreds and their contempt for liberal or humanist values reasserted themselves in the killing fields of Libya, Ethiopia, Poland, and the Soviet Union.[81]

Introduction

Although the study of fascist ideology helps elucidate beginnings and endings, it is much less helpful in understanding the middle ranges of the fascist cycle. In order to become a major political player, to gain power, and to exercise it, the fascist leaders engaged in alliance building and political compromises, thereby putting aside parts of their program, and accepting the defection or marginalization of some of their early militants. I will examine that experience more closely in chapters 3 and 4.

No sound strategy for studying fascism can fail to examine the entire context in which it was formed and grew. Some approaches to fascism start with the crisis to which fascism was a response, at the risk of making the crisis into a cause. A crisis of capitalism, according to Marxists, gave birth to fascism. Unable to assure ever-expanding markets, ever-widening access to raw materials, and ever-willing cheap labor through the normal operation of constitutional regimes and free markets, capitalists were obliged, Marxists say, to find some new way to attain these ends by force.

Others perceive the founding crisis as the inadequacy of liberal state and society (in the laissez-faire meaning of liberalism current at that time) to deal with the challenges of the post-1914 world. Wars and revolutions produced problems that parliament and the market—the main liberal solutions—appeared incapable of handling: the distortions of wartime command economies and the mass unemployment attendant upon demobilization; runaway inflation; increased social tensions and a rush toward social revolution; extension of the vote to masses of poorly educated citizens with no experience of civic responsibility; passions heightened by wartime propaganda; distortions of international trade and exchange by war debts and currency fluctuations. Fascism came forward with new solutions for these challenges. I will examine this crucial matter further in chapter 3.

Fascists hated liberals as much as they hated socialists, but for different reasons. For fascists, the internationalist, socialist Left was the enemy and the liberals were the enemies' accomplices. With their hands-off government, their trust in open discussion, their weak hold over mass opinion, and their reluctance to use force, liberals were, in fascist eyes, culpably incompetent guardians of the nation against the class warfare waged by the socialists. As for beleaguered middle-class liberals themselves, fearful of a rising Left, lacking the secret of mass appeal, facing the unpalatable choices offered them by the twentieth century, they have sometimes been as ready as conservatives to cooperate with fascists.

Every strategy for understanding fascism must come to terms with the wide diversity of its national cases. The major question here is whether fascisms are more disparate than the other "isms."

This book takes the position that they are, because they reject any universal value other than the success of chosen peoples in a Darwinian struggle for primacy. The community comes before humankind in fascist values, and respecting individual rights or due process gave way to serving the destiny of the *Volk* or *razza*.[82] Therefore each individual national fascist movement gives full expression to its own cultural particularism. Fascism, unlike the other "isms," is not for export: each movement jealously guards its own recipe for national revival, and fascist leaders seem to feel little or no kinship with their foreign cousins. It has proved impossible to make any fascist "international" work.[83]

Instead of throwing up our hands in despair at fascism's radical disparities, let us make a virtue of this necessity. For variety invites comparison. It is precisely the differences that separated Hitler's Nazism from Mussolini's Fascism, and both of them from, say, the religious messianism of Corneliu Codreanu's Legion of the Archangel Michael in Romania, that give bite to comparison. Comparison, as Marc Bloch reminded us, is most useful for eliciting differences.[84] I use comparison that way. I shall not be very interested in finding similarities—deciding whether some regime falls within the definition of some fascist essence. That kind of taxonomy, so widespread in the literature about fascism, does not lead very far. Instead, I will search as precisely as possible for the reasons behind differing outcomes. Movements that called themselves fascist or that deliberately modeled themselves on Mussolini existed in every Western country after World War I, and in some cases outside the Western world. Why did movements of similar inspiration have such different outcomes in different societies? Comparison used in this way will be a central strategy in this work.

Where Do We Go from Here?

Faced with the great variety of fascisms and the elusiveness of the "fascist minimum," there have been three sorts of response. As we saw at the outset, some scholars, exasperated with the sloppiness of the term *fascism* in common usage, deny that it has any useful meaning at all. They have seriously proposed limiting it to Mussolini's particular case.[85] If we followed their advice, we would call Hitler's regime Nazism, Mussolini's regime

Fascism, and each of the other kindred movements by its own name would treat each one as a discrete phenomenon.

This book rejects such nominalism. The term *fascism* needs to be rescued from sloppy usage, not thrown out because of it. It remains indispensable. We need a generic term for what is a general phenomenon, indeed the most important political novelty of the twentieth century: a popular movement against the Left and against liberal individualism. Contemplating fascism, we see most clearly how the twentieth century contrasted with the nineteenth, and what the twenty-first century must avoid.

The wide diversity among fascisms that we have already noted is no reason to abandon the term. We do not doubt the utility of *communism* as a generic term because of its profoundly different expressions in, say, Russia, Italy, and Cambodia. Nor do we discard the term *liberalism* because liberal politics took dissimilar forms in free-trading, Bible-reading Victorian Britain, in the protectionist, anticlerical France of the Third Republic, or in Bismarck's aggressively united German Reich. Indeed "liberalism" would be an even better candidate for abolition than "fascism," now that Americans consider "liberals" the far Left while Europeans call "liberals" advocates of a hands-off laissez-faire free market such as Margaret Thatcher, Ronald Reagan, and George W. Bush. Even fascism isn't as confusing as that.

A second response has been to accept fascism's variety and compile an encyclopedic survey of its many forms.[86] Encyclopedic description provides enlightening and fascinating detail but leaves us with something that recalls a medieval bestiary, with its woodcut of each creature, classified by external appearances, fixed against a stylized background of branch or rock.

A third approach finesses variety by constructing an "ideal type" that fits no case exactly, but lets us posit a kind of composite "essence." The most widely accepted recent concise definition of fascism as an "ideal type" is by the British scholar Roger Griffin: "Fascism is a genus of political ideology whose mythic core in its various permutations is a palingenetic form of populist ultranationalism."[87]

This book proposes to set aside, for a moment, both the bestiary and the essence. These condemn us to a static view, and to a perspective that encourages looking at fascism in isolation. Let us instead watch fascism in action, from its beginnings to its final cataclysm, within the complex web of interaction it forms with society. Ordinary citizens and the holders of political, social, cultural, and economic power who assisted, or failed to resist, fascism belong to the story. When we are done, we may be better able to give fascism an appropriate definition.

We will need a clear understanding of fascism's two principal coalition partners, liberals and conservatives. In this book I use *liberalism* in its original meaning, the meaning in use at the time when fascism rose up against it, rather than the current American usage noted above. European liberals of the early twentieth century were clinging to what had been progressive a century earlier, when the dust was still settling from the French Revolution. Unlike conservatives, they accepted the revolution's goals of liberty, equality, and fraternity, but they applied them in ways suitable for an educated middle class. Classical liberals interpreted liberty as individual personal freedom, preferring limited constitutional government and a laissez-faire economy to any kind of state intervention, whether mercantilist, as in the early nineteenth century, or socialist, as later on. Equality they understood as opportunity made accessible to talent by education; they accepted inequality of achievement and hence of power and wealth. Fraternity they considered the normal condition of free men (and they tended to regard public affairs as men's business), and therefore in no need of artificial reinforcement, since economic interests were naturally harmonious and the truth would out in a free marketplace of ideas. This is the sense in which I use the term *liberal* in this book, and never in its current American meaning of "far Left." Conservatives wanted order, calm, and the inherited hierarchies of wealth and birth. They shrank both from fascist mass enthusiasm and from the sort of total power fascists grasped for. They wanted obedience and deference, not dangerous popular mobilization, and they wanted to limit the state to the functions of a "night watchman" who would keep order while traditional elites ruled through property, churches, armies, and inherited social influence.[88]

More generally, conservatives in Europe still rejected in 1930 the main tenets of the French Revolution, preferring authority to liberty, hierarchy to equality, and deference to fraternity. Although many of them might find fascists useful, or even essential, in their struggle for survival against dominant liberals and a rising Left, some were keenly aware of the different agenda of their fascist allies and felt a fastidious distaste for these uncouth outsiders.[89] Where simple authoritarianism sufficed, conservatives much preferred that. Some of them maintained their antifascist posture to the end. Most conservatives, however, were sure that communism was worse. They would work with fascists if the Left looked otherwise likely to win. They made common cause with the fascists in the spirit of Tancredi, the recalcitrant aristocratic youth in Giuseppe di Lampedusa's great novel of the decay of a noble Sicilian family, *The Leopard:* "If we want things to stay as they are, things will have to change."[90]

The fascisms we have known have come into power with the help of frightened ex-liberals and opportunist technocrats and ex-conservatives, and governed in more or less awkward tandem with them. Following these coalitions vertically through time, as movements turned into regimes, and horizontally in space, as they adapted to the peculiarities of national settings and momentary opportunities, requires something more elaborate than the traditional movement/regime dichotomy. I propose to examine fascism in a cycle of five stages: (1) the creation of movements; (2) their rooting in the political system; (3) their seizure of power; (4) the exercise of power; (5) and, finally, the long duration, during which the fascist regime chooses either radicalization or entropy. Though each stage is a prerequisite for the next, nothing requires a fascist movement to complete all of them, or even to move in only one direction. Most fascisms stopped short, some slipped back, and sometimes features of several stages remained operative at once. Whereas most modern societies spawned fascist movements in the twentieth century, only a few had fascist regimes. Only in Nazi Germany did a fascist regime approach the outer horizons of radicalization.

Separating the five stages of fascism offers several advantages. It permits plausible comparison between movements and regimes at equivalent degrees of development. It helps us see that fascism, far from static, was a succession of processes and choices: seeking a following, forming alliances, bidding for power, then exercising it. That is why the conceptual tools that illuminate one stage may not necessarily work equally well for others. The time has come to examine each of the five stages in turn.

CHAPTER 2

Creating Fascist Movements

If something begins when it acquires a name, we can date the beginnings of fascism precisely. It began on Sunday morning, March 23, 1919, at the meeting on the Piazza San Sepolcro in Milan already described in chapter 1. But Mussolini's Fasci Italiani di Combattimento were not alone. Something broader was afoot. Quite independently of Mussolini, similar groups were coming together elsewhere in Europe.

Hungary was another fertile setting for the spontaneous growth — copied from no one — of something that did not yet call itself fascism, but bears a strong family resemblance. Hungary suffered the most calamitous territorial losses from World War I of any participant — worse even than Germany. Before the war, it had been a ruling partner in the mighty Dual Monarchy of Austria-Hungary, or the Habsburg empire. The Hungarian half of the empire — the kingdom of Hungary — had ruled a multilingual world of South Slavs, Romanians, Slovaks, and many others, among whom the Hungarians enjoyed a privileged position. During the closing months of World War I, the Habsburg empire dissolved as its component nationalities claimed independence. Hungary — once the greatest beneficiary of the multinational empire — became the greatest loser in its dissolution. The victorious Allies eventually amputated 70 percent of Hungary's prewar territory and almost two thirds of its population by the punitive Treaty of the Trianon, signed under protest on June 4, 1920.

During the chaotic days after the armistice of November 1918, as the subject peoples of the Hungarian half of the Austro-Hungarian empire — Romanians, South Slavs, Slovaks — began to govern their own territories under Allied protection, a maverick progressive nobleman, Count Michael

24

Károlyi, tried to save the Hungarian state by dramatic reforms. Károlyi gambled that establishing full democracy within a federal Hungary whose subject peoples would enjoy extensive self-government would soften the Allies' hostility, and win their acceptance of Hungary's historic borders. Károlyi lost his gamble. French and Serb armies occupied the southern third of Hungary while Romanian armies, supported by the Allies, occupied the wide plains of Transylvania. These annexations looked permanent. Unable to persuade the French authorities to stop them, Count Károlyi abandoned his tenuous grip on power at the end of March 1919.

A socialist-communist coalition then assumed power in Budapest. Headed by a Jewish revolutionary intellectual, Béla Kun, the new government briefly drew support even from some army officers by his promise that Bolshevik Russia would be a better bet than the Allies to help Hungary survive. Lenin was in no position to assist the Hungarians, however, and although Kun's government managed to reconquer some Slovak-occupied territories, it simultaneously adopted radical socialist measures. Kun proclaimed a Soviet republic in Budapest in May 1919 and the dictatorship of the proletariat on June 25.

Faced with these combined and unprecedented challenges of territorial dismantlement and social revolution, the Hungarian elites chose to fight the latter more vigorously than the former. They set up a provisional government in the southwestern provincial city of Szeged, then under French and Serb occupation, and stood by while the Romanians advanced in early August 1919 to occupy Budapest, from which Kun had already fled. A bloody counterrevolution followed, and claimed some five to six thousand victims, ten times as many as the Soviet regime had killed.

The Hungarian counterrevolution had two faces. Its top leadership was composed of the traditional elite, within which the last commander of the Austro-Hungarian navy, Admiral Miklós Horthy, emerged as the dominant figure. A second component was those who believed that traditional authority was no longer sufficient to deal with Hungary's emergency. A group of young officers headed by Captain Gyula Gömbös founded a movement with many of the characteristics of fascism.

Gömbös's officers wanted to mobilize a mass base for a militant movement of nationalist renovation, different from both parliamentary liberalism (for Count Károlyi's democracy was now as discredited as Kun's Soviet), and from an old-fashioned dictatorship that ruled from above. Their Anti-Bolshevik Committee was virulently anti-Semitic (not only Béla Kun but thirty-two of his forty-five commissars had been Jewish).[1]

s officers did not want to restore traditional authority but to
it with something more dynamic, rooted in popular nationalist
ophobic passions and expressed in traditional Hungarian symbols
anu .. yths.[2] For the moment, Admiral Horthy and the conservatives were
able to rule without having to call upon the young officers, though Gömbös served as prime minister under Horthy in 1932–35 and built an
alliance with Mussolini to counter growing German power.

In the Austrian half of the Habsburg monarchy, German nationalists
had been alarmed even before World War I by the gains of Czechs and
other minorities toward more administrative and linguistic autonomy.
Before 1914 they were already developing a virulent strain of working-
class nationalism. German-speaking workers came to look upon Czech-
speaking workers as national rivals rather than as fellow proletarians. In
Habsburg Bohemia, on the eve of World War I, nation already trumped
class.

The German nationalists of the Habsburg empire had since the late
nineteenth century built upon the populist pan-Germanism of Georg von
Schönerer, whom I will treat in more detail shortly.[3] They reached effective political power in the capital, Vienna, when Karl Lueger became
mayor in 1897. Lueger built his long mayoralty solidly upon a populist
mixture of anti-Semitism, anticorruption, defense of artisans and small
shopkeepers, catchy slogans and songs, and efficient municipal services.

Adolf Hitler, a young drifter and would-be art student from fifty miles
upriver in Linz, soaked up the atmosphere of Lueger's Vienna.[4] He was
not the only one. The nationalist German Workers' Party, led by a Vienna
lawyer and a railroad employee, had already earned three seats in the Austrian Diet by 1911. Revived in May 1918 as the German National Socialist
Workers' Party, it began using the *Hakenkreuz*, or swastika, as its symbol.[5]

Postwar Germany offered particularly fertile soil to popular-based
antisocialist movements of national revival. Germans had been shaken to
their roots by defeat in 1918. The emotional impact was all the more
severe because German leaders had been trumpeting victory until a few
weeks before. So unbelievable a calamity was easily blamed on traitors.
The plummet in German fortunes from the bold Great Power of 1914
to the stunned, hungry loser of 1918 shattered national pride and self-
confidence. Wilhelm Spannaus later described his feelings upon returning to his hometown in 1921 after years of teaching in a German school in
South America:

It was shortly after the Spartakus uprising in the Rhineland: practically every windowpane was broken on the train in which I reentered Germany, and the inflation was reaching fantastic proportions. I had left Germany at the height of the power and glory of the Wilhelmine Reich. I came back to find the Fatherland in shambles, under a Socialist republic.[6]

Spannaus became the first respectable citizen of his town to join the Nazi Party, and, as an intellectual leader (he owned the local bookstore), he carried many other citizens with him.

Footloose veterans, their units melting away, unable to find work or even food, were available for extremism of either Left or Right. Some turned to Bolshevik Russia for their inspiration, as in the short-lived Munich Soviet Republic of spring 1919. Others clung to the nationalism already spread by the wartime propaganda movement, the Fatherland Front. Some of these nationalist veterans joined mercenary units (Freikorps) formed under the command of regular army officers to fight what they regarded as Germany's internal enemies. In January 1919 they murdered the socialist leaders Rosa Luxemburg and Karl Liebknecht in revolutionary Berlin. The following spring they crushed socialist regimes in Munich and elsewhere. Other Freikorps units continued battling Soviet and Polish armies along the still-undemarcated Baltic frontier well after the armistice of November 1918.[7]

Corporal Adolf Hitler,[8] back on active duty with Army Group Command IV in Munich after recovering from the hysterical blindness he suffered upon learning of German defeat, was sent by Army Intelligence in September 1919 to investigate one of the many nationalist movements that were sprouting in the postwar disorder. The German Workers' Party (DAP) had been created at the end of the war by a patriotic locksmith, Anton Drexler. Finding a handful of artisans and journalists who dreamed of winning workers to the nationalist cause but had no idea of how to go about it, Hitler joined them and received party card No. 555. He soon became one of the movement's most effective speakers and a member of its directing committee.

In early 1920 Hitler was put in charge of the DAP's propaganda. With the help of sympathetic army officers such as Captain Ernst Röhm and some wealthy Munich backers,[9] Hitler greatly expanded the party's audience. Before nearly two thousand people in a big Munich beer cellar, the

Hofbräuhaus, on February 24, 1920, Hitler gave the movement a new name—the Nationalsozialistische Deutsche Arbeiterpartei (NSDAP, or "Nazi" Party, for short)—and presented a program of twenty-five points mixing nationalism, anti-Semitism, and attacks on department stores and international capital. The following April 1, he left the army to devote himself full-time to the NSDAP. He was increasingly recognized as its leader, its *Führer*.[10]

As the immediate postwar turmoil eased, such activist nationalist sects faced less hospitable conditions in Europe. Governments gradually established a toehold on legitimacy. Borders were set. Bolshevism was contained within its Russian birthplace. Some semblance of peacetime normalcy returned to most parts of Europe. Even so, the Italian Fascists, the Hungarian officers, and the Austrian and German National Socialists persisted. Similar movements arose in France[11] and elsewhere. They clearly expressed something more enduring than a momentary nationalist spasm accompanying the final paroxysm of the war.

The Immediate Background

A political space[12] for mass-based nationalist activism, mobilized against both socialism and liberalism, had been only dimly visible in 1914. It became a yawning gap during World War I. That conflict did not so much create fascism as open up wide cultural, social, and political opportunities for it. Culturally, the war discredited optimistic and progressive views of the future, and cast doubt upon liberal assumptions about natural human harmony. Socially, it spawned armies of restless veterans (and their younger brothers)[13] looking for ways to express their anger and disillusion without heed for old-fashioned law or morality. Politically, it generated economic and social strains that exceeded the capacity of existing institutions— whether liberal or conservative—to resolve.

The experience of World War I was the most decisive immediate precondition for fascism. The successful campaign to bring Italy into the war in May 1915 (the "radiant May" of Fascist mythology) first brought together the founding elements of Italian Fascism. "The right to the political succession belongs to us," proclaimed Mussolini at the founding meeting of the Fasci di Combattimento in March 1919, "because we were the ones who pushed the country into war and led it to victory."[14]

The Great War was also, it must be added, at the root of much else that was violent and angry in the postwar world, from Bolshevism to expressionist painting. Indeed, for some authors, the Great War by itself suffices to explain both Fascism and Bolshevism.[15] Four years of industrialized slaughter had left little of Europe's legacy unaltered and nothing of its future certain.

Before 1914, no living European could have imagined such brutality in what was then considered the most civilized part of the globe. Wars had become rare, localized, and short in Europe in the nineteenth century, fought out by professional armies that impinged little on civilian society. Europe had been spared the likes of the American Civil War or the War of the Triple Alliance (Brazil, Argentina, and Uruguay) against Paraguay, which reduced the Paraguayan population by half between 1864 and 1870. When, in August 1914, a petty Balkan conflict erupted out of control into a total war among the European Great Powers, and when those powers managed to sustain the slaughter of an entire generation of young men over four years, it seemed to many Europeans that their civilization itself, with its promise of peace and progress, had failed.

The Great War had also lasted far longer than most people had imagined possible for urbanized industrial countries. Most Europeans had assumed that highly differentiated populations packed into cities, dependent upon massive exchanges of consumer goods, would be simply incapable of enduring years of massive destruction. Only primitive societies, they thought, could support long wars. Contrary to expectations, Europeans discovered, beginning in 1914, how to mobilize industrial productivity and human wills for long years of sacrifice. As trench warfare approached the limits of human endurance, so war governments approached the limits of regimentation of life and thought.[16]

All the belligerent governments had experimented with the manipulation of public opinion. Germany's attempt to motivate the entire civilian population in the Fatherland Front was one of the most coercive examples, but all of them worked to shape their citizens' knowledge and opinions. The economies and societies of all the belligerent countries, too, had been deeply transformed. European peoples had endured their first prolonged experience of universal national service, rationing of food, energy, and clothing, and full-scale economic management. Despite these unprecedented efforts, however, none of the belligerents had achieved its goals. Instead of a short war with clear results, this long and labor-intensive carnage had ended in mutual exhaustion and disillusion.

The war posed such a redoubtable challenge that even the best-integrated and best-governed countries barely managed to meet its strains.

Badly integrated and governed countries failed altogether to meet them. Britain and France allocated materiel, assigned people to duties, distributed sacrifice, and manipulated the news just successfully enough to retain the allegiance of most of their citizens. The recently unified German empire and Italian monarchy did less well. The Habsburg empire broke apart into its constituent nationalities. Tsarist Russia collapsed into chaos. Those dislocated countries where a landless peasantry was still numerous and where a disfranchised middle class still lacked basic liberties polarized to the Left (as in Russia). Those with a large but threatened middle class, including family farmers, polarized against the Left and looked for new solutions.[17]

At the end of the war, Europeans were torn between an old world that could not be revived and a new world about which they disagreed bitterly. As war economies were dismantled too quickly, wartime inflation spun out of control, making a mockery of the bourgeois virtues of thrift and savings. A population that had come to expect public solutions to economic problems was thrown into uncertainty.

Compounding these social and economic strains, the war also deepened political divisions. Because trench warfare had been a brutalizing experience beyond previous imagining, even the most equitable apportionment of the burdens of war making had divided civilians from soldiers, battlefront from home front. Those who had survived the trenches could not forgive those who had sent them there. Veterans inured to violence asserted what they regarded as their well-earned right to rule the countries they had bled for.[18] "When I returned from the war," wrote Italo Balbo, "just like so many others, I hated politics and politicians who, in my opinion, had betrayed the hopes of soldiers, reducing Italy to a shameful peace and to a systematic humiliation Italians who maintained the cult of heroes. To struggle, to fight in order to return to the land of Giolitti, who made a merchandise of every ideal? No. Rather deny everything, destroy everything, in order to renew everything from the foundations."[19] Balbo, a twenty-three-year-old demobilized veteran in 1919 of antisocialist but Mazzinian convictions, who had needed four attempts to pass his law exams and had worked for a while editing a weekly soldiers' newspaper, *L'Alpino*, had few prospects until he was hired in January 1921 as the paid secretary of the Ferrara *fascio*.[20] He was on his way to becoming one of Mussolini's right-hand men and potential rivals.

Three grand principles of world order contended for influence as postwar Europe bandaged its wounds: liberalism, conservatism, and communism. Liberals (joined by some democratic socialists) wanted to organize the postwar world by the principle of the self-determination of nations. Satisfied nationalities, each with its own state, would coexist in such natural harmony, according to liberal doctrine, that no external force would be needed to keep the peace. U.S. president Woodrow Wilson's idealistic but ill-conceived Fourteen Points of January 1918 was its most concrete expression.

Conservatives said little in 1918, but tried quietly to restore a world in which armed force settled relations among states. The French prime minister Georges Clemenceau and his chief of staff General Ferdinand Foch tried (with some disagreement between themselves about how far they could go) to establish permanent French military supremacy over a weakened Germany.

The third contender was the world's first functioning socialist regime, installed in Russia by the Bolshevik Revolution of November 1917. Lenin demanded that socialists elsewhere follow his successful example, set democracy aside, and create dictatorial conspiratorial parties on the Bolshevik model capable of spreading revolution to the more advanced capitalist states. For the moment he carried with him some Western democratic socialists who did not want to miss the long-awaited revolutionary train. Where liberals wanted to keep the peace by satisfying national claims and conservatives wanted to keep it by military preparedness, Lenin wanted to establish a worldwide communist society that would transcend national states altogether.[21]

No camp had complete success. Lenin's project was contained by late 1919 within Russia, after liberals and conservatives together had crushed brief local Soviet regimes in Budapest and Munich and risings elsewhere in Germany and in Italy. It survived in Russia, however—the first socialist state—and in communist parties around the world. Wilson's project was supposedly put into effect by the peace treaties of 1919–20. In practice, however, it had been partially modified in a conservative direction by the national interests of the Great Powers and by the hard facts of contested national and ethnic frontiers. Instead of a world of either satisfied nationalities or dominant powers, the peace treaties created one divided between the victor powers and their client states, artificially swollen to include other national minorities (Poland, Czechoslovakia, Yugoslavia, and Romania), and vengeful loser states (defeated Germany, Austria, and

Hungary, and unsatisfied Italy). Torn between a distorted Wilsonianism and an unfulfilled Leninism, Europe seethed after 1919 with unresolved territorial and class conflicts.

This mutual failure left political space available for a fourth principle of world order. The fascists' new formula promised, like that of the conservatives, to settle territorial conflicts by allowing the strong to triumph. Unlike conservatives, they measured strong states not only by military might but by the fervor and unity of their populations. They proposed to overcome class conflict by integrating the working class into the nation, by persuasion if possible and by force if necessary, and by getting rid of the "alien" and the "impure." The fascists did not want to keep the peace at all. They expected that inevitable war would allow the master races, united and self-confident, to prevail, while the divided, "mongrelized," and irresolute peoples would become their handmaidens.

Fascism had become conceivable, as we will soon see, before 1914. But it was not realizable in practical terms until the Great War had wrenched Europe into a new era. The "epoch" of fascism, to quote the German title of the philosopher-historian Ernst Nolte's classic work of 1963, "fascism in its epoch,"[22] opened in 1918.

Intellectual, Cultural, and Emotional Roots

How Europeans understood their war ordeal amidst the wreckage of 1919 was shaped, of course, by prior mental preparation. Deeper preconditions of fascism lay in the late-nineteenth-century revolt against the dominant liberal faith in individual liberty, reason, natural human harmony, and progress. Well before 1914 newly stylish antiliberal values, more aggressive nationalism and racism, and a new aesthetic of instinct and violence began to furnish an intellectual-cultural humus in which fascism could germinate.

We can begin with what the first fascists read. Mussolini was a serious reader. The young Italian schoolteacher and socialist organizer read not so much Marx as Nietzsche, Gustave Le Bon, and Georges Sorel. Hitler absorbed rather by osmosis the fevered pan-German nationalism and anti-Semitism of Georg von Schönerer, Houston Stewart Chamberlain,[23] Mayor Lueger, and the Vienna streets, elevated into ecstasy in his mind by the music of Richard Wagner.

Friedrich Nietzsche (1844–1900) has so often been accused of being fascism's progenitor that his case requires particular care. Intended for the Lutheran pastorate, the young Nietzsche lost his faith and became a professor of classical philology while still extraordinarily young. For his remaining good years (he suffered permanent mental breakdown at fifty, perhaps related to syphilis) he invested all his brilliance and rage in attacking complacent and conformist bourgeois piety, softness, and moralism in the name of a hard, pure independence of spirit. In a world where God was dead, Christianity weak, and Science false, only a spiritually free "superman" could fight free of convention and live according to his own authentic values. At first Nietzsche inspired mostly rebellious youth and shocked their parents. At the same time, his writing contained plenty of raw material for people who wanted to brood on the decline of modern society, the heroic effort of will needed to reverse it, and the nefarious influence of Jews. Nietzsche himself was scornful of patriotism and the actual anti-Semites he saw around him, and imagined his superman a "free spirit, the enemy of fetters, the non-worshipper, the dweller in forests."[24] His white-hot prose exerted a powerful intellectual and aesthetic influence across the political spectrum, from activist nationalists like Mussolini and Maurice Barrès to nonconformists like Stefan George and André Gide, to both Nazis and anti-Nazis, and to several later generations of French iconoclasts from Sartre to Foucault. "Nietzsche's texts themselves provide a positive goldmine of varied possibilities."[25]

Georges Sorel (1847–1922) exerted a more direct and practical influence on Mussolini. A retired French engineer and amateur social theorist, Sorel was fascinated by what kinds of causes were capable of awakening "in the depths of the soul a sentiment of the sublime proportionate to the conditions of a gigantic struggle" so that "the European nations, stupefied by humanitarianism, can recover their former energy."[26] He found the best examples at first in the revolutionary syndicalism we have already encountered as Mussolini's first spiritual home. The syndicalist dream of "one big union," whose all-out general strike would sweep away capitalist society in "one big night" and leave the unions in charge, was what Sorel called a "myth"—a galvanizing ideal capable of rousing people to perform beyond their everyday capacities. Later, at the end of the war, Sorel concluded that Lenin best embodied this ideal. Still later he was briefly impressed by Mussolini (who was, in turn, Sorel's most successful disciple).[27]

Also important for the fascist assault on democracy were social theorists who raised pragmatic doubts about the workability of this relatively young form of government. Mussolini referred often to Gustave Le Bon's

La Psychologie des foules (The Psychology of Crowds, 1895). Le Bon took a cynical look at how passions rose and fused within a mass of people who could then be easily manipulated.[28] Mussolini also enrolled in the courses of Vilfredo Pareto at the University of Lausanne in 1904 when he was living in exile to escape Italian military service. Pareto (1848–1923), son of a Mazzinian exile in France and a French mother, was a liberal economist so frustrated by the spread of protectionism in the late nineteenth century that he constructed a political theory about how the superficial rules of electoral and parliamentary democracy were inevitably subverted in practice by the permanent power of elites and by the irrational "residues" of popular feelings.

At the summit of the intellectual scale, the major intellectual development of the end of the nineteenth century was the discovery of the reality and power of the subconscious in human thought and the irrational in human action. While Bergson and Freud had absolutely nothing to do with fascism, and indeed suffered personally from it, their work helped undermine the liberal conviction that politics means free people choosing the best policies by the simple exercise of their reason.[29] Their findings—particularly Freud's—were spread and popularized after 1918 by direct wartime experiences such as battlefield emotional trauma, for which the term "shell shock" was invented.

At the bottom of the intellectual scale, a host of popular writers reworked an existing repertory of themes—race, nation, will, action— into harder, more aggressive forms as the ubiquitous social Darwinism.[30] Race, hitherto a rather neutral term for any animal or human grouping, was given a more explicitly biological and hereditarian form in the late nineteenth century. Charles Darwin's cousin Francis Galton suggested in the 1880s that science gave mankind the power to improve the race by urging "the best" to reproduce; he invented the word "eugenics" for this effort.[31] The nation—once, for progressive nationalists like Mazzini, a framework for progress and fraternity among peoples—was made more exclusive and ranked in a hierarchy that gave "master races" (such as the "Aryans," a figment of nineteenth-century anthropological imagination)[32] the right to dominate "inferior" peoples. Will and action became virtues in themselves, independently of any particular goal, linked to the struggle among the "races" for supremacy.[33]

Even after the horrors of 1914–18 had made it harder to think of war as the sort of bracing exploit admired by Rudyard Kipling, Theodore Roosevelt, or the early Boy Scout movement, some still considered it the highest human activity. If the nation or *Volk* was mankind's highest attainment, violence in its cause was ennobling. Beyond that, a few aesthetes of violence found beauty in the very extremity of masculine will and endurance demanded by trench warfare.[34]

New forms of anxiety appeared with the twentieth century, to which fascism soon promised remedies. Looking for fears, indeed, may be a more fruitful research strategy than a literal-minded quest for thinkers who "created" fascism. One such fear was the collapse of community under the corrosive influences of free individualism. Rousseau had already worried about this before the French Revolution.[35] In the mid-nineteenth century and after, the fear of social disintegration was mostly a conservative concern. After the turbulent 1840s in England, the Victorian polemicist Thomas Carlyle worried about what force would discipline "the masses, full of beer and nonsense," as more and more of them received the right to vote.[36] Carlyle's remedy was a militarized welfare dictatorship, administered not by the existing ruling class but by a new elite composed of selfless captains of industry and other natural heroes of the order of Oliver Cromwell and Frederick the Great. The Nazis later claimed Carlyle as a forerunner.[37]

Fear of the collapse of community solidarity intensified in Europe toward the end of the nineteenth century, under the impact of urban sprawl, industrial conflict, and immigration. Diagnosing the ills of community was a central project in the creation of the new discipline of sociology. Émile Durkheim (1858–1917), the first French holder of a chair in sociology, diagnosed modern society as afflicted with "anomie"—the purposeless drift of people without social ties—and reflected on the replacement of "organic" solidarity, the ties formed within natural communities of villages, families, and churches, with "mechanical" solidarity, the ties formed by modern propaganda and media such as fascists (and advertisers) would later perfect. The German sociologist Ferdinand Tönnies regretted the supplanting of traditional, natural societies (*Gemeinschaften*) by more differentiated and impersonal modern societies (*Gesellschaften*) in *Gemeinschaft und Gesellschaft* (1887), and the Nazis borrowed his term for the "people's community" (*Volksgemeinschaft*) they wanted to form. The early-twentieth-century sociologists Vilfredo Pareto, Gaetano Mosca, and Roberto Michels contributed more directly to fascist ideas.[38]

Another late-nineteenth-century anxiety was decadence: the dread that great historic nations were doomed by their own comfort and complacency to declining birth rates[39] and diminished vitality. The best known prediction of decline, whose title everyone knew even if few waded through its prose, was Oswald Spengler's *Der Untergang des Abendlandes* (Decline of the West, 1918). Spengler, a German high school history teacher, argued that cultures have life cycles like organisms, passing from a heroic and creative "Age of Culture" to a corrupt "Age of Civilization" when rootless masses, huddled in cities, lose contact with the soil, think only of money, and become incapable of great actions. Thus Germany was not alone in its decline. In a second volume (1922), he suggested that a heroic "Caesarism" might still manage to save things in Germany. Modernization, Spengler feared, was sweeping away rooted traditions. Bolshevism would carry destruction even further. He advocated a spiritual revolution that would revitalize the nation without altering its social structure.[40]

Enemies were central to the anxieties that helped inflame the fascist imagination. Fascists saw enemies within the nation as well as outside. Foreign states were familiar enemies, though their danger seemed to intensify with the advance of Bolshevism and with the exacerbated border conflicts and unfulfilled national claims that followed World War I. Internal enemies grew luxuriantly in number and variety in the mental landscape as the ideal of the homogeneous national state made difference more suspect. Ethnic minorities had been swollen in western Europe after the 1880s by an increased number of refugees fleeing pogroms in eastern Europe.[41] Political and cultural subversives—socialists of various hues, avant-garde artists and intellectuals—discovered new ways to challenge community conformism. The national culture would have to be defended against them. Joseph Goebbels declared at a book-burning ceremony in Berlin on May 10, 1933, that "the age of extreme Jewish intellectualism has now ended, and the success of the German revolution has again given the right of way to the German spirit."[42] Though Mussolini and his avant-garde artist friends worried less than the Nazis about cultural modernism, Fascist squads made bonfires of socialist books in Italy.

The discovery of the role of bacteria in contagion by the French biologist Louis Pasteur and the mechanisms of heredity by the Austrian monk-botanist Gregor Mendel in the 1880s made it possible to imagine whole new categories of internal enemy: carriers of disease, the unclean, and the hereditarily ill, insane, or criminal. The urge to purify the community medically became far stronger in Protestant northern Europe than in Catholic southern Europe. This agenda influenced liberal states, too. The United States and Sweden led the way in the forcible sterilization of habitual offenders (in the American case, especially African Americans), but Nazi Germany went beyond them in the most massive program of medical euthanasia yet known.[43]

Fascist Italy, by contrast, though it promoted the growth of *la razza*, understood in cultural-historical terms,[44] remained little touched by the northern European and American vogue for biological purification. This difference rested upon cultural tradition. The German Right had traditionally been *völkisch*, devoted to the defense of a biological "people" threatened by foreign impurities, socialist division, and bourgeois softness.[45] The new Italian nationalism was less biological and more political in its determination to "do over" the Risorgimento that had been corrupted by liberals and weakened by socialists. It claimed the right of Italians as a "proletarian nation" to a share of the world's colonies. If it were true that every nation, whatever its superficial democratic gadgetry, was really run by an elite, as the sociologists Vilfredo Pareto, Gaetano Mosca, and the disillusioned German socialist émigré Roberto Michels were telling Italians at the end of World War I, then Italy must look to the creation of a worthy new elite capable of running its new state and leading Italian opinion, by "myths" if necessary.[46]

Fascists need a demonized enemy against which to mobilize followers, but of course the enemy does not have to be Jewish. Each culture specifies the national enemy. Even though in Germany the foreign, the unclean, the contagious, and the subversive often mingled in a single diabolized image of the Jew, Gypsies and Slavs were also targeted. American fascists diabolized blacks and sometimes Catholics as well as Jews. Italian Fascists diabolized their South Slav neighbors, especially the Slovenes, as well as the socialists who refused the war of national revival. Later they easily added to their list the Ethiopians and the Libyans, whom they tried to conquer in Africa.

Fascist anxieties about decline and impurity did not necessarily point toward the restoration of some antique golden age. Isaiah Berlin was surely stretching a point when he found a precursor to fascism in Joseph de Maistre in Restoration France, not so much by virtue of his conviction of human depravity and the need for authority as because of his "preoccupation with blood and death," his fascination with punishment, and his prophecy of "totalitarian society."[47] But de Maistre offered only old-fashioned solutions: the unlimited authority of Church and King. Zeev Sternhell has established that socialist heresies belong among the roots of fascism, though they were not alone, of course.[48] Other elements of the fascist mental universe—national unity, citizen participation—came from the bosom of liberal values.

Fascism's place in the European intellectual tradition is a matter of heated dispute. Two extreme positions have been staked out. Zeev Stern-hell considers fascism a coherent ideology that formed "an integral part of the history of European culture."[49] According to Hannah Arendt, Nazism "owed nothing to any part of the Western tradition, be it German or not, Catholic or Protestant, Christian, Greek or Roman. . . . On the contrary Nazism is actually the breakdown of all German and European traditions, the good as well as the bad . . . basing itself on the intoxication of destruction as an actual experience, dreaming the stupid dream of producing the void."[50]

In support of Sternhell, a whole repertory of themes had become available to fascism within European culture by 1914—the primacy of the "race" or the "community" or "the people" (the *Volk*, for Germans) over any individual rights; the right of the strongest races to fight it out for primacy; the virtue and beauty of violent action on behalf of the nation; fear of national decline and impurity; contempt for compromise; pessimism about human nature.

It is wrong, however, to construct a kind of intellectual teleology that starts with the fascist movement and reads backwards, selectively, rounding up every text or statement that seems to be pointing toward it. A linear pedigree that leads directly from pioneer thinkers to a finished fascism is pure invention. For one thing, nineteenth-century and early-twentieth-century rebels against conformist liberalism, such as Nietzsche, and against reformist socialism, such as Sorel, are not seen whole if we pick out the parts that seem to presage fascism. Fascist pamphleteers who quoted from them later were wrenching fragments out of context.

Antifascists, too, drew on these authors. Even some German *völkisch* writers rejected Nazism. Oswald Spengler, for example, despite the Nazis' enthusiasm for his work, always refused to endorse National Socialism. "Enthusiasm," he wrote in 1932, apparently with Hitler in mind, "is a dangerous burden on the road of politics. The pathfinder must be a hero, not a heroic tenor."[51] The poet Stefan George, whose dream of a purified community of peasants and artists led by a cultivated elite was attractive to some Nazis, refused their offer of the presidency of the German Academy. Horrified by the coarse violence of the Storm Troopers (*Sturmabteilungen*, or SA), George went into voluntary exile in Zürich, where he died in

December 1933.[52] One of his former disciples, Colonel Count Klaus Schenk von Stauffenberg, tried to assassinate Hitler in July 1944. Ernst Niekisch (1889–1967), whose radical rejection of bourgeois society was linked to a passionate German nationalism, cooperated briefly with Nazism in the middle 1920s before becoming a bitter opponent on the Left. The Austrian theorist of corporatism Othmar Spann was enthusiastic for Nazism in 1933, but the Nazi leadership judged his form of corporatism too anti-statist and they arrested him when they took over Austria in 1938.[53]

In Italy, Gaetano Mosca, who influenced Fascists by his analysis of the inevitable "circulation of elites" even within democracies, was one of the senators who stood up to Mussolini in 1921. He signed Croce's Anti-Fascist Manifesto in 1925. Giovanni Prezzolini, whose zeal to redo the Risorgimento had inspired the young Mussolini,[54] grew reserved and left to teach in the United States.

Intellectual and cultural preparation may have made it possible to imagine fascism, but they did not thereby bring fascism about. Even for Sternhell, the ideology of fascism, fully formed, he believes, by 1912, did not shape fascist regimes all by itself. Fascist regimes had to be woven into societies by choices and actions.[55]

The intellectual and cultural critics who are sometimes considered the creators of fascism actually account better for the space made available for fascism than they do fascism itself. They explain most directly the weakness of fascism's rivals, the previously ascendant bourgeois liberalism and the powerful reformist socialism of pre-1914 Europe. Concrete choices and actions were necessary before fascism could come into being, exploit that weakness, and occupy those spaces.

A further difficulty with tracing the intellectual and cultural roots of fascism is that the national cases differ so widely. That should not be surprising, for two reasons. Some national settings, most notably successful democracies but also troubled countries like Russia where dissent and anger still polarized to the Left, offered fascism few openings. Moreover, fascists do not invent the myths and symbols that compose the rhetoric of their movements but select those that suit their purposes from within the national cultural repertories. Most of these have no inherent or necessary link to fascism. The Russian Futurist poet Vladimir Mayakovsky, whose love of machines and speed equaled that of Marinetti, found his outlet as a fervent Bolshevik.

In any event, it is not the particular themes of Nazism or Italian Fascism that define the nature of the fascist phenomenon, but their function. Fascisms seek out in each national culture those themes that are best capable of mobilizing a mass movement of regeneration, unification, and purity, directed against liberal individualism and constitutionalism and against Leftist class struggle. The themes that appeal to fascists in one cultural tradition may seem simply silly to another. The foggy Norse myths that stirred Norwegians or Germans sounded ridiculous in Italy, where Fascism appealed rather to a sun-drenched classical *Romanità*.[56]

Nevertheless, where fascism appealed to intellectuals it did so most widely in its early stages. Its latitudinarian hospitality to disparate intellectual hangers-on was at its broadest then, before its antibourgeois animus was compromised by the quest for power. In the 1920s, it seemed the very essence of revolt against stuffy bourgeois conformity. The Vorticist movement, founded in London in 1913 by the American poet Ezra Pound and the Canadian-British writer and painter Wyndham Lewis,[57] was sympathetic to Italian Fascism in the 1920s. Its champions showed just as well as Marinetti's Futurism that one could be rebellious and avant-garde without having to swallow the leveling, the cosmopolitanism, the pacifism, the feminism, or the earnestness of the Left.

But the intellectual and cultural changes that helped make fascism conceivable and therefore possible were both broader and narrower, simultaneously, than the fascist phenomenon itself. On the one hand, many people shared in those currents without ever becoming fascist supporters. The British novelist D. H. Lawrence sounded like an early fascist in a letter to a friend, twenty months before the outbreak of World War I: "My great religion is a belief in the blood, the flesh, as being wiser than the intellect. We can go wrong in our minds, but what our blood feels and believes and says is always true."[58] But when the war began, Lawrence, married to a German woman, was horrified by the killing and declared himself a conscientious objector.

On the other hand, fascism became fully developed only after its practitioners had quietly closed their eyes to some of their early principles, in the effort to enter the coalitions necessary for power. Once in power, as we will see, fascists played down, marginalized, or even discarded some of the intellectual currents that had helped open the way.

To focus only on the educated carriers of intellect and culture in the search for fascist roots, furthermore, is to miss the most important register: subterranean passions and emotions. A nebula of attitudes was taking shape, and no one thinker ever put together a total philosophical system to support fascism. Even scholars who specialize in the quest for fascism's intellectual and cultural origins, such as George Mosse, declare that the establishment of a "mood" is more important than "the search for some individual precursors."[59] In that sense too, fascism is more plausibly linked to a set of "mobilizing passions" that shape fascist action than to a consistent and fully articulated philosophy. At bottom is a passionate nationalism. Allied to it is a conspiratorial and Manichean view of history as a battle between the good and evil camps, between the pure and the corrupt, in which one's own community or nation has been the victim. In this Darwinian narrative, the chosen people have been weakened by political parties, social classes, unassimilable minorities, spoiled rentiers, and rationalist thinkers who lack the necessary sense of community. These "mobilizing passions," mostly taken for granted and not always overtly argued as intellectual propositions, form the emotional lava that set fascism's foundations:

- a sense of overwhelming crisis beyond the reach of any traditional solutions;
- the primacy of the group, toward which one has duties superior to every right, whether individual or universal, and the subordination of the individual to it;
- the belief that one's group is a victim, a sentiment that justifies any action, without legal or moral limits, against its enemies, both internal and external;[60]
- dread of the group's decline under the corrosive effects of individualistic liberalism, class conflict, and alien influences;
- the need for closer integration of a purer community, by consent if possible, or by exclusionary violence if necessary;
- the need for authority by natural leaders (always male), culminating in a national chief who alone is capable of incarnating the group's destiny;
- the superiority of the leader's instincts over abstract and universal reason;
- the beauty of violence and the efficacy of will, when they are devoted to the group's success;
- the right of the chosen people to dominate others without restraint from any kind of human or divine law, right being decided by the sole criterion of the group's prowess within a Darwinian struggle.

The "mobilizing passions" of fascism are hard to treat historically, for many of them are as old as Cain. It seems incontestable, however, that the fevers of increased nationalism before World War I and the passions aroused by that war sharpened them. Fascism was an affair of the gut more than of the brain, and a study of the roots of fascism that treats only the thinkers and the writers misses the most powerful impulses of all.

Long-Term Preconditions

Longer-term shifts in fundamental political, social, and economic structures also helped prepare the way for fascism. As I pointed out at the beginning, fascism was a latecomer among political movements.[61] It was simply inconceivable before a number of basic preconditions had been put in place.

One necessary precondition was mass politics. As a mass movement directed against the Left, fascism could not really exist before the citizenry had become involved in politics. Some of the first switches on the tracks leading to fascism were thrown with the first enduring European experiments with manhood suffrage following the revolutions of 1848.[62] Up to that time, both conservatives and liberals had generally tried to limit the electorate to the wealthy and the educated—"responsible" citizens, capable of choosing among issues of broad principle. After the revolutions of 1848, while most conservatives and cautious liberals were trying to restore limits to the right to vote, a few bold and innovative conservative politicians chose instead to gamble on accepting a mass electorate and trying to manage it.

The adventurer Louis Napoleon was elected president of the Second French Republic in December 1848 by manhood suffrage, using simple imagery and what is called today "name recognition" (his uncle was the world-shaking Emperor Napoleon Bonaparte). Confronted with a liberal (in the nineteenth-century meaning of the term) legislature that tried in 1850 to disenfranchise poor and itinerant citizens, President Louis Napoleon boldly championed manhood suffrage. Even after he had made himself Emperor Napoleon III in a military coup d'état in December 1851, he let all male citizens vote for a phantom parliament. Against the liberals' preference for a restricted, educated electorate, the emperor pioneered the skillful use of simple slogans and symbols to appeal to the poor and little educated.[63]

Similarly, in the new German empire he completed in 1871, Bismarck chose to manipulate a broad suffrage in his battles against liberals. It would be absurd to call these authoritarians "fascists,"[64] but they were clearly pioneering in terrain that fascists would later master. By choosing to manipulate a mass electorate rather than to disenfranchise it, they parted company with both conservatives and liberals and with politics as then practiced, in the form of learned discussion among notables chosen by a deferential public to govern on its behalf.

Unlike conservatives and cautious liberals, fascists never wanted to keep the masses out of politics. They wanted to enlist, discipline, and energize them. In any event, by the end of World War I, there was no possible turning back to a narrow suffrage. Young men almost everywhere had been summoned to die for their countries, and one could hardly deny the full rights of citizenship to any of them. Women, too, whose economic and social roles the war had expanded enormously, received the vote in many northern European countries (though not yet in France, Italy, Spain, or Switzerland). While fascists sought to restore patriarchy in the family and the workplace, they preferred to mobilize sympathetic women rather than disfranchise them, at least until they could abolish voting altogether.[65]

European political culture also had to change before fascism became possible. The Right had to recognize that it could no longer avoid participating in mass politics. This transition was made easier by the gravitation of increasing numbers of middle-class citizens into conservative ranks, as their limited political demands were satisfied and as threatening new socialist demands took shape. By 1917 (if not before), the revolutionary project was immediate enough to alienate much of the middle class from the Left allegiance of its democratic grandparents of 1848. Conservatives could begin to dream of managing electoral majorities.

The democratic and socialist Lefts, still united in 1848, had to split apart before fascism could become possible. The Left also had to lose its position as the automatic recourse for all the partisans of change—the dreamers and the angry, among the middle class as well as the working class. Fascism is therefore inconceivable in the absence of a mature and expanding socialist Left. Indeed fascists can find their space only after socialism has become powerful enough to have had some share in governing, and thus to have disillusioned part of its traditional working-class and intellectual clientele. So we can situate fascism in time not only after the irreversible establishment of mass politics, but indeed late in that process, when socialists have reached the point of participating in government—and being compromised by it.

That threshold was crossed in September 1899, when the first European socialist accepted a position in a bourgeois cabinet, in order to help support French democracy under attack during the Dreyfus Affair, thereby earning the hostility of some of his movement's moral purists.[66] By 1914, part of the Left's traditional following had become disillusioned with what they considered the compromises of moderate parliamentary socialists. After the war, looking for something more uncompromisingly revolutionary, they went over to Bolshevism, or, as we have seen, via national syndicalism to fascism.

After 1917, of course, the Left was no longer gathering itself and waiting for its moment, as it had been doing before 1914. It was threatening to march across the world at the head of a seemingly irresistible Bolshevik Revolution. The fright given the entire middle and upper classes by Lenin's victory in Russia, and the anticipated success of his followers in more industrialized Germany, is crucial for understanding the panicky search during 1918–22 for some new kind of response to Bolshevism.

The fire-bells set off by Bolshevism transformed into emergencies the difficulties already faced by liberal values and institutions in the aftermath of World War I.[67] All three key liberal institutions—parliament, market, school—dealt poorly with these emergencies. Elected representatives struggled to find the necessary minimum of common ground to make difficult policy choices. Assumptions about the adequacy of a self-regulating market, even if believable in the long run, seemed laughably inadequate in the face of immediate national and international economic dislocations. Free schooling no longer seemed sufficient by itself to integrate communities shaken by the cacophony of opposing interests, cultural pluralism, and artistic experiment. The crisis of liberal institutions did not affect every country with exactly the same intensity, however, and I will explore these varying national experiences in the next chapter.

Precursors

We have already noted that fascism was unexpected. It is not the linear projection of any one nineteenth-century political tendency. It is not easily comprehensible in terms of any of the major nineteenth-century paradigms: liberalism, conservatism, socialism. There were neither words nor concepts for it before Mussolini's movement and others like it were created in the aftermath of World War I.

There had been straws in the wind, however. Late in the nineteenth century came the first signs of a "Politics in a New Key":[68] the creation of the first popular movements dedicated to reasserting the priority of the nation against all forms of internationalism or cosmopolitanism. The decade of the 1880s—with its simultaneous economic depression and broadened democratic practice—was a crucial threshold.

That decade confronted Europe and the world with nothing less than the first globalization crisis. In the 1880s new steamships made it possible to bring cheap wheat and meat to Europe, bankrupting family farms and aristocratic estates and sending a flood of rural refugees into the cities. At the same time, railroads knocked the bottom out of what was left of skilled artisanal labor by delivering cheap manufactured goods to every city. At the same ill-chosen moment, unprecedented numbers of immigrants arrived in western Europe—not only the familiar workers from Spain and Italy, but also culturally exotic Jews fleeing oppression in eastern Europe. These shocks form the backdrop to some developments in the 1880s that we can now perceive as the first gropings toward fascism.

The conservative French and German experiments with a manipulated manhood suffrage that I alluded to earlier were extended in the 1880s. The third British Reform Bill of 1884 nearly doubled the electorate to include almost all adult males. In all these countries, political elites found themselves in the 1880s forced to adapt to a shift in political culture that weakened the social deference that had long produced the almost automatic election of upper-class representatives to parliament, thereby opening the way to the entry of more modest social strata into politics: shopkeepers, country doctors and pharmacists, small-town lawyers—the "new layers" (*nouvelles couches*) famously summoned forth in 1874 by Léon Gambetta, soon to be himself, the son of an immigrant Italian grocer, the first French prime minister of modest origins.

Lacking personal fortunes, this new type of elected representative lived on their parliamentarians' salary and became the first professional politicians.[69] Lacking the hereditary name recognition of the "notables" who had dominated European parliaments up to then, the new politicians had to invent new kinds of support networks and new kinds of appeal. Some of them built political machines based upon middle-class social clubs, such as Freemasonry (as Gambetta's Radical Party did in France); others, in both Germany and France, discovered the drawing power of anti-Semitism and nationalism.[70]

Rising nationalism penetrated at the end of the nineteenth century even into the ranks of organized labor. I referred earlier in this chapter to the hostility between German-speaking and Czech-speaking wage earners in Bohemia, in what was then the Habsburg empire. By 1914 it was going to be possible to use nationalist sentiment to mobilize parts of the working class against other parts of it, and even more so after World War I.

For all these reasons, the economic crisis of the 1880s, as the first major depression to occur in the era of mass politics, rewarded demagoguery. Henceforth a decline in the standard of living would translate quickly into electoral defeats for incumbents and victories for political outsiders ready to appeal with summary slogans to angry voters.

Several notorious mass-based populist nationalist movements arose in Europe during the 1880s. France, precocious in so many political experiments, was also a pioneer in this one. The glamorous General Boulanger, made minister of war in January 1886 by the moderately Left-leaning government of Charles de Freycinet, was idolized in Paris because he had stood up to the Germans and had treated his soldiers considerately, and because his blond beard and black horse looked splendid in patriotic parades. The general was dismissed as minister of war in May 1887, however, for excessively bellicose language during a period of tension with Germany. His departure for a provincial reassignment triggered a gigantic popular demonstration as his Parisian fans lay down on the rails to block his train. Boulanger had originally been close to the anticlerical moderate Left ("Radicals," in the French political terminology of the day), but he now allowed himself to become the center of a political agitation that drew from both Left and Right. While he continued to support Radical proposals such as the abolition of the indirectly elected senate, his advocacy of sweeping constitutional changes now acquired an odor of conspiracy by a providential man.

When the alarmed government dismissed Boulanger from the army, the ex-general was now free to indulge his newfound political ambitions. His strategy was to run in every by-election that occurred whenever a parliamentary seat became vacant through death or resignation. Boulanger turned out to have wide popular appeal in working-class districts. Monarchists as well as Bonapartists gave him money because his success seemed more likely to damage the Republic than to reform it. In January 1889, after he had won a by-election in Paris by a considerable majority, Boulanger's supporters urged him to carry out a coup d'état against a French Republic already reeling under financial scandals and economic depression. At the climactic moment, however, the providential man faltered. Threatened with government prosecution, he fled to Belgium on April 1, where he later committed suicide on the grave of his mistress. Boulangism turned out to be a flash in the pan.[71] But for the first time in Europe the ingredients had been assembled for a mass-based, populist nationalist gathering around a charismatic figure.

Similar ingredients mingled in the popular emotions aroused in France after 1896 against Captain Alfred Dreyfus, a Jewish staff officer wrongly accused of spying for Germany. The case convulsed France until 1906. The anti-Dreyfus camp enlisted in defense of the authority of the state and the honor of the army both conservatives and some Leftists influenced by traditional anticapitalist anti-Semitism and Jacobin forms of nationalism. The pro-Dreyfus camp, mostly from Left and center, defended a universal standard of the rights of man. The nation took precedence over any universal value, proclaimed the anti-Dreyfusard Charles Maurras, whose Action Française movement is sometimes considered the first authentic fascism.[72] When a document used to incriminate Dreyfus turned out to have been faked, Maurras was undaunted. It was, he said, a "patriotic forgery," a *faux patriotique.*

Austria-Hungary was another setting where forerunner movements successfully pioneered in the terrain of populist nationalism. Georg von Schönerer (1842–1921), a wealthy landowner and apostle of pan-Germanism from the Sudetenland, along the western fringes of Bohemia, urged the German speakers of the Habsburg empire to work for union with the German empire and to fight Catholic and Jewish influence.[73] We have already noted how Karl Lueger was elected mayor of Vienna in 1897, over the opposition of the emperor and traditional liberals, and governed invincibly until his death in 1910 with a path-breaking mixture of "municipal socialism" (public gas, water, electricity, hospitals, schools, and parks) and anti-Semitism.[74]

German politicians, too, experimented in the 1880s with the appeal of anti-Semitism. The Protestant court pastor Adolf Stöcker used it in his Christian Social Party in an attempt to draw voters from the working and lower middle classes to conservatism. A new generation of liberals drawn from outside the old circles of aristocrats and big planters, lacking the old mechanisms of social deference, used it as a new way to manage mass politics.[75] But these tests of overtly anti-Semitic politics in Germany had shrunk to insignificance by the early twentieth century. Such forerunner movements showed that while many elements of later fascism already existed, conditions were not ripe to put them together and gain a substantial following.[76]

Arguably the first concrete example of "national socialism" in practice was the Cercle Proudhon in France in 1911, a study group designed to "unite nationalists and left-wing anti-democrats" around an offensive against "Jewish capitalism."[77] It was the creation of Georges Valois, a former militant of Charles Maurras's Action Française who broke away from his master in order to concentrate more actively on converting the working class from Marxist internationalism to the nation. It proved too early, however, to rally more than a few intellectuals and journalists to Valois's "triumph of heroic values over the ignoble bourgeois materialism in which Europe is now stifling . . . [and] . . . the awakening of Force and Blood against Gold."[78]

The term *national socialism* seems to have been invented by the French nationalist author Maurice Barrès, who described the aristocratic adventurer the Marquis de Morès in 1896 as the "first national socialist."[79] Morès, after failing as a cattle rancher in North Dakota, returned to Paris in the early 1890s and organized a band of anti-Semitic toughs who attacked Jewish shops and offices. As a cattleman, Morès found his recruits among slaughterhouse workers in Paris, to whom he appealed with a mixture of anticapitalism and anti-Semitic nationalism.[80] His squads wore the cowboy garb and ten-gallon hats that the marquis had discovered in the American West, which thus predate black and brown shirts (by a modest stretch of the imagination) as the first fascist uniform. Morès killed a popular Jewish officer, Captain Armand Meyer, in a duel early in the Dreyfus Affair, and was himself killed by his Touareg guides in the Sahara in 1896 on an expedition to "unite France to Islam and to Spain."[81] "Life is valuable only through action," he had proclaimed. "So much the worse if the action is mortal."[82]

Some Italians were moving in the same direction. Some Italian disciples of Sorel found in the nation the kind of mobilizing myth that the proletarian revolution was failing to provide.[83] Those who, like Sorel, wanted to retain the purity of motive and intensity of commitment that socialism had offered when it was a hounded opposition, now joined those who despised the compromises of parliamentary socialism and those who were becoming disillusioned by the failure of general strikes—climaxing in the terrible defeat of "red week" in Milan in June 1914. They thought that productivism[84] and expansionist war for "proletarian" Italy (as in Libya in 1911) might replace the general strike as the most effective mobilizing myth for revolutionary change in Italy. Another foundation stone had been laid for the edifice that fascists would build: the project of winning the socialists' clientele back to the nation via a heroic antisocialist "national syndicalism."

Considering these precursors, a debate has arisen about which country spawned the earliest fascist movement. France is a frequent candidate.[85] Russia has been proposed.[86] Hardly anyone puts Germany first.[87] It may be that the earliest phenomenon that can be functionally related to fascism is American: the Ku Klux Klan. Just after the Civil War, some former Confederate officers, fearing the vote given to African Americans in 1867 by the Radical Reconstructionists, set up a militia to restore an overturned social order. The Klan constituted an alternate civic authority, parallel to the legal state, which, in the eyes of the Klan's founders, no longer defended their community's legitimate interests. By adopting a uniform (white robe and hood), as well as by their techniques of intimidation and their conviction that violence was justified in the cause of their group's destiny,[88] the first version of the Klan in the defeated American South was arguably a remarkable preview of the way fascist movements were to function in interwar Europe. It should not be surprising, after all, that the most precocious democracies—the United States and France—should have generated precocious backlashes against democracy.

Today we can perceive these experiments as harbingers of a new kind of politics to come. At the time, however, they seemed to be personal aberrations by individual adventurers. They were not yet perceptible as examples of a new system. They become visible this way only in retrospect, after all the pieces have come together, a space has opened up, and a name has been invented.

Recruitment

We have repeatedly encountered embittered war veterans in our account of the founding of the first fascist movements. Fascism would have remained a mere pressure group for veterans and their younger brothers, however, if it had not drawn in many other kinds of recruits.[89]

Above all, the early fascists were young. Many of the new generation were convinced that the white-bearded men responsible for the war, who still clung to their places, understood nothing of their concerns, whether they had experienced the front or not. Young people who had never voted before responded enthusiastically to fascism's brand of antipolitical politics.[90]

Several features distinguished the most successful fascisms from previous parties. Unlike the middle-class parties led by "notables" who condescended to contact their publics only at election time, the fascist parties swept their members up into an intense fraternity of emotion and effort.[91] Unlike the class parties—socialist or bourgeois—fascist parties managed to realize their claim to bring together citizens from all social classes. These were attractive features for many.[92]

Early fascist parties did not recruit from all classes in the same proportions, however. It was soon noticed that fascist parties were largely middle class, to the point where fascism was perceived as the very embodiment of lower-middle-class resentments.[93] But, after all, all political parties are largely middle class. On closer inspection, fascism turned out to appeal to upper-class members and voters as well.[94]

Early fascism also won more working-class followers than used to be thought, though these were always proportionally fewer than their share in the population.[95] The relative scarcity of working-class fascists was not due to some proletarian immunity to appeals of nationalism and ethnic cleansing. It is better explained by "immunization" and "confessionalism":[96] those already deeply engaged, from generation to generation, in the rich subculture of socialism, with its clubs, newspapers, unions, and rallies, were simply not available for another loyalty.

Workers were more available for fascism if they stood outside the community of socialists. It helped if they had a tradition of direct action, and of hostility to parliamentary socialism: in Italy, blackleg marble workers in traditionally anarchist Carrara,[97] for example, or the Genoese seamen organized by Captain Giuseppe Giulietti, who followed first D'Annunzio and then Mussolini. The unemployed, too, had been separated from organized socialism (which, under the harsh and divisive conditions of economic depression, appeared to value employed workers more than the unemployed). The unemployed were more likely to join the communists than the fascists, however, unless they were first-time voters or from the middle class.[98] A similar rootedness in the parish community probably explains the smaller proportion of Catholics than Protestants among the Nazi electorate.

Special local conditions could draw proletarians to fascism. A third of the members of the British Union of Fascists in rundown East London were unskilled or semiskilled workers, recruited through resentment at recent Jewish immigrants, disillusion with the feckless Labour Party, or anger at communist and Jewish assaults upon BUF parades.[99] The Hungarian Arrow Cross won a third of the votes in heavily industrial central Budapest (Csepel Island), and had success in some rural mining areas, in the absence of a plausible Left alternative for an antigovernment protest vote.[100]

Whether fascism recruited more by an appeal to reason than to the emotions is hotly debated.[101] The evident power of emotions within fascism has tempted many to believe that fascism recruited the emotionally disturbed or the sexually deviant. I will consider some of the pitfalls of psychohistory in chapter 8. It needs to be reemphasized that Hitler himself, while driven by hatreds and abnormal obsessions, was capable of pragmatic decision-making and rational choices, especially before 1942. To conclude that Nazism or other forms of fascism are forms of mental disturbance is doubly dangerous: it offers an alibi to the multitude of "normal" fascists, and it ill prepares us to recognize the utter normality of authentic fascism. Most fascist leaders and militants were quite ordinary people thrust into positions of extraordinary power and responsibility by processes that are perfectly comprehensible in rational terms. Putting fascism on the couch can lead us astray. Suspicions about Hitler's own perverse sexuality rest on no firm evidence,[102] though he was notoriously no conventional family man. Both homosexuals (such as Ernst Röhm and Edmund Heines of the SA) and violent homophobes (Himmler, for example) were prominent in the masculine fraternity that was Nazism. But there is no evidence that the proportion of homosexuals was higher among Nazis than in the general population. The issue has not risen for Italian Fascism.

The fascist leaders were outsiders of a new type. New people had forced their way into national leadership before. There had long been hard-bitten soldiers who fought better than aristocratic officers and became indispensable to kings. A later form of political recruitment came from young men of modest background who made good when electoral politics broadened in the late nineteenth century. One thinks of the aforementioned French politician Léon Gambetta, the grocer's son, or the beer wholesaler's son Gustav Stresemann, who became the preeminent statesman of Weimar Germany. A third kind of successful outsider in modern times has been clever mechanics in new industries (consider those entrepreneurial bicycle makers Henry Ford, William Morris, and the Wrights).

But many of the fascist leaders were marginal in a new way. They did not resemble the interlopers of earlier eras: the soldiers of fortune, the first upwardly mobile parliamentary politicians, or the clever mechanics. Some were bohemians, lumpen-intellectuals, dilettantes, experts in nothing except the manipulation of crowds and the fanning of resentments: Hitler, the failed art student; Mussolini, a schoolteacher by trade but mostly a restless revolutionary, expelled for subversion from Switzerland and the Trentino; Joseph Goebbels, the jobless college graduate with literary ambitions; Hermann Goering, the drifting World War I fighter ace; Heinrich Himmler, the agronomy student who failed at selling fertilizer and raising chickens.

Yet the early fascist cadres were far too diverse in social origins and education to fit the common label of marginal outsiders.[103] Alongside street-brawlers with criminal records like Amerigo Dumini[104] or Martin Bormann one could find a professor of philosophy like Giovanni Gentile[105] or even, briefly, a musician like Arturo Toscanini.[106] What united them was, after all, values rather than a social profile: scorn for tired bourgeois politics, opposition to the Left, fervent nationalism, a tolerance for violence when needed.

Someone has said that a political party is like a bus: people are always getting on and off. We will see as we go along how fascist clientele altered over time, from early radicals to later careerists. Here, too, we cannot see the fascist phenomenon in full by looking only at its beginnings.

Understanding Fascism by Its Origins

In this chapter we have looked at the times, the places, the clientele, and the rhetoric of the first fledgling fascist movements. Now we are forced to admit that the first movements do not tell the whole story. The first fascisms were going to be transformed by the very enterprise of trying to be more than a marginal voice. Wherever they became more active claimants for power, that effort was to turn them into something strikingly different from the radical early days. Understanding the first movements gives us only a partial and incomplete understanding of the whole phenomenon.

It is curious what a disproportionate amount of historical attention has been lavished on the beginnings of fascism. There are several reasons for this. One is the latent (but misleading) Darwinian convention that if we study the origins of something we grasp its inner blueprint. Another is the availability of a profusion of fascist words and cultural artifacts from the early stages which are grist for historians' mills; the subtler, more secretive, and more sordid business of negotiating deals to reach or exercise power somehow seems a less alluring subject (erroneously so!).

A solid pragmatic reason why so many works about fascism concentrate on the early movements is that most fascist movements never got any further. To write of fascism in Scandinavia, Britain, the Low Countries, or even France is necessarily to write of movements that never developed beyond founding a newspaper, staging some demonstrations, speaking on street corners. José Antonio Primo de Rivera in Spain, Mosley in Britain, and the most outspokenly fascist movements in France never even participated in the electoral process.[107]

Looking mainly at early fascism starts us down several false trails. It puts intellectuals at the center of an enterprise whose major decisions were made by power-seeking men of action. The intellectual fellow travelers had diminishing influence in the rooting and regime stages of the fascist cycle, although certain ideas reasserted themselves in the radicalization stage (see chapter 6). Further, concentrating on origins puts misleading emphasis on early fascism's antibourgeois rhetoric and its critique of capitalism. It privileges the "poetic movement" of José Antonio Primo de Rivera that would impose "hard and just sacrifices . . . on many of our own class," and "reach the humble as well as the powerful with its benefits,"[108] and the "great red fascism of our youth," as Robert Brasillach remembered it with fond nostalgia shortly before his execution for treason in Paris in February 1945.[109]

Comparison, finally, has little bite at the early stages, for every country with mass politics had a fledgling fascist movement at some point after 1918. Comparison does show that the map of fascist intellectual creativity does not coincide with the map of fascist success. Some observers contend that fascism was invented in France, and attained its fullest intellectual flowering there.[110] But fascism did not come close to power in France until after military defeat in 1940, as we will see in more detail below.

The first to test early fascism at the ballot box was Mussolini. He imagined that his antisocialist but antibourgeois "antiparty" would draw in all the veterans of Italy and their admirers and turn his Fasci di Combattimento into a mass catch-all party. Running for parliament in Milan on November 16, 1919, on the original San Sepolcro program, with its mixture of radical domestic change and expansionist nationalism, he received a total of 4,796 votes out of 315,165.[111] Before becoming a major contender in Italian political life, he would have to make adjustments.

To understand fascism whole, we need to spend as much energy on the later forms as on the beginnings. The adaptations and transformations that mark the path followed by some fascisms from movement to party to regime to final paroxysm will occupy much of the rest of this book.

CHAPTER 3

Taking Root

Successful Fascisms

Between the two world wars, almost every nation on earth, and certainly all those with mass politics, generated some intellectual current or activist movement akin to fascism. Nearly ubiquitous but mostly ephemeral, movements like the Greyshirts of Iceland[1] or the New Guard of New South Wales (Australia)[2] would not interest us urgently today had not a few of their kind grown big and dangerous. A few fascist movements became much more successful than the general run of fascist street-corner orators and bullies. By becoming the carriers of substantial grievances and interests, and by becoming capable of rewarding political ambitions, they took root within political systems. A handful of them played major roles in public life. These successful fascisms elbowed a space among the other contending parties or interest groups, and persuaded influential people that they could represent their interests and feelings and fulfill their ambitions better than any conventional party. The early ragtag outsiders thus transformed themselves into serious political forces capable of competing on equal terms with longer-established parties or movements. Their success influenced entire political systems, giving them a more intense and aggressive tone and legitimating open expressions of extreme nationalism, Left-baiting, and racism. This bundle of processes—how fascist parties take root—is the subject of the present chapter.

Becoming a successful participant in electoral or pressure-group politics forced young fascist movements to focus their words and actions more precisely. It became harder for them to indulge their initial freedom to mobilize a wide range of heterogeneous complaints, and to voice the scattered resentments of everyone (except socialists) who felt aggrieved but unrepresented. They had to make choices. They had to give up the amorphous realms of indiscriminate protest and locate a definite political space[3] in which they could obtain positive practical results. In order to form effective working relations with significant partners, they had to make themselves useful in measurable ways. They had to offer their followers concrete advantages and engage in specific actions whose beneficiaries and victims were obvious.

These more focused steps forced the fascist parties to make their priorities clearer. At this stage, one can begin to test fascist rhetoric against fascist actions. We can see what really counted. The radical rhetoric never disappeared, of course: as late as June 1940 Mussolini summoned "Proletarian and Fascist Italy" and "the Blackshirts of the Revolution" to "the battlefield against the plutocratic and reactionary democracies of the West."[4] As soon as the fascist parties began to take root in concrete political action, however, the selective nature of their antibourgeois rhetoric became clearer.

It turned out in practice that fascists' anticapitalism was highly selective.[5] Even at their most radical, the socialism that the fascists wanted was a "national socialism": one that denied only foreign or enemy property rights (including that of internal enemies). They cherished national producers.[6] Above all, it was by offering an effective remedy against socialist revolution that fascism turned out in practice to find a space. If Mussolini retained some lingering hopes in 1919 of founding an alternative socialism rather than an antisocialism, he was soon disabused of those notions by observing what worked and what didn't work in Italian politics. His dismal electoral results with a Left-nationalist program in Milan in November 1919[7] surely hammered that lesson home.

The pragmatic choices of Mussolini and Hitler were driven by their urge for success and power. Not all fascist leaders had such ambitions. Some of them preferred to keep their movements "pure," even at the cost of remaining marginal. José Antonio Primo de Rivera, founder of the Falange Española, saw his mission as the reconciliation of workers and employers by replacing materialism—the fatal flaw of both capitalism and socialism—with idealism in the service of Nation and Church, though his early death in November 1936 before a Republican firing squad saved him from the hard choices Franco's success would have forced on him.[8] Charles Maurras, whose Action Française was a pioneer of populist anti-Left nationalism, let his followers run for office only once, in 1919, when his chief lieutenant, the journalist Léon Daudet, and a handful of provincial sympathizers were elected to the French Chamber of Deputies. Colonel François de La Rocque's Croix de Feu disdained elections, but its more moderate successor, the Parti Social Français, began running candidates in by-elections in 1938.[9] Ferenc Szálasi, the former staff officer who headed the Hungarian Arrow Cross, refused ever to run for office again after two defeats, and preferred nebulous philosophizing to maneuvers for power.

Hitler and Mussolini, by contrast, not only felt destined to rule but shared none of the purists' qualms about competing in bourgeois elections. Both set out—with impressive tactical skill and by rather different routes, which they discovered by trial and error—to make themselves indispensable participants in the competition for political power within their nations.

Becoming a successful political player inevitably involved losing followers as well as gaining them. Even the simple step of becoming a party could seem a betrayal to some purists of the first hour. When Mussolini decided to change his movement into a party late in 1921, some of his idealistic early followers saw this as a descent into the soiled arena of bourgeois parliamentarism.[10] Being a party ranked talk above action, deals above principle, and competing interests above a united nation. Idealistic early fascists saw themselves as offering a new form of public life—an "antiparty"[11]—capable of gathering the entire nation, in opposition to both parliamentary liberalism, with its encouragement of faction, and socialism, with its class struggle. José Antonio described the Falange Española as "a movement and not a party—indeed you could almost call it an anti-party . . . neither of the Right nor of the Left."[12] Hitler's NSDAP, to be sure, had called itself a party from the beginning, but its members, who knew it was not like the other parties, called it "the movement" *(die Bewegung)*. Mostly fascists called their organizations movements[13] or camps[14] or bands[15] or *rassemblements*[16] or *fasci*: brotherhoods that did not pit one interest against others, but claimed to unite and energize the nation.

Conflicts over what fascist movements should call themselves were relatively trivial. Far graver compromises and transformations were involved in the process of becoming a significant actor in a political arena. For that process involved teaming up with some of the very capitalist speculators and bourgeois party leaders whose rejection had been part of the early movements' appeal. How the fascists managed to retain some of their antibourgeois rhetoric and a measure of "revolutionary" aura while forming practical political alliances with parts of the establishment constitutes one of the mysteries of their success.

Becoming a successful contender in the political arena required more than clarifying priorities and knitting alliances. It meant offering a new political style that would attract voters who had concluded that "politics" had become dirty and futile. Posing as an "antipolitics" was often effective with people whose main political motivation was scorn for politics. In situations where existing parties were confined within class or confessional boundaries, like Marxist, smallholders', or Christian parties, the fascists could appeal by promising to unite a people rather than divide it. Where existing parties were run by parliamentarians who thought mainly of their own careers, fascist parties could appeal to idealists by being "parties of engagement," in which committed militants rather than careerist politicians set the tone. In situations where a single political clan had monopolized power for years, fascism could pose as the only nonsocialist path to renewal and fresh leadership. In such ways, fascists pioneered in the 1920s by creating the first European "catch-all" parties of "engagement,"[17] readily distinguished from their tired, narrow rivals as much by the breadth of their social base as by the intense activism of their militants.

Comparison acquires some bite at this point: only some societies experienced so severe a breakdown of existing systems that citizens began to look to outsiders for salvation. In many cases fascist establishment failed; in others it was never really attempted. Fully successful fascist implantation occurred in only a few cases in Europe between the wars. I propose to discuss three cases in this chapter: two successful and one unsuccessful. Then we will be in a better position to see clearly what conditions helped fascist movements to become implanted in a political system.

(1) The Po Valley, Italy, 1920–22

Mussolini was saved from oblivion after the nearly terminal disaster of the elections of November 1919 by a new tactic invented by some of his followers in rural northern Italy: *squadrismo*. Some of his more aggressive disciples there formed strong-arm squads, *squadre d'azione*, and applied the tactics they had learned as soldiers to attacking the internal enemies (in their view) of the Italian nation. Marinetti and some other friends of Mussolini had set the example in their April 1919 raid on *Avanti*.[18]

The *squadre* started their career in the nationalist cauldron of Trieste, a polyglot Adriatic port taken from Austria-Hungary by Italy according to the terms of the postwar settlement. To establish Italian supremacy in this cosmopolitan city, a fascist squad burned the Balkan Hotel, where the Slovene Association had its headquarters, in July 1920, and intimidated Slovenes in the street.

Mussolini's Blackshirts were not alone in using direct action for nationalist aims in postwar Italy. Mussolini's most serious rival was the writer-adventurer Gabriele D'Annunzio. In 1919–20 D'Annunzio was, in fact, a far greater celebrity than the leader of the tiny Fascist sect. He was already notorious in Italy not only for his bombastic plays and poems and his extravagant life, but also for leading air raids over Austrian territory during World War I (in which he lost an eye).

In September 1919, D'Annunzio led a band of nationalists and war veterans into the Adriatic port of Fiume, which the peacemakers at Versailles had awarded to the new state of Yugoslavia. Declaring Fiume the "Republic of Carnaro," D'Annunzio invented the public theatricality that Mussolini was later to make his own: daily harangues by the *Comandante* from a balcony, lots of uniforms and parades, the "Roman salute" with arm outstretched, the meaningless war cry *"Eia, eia, alalà."*

As the occupation of Fiume turned into an international embarrassment for Italy, D'Annunzio defied the government in Rome and his more conservative nationalist backers drifted away. The Fiume regime drew its support increasingly from the nationalist Left. Alceste De Ambris, for example, an interventionist syndicalist and friend of Mussolini, drafted its new constitution, the Charter of Carnaro. D'Annunzian Fiume became a kind of martial populist republic whose chief drew directly upon a popular will affirmed in mass rallies, and whose labor unions sat alongside management in official "corporations" that were supposed to manage the economy together. An international "Fiume League" attempted to assemble the national liberation movements of the world as a rival to the League of Nations.[19]

Mussolini uttered only mild protests when the old master political fixer Giovanni Giolitti, once again prime minister of Italy, at the age of eighty, negotiated a settlement with Yugoslavia in November 1920 that made Fiume an international city, and then sent the Italian navy at Christmas to disperse D'Annunzio's volunteers. This did not mean that Mussolini was uninterested in Fiume. Once in power, he forced Yugoslavia to recognize the city as Italian in 1924.[20] But Mussolini's ambitions gained from D'Annunzio's humiliation. Adopting many of the

Comandante's mannerisms, Mussolini managed to draw back to his own movement many veterans of the Fiume adventure, including Alceste De Ambris.

Mussolini succeeded where D'Annunzio failed by more than mere luck or style. Mussolini was sufficiently thirsty for power to make deals with leading centrist politicians. D'Annunzio gambled all or nothing on Fiume, and he was more interested in the purity of his gestures than in the substance of power. He was also fifty-seven years old in 1920. Once in office, Mussolini easily bought him off with the title of prince of Monte Nevoso and a castle on Lake Garda.[21] D'Annunzio's failure is a warning to those who wish to interpret fascism primarily in terms of its cultural expressions. Theater was not enough.

Above all Mussolini bested D'Annunzio by serving economic and social interests as well as nationalist sentiment. He made his Blackshirts available for action against socialists as well as against the South Slavs of Fiume and Trieste. War veterans had hated the socialists since 1915 for their "antinational" stance during the war. Big planters in the Po Valley, Tuscany, Apulia, and other regions of large estates hated and feared the socialists for their success at the end of the war in organizing the *braccianti,* or landless laborers, to press for higher wages and better working conditions. *Squadrismo* was the conjunction of these two hatreds.

Following their victory in the first postwar election (November 1919), the Italian socialists had used their new power in local government to establish de facto control over the agricultural wage-labor market. In the Po Valley in 1920, every farmer who needed workmen for planting or harvesting had to visit the socialist Labor Exchange. The Labor Exchanges made the most of their new leverage. They forced the farmers to hire workers year-round rather than only seasonally, and with better wages and working conditions. The farmers were financially squeezed. They had invested considerable sums before the war in transforming Po Valley marshlands into cultivable farms; their cash crops earned little money in the difficult conditions of the Italian postwar economy. The socialist unions also undermined the farmers' personal status as masters of their domains.

Frightened and humiliated, the Po Valley landowners looked frantically for help.[22] They did not find it in the Italian state. Local officials were either socialists themselves, or little inclined to do battle with them. Prime Minister Giolitti, a true practitioner of laissez-faire liberalism, declined to use national forces to break strikes. The big farmers felt abandoned by the Italian liberal state.

In the absence of help from the public authorities, the large landowners of the Po Valley turned to the Blackshirts for protection. Glad for an excuse to attack their old pacifist enemies, fascist *squadre* invaded the city hall in Bologna, where socialist officials had hung up a red banner, on November 21, 1920. Six were killed. From there, the movement quickly spread throughout the rich agricultural country in the lower Po River delta. Black-shirted *squadristi* mounted nightly expeditions to sack and burn Labor Exchanges and local socialist offices, and beat and intimidate socialist organizers. Their favorite forms of humiliation were administering uncontainable doses of castor oil and shaving off half of a proud Latin moustache. In the first six months of 1921, the squads destroyed 17 newspapers and printing works, 59 Peoples' Houses (socialist headquarters), 119 Chambers of Labor (socialist employment offices), 107 cooperatives, 83 Peasants' Leagues, 151 socialist clubs, and 151 cultural organizations.[23] Between January 1 and April 7, 1921, 102 people were killed: 25 fascists, 41 socialists, 20 police, and 16 others.[24]

The Po Valley Blackshirts' success was not based on force alone. The Fascists also gave some peasants what they wanted most: jobs and land. Turning the tables on the socialists, the Fascists established their own monopoly over the farm labor market. By offering a few peasants their own small parcels of land, donated by farsighted owners, they persuaded large numbers of landless peasants to abandon the socialist unions. Land had been the heart's desire of all Po Valley peasants who had too little (as smallholders, sharecroppers, or renters) or none at all (as day laborers). The socialists quickly lost their hold on these categories of farmworkers, not only because they had been exposed as unable to defend their postwar gains, but also because their long-term goal of collectivized farms was unattractive to the land-hungry rural poor.

At the same time, the *squadristi* succeeded in demonstrating the incapacity of the state to protect the landowners and maintain order. They even began to supplant the state in the organization of public life and to infringe on its monopoly of force. As they became more daring, the Blackshirts occupied whole cities. Once installed in Ferrara, say, they would force the town to institute a program of public works. By early 1922, the Fascist squads and their truculent leaders, such as Italo Balbo in Ferrara and Roberto Farinacci in Cremona—called *ras* after Ethiopian chieftains—were a de facto power in northeastern Italy with which the state had to reckon, without whose goodwill local governments could not function normally.

Landowners were not the only ones who helped the Blackshirts of the Po Valley smash socialism. Local police and army commanders lent them arms and trucks, and some of their younger personnel joined the expeditions. Some local prefects, resentful of the pretensions of new socialist mayors and town councils, turned a blind eye to these nightly forays, or even supplied vehicles.

Although the Po Valley Fascists still advocated some policies—public works for the unemployed, for example—that recalled the movement's initial radicalism, the *squadristi* were widely viewed as the strong-arm agents of the big landowners. Some idealistic early Fascists were horrified by this transformation. They appealed to Mussolini and the Milan leadership to stop this drift toward complicity with powerful local interests. Barbato Gatelli, one of the disillusioned, complained bitterly that Fascism had lost its original ideals and had become "the bodyguard of the profiteers." He and his friends tried to organize a rival Fascist movement and a new newspaper *(L'Idea Fascista)* to recover the old spirit, but Mussolini sided with the *squadristi*.[25] The purists eventually left the party or were pushed out of it. They were replaced by sons of landowners, younger policemen, army officers and NCOs, and other supporters of *squadrismo*. D'Annunzio, to whom some of the disgruntled idealists looked to replace Mussolini, grumbled that Fascism had come to mean "agrarian slavery."[26] That was neither the first nor the last time fascist movements lost part of their first clientele and recruited a new one,[27] in the process of positioning themselves to become rooted in a profitable political space.

As we saw in the previous chapter, the first Fascists had been recruited among radical veterans, national syndicalists, and Futurist intellectuals— young antibourgeois malcontents who wanted social change along with national grandeur. In many cases it was only nationalism that separated them from socialists and the radical wing of the new Catholic party, the Partito Popolare Italiano ("Popolari").[28] Indeed, many had come from the Left—like Mussolini himself. *Squadrismo* altered the movement's social composition toward the Right. Sons of landowners, even some criminal elements, now joined. But Fascism still retained its youthful quality: the new Fascism remained a generational revolt against the elders.

Mussolini chose to adapt his movement to opportunity rather than cling to the failed Left-nationalist Fascism of Milan in 1919. We can follow his evolution in the drift of fascist positions rightwards in the speeches and programs of 1920–22.[29] The first idea to disappear was the first Fascism's rejection of war and imperialism—the "pacifism of the trenches" so widespread among veterans when their memory of combat was still fresh. The San Sepolcro program accepted the League of Nations' "supreme postulate of . . . the integrity of each nation" (though affirming Italy's right to Fiume and the Dalmatian coast). The league disappeared from the program of June 1919, though the Fascists still called for the replacement of the professional army by a defensive militia, and the nationalization of arms and munitions factories. The program of the transformed Fascist Party in November 1921 attacked the League of Nations for partiality, asserted Italy's role as a "bulwark of Latin civilization in the Mediterranean" and of *italianità* in the world, called for the development of Italy's colonies, and advocated a large standing army.

Early Fascism's radical proposals for nationalizations and heavy taxes were watered down by 1920 to the right of workers to defend strictly economic goals, but not "demagogic" ones. The representation of workers in management was limited by 1920 to personnel matters. By 1921, the Fascists rejected "progressive and confiscatory taxation" as "fiscal demagoguery that discourages initiative," and set productivity as the highest goal of the economy. A lifelong atheist, Mussolini had urged in 1919 the confiscation of all properties belonging to religious congregations and the sequestration of all the revenues of episcopal sees. In his first speech in the Chamber of Deputies, however, on June 21, 1921, he said that Catholicism represents "the Latin and imperial tradition of Rome," and called for a settlement of differences with the Vatican. As for the monarchy, Mussolini declared in 1919 that "the present regime in Italy has failed." In 1920 he softened his initial republicanism to an agnostic position in favor of any constitutional regime that best served the moral and material interests of the nation. In a speech on September 20, 1922, Mussolini publicly denied any intention to call into question the monarchy or the ruling House of Savoy. "They ask us what is our program," said Mussolini. "Our program is simple. We want to govern Italy."[30]

Long after his regime had settled into routine, Mussolini still liked to refer to the "Fascist revolution." But he meant a revolution against socialism and flabby liberalism, a new way of uniting and motivating Italians, and a new kind of governmental authority capable of subordinating private liberties to the needs of the national community and of organizing mass assent while leaving property intact. The major point is that the Fascist movement was reshaped in the process of growing into the available space. The antisocialism already present in the initial movement became central, and many antibourgeois idealists left or were pushed out. The radical anticapitalist idealism of early Fascism was watered down, and we must not let its conspicuous presence in early texts confuse us about what Fascism later became in action.

The de facto power of Fascism in rural northeastern Italy—especially Emilia-Romagna and Tuscany—had become by 1921 too substantial for national politicians to ignore. When Prime Minister Giolitti prepared new parliamentary elections in May 1921, grasping at any resource to roll back the large vote earned in November 1919 by the socialists and the Popolari, he included Mussolini's Fascists in his electoral coalition alongside liberals and nationalists. Thanks to this arrangement, thirty-five PNF candidates were elected to the Italian chamber on Giolitti's list, including Mussolini himself. This number was not large, and many contemporaries thought that Mussolini's movement was too incoherent and contradictory to last.[31] Nevertheless, it showed that Mussolini had become a vital part of the Italian antisocialist coalition on a national level. It was the first step in that advance toward national power that was now Mussolini's one guiding principle.

The transformation of Italian Fascism set in motion by success in the Po Valley in 1920–22 shows us why it is so hard to find a fixed "essence" in early Fascist programs or in the movement's first young antibourgeois rebels, and why one must follow the movement's trajectory as it found a political space and adapted to fit it. Without the Po Valley transformation (paralleled in other regions where Fascism won local landowner support like Tuscany and Apulia),[32] Mussolini would have remained an obscure Milan agitator who failed.

(2) Schleswig-Holstein, Germany, 1928–33

Schleswig-Holstein was the only German state (Land) to give the Nazis an outright majority in any free election: it voted 51 percent Nazi in the parliamentary election of July 31, 1932. Hence it offers us an obvious second example of a fascist movement successfully becoming a major political actor.

The German fascist movement had failed to establish itself during the first postwar crisis of 1918–23, when the Freikorps's bloody repression of the Munich soviet and other socialist risings offered an opening. The next opportunity arrived with the Depression. Having done very poorly with an urban strategy in the elections of 1924 and 1928, the Nazi Party turned to the farmers.[33] They chose well. Agriculture had prospered nowhere in the 1920s, because world markets were flooded by new producers in the United States, Argentina, Canada, and Australia. Agricultural prices tumbled further in the late 1920s, even before the 1929 crash; that was only the final blow to the world's farmers.

In the sandy cattle-raising country of interior Schleswig-Holstein, near the Danish frontier, farmers had traditionally supported the conservative nationalist party (DNVP).[34] At the end of the 1920s, they lost faith in the capacity of traditional parties and of the national government to help them. The Weimar Republic was triply damned in their eyes: dominated by distant Prussia, by sinful and decadent Berlin, and by "reds" who thought only of cheap food for urban workers. As the collapse of farm prices after 1928 forced many of them into debt and foreclosure, desperate Schleswig-Holstein cattle farmers abandoned the DNVP and turned to the Landbund, a violent peasant self-help league. Its localized tax strikes and protests against banks and middlemen were ineffective, for lack of any nationally organized support. So in July 1932, 64 percent of the rural vote in Schleswig-Holstein went to the Nazis. The cattle farmers would likely have switched again to some newer nostrum (their commitment to Nazism was already beginning to fade in the November 1932 election) if Hitler's appointment to the office of chancellor in January 1933 had not frozen things in place.

The first process one observes at work here is the humiliation of existing political leaders and organizations in the crisis of the world Depression of 1929. Space was opened up by their helplessness in the face of collapsed prices, glutted markets, and farms seized and sold by banks for debt.

The Schleswig-Holstein cattle raisers comprised only one part—the most successful part—of the broad stream of particular and sometimes incompatible grievances that Hitler and the Nazis managed to assemble into an electoral tidal wave between 1929 and July 1932. The growth of the Nazi vote from the ninth party in Germany in 1928 to the first in 1932 showed how successfully Hitler and his strategists profited from the discredit of the traditional parties by devising new electoral techniques and directing appeals to specific constituencies.[35]

Hitler knew how to work a mass electorate. He played skillfully upon the resentments and fears of ordinary Germans, in incessant public meetings spiced up by uniformed strong-arm squads, the physical intimidation of enemies, the exhilaration of excited crowds and fevered harangues, and dramatic arrivals by airplane and fast, open Mercedeses. The traditional parties stuck doggedly to the long bookish speeches appropriate for a small educated electorate. The German Left did adopt salutes and shirts,[36] but it could not recruit far outside the working class. While the other parties were firmly identified with one interest, one class, or one political approach, the Nazis managed to promise something for everyone. They were the first party in Germany to target different occupations with tailor-made appeals, paying little heed if one contradicted another.[37]

All of this cost a lot of money, and it has often been alleged that German businessmen paid the bills. The orthodox Marxist version of this view holds that Hitler was virtually created by businessmen as a kind of private anticommunist army. It is indeed possible to discover German businessmen (usually from small business) who were attracted by Hitler's expansionist nationalism and antisocialism and deceived by his carefully tailored addresses to business audiences which downplayed anti-Semitism and suppressed any reference to the radical clauses in the 25 Points. The steel manufacturer Fritz Thyssen, whose ghostwritten book *I Paid Hitler* (1941) provided ammunition for the Marxist case, turns out to be exceptional, both in his early support for Nazism and in his break with Hitler and exile after 1939.[38] Another famous businessman, the aged coal magnate Emil Kirdorf, joined the Nazi Party in 1927 but left it angrily in 1928 over Nazi attacks on the coal syndicate, and he supported the conservative DNVP in 1933.[39]

Close scrutiny of business archives shows that most German businessmen hedged their bets, contributing to all the nonsocialist electoral formations that showed any signs of success at keeping the Marxists out of power. Though some German firms contributed some money to the Nazis, they always contributed more to traditional conservatives. Their favorite was Franz von Papen. When Hitler grew too important to ignore, they were alarmed by the anticapitalist tone of some of his radical associates such as the interest-rate crank Gottfried Feder, the "salon bolshevik" Otto Strasser (as an irritated Hitler once called him), and a violence-prone organization of anti-Semitic shopkeepers, the Fighting League of the Commercial Middle Class. Even the head of the Nazi Party administrative apparatus, Gregor Strasser, though more moderate than his brother Otto, proposed radical job-creation measures.[40] Nazi radicalism actually increased in late 1932, when the party sponsored legislation to abolish all trusts and cooperated with the communists in a transport workers' strike in

Berlin. Some important firms, such as I. G. Farben, contributed almost nothing to the Nazis before 1933.[41] An important share of Nazi funds came instead from entry fees at mass rallies, the sale of Nazi pamphlets and memorabilia, and small contributions.[42]

Hitler thus built Nazism by July 1932 into the first catch-all party in German history and the largest party so far seen there. His Storm Troopers aroused both fear and admiration by their readiness to beat up socialists, communists, pacifists, and foreigners. Direct action and electioneering were complementary, not contradictory, tactics. Violence—selective violence against "antinational" enemies who were perceived by many Germans as outside the fold—helped win the votes that allowed Hitler to pretend that he was working for power by legal means.

One reason why the Nazis succeeded in supplanting the liberal middle-class parties was the liberals' perceived failure to deal with the twin crises Germany faced in the late 1920s. One crisis was many Germans' sense of national humiliation by the Treaty of Versailles. The contentious issue of treaty fulfillment became acute again in January 1929 when an international commission under the American banker Owen D. Young began another attempt to settle the problem of German payment of reparations for World War I. When the German government signed the Young Plan in June, German nationalists attacked it bitterly for its continued recognition of Germany's duty to pay something, even though the sums had been reduced. The second crisis was the Depression that began in 1929. The German economic collapse was the most catastrophic of any major country, depriving a quarter of the population of work. All the anti-system parties joined in blaming the Weimar Republic for its failure to cope with either crisis.

For the moment, I leave this story in July 1932, with the Nazi Party the largest in Germany, with 37 percent of the vote. The Nazis had not gained a majority at the ballot box—they never would—but they had made themselves indispensable to any nonsocialist coalition that wished to govern with a popular majority rather than through presidential emergency-decree powers, as had been the case since the last normal government fell in March 1930 (we will examine this matter more closely in the next chapter).

Fascism was not yet in power in Germany, however. In November 1932, the Nazi vote slipped in further parliamentary elections. The Nazi Party was losing its most precious asset: momentum. Money was running out. Hitler, gambling all or nothing on the position of chancellor, refused all lesser offers to become vice-chancellor in a coalition government. The Nazi rank and file grew restive as the chances for jobs and places seemed to be slipping away. Gregor Strasser, head of the party organization and a leader of the movement's anticapitalist wing, was expelled for independent negotiations with the new chancellor, General Kurt von Schleicher. The movement might have ended as a footnote to history had it not been saved in the opening days of 1933 by conservative politicians who wanted to pilfer its following and use its political muscle for their own purposes. The specific path by which the fascists arrived in power in both Italy and Germany is the subject of the next chapter. But not until we have examined a third case, the failure of fascism in France.

An Unsuccessful Fascism: France, 1924–40

Not even the victor nations were immune to the fascist virus after World War I. Outside Italy and Germany, however, although fascists could be noisy or troublesome, they did not get close to power. That does not mean we should ignore these other cases. Failed fascist movements may tell us as much about what was needed for taking root as successful ones.

France offers an ideal example. Though France seems typified for many by the fall of the Bastille, the Rights of Man, and the "Marseillaise," numerous French monarchists and authoritarian nationalists had never been reconciled to a parliamentary republic as appropriate for *la grande nation*. When the republic coped badly between the wars with the triple crisis of revolutionary threat, economic depression, and German menace, that discontent hardened into outright disaffection.

The extreme Right expanded in interwar France in reaction to electoral successes by the Left. When a center-Left coalition, the Cartel des Gauches, won the 1924 parliamentary election, Georges Valois, whom we encountered in chapter 2 as the founder of the Cercle Proudhon for nationalist workers in 1911,[43] founded the Faisceau, whose name and behavior were borrowed straight from Mussolini. Pierre Taittinger, a champagne magnate, formed the more traditionally nationalist Jeunesses Patriotes. And the new Fédération Nationale Catholique took on a passionately antirepublican tone under General Noël Currières de Castelnau.

In the 1930s, as the Depression bit, as Nazi Germany dismantled the safeguards of the 1918 peace settlement, and as the Third Republic's center-Left majority (renewed in 1932) became tarnished by political corruption, a new crop of radical Right "leagues" (they rejected the word *party*) blossomed. In massive street demonstrations on February 6, 1934, before the Chamber of Deputies in which sixteen people were killed, they proved that they were strong enough to topple a French government but not strong enough to install another one in its place.

In the period of intense polarization that followed, it was the Left that drew more votes. The Popular Front coalition of socialists, Radicals, and communists won the elections of May 1936, and Prime Minister Léon Blum banned paramilitary leagues in June, something German chancellor Heinrich Brüning had failed to do in Germany four years earlier.

The Popular Front's victory had been narrow, however, and the presence of a Jew supported by communists in the prime minister's office raised the extreme Right to a paroxysm of indignation. Its true strength in 1930s France has been the subject of a particularly intense debate.[44] Some scholars have argued that France had no indigenous fascism, but, at most, a little "whitewash" splashed from foreign examples onto a homegrown Bonapartist tradition.[45] At the opposite extreme are those who consider that France was the "true cradle of fascism."[46] Contemplating this undeniably noisy and vigorous far Right and the ease with which democracy was overthrown after French defeat in June 1940, Zeev Sternhell concluded that fascism had "impregnated" by then the language and attitudes of French public life. He supported his case by labeling as fascist a broad range of criticisms of the way democracy was working in France in the 1930s made by a wide spectrum of French commentators, some of whom expressed some sympathy for Mussolini but almost none for Hitler.[47] Most French and some foreign scholars thought Sternhell's "fascist" category was far too loose and his conclusions excessive.[48]

It is not enough, of course, to simply count up the number of prominent French intellectuals who spoke a language that sounded fascist, along with the colorful array of movements that demonstrated and pontificated in 1930s France. Two questions arise: Were they as significant as they were noisy, and were they really fascist? It is important to note that the more closely a French movement imitated the Hitlerian or (more frequently) the Mussolinian model, as did the tiny blue-shirted Solidarité Française or the narrowly localized Parti Populaire Français of Jacques Doriot,[49] the less successful it was, while the one far Right movement that approached mass catch-all party status between 1936 and 1940, Colonel François de La Rocque's Parti Social Français, tried to look moderate and "republican."

Any assessment of fascism in France turns on La Rocque. If his move-

THE ANATOMY OF FASCISM

ments were fascist, fascism was powerful in 1930s France; if they were not, fascism was limited to the margins. La Rocque, a career army officer from a monarchist family, took over in 1931 the Croix de Feu, a small veterans' association of those decorated with the Croix de Guerre for heroism under fire, and developed it into a political movement. He drew in a wider membership and denounced the weakness and corruption of parliament, warned against the threat of Bolshevism, and advocated an authoritarian state and greater justice for workers integrated into a corporatist economy. His paramilitary force, called *dispos* (from the French word *disponible*, or "ready"), embarked on militaristic automobile rallies in 1933 and 1934. They mobilized with precision to pick up secret orders at remote destinations for *"le jour J"* (D day) and *"l'heure H"* (H hour) in apparent training to combat by force a communist insurrection.[50]

The Left, made jittery by supposed fascist marches on Rome, Berlin, Vienna, and Madrid, branded the Croix de Feu fascist. That impression was fortified when the Croix de Feu participated in the march on the Chamber of Deputies in the night of February 6, 1934. Colonel de La Rocque kept his forces separate from the others on a side street, however, and in all his public statements he gave the impression of strict discipline and order more than of unbridled street violence. Unusually for the French Right, he rejected anti-Semitism and even recruited some notable patriotic Jews (though his sections in Alsace and Algeria were anti-Semitic). Although he found good in Mussolini (except for what he saw as excessive statism), he retained the anti-Germanism of most French nationalists.

When the Popular Front government dissolved the Croix de Feu along with other right-wing paramilitary groups in June 1936, Colonel de La Rocque replaced it with an electoral party, the Parti Social Français (PSF). The PSF abandoned paramilitary rallies and emphasized national reconciliation and social justice under a strong but elected leader. This move toward the center was enthusiastically ratified by rapidly growing membership. The PSF was probably the largest party in France on the eve of the war. It is very hard to measure the size of any of the French far Right movements, however, in the absence of electoral results or audited circulation figures for their newspapers. The parliamentary elections scheduled for 1940, in which La Rocque's party was expected to do well, were canceled by the war.

As France regained some calm and stability in 1938–39 under an energetic center-Left prime minister, Édouard Daladier, all the far Right movements except the most moderate one, La Rocque's PSF, lost ground. After the defeat of 1940, it was the traditional Right, and not the fascist Right, that established and ran the collaborationist Vichy government.[51] What was left of French fascism completed its discredit by reveling in occupied Paris on the Nazi payroll during 1940–44. For a generation after the liberation of 1945, the French extreme Right was reduced to the dimensions of a sect.

The failure of fascism in France was not due to some mysterious allergy,[52] though the importance of the republican tradition for a majority of French people's sense of themselves cannot be overestimated. The Depression, for all its ravages, was less severe in France than in more industrially concentrated Britain and Germany. The Third Republic, for all its lurching, never suffered deadlock or total paralysis. Mainstream conservatives did not feel sufficiently threatened in the 1930s to call on fascists for help. Finally, no one preeminent personage managed to dominate the small army of rival French fascist *chefs*, most of whom preferred intransigent doctrinal "purity" to the kind of deal making with conservatives that Mussolini and Hitler practiced.

We can put a bit more flesh on these bare bones of analysis by examining one movement more closely. The Greenshirts were a farmers' movement in northwestern France in the 1930s, overtly fascist at least in its early days, which succeeded in sweeping some embittered farmers into direct action, but failed to construct a permanent movement or to spread outside the Catholic northwest to become a truly national contender.[53] It is important to investigate rural fascism in France, since it was among farmers that Italian and German fascisms first successfully implanted themselves. Moreover, in a country that was more than half rural, the potential for fascism in France would rest upon what it could do in the countryside. That being the case, it is curious that all previous studies of French fascism have examined only the urban movements.

Space opened up in rural France at the beginning of the 1930s because both the government and the traditional farmers' organizations, as in Schleswig-Holstein, were discredited by their utter helplessness in the collapse of farm prices.

The Greenshirts' leader, Henry Dorgères (the pen name of an agricultural journalist who discovered a talent for whipping up peasant anger on market day), openly praised Fascist Italy in 1933 and 1934 (though he later declared it too statist), and he adopted a certain number of fascist mannerisms: the colored shirt, the inflamed oratory, nationalism, xenophobia, and anti-Semitism. At peak form in 1935, he was capable of gathering the largest crowds ever seen in distressed French rural market towns.

There was even a space in France that superficially resembled the opportunities offered to direct action by Italian Fascists in the Po Valley: in the summers of 1936 and 1937, when massive strikes of farm laborers on the big farms of the northern plains of France at crucial moments—thinning the sugar beets, harvesting the beets and wheat—threw farm owners into panic. The Greenshirts organized volunteers to carry out the harvest, recalling the Blackshirts' rescue of Po Valley farmers. They had a keen sense of theater: at the end of the day, they gathered at a memorial to the dead of World War I and laid a wheat sheaf there.

Direct action by Dorgères's harvest volunteers led nowhere, however, and these tiny groups that bore a family resemblance to Mussolini's *squadristi* never became a de facto local power in France. A major reason for this was that the French state dealt much more aggressively than the Italian one with any threat to the harvest. Even Léon Blum's Popular Front sent the gendarmes instantly whenever farmworkers went out on strike at harvest time. The French Left had always put high priority on feeding the cities, since the days in 1793 when Robespierre's Committee of Public Safety had sent out "revolutionary armies" to requisition grain.[54] French farmers had less fear than the Po Valley ones of being abandoned by the state, and felt less need for a substitute force of order.

Moreover, over the course of the 1930s, the powerful French conservative farm organizations held their own much better than in Schleswig-Holstein. They organized successful cooperatives and supplied essential services, while the Greenshirts offered only a vent for anger. In the end, the Greenshirts were left on the margins. The crucial turning point arrived when Jacques Le Roy Ladurie, president of the powerful French Farmers' Federation (FNEA, Fédération Nationale des Exploitants Agricoles), who had earlier helped Dorgères work up rural crowds, decided in 1937 that it would be more efficacious to construct a powerful farmers' lobby capable of influencing the state administration from within. The power of entrenched conservative farm organizations like the FNEA and the mighty cooperative movement based at Landerneau in Brittany was such that the Greenshirts found little space available.

This suggests that fascist interlopers cannot easily break into a political system that is functioning tolerably well. Only when the state and existing institutions fail badly do they open opportunities for newcomers. Another shortcoming of Dorgères's Greenshirts was their inability to form the basis for a catch-all party. While Dorgères was a genius at arousing farmers' anger, he almost never addressed the woes of the urban middle class. As an essentially ruralist agitator, he tended to see urban shopkeepers as part of the enemy rather than as potential alliance partners in a fully developed fascism.

Still another reason for Dorgères's failure was that large areas of rural France were closed to the Greenshirts by long-standing attachment to the traditions of the French Revolution, which had given French peasants full title to their little plots of land. While peasants of republican southern and southwestern France could become violently angry, their radicalism was channeled away from fascism by the French Communist Party, which was rather successful among French small farmers of traditionally Left-leaning regions.[55] And so rural France, despite its intense suffering in the Depression of the 1930s, was not a setting in which a powerful French fascism could germinate.

Some Other Unsuccessful Fascisms

Outside Italy and Germany, only a rather limited number of nations offered conditions that enabled fascism to win large electoral support, along with eager conservative coalition partners. Next after Germany in order of electoral success came the Arrow Cross Party–Hungarist Movement of Ferenc Szálasy, which won about 750,000 votes out of 2 million in the Hungarian elections of May 1939.[56] The government, however, was already firmly in the hands of the conservative military dictatorship of Admiral Horthy, who had both no intention of sharing power and no need to do so. The other important vote winner in eastern Europe was the Legion of the Archangel Michael in Romania, which, running under the label "All for the Fatherland," was the third largest party in the general election of 1937, with 15.38 percent of the vote, and 66 seats out of 390 in the legislature.[57]

The most successful fascist vote winner in western Europe, at least momentarily, was Léon Degrelle's Rexist movement in Belgium. Degrelle began by organizing Catholic students and running a Catholic publishing house (Christus Rex), and then developed wider ambitions. In 1935 he embarked on a campaign to persuade Belgian voters that the traditional parties (including the Catholic Party) were mired in corruption and routine at a moment that demanded dramatic action and vigorous leadership. In the national parliamentary elections of May 1936 the Rexists campaigned with a simple but eloquent symbol: a broom. A vote for Rex would sweep the old parties away. They also called for unity. The old parties divided Belgium, for they gathered voters on confessional or ethnic or class lines. Rex promised—as all effective fascist movements did—to gather citizens of all classes in a unifying *"rassemblement"* rather than a divisive "party."

These appeals struck home in a country plagued by ethnic and linguistic division aggravated by economic depression. The Rexists won 11.5 percent of the popular vote in May 1936 and 21 out of 202 seats in the legislature. Degrelle was not able to hold on to his mushroom vote, however. The conservative establishment united against him, and Church leaders disavowed him. When Degrelle ran in a by-election in Brussels in April 1937, the entire political class from communists to Catholics united behind a popular young opponent, the future prime minister Paul Van Zeeland, and Degrelle lost his own parliamentary seat.[58]

Degrelle's rapid rise and equally rapid decline reveals how hard it is for a fascist leader to keep the bubble intact after managing to assemble a heterogeneous protest vote. Rapid flows of the vote into a new catch-all party could be a two-way current. The feverish swelling of the party could be followed by an equally rapid collapse if it did not establish itself as capable of representing some important interests and gratifying ambitious career politicians. One big vote was not enough to root a fascist party.

Other western European fascist movements had less electoral success. The Dutch Nationaal Socialistische Beweging (NSB) won 7.94 percent of the votes in the national election of 1935, but declined rapidly thereafter.[59] Vidkun Quisling's Nasjonal Samling received only 2.2 percent of the Norwegian vote in 1933 and 1.8 percent in 1936, though in the port of Stavanger and in two rural localities the vote was as high as 12 percent.[60]

Sir Oswald Mosley's British Union of Fascists was one of the most interesting failures, not least because Mosley probably had the greatest intellectual gifts and the strongest social connections of all the fascist chiefs. As a promising junior minister in the Labour government of 1929, he put forward a bold plan in early 1930 to combat the Depression by making the empire a closed economic zone and by spending (into deficit, if need be) for job-creating public works and consumer credit. When the leaders of the Labour Party rebuffed these unorthodox proposals, Mosley resigned and formed his own New Party in 1931, taking a few left-wing Labour MPs with him. The New Party won no seats, however, in the parliamentary election of October 1931. A visit to Mussolini persuaded the frustrated Mosley that fascism was the wave of the future, and his own personal way forward.

Mosley's British Union of Fascists (October 1932) won some important early converts, like Lord Rothermere, publisher of the mass-circulation London *Daily Mail*. Mosley's movement aroused revulsion, however, when his black-shirted guards spotlighted and beat up opponents at a large public meeting at the Olympia exhibition hall in London in June 1934. Hitler's Night of the Long Knives, at the end of the same month, provoked the departure of 90 percent of the BUF's fifty thousand members,[61] including Lord Rothermere. At the end of 1934, Mosley took an actively anti-Semitic tack and sent his Blackshirts to swagger through London's East End, where they fought with Jews and Communists, building a new clientele among unskilled workers and struggling shopkeepers there. The Public Order Act, passed soon after the "Battle of Cable Street" with antifascists on October 4, 1936, outlawed political uniforms and deprived the BUF of its public spectacles, but it grew again to about twenty thousand with a campaign against war in 1939. Mosley's black shirts, violence, and overt sympathy for Mussolini and Hitler (he was married to Diana Mitford in Hitler's presence at Munich in 1936) seemed alien to most people in Britain, and gradual economic revival after 1931 under the broadly accepted National Government, a coalition dominated by conservatives, left him little political space.

Some of the European imitators of fascism in the 1930s were little more than shadow movements, like Colonel O'Duffy's Blueshirts in Ireland, though the poet W. B. Yeats agreed to write his anthem and he sent three hundred volunteers to help Franco in Spain. Most of these feeble imitations showed that it was not enough to don a colored shirt, march about, and beat up some local minority to conjure up the success of a Hitler or a Mussolini. It took a comparable crisis, a comparable opening of political space, comparable skill at alliance building, and comparable cooperation from existing elites. These imitations never got beyond the founding stage, and so underwent none of the transformations of the successful movements. They remained "pure"—and insignificant.

Comparisons and Conclusions

Fascist movements appeared so widely in the early twentieth century that we cannot learn much about their nature from the mere fact of their foundation. But they grew at different rates and succeeded to different degrees. A comparative look at their successes and failures suggests that the major differences lay not only in the movements themselves but also, and significantly, in the opportunities offered. To understand the later stages of fascism, we will have to look beyond the parties themselves to the settings that offered space (or not) and to the sorts of helpers who were (or were not) available.

Intellectual history, vital for the first formation of fascist movements, offers us less help at this stage. Fascism remained marginal in some nations that would seem, at first glance, to have had powerful intellectual and cultural preparation for it. In France, for example, the richness, fervor, and celebrity of the intellectual revolt against classical liberal values in the early twentieth century would seem, on intellectual history grounds alone, to make that country a prime candidate for the successful establishment of fascist movements.[62] We have seen why it did not happen.[63] Indeed, all European countries produced thinkers and writers in whom we can perceive today a strong current of fascist sensibility. It is therefore difficult to argue that one country was more "predisposed" than another by its intellectuals to give an important role to fascist parties.

Anti-Semitism needs special mention. It is not clear that cultural preparation is the most important predictor of which country would carry measures against Jews to extremes. If one had been asked around 1900 to identify the European nation where the menace of anti-Semitism seemed most acute, who would have chosen Germany? It was in France after 1898, during the Dreyfus frenzy, that Jewish shops were looted, and in French Algeria that Jews were murdered.[64] Ugly anti-Semitic incidents occurred in Britain at the turn of the century,[65] and in the United States, such as the notorious lynching of Leo Frank in Atlanta,[66] not to mention those traditionally rabid centers of endemic anti-Jewish violence in Poland and Russia, where the very word *pogrom* was invented.

In Germany, by contrast, organized anti-Semitism, vigorous in the 1880s, lost steam as a political tactic in the decades before World War I.[67] After the war, Jewish advancement into posts like university teaching became easier in Weimar Germany than in the United States of Harding and Coolidge. Even Wilhelmian Germany may have been more open to

Jewish professional advancement than the United States of Theodore Roosevelt, with important exceptions such as the officer corps. What comparison reveals about Wilhelmian Germany is not that it had more numerous or more powerful anti-Semites and rebels against "modernity" than other European states, but that in a political crisis the German army and bureaucracy were less subject to effective judicial or political oversight.[68]

Nevertheless, there are connections between intellectual preparation and the later success of fascism, and we need to be very precise about what they are. The role of intellectuals was crucial at three points already suggested in chapter 1: in discrediting previous liberal regimes; in creating new poles outside the Left around which anger and protest (until recently a monopoly of the Left) could be mobilized; and in making fascist violence respectable. We need also to study the cultural and intellectual preparation of those sectors of the old elites that were ready to cooperate with the fascists (or at least to try to coopt them). The European states resembled each other rather closely in their luxuriant growth of antiliberal criticism as the twentieth century opened. Where they differed was in those political, social, and economic preconditions that seem to distinguish the states where fascism, exceptionally, was able to become established.

One of the most important preconditions was a faltering liberal order.[69] Fascisms grew from back rooms to the public arena most easily where the existing government functioned badly, or not at all. One of the commonplaces of discussions of fascism is that it thrived upon the crisis of liberalism. I hope here to make that vague formulation somewhat more concrete.

On the eve of World War I the major states of Europe were either governed by liberal regimes or seemed headed that way. Liberal regimes guaranteed freedoms both for individuals and for contending political parties, and allowed citizens to influence the composition of governments, more or less directly, through elections. Liberal government also accorded a large measure of freedom to citizens and to enterprises. Government intervention was expected to be limited to the few functions individuals could not perform for themselves, such as the maintenance of order and the conduct of war and diplomacy. Economic and social matters were supposed to be left to the free play of individual choices in the market, though liberal regimes did not hesitate to protect property from worker protests and from foreign competition. This kind of liberal state ceased to exist during World War I, for total war could be conducted only by massive government coordination and regulation.

After the war was over, liberals expected governments to return to liberal policies. The strains of war making, however, had created new conflicts, tensions, and malfunctions that required sustained state intervention. At the war's end, some of the belligerent states had collapsed. In Russia (only partially a liberal state in 1914), power was taken by the Bolsheviks. In Italy, and later Germany, it was taken by fascists. Between the wars parliamentary governments gave way to authoritarian regimes in Spain, Portugal, Poland, Romania, Yugoslavia, Estonia, Lithuania, and Greece, to mention only the European cases. What had gone wrong with the liberal recipe for government?

We must not view this as exclusively a matter of ideas. What was at stake was a technique of government: rule by notables, where the well-born and well-educated could rely on social prestige and deference to keep them elected. Notable rule, however, came under severe pressure from the "nationalization of the masses."[70] After 1918, politicians, including anti-Left politicians, would have to learn to deal with a mass electorate or fail. Where the mass vote was new and unruly, as in Italy (all men received the vote there only in 1912), and in the Prussian state within Germany (where the old three-class voting system in local elections was abolished only in 1918), many old-fashioned politicians, whether liberal or conservative, had not the faintest idea how to appeal to a crowd. Even in France, where conservatives had learned in the nineteenth century to tame at least the rural part of a mass electorate by exploiting social influence and traditions of deference, they had trouble after 1918 understanding that these influences no longer worked. When the nationalist conservative Henri de Kérillis tried to deal with the new challenges of mass politics by setting up a "Propaganda Center for National Republicans" in 1927, hidebound conservatives scoffed that his methods were more appropriate for selling a new brand of chocolate than for politics.[71]

Fascists quickly profited from the inability of centrists and conservatives to keep control of a mass electorate. Whereas the notable dinosaurs disdained mass politics, fascists showed how to use it for nationalism and against the Left. They promised access to the crowd through exciting political spectacle and clever publicity techniques; ways to discipline that crowd through paramilitary organization and charismatic leadership; and the replacement of chancy elections by yes-no plebiscites.[72] Whereas citizens in a parliamentary democracy voted to choose a few fellow citizens to serve as their representatives, fascists expressed their citizenship directly by participating in ceremonies of mass assent. The propagandistic manipulation of public opinion replaced debate about complicated issues among a small group of legislators who (according to liberal ideals) were supposed to be better informed than the mass of the citizenry. Fascism could well seem to offer to the opponents of the Left efficacious new techniques for controlling, managing, and channeling the "nationalization of the masses," at a moment when the Left threatened to enlist a majority of the population around two nonnational poles: class and international pacifism.

One may also perceive the crisis of liberalism after 1918 in a second way, as a "crisis of transition," a rough passage along the journey into industrialization and modernity. It seems clear that nations that industrialized late faced more social strains than did Britain, the first to industrialize. For one thing, the pace was faster for the latecomers; for another, labor was by then much more powerfully organized. One does not have to be a Marxist to perceive the crisis of the liberal state in terms of a stressful transition to industrialization, unless one injects inevitability into the explanatory model. Marxists, until fairly recently, saw this crisis as an ineluctable stage in capitalist development, where the economic system can no longer function without reinforced discipline of the working class and/or a forceful conquest of external resources and markets. One can argue, much less sweepingly, that the latecomers simply faced higher levels of social turmoil which required new forms of control.

A third way of looking at the crisis of the liberal state envisions the same problem of late industrialization in social terms. Certain liberal states, according to this version, were unable to deal with either the "nationalization of the masses" or the "transition to industrial society" because their social structure was too heterogeneous, divided between pre-industrial groups that had not yet disappeared—artisans, great landowners, rentiers—alongside new industrial managerial and working classes. Where the pre-industrial middle class was particularly powerful, according to this reading of the crisis of the liberal state, it could block peaceful settlement of industrial issues, and could provide manpower to fascism in order to save the privileges and prestige of the old social order.[73]

Yet another "take" on the crisis of the liberal order focuses on stressful transitions to modernity in cultural terms. According to this reading, universal literacy, cheap mass media, and invasive alien cultures (from within as well as from without) made it harder as the twentieth century opened for the liberal intelligentsia to perpetuate the traditional intellectual and cultural order.[74] Fascism offered the defenders of a cultural canon new propaganda skills along with a new shamelessness about using them.

It may not be absolutely necessary to choose only one among these various diagnoses of the difficulties faced by the liberal regimes of Europe after the end of World War I. Italy and Germany do indeed seem to fit all four. They were among the last major states in Europe to learn to live with a mass electorate: Italy in 1912, Germany only fully in 1919. Russia, another newcomer to mass politics, fell to the Left as befitted an even less developed society where even the middle class was not yet fully enfranchised. Industrially, Italy, as "the least of the Great Powers,"[75] had been engaged in an energetic catching-up sprint since the 1890s. Germany, to be sure, was already a highly industrial nation in 1914, but it had been the last of the Great Powers to industrialize, after the 1860s, and then, after the defeat of 1918, desperately needed repair and reconstruction. In social structure, both Italy and Germany contained large pre-industrial sectors (though so did France and even England).[76] Cultural conservatives in both countries felt intensely threatened by artistic experiment and popular culture; Weimar Germany was indeed at the very epicenter of postwar cultural experimentalism.[77]

One needs to interject a warning at this point against inevitability. Identifying the crisis of liberal regimes as crucial to the success of fascism suggests that some kind of environmental determinism is at work. If the setting is conducive, according to this way of thinking, one gets fascism. I prefer to leave space for national differences and for human choices in our explanation.

In the shorter term, the European states had undergone vastly different national experiences since 1914. Most obviously, some countries had won the war while others had lost it. Two maps of Europe help explain where fascism would grow most rankly. Fascist success follows closely but not exactly the map of defeat in World War I. Germany, with its stab-in-the-back legend, was the classic case. Italy, exceptionally, had belonged to the victorious alliance, but it had failed to achieve the national expansion that the Italian nationalists-who had led Italy into the war had counted on. The victory was in their eyes a *vittoria mutilata*. Spain had been neutral in 1914–18, but its loss of empire in the Spanish-American War of 1898 branded the whole generation that followed with national humiliation. The Spanish radical Right grew partly in fear that the new republic founded in 1931 was letting separatist movements get the upper hand in Catalonia and the Basque country. In Spain, however, defeat and fears of decline led to Franco's military dictatorship rather than to power for the leader of the fascist Falange, José Antonio Primo de Rivera. Fascism is never an inevitable outcome.

Fascist success also followed fairly closely another map: that of attempts at Bolshevik revolution—or fear of it—during the period when communism seemed likely to spread beyond its Russian home base. Germany, Italy, and Hungary had all had particularly close calls with the "red menace" after the war. The fit is not precise here, either, for fascism also flourished in states more threatened by ethnic division than by class conflict—Belgium, for example.

In settings where a large landless peasantry added massive numbers to a revolutionary movement, and where large portions of the middle class were still struggling for the most elementary rights (rather than defending established privileges), as in Russia in 1917, mass protest gathered on the Left. Communism, not fascism, was the winner. Revolutionary Russia did contain anti-Bolshevik squads that resembled the German Freikorps,[78] but a society where landless peasants far outnumbered an insecure middle class offered no mass following to fascism. Russia came close to a military dictatorship in July 1917 when General Lavr Georgyevich Kornilov tried to march on Moscow, and that would have been a likely outcome if Bolshevism had failed in Russia.

A typology of crises that could give fascism an opening is not enough. An equally important consideration is the capacity of liberal and democratic regimes to respond to these crises. Leon Trotsky's metaphor of the "least-barricaded gate" works just as well for fascism as it did, in Trotsky's opinion, for Bolshevism. Trotsky used this metaphor to help explain how Bolshevism made its first breakthrough to power in a relatively unindustrialized country, rather than, as more literal-minded Marxists expected, in highly industrialized countries with powerful working-class organizations such as Germany.[79] Fascism, too, has historically been a phenomenon of weak or failed liberal states and belated or damaged capitalist systems rather than of triumphant ones. The frequent assertion that fascism stems from a crisis of liberalism might well be amended to specify crises in *weak* or *failed* liberalisms.

There are several false trails in the common understanding of why fascism took root in some places and not in others. Looking for assets for fascism in national character or in the hereditary predilections of a particular people comes perilously close to a reverse racism.[80] It is nonetheless true that democracy and human rights were less solidly implanted in some national traditions than in others. While democracy, the rights of citizens, and the rule of law were associated historically with national greatness in France and Britain, they seemed foreign imports to many Germans. The Weimar Republic's association with defeat and national humiliation, coupled with its political and economic inefficacy and cultural libertinism, destroyed its legitimacy for many old-fashioned Germans.

It is legitimate to ask why the clamors of the post-1918 world could not be expressed within one of the great nineteenth-century political ideological families—conservatism, liberalism, socialism—which until so recently had offered a full gamut of political choices. The exhaustion of older political options, now apparently incapable of offering satisfying expression to all the postwar feelings, is an important part of the story.

Conservatives would have preferred a traditional solution to the stresses of the post-1918 world: tranquilize the overexcited crowd and return public affairs to a gentlemanly elite. That solution was unthinkable, however, after so much emotional engagement in wartime propaganda and in the rejection of it. The immediate postwar world was a moment of intense public engagement, and conservatives, unable to abolish mass society and mass politics, would have to learn to manage them.

Liberals, too, as we have seen, had their solution: return to the nineteenth-century doctrine of the omnipotent market. Unregulated markets functioned so badly in economies distorted by war making and revolutionary pressures that even liberals wanted some regulation—but not enough to satisfy all their own followers. We saw earlier how the Italian liberal state lost its legitimacy among the landowners of the Po Valley by failing to protect them against the Left. Convinced that public order was absent, the landowners enlisted a private vigilante force in the form of *squadrismo*. Liberals offered Mill's pallid "marketplace of ideas" to people whose ears were ringing with nationalist and revolutionary propaganda. But it was liberal Europe itself that had violated all its own principles by letting itself be swept into the barbarity of a long war that it was then incapable of managing.

As for the Left, a new era was opening in the history of dissidence in Europe. In the nineteenth century, whenever anger and protest arose, the Left more or less automatically spoke for them. In the mid-nineteenth century, the Left was still a capacious family: it could include nationalists and anti-Semites, artisans and industrial workers, middle-class democrats and advocates of collective ownership. It was the coalition of virtually all the discontented. The Left could no longer play that role in 1919. As its organizations became disciplined and domesticated by Marxism after the 1880s, it tried to expel the old working-class xenophobia it had once tolerated. Especially in 1920, reacting against the patriotic brainwashing of the war and awaiting world revolution expectantly, the Left had no room for the Nation within the international revolutionary cause.

Noncommunist socialists, somewhat tarnished by having participated in war government and by appearing to have missed the revolutionary boat in 1917, were now less frequently able to stir young people in the pit of their stomachs. In the nineteenth century, the angry and the discontented had normally looked to the Left, and so had those intoxicated with the kind of insurrectionary ecstasy once expressed in Chopin's Revolutionary Étude, Wordsworth's "Bliss was it in that dawn to be alive, but to be young was very heaven,"[81] or Delacroix's *Revolution Leading the People*. As the twentieth century opened, the Left no longer had a monopoly on youths who wanted to change the world. Following World War I, what the French author Robert Brasillach recalled as the "great red fascism" of his youth[82] could compete with communism in offering a haven for the angry, an ecstatic experience on the barricades, the lure of untried possibility. Those young people and intellectuals who were heated by insurrectionary fevers but still clung to the Nation found a new home in fascism.

Before fascism could become a serious contender, one chief would have to emerge as the "gatherer"—the one able to shove his rivals aside and assemble in one tent all the (nonsocialist) discontented. For the problem at first was not a lack of would-be *Führers* but a plethora of them. Both Hitler and Mussolini faced rivals at the beginning. D'Annunzio, as we saw, understood how to dramatize a coup but not how to forge a coalition; Hitler's competitors in post-defeat Germany did not know how to arouse a crowd or build a catch-all party.

A successful "chief" was able to reject "purity" and engage in the compromises and deals needed to fit into the space available. The Italian Fascist Party, having discovered that in its first identity as a Left-nationalist movement the space it coveted was already occupied by the Left, underwent the necessary transformations to become a local power in the Po Valley. The Nazi Party broadened its appeal after 1928 to court farmers desperate over going broke and losing their farms. Both Mussolini and Hitler could perceive the space available, and were willing to trim their movements to fit.

The space was partly symbolic. The Nazi Party early shaped its identity by staking a claim to the street and fought with communist gangs for control of working-class neighborhoods of Berlin.[83] At issue was not merely a few meters of urban "turf." The Nazis sought to portray themselves as the most vigorous and effective force against the communists—and, at the same time, to portray the liberal state as incapable of preserving public security. The communists, at the same time, were showing that the Social Democrats were unequipped to deal with an incipient revolutionary situation that needed a fighting vanguard. Polarization was in the interest of both.

Fascist violence was neither random nor indiscriminate. It carried a well-calculated set of coded messages: that communist violence was rising, that the democratic state was responding to it ineptly, and that only the fascists were tough enough to save the nation from antinational terrorists. An essential step in the fascist march to acceptance and power was to persuade law-and-order conservatives and members of the middle class to tolerate fascist violence as a harsh necessity in the face of Left provocation.[84] It helped, of course, that many ordinary citizens never feared fascist violence against themselves, because they were reassured that it was reserved for national enemies and "terrorists" who deserved it.[85]

Fascists encouraged a distinction between members of the nation who merited protection and outsiders who deserved rough handling. One of the most sensational cases of Nazi violence before power was the murder of a communist laborer of Polish descent in the town of Potempa, in Silesia, by five SA men in August 1932. It became sensational when the killers' death sentences were commuted, under Nazi pressure, to life imprisonment. Party theorist Alfred Rosenberg took the occasion to underscore the difference between "bourgeois justice," according to which "one Polish Communist has the same weighting as five Germans, front-soldiers," and National Socialist ideology, according to which "one soul does not equal another soul, one person not another." Indeed, Rosenberg went on, for National Socialism, "there is no 'law as such.' "[86] The legitimation of violence against a demonized internal enemy brings us close to the heart of fascism.

For some, fascist violence was more than useful: it was beautiful. Some war veterans and intellectuals (Marinetti and Ernst Jünger were both) indulged in the aesthetics of violence. Violence often appealed to men too young to have known it in 1914–18 and who felt cheated of their war. It appealed to some women, too.[87] But it is a mistake to regard fascist success as solely the triumph of the D'Annunzian hero. It was the genius of fascism to wager that many an orderly bourgeois (or even bourgeoise) would take some vicarious satisfaction in a carefully selective violence, directed only against "terrorists" and "enemies of the people."

A climate of polarization helped the new fascist catch-all parties sweep up many who became disillusioned with the old deference *("honoratioren")* parties. This was risky, of course. Polarization could send the mass of angry protesters to the Left under certain conditions (as in Russia in 1917). Hitler and Mussolini understood that while Marxism now appealed mainly to blue-collar workers (and not to all of them), fascism was able to appeal more broadly across class lines. In postrevolutionary western Europe, a climate of polarization worked in fascism's favor.

One device used by fascist parties, but also by Marxist revolutionaries who have given serious thought to the conquest of power, was parallel structures. An outsider party that wants to claim power sets up organizations that replicate government agencies. The Nazi Party, for example, had its own foreign policy agency that, at first, soon after the party had achieved power, had to share power with the traditional Foreign Office. After its head, Joachim von Ribbentrop, became foreign minister in 1938, the party's foreign policy office increasingly supplanted the professional diplomats of the Foreign Office. A particularly important fascist "parallel organization" was the party police. Fascist parties that aspired to power tended to use their party militias to challenge the state's monopoly of physical force.

The fascist parties' parallel structures challenged the liberal state by claiming that they were capable of doing some things better (bashing communists, for instance). After achieving power, the party could substitute its parallel structures for those of the state.

We will encounter the parallel structures again in the course of observing the process of achieving power, and of exercising power. It is one of the defining characteristics of fascism. Leninist parties did the same during the conquest of power, but then in power the single party totally eclipsed the traditional state. Fascist regimes, as we will see in chapter 5, retained both the parallel structures and the traditional state, in permanent tension, which made them function very differently from the Bolshevik regime once in power.

Fascist success depended as much on allies and accomplices as on the tactics or special qualities of the movements themselves. The assistance given to Mussolini's *squadristi* in the Po Valley by elements of the police, the army, and the prefectoral administration has already been noted. Wherever public authorities winked at direct action against communists or socialists without troubling themselves too much about the niceties, a door was opened to fascism. At this point, judicial and administrative due process was fascism's worst enemy.

In the Italian case, the old centrist deal maker Giovanni Giolitti took an additional step to give Mussolini legitimacy. Pursuing the hallowed Italian parliamentary tradition of *trasformismo*,[88] he brought Mussolini into his centrist-nationalist coalition in the parliamentary elections of 1921 to help fight the socialists and the Popolari. Mussolini, who had refused to be coopted as a young socialist, accepted with alacrity as a Fascist, though this aroused some opposition among party purists. Mussolini's thirty-five seats brought the gift of respectability. Now he was available for all anti-socialist coalition builders. Bringing new parties into the system is usually a profoundly wise political step, but not when it rewards violence and an unrepentant determination to abolish democracy.

Having assembled a catalogue of preconditions, intellectual roots, and longer-term structural preconditions, we might be tempted to believe we can foresee exactly where fascism is likely to appear, grow, and take power. But that would mean falling into a determinist trap. There remains the element of human choice. It was by no means guaranteed that a nation fitted with all the preconditions would become fascist. Only the "vulgar" Marxist interpretation holds that capitalism will eventually get into trouble and inevitably need to adopt a fascist formula to save itself, and even sophisticated Marxists have ceased to believe in such inevitability.

As we will see in the next chapter, it took the decisions of powerful individuals to open the gates to fascism. That was the final essential precondition of successful fascism: decision-makers ready to share power with fascist challengers.

CHAPTER 4

Getting Power

Mussolini and the "March on Rome"

The myth that Mussolini's Fascists conquered power by their sole heroic exploits was propaganda—one of their most successful themes, evidently, for many people still believe it. Since Mussolini's "March on Rome" lies behind the widespread misinterpretation of the Fascist entry into office as a "seizure," we need to scrutinize that event stripped of its mythology.

During 1922 the *squadristi* escalated from sacking and burning local socialist headquarters, newspaper offices, labor exchanges, and socialist leaders' homes to the violent occupation of entire cities, all without serious hindrance from the authorities. They took Fiume back from its international administration on March 3 and assaulted Ferrara and Bologna in May, chasing out socialist city governments and imposing their own programs of public works. On July 12, they occupied Cremona and burned the headquarters of both socialist and Catholic unions and devastated the home of Guido Miglioli, a Left Catholic leader who had organized dairy farm laborers in the region. A "column of fire" through the Romagna arrived in Ravenna on July 26. Trent and Bolzano, with their large German-speaking minorities, were "Italianized" in early October. The Blackshirts had developed such formidable momentum that the capital city of Rome could hardly fail to be next.

When the annual Fascist Congress convened on October 24 in Naples—its first foray into the south—Mussolini was ready to see how far the wave would take him. He ordered the Blackshirts to seize public buildings, commandeer trains, and converge on three points surrounding Rome. The "March" was led by four militants who represented the multiple strands of fascism: Italo Balbo, war veteran and *squadrist* boss of

Ferrara; General Emilio De Bono; Michele Bianchi, ex-syndicalist and founder of the interventionist Fascio of Milan in 1915; and Cesare Maria De Vecchi, the monarchist leader of Piedmontese Fascism. Mussolini himself waited prudently in his Milan newspaper offices, not far from a possible Swiss refuge in case things went wrong. On October 27, *squadristi* seized post offices and train stations in several northern Italian cities without opposition.

The Italian government was ill-equipped to meet this challenge. Indeed, an effective government had hardly existed since February 1922. We noted in the last chapter how postwar dreams of profound change brought a large left-wing majority into the Italian parliament in the first postwar election, on November 16, 1919. But this Left majority, fatally divided into two irreconcilable parts, could not govern. The Marxist Partito Socialista Italiano (PSI) held about a third of the seats. Many of the Italian socialists—the "maximalists"—were hypnotized by Bolshevik success in Russia, and felt that mere reform was a betrayal of this moment of opportunity. Another third of the Italian chamber was held by a new Catholic party, parent of the powerful post-1945 Christian Democrats, the Partito Popolare Italiano (PPI), some of whose members wanted radical social reform within a Catholic context. Catholics, even those favoring profound changes in Italian land tenure and class relations, disagreed passionately with the atheistic Marxists over religion in the schools. No alliance was possible, therefore, between the two halves of what might otherwise have comprised a progressive majority. In the absence of other workable alternatives, a heterogeneous coalition of liberals (in that period's sense of the word) and conservatives struggled after 1919 to govern without a solid majority.

As we saw in the last chapter, the solution adopted by Prime Minister Giolitti was to include the Fascists on his ticket (the "National Bloc") for new elections in May 1921. This was the first of several crucial steps by which the Italian Establishment tried to coopt Fascist energy and numbers for their own survival. While the temptations of office might have "transformed" the Fascists in normal times, as it had domesticated and divided Italian socialists before 1914, Italy was not living in normal times in 1921.

When the government of the well-meaning but overwhelmed Ivanoe Bonomi, an associate of Giolitti's center-Left, lost a vote of confidence in February 1922, it took three weeks to find a successor. Finally an even more subaltern Giolitti lieutenant, Luigi Facta, reluctantly assumed the prime ministry. His government lost its majority on July 19. When the emergency came, Facta was serving in only a caretaker capacity.

Nevertheless, the prime minister began vigorous countermeasures. With the king's approval, Facta had already reinforced the Rome garrison with five battalions of disciplined Alpine troops. Now he ordered police and railroad officials to stop the Fascist trains at five checkpoints and began preparations to impose martial law.

Meanwhile Mussolini quietly left the door open for a political deal. Several old political warhorses were trying to defuse the crisis by "transforming" Mussolini into a mere minister within yet another liberal-conservative coalition cabinet. The aged deal maker Giolitti was widely regarded as the most plausible savior (he had evicted D'Annunzio by force in 1920, and had included Mussolini in his 1921 electoral list), but he was in no hurry to reassume office, and Mussolini remained noncommittal in meetings with his representatives. Further to the right, the nationalist former prime minister Antonio Salandra also offered cabinet seats to Mussolini's party. By the time the *squadristi* began mobilizing, these negotiations had become becalmed by mutual rivalries, by the refusal of most socialists to support a "bourgeois" government, by indecision about whether to include Mussolini or not, and by Mussolini's calculated hesitations.

The socialists contributed their bit to the emergency. Although nearly half the socialist deputies, led by Filippo Turati, finally agreed on July 28 to support a centrist government without Mussolini if one could be formed, the other half expelled them from the party for treasonous class collaboration. What the Italian Left *could* agree on was a general strike on July 31. Although this was billed as a "strike for legality," intended to reinforce constitutional authority, it had the effect of inflating Mussolini's appeal as a bulwark against revolution. Its speedy collapse also revealed the Left's weakness.

Prime Minister Facta's emergency measures nearly succeeded in blocking the Fascist march in October. Four hundred police stopped trains carrying twenty thousand Blackshirts at three of the checkpoints — Civita Vecchia, Orte, and Avezzano. About nine thousand Blackshirts who evaded the checkpoints or continued on foot formed a motley crowd at the gates of Rome on the morning of October 28,[1] poorly armed, wearing makeshift uniforms, short of food and water, and milling about in a discouraging rain. "In ancient and modern history, there was hardly any attempt on Rome that failed so miserably at its beginning."[2]

At the last moment King Victor Emmanuel III balked. He decided not to sign Prime Minister Facta's martial law decree. He refused to call Mussolini's bluff and use the readily available force to exclude the Black-shirts from Rome. He rejected Salandra's last-minute efforts to form a new conservative government without Mussolini, who had by now refused Salandra's offer of a coalition. Instead he offered the prime ministry directly to the young upstart Fascist leader.

Mussolini arrived in Rome from Milan on the morning of October 30, not at the head of his Blackshirts, but by railway sleeping car. He called upon the king clad incongruously in morning coat and black shirt, a sartorial reflection of his ambiguous situation: partly a legal claimant to office, partly the leader of an insurrectionary band. "Sire, forgive my attire," he is said to have told the king, mendaciously, "I come from the battlefields."

Why did the king thus rescue Mussolini from a rashly overplayed hand? Mussolini had cleverly confronted the sovereign with a hard choice. Either the government must use force to disperse thousands of Blackshirts converging on Rome, with considerable risk of bloodshed and bitter inter-nal dissension, or the king must accept Mussolini as head of government.

The most likely explanation for the king's choice of the second option is a private warning (of which no archival trace remains) by the army commander-in-chief, Marshal Armando Diaz, or possibly another senior military officer, that the troops might fraternize with the Blackshirts if ordered to block them. According to another theory, the king feared that if he tried to use force against Mussolini, his cousin, the duke of Aosta, reputed to be sympathetic to the Fascists, might make a bid for the throne by siding with them. We will probably never know for sure. What seems certain is that Mussolini had correctly surmised that the king and the army would not make the hard choice to resist his Blackshirts by force. It was not Fascism's force that decided the issue, but the conservatives' unwillingness to risk their force against his. The "March on Rome" was a gigantic bluff that worked, and still works in the general public's percep-tions of Mussolini's "seizure of power."

It was only on October 31, with Mussolini already in office, that about ten thousand Blackshirts, finally fed and given dry clothes, were accorded a compensatory parade through the streets of Rome, where they provoked bloody incidents.[3] That very evening the new prime minister bustled his awkward squads out of town in fifty special trains.

Mussolini later worked hard to establish the myth that his Blackshirts had taken power by their own will and force. The first anniversary of what was supposed to have been their arrival in Rome was commemorated in 1923 with four days of pageantry, and that date — October 28 — became a national holiday. It also became the first day of the Fascist New Year when the new calendar was introduced in 1927.[4] On the tenth anniversary, in October 1932, a national exhibition, the Mostra della Rivoluzione Fascista, had as its centerpiece the heroic deeds of the march's "martyrs."[5]

Hitler and the "Backstairs Conspiracy"

Only in Italy did fascism come to power in its first élan, in the turbulent days following World War I. Elsewhere, except in Russia, traditional elites found less disruptive ways to reestablish stability and recover some semblance of normalcy after the earthquake of World War I.[6] The other early fascist movements, offspring of crises, shrank into insignificance as normal life returned in the 1920s.

But first Hitler, taken in by Mussolini's mythmaking, attempted a "march" of his own. On November 8, 1923, during a nationalist rally in a Munich beer hall, the Bürgerbräukeller, Hitler attempted to kidnap the leaders of the Bavarian government and force them to support a coup d'état against the federal government in Berlin. He believed that if he took control of Munich and declared a new national government, the Bavarian civil and military leaders would be forced by public opinion to support him. He was equally convinced that the local army authorities would not oppose the Nazi coup because the World War I hero General Ludendorff was marching beside him.[7]

Hitler underestimated military fidelity to the chain of command. The conservative Bavarian minister-president Gustav von Kahr gave orders to stop Hitler's coup, by force if necessary. The police fired on the Nazi marchers on November 9 as they approached a major square (possibly returning a first shot from Hitler's side). Fourteen putschists and four policemen were killed. Hitler was arrested and imprisoned,[8] along with other Nazis and their sympathizers. The august General Ludendorff was released on his own recognizance. Hitler's "Beer Hall Putsch" was thus put down so ignominiously by the conservative rulers of Bavaria that he resolved never again to try to gain power through force. That meant remaining at least superficially within constitutional legality, though the Nazis never gave up the selective violence that was central to the party's appeal, or hints about wider aims after power.[9]

Hitler's opportunity came around with the next crisis: the economic crash of the 1930s. As millions of people lost their jobs, fascist movements everywhere recovered their momentum. Governments of all sorts, democracies more publicly and noisily than the rest, became paralyzed by awkward choices. The Italian model made fascist movements look plausible again, as a new way to provide mass assent for a restoration of order, national authority, and economic productivity.

The Weimar Republic's constitutional system had never achieved general legitimacy in Germany; many Germans considered it the offspring of foreign domination and internal treason. Weimar democracy resembled a candle burning at both ends. Eaten away from both right and left by antisystem Nazis and communists, the dwindling center was obliged to form heterogeneous coalitions pairing such incompatible partners as socialists with laissez-faire moderates and clericals with anticlericals in its doomed quest for a working parliamentary majority.

A political system that obliged such a cacophony of parties to work together would inevitably have trouble agreeing on sensitive issues, even in good times. After 1929 German governments had to make increasingly divisive political and economic choices. In June of that year came the Young Plan, an international agreement by which Germany promised to continue paying reparations for World War I to the Allies, though at a reduced rate. Although German diplomacy had successfully lowered the payments, the Young Plan's confirmation of the principle of reparations aroused a nationalist outcry. In October came the Wall Street crash. In 1930, as unemployment soared, the government had to decide whether to extend unemployment benefits (as socialists and Left Catholics wanted) or balance the budget to satisfy foreign creditors (as middle-class and conservative parties wanted). A clear choice, but one about which no majority available in Germany would be able to agree.

When the government of Chancellor Hermann Müller fell on March 27, 1930, the German governing system seized up in terminal deadlock. Müller, a reformist socialist, had presided since June 1928 over a five-party Great Coalition stretching from the socialists through the Catholic Center Party to the moderate centrist Democratic Party and the internationalist but conservative People's Party. The Great Coalition lasted longer than any other government of the Weimar Republic, twenty-one months (June 1928–March 1930).[10]

Instead of being a sign of strength, however, this longevity signaled the absence of alternatives. Deep policy disagreements that had made governing hard enough when the Great Coalition was first formed, in the relatively calm days of June 1928, made it impossible two years later after the Depression had thrown millions out of work. The Left wanted to raise taxes to maintain unemployment compensation; moderates and conservatives wanted to reduce social spending in order to cut taxes. The Great Coalition foundered on these reefs of social entitlement and tax burdens. After March 1930 no parliamentary majority could be cobbled together in Germany. The Catholic trade union official Heinrich Brüning governed as chancellor without a majority, relying upon President Hindenburg to sign legislation into law without a majority vote, under emergency powers granted him by Article 48 of the constitution. Thereafter Germans endured nearly three years of this awkward emergency government, with no parliamentary majority, before Hitler had his chance. In a curious irony, Hitler's arrival in power seemed to permit, at long last, a return to majority government. Hitler was a godsend for conservatives because, as the head of what was since July 1932 Germany's largest party, he held out the possibility for the first time of a parliamentary majority that excluded the Left.

At the moment when deadlock gripped the German political system, on March 27, 1930, the Nazi Party was still quite small (only 2.8 percent of the popular vote in the parliamentary elections of May 1928). But nationalist agitation over the Young Plan plus the collapse of farm prices and urban employment catapulted it in the September 1930 elections from 12 to 107 seats out of 491—already the second largest party. After that, any parliamentary majority in Germany had to include either the socialists or the Nazis. The Left (even assuming that the socialists, communists, and Left Catholics could overcome their crippling divisions sufficiently to govern) was excluded out of hand by President Hindenburg and his advisors.

The myth of the Fascist coup in Italy also misled the German Left, and helped assure the fatal passivity of the German Socialist Party (SPD) and the German Communist Party (KPD) in late 1932 and early 1933. Both expected the Nazis to attempt a coup, though their analyses of the situation were otherwise totally different. For the SPD, the expected Nazi uprising would be their signal to act without bearing the onus of illegality, as they had successfully done with a general strike against the "Kapp Putsch" of 1920, when Freikorps units had tried to take over the government. Given that frame of mind, they never identified an opportune moment for counteraction against Hitler.

The nearest thing to a putsch in Weimar Germany in the early 1930s came not from the Nazis but from their conservative predecessor, Chancellor Franz von Papen. On July 20, 1932, von Papen deposed the legitimately elected government of the state (Land) of Prussia, a coalition of socialists and the Catholic Center Party, and prevailed upon President Hindenburg to use his emergency powers to install a new state administration headed by von Papen. That act might legitimately have triggered strong counteraction from the Left. The SPD leaders, however, deterred by strong legalitarian convictions, advancing age,[11] the futility of the strike weapon during mass unemployment, and perhaps legitimate fears that action by the Left might perversely throw even more middle-class Germans into the arms of the Nazis, limited their response to a futile lawsuit against Chancellor von Papen. Having failed to offer effective opposition to von Papen's illegal action in July 1932, the socialists—still the second largest party in Germany—had even less occasion to act against Hitler, who avoided any direct assault on legality until he was already in unshakable control in spring 1933.[12]

The communists followed a totally different logic, based upon their conviction that social revolution was at hand. In that perspective, Nazi success might actually help the communist cause by setting off a pendulum movement, first to the Right and then, inexorably, to the Left. KPD strategists, focused firmly on the coming revolution, saw SPD efforts to save Weimar democracy as "objectively" counterrevolutionary. They denounced the socialists as "social fascists." Convinced that the SPD was no less their enemy than the Nazis and competing with the Nazis for the same volatile membership (especially the unemployed), the KPD even cooperated with the Nazis in a wildcat strike against the Berlin transport system in November 1932. The last thing the German communists were going to do was help the SPD save democratic institutions.[13]

Hitler's electoral success—far greater than Mussolini's—allowed him more autonomy in bargaining with the political insiders whose help he needed to reach office. Even more than in Italy, as German governmental mechanisms jammed after 1930, responsibility for finding a way out narrowed to a half-dozen men: President Hindenburg, his son Oskar and other intimate advisors, and the last two Weimar chancellors, Franz von Papen and Kurt von Schleicher. At first they tried to keep the uncouth Austrian ex-corporal out. One must recall that in the 1930s cabinet ministers were still supposed to be gentlemen. Bringing raw fascists into government was a measure of their desperation.

The Catholic aristocrat Franz von Papen tried as chancellor (July–November 1932) to govern without politicians, through a so-called Cabinet of Barons composed of technical experts and nonpolitical eminences. His gamble at holding national elections in July let the Nazis become the largest party. Von Papen then tried to bring Hitler in as vice chancellor, a position without authority, but the Nazi leader had enough strategic acumen and gambler's courage to accept nothing but the top office. This path forced Hitler to spend the tense fall of 1932 in an agony of suspenseful waiting, trying to quiet his restless and office-hungry militants while he played for all or nothing.

Hoping to deepen the crisis, the Nazis (like the Fascists before them) increased their violence, carefully choosing their targets. The apogee of Nazi street violence in Germany came after June 16, 1932, when Chancellor von Papen lifted the ban on SA uniforms that Brüning had imposed in April. During several sickening weeks, 103 people were killed and hundreds were wounded.[14]

Mussolini had played a weaker hand in his negotiations for power, and it had rested more than Hitler's on overt violence. We often forget that Mussolinian Fascism was more violent than Nazism on its way to power. On May 5, 1921, alone, election day, 19 people were killed in political violence in Italy and 104 wounded.[15] Though the statistics are unreliable, plausible estimates of the dead in political violence in Italy during 1920–22 include five to six hundred Fascists and two thousand anti-Fascists and non-Fascists, followed by another one thousand of the latter in 1923–26.[16]

Von Papen's expedient of new elections on November 6 diminished the Nazi vote somewhat (the communists gained again), but did nothing to extract Germany from constitutional deadlock. President Hindenburg replaced him as chancellor on December 2 with a senior army officer regarded as more technocratic than reactionary, General Kurt von Schleicher. During his brief weeks in power (December 1932–January 1933), Schleicher prepared an active job-creation program and mended relations with organized labor. Hoping to obtain Nazi neutrality in parliament, he flirted with Gregor Strasser, head of the party administration and a leader of its anticapitalist current (Hitler never forgot and never forgave Strasser's "betrayal").

At this point, Hitler was in serious difficulty. In the elections of November 6, his vote had dropped for the first time, costing him his most precious asset—momentum. The party treasury was nearly empty. Gregor

Strasser was not the only senior Nazi who, exhausted by Hitler's all-or-nothing strategy, was considering other options.

The Nazi leader was rescued by Franz von Papen. Bitter at Schleicher for taking his place, von Papen secretly arranged a deal whereby Hitler would be chancellor and he, von Papen, deputy chancellor—a position from which von Papen expected to run things. The aged Hindenburg, convinced by his son and other intimate advisors that Schleicher was planning to depose him and install a military dictatorship, and convinced by von Papen that no other conservative option remained, appointed the Hitler–von Papen government on January 30, 1933.[17] Hitler, concluded Alan Bullock, had been "hoist" into office by "a backstairs conspiracy."[18]

What Did Not Happen:
Election, Coup d'État, Solo Triumph

German voters never gave the Nazis a majority of the popular vote, as is still sometimes alleged. As we saw in the last chapter, the Nazis did indeed become the largest party in the German Reichstag in the parliamentary election of July 31, 1932, with 37.2 percent of the vote. They then slipped back to 33.1 percent in the parliamentary election of November 6, 1932. In the parliamentary election of March 6, 1933, with Hitler as chancellor and the Nazi Party in command of all the resources of the German state, its score was a more significant but still insufficient 43.9 percent.[19] More than one German in two voted against Nazi candidates in that election, in the teeth of intimidation by Storm Troopers. The Italian Fascist Party won 35 out of 535 seats, in the one free parliamentary election in which it participated, on May 15, 1921.[20]

At the other extreme, neither Hitler nor Mussolini arrived in office by a coup d'état. Neither took the helm by force, even if both had used force before power in order to destabilize the existing regime, and both were to use force again, after power, in order to transform their governments into dictatorships (as we will see shortly). Even the most scrupulous authors refer to their "seizure of power,"[21] but that phrase better describes what the two fascist leaders did after reaching office than how they got into office.

Both Mussolini and Hitler were invited to take office as head of government by a head of state in the legitimate exercise of his official functions, on the advice of civilian and military counselors. Both thus became heads of government in what appeared, at least on the surface, to be legiti-

mate exercises of constitutional authority by King Victor Emmanuel III
and President Hindenburg. Both these appointments were made, it must
be added at once, under conditions of extreme crisis, which the fascists
had abetted. I will consider the kind of crisis that opens the way to fascism
below.

Indeed no insurrectionary coup against an established state has ever
so far brought fascists to power. Authoritarian dictatorships have several
times crushed such attempts.[22] This happened three times to the Romanian Legion of the Archangel Michael, the most ecstatically religious of all
fascist parties and one of the readiest to murder Jews and bourgeois politicians. In a Romania wretchedly governed by a corrupt and narrow oligarchy, the legion had a fervent rapport with its popular following, mostly
hitherto apolitical peasants dazzled by the youthful Corneliu Codreanu
and his disciples, touring remote villages on horseback, decked out with
green shirts and religious and patriotic banners.[23]

After a particularly sterile period of parliamentary infighting and
cronyism, Romanian King Carol assumed dictatorial powers on February
10, 1938. In November, having tried and failed to coopt the increasingly
violent legion into his official Front of National Rebirth, Carol arrested
Codreanu, who was subsequently killed, along with some associates, "while
trying to escape." Codreanu's successor Horia Sima responded in January
1939 with an insurrection, which the royal dictatorship repressed firmly.

Carol abdicated in September 1940 after victorious Germany had
forced Romania to cede territories to Hungary and Bulgaria. The new
Romanian dictator, General (later Marshal) Ion Antonescu, in another
attempt to harness the legion's popular following, made it the sole party in
the "National Legionary State" he formed on September 15, 1940. Horia
Sima, the legion's impetuous new head, set up "parallel" police and labor
organizations and began the confiscation of Jewish property, so disorgan-
izing the Romanian state and economy that Antonescu, with Hitler's
approval, began in January 1941 to curtail Horia's powers. A full-scale
revolt and pogrom launched by the legion on January 21 was bloodily
crushed by Antonescu in "the most extreme example"[24] of a conservative repression of fascism. Antonescu liquidated the legion and replaced
the National Legionary State with a pro-German but nonfascist military
dictatorship.[25]

Other fascist coup attempts fared no better. While the July 25, 1934,
coup by the Austrian Nazi Party succeeded in murdering Chancellor
Engelbert Dollfuss, his successor, Kurt von Schuschnigg, repressed Nazism

in Austria and governed through a single clerical-authoritarian party, the Fatherland Front.

Although conservatives might accept violence against socialists and trade unionists, they would not tolerate it against the state. For their part, most fascist leaders have recognized that a seizure of power in the teeth of conservative and military opposition would be possible only with the help of the street, under conditions of social disorder likely to lead to wildcat assaults on private property, social hierarchy, and the state's monopoly of armed force. A fascist resort to direct action would thus risk conceding advantages to fascism's principal enemy, the Left, still powerful in the street and workplace in interwar Europe.[26] Such tactics would also alienate those very elements—the army and the police—that the fascists would need later for planning and carrying out aggressive national expansion. Fascist parties, however deep their contempt for conservatives, had no plausible future aligning themselves with any groups who wanted to uproot the bases of conservative power.

Since the fascist route to power has always passed through cooperation with conservative elites, at least in the cases so far known, the strength of a fascist movement in itself is only one of the determining variables in the achievement (or not) of power, though it is surely a vital one. Fascists did have numbers and muscle to offer to conservatives caught in crisis in Italy and Germany, as we have seen. Equally important, however, was the conservative elites' willingness to work with fascism; a reciprocal flexibility on the fascist leaders' part; and the urgency of the crisis that induced them to cooperate with each other.

It is therefore essential to examine the accomplices who helped at crucial points. To watch only the fascist leader during his arrival in power is to fall under the spell of the *"Führer* myth" and the *"Duce* myth" in a way that would have given those men immense satisfaction. We must spend as much time studying their indispensable allies and accomplices as we spend studying the fascist leaders, and as much time studying the kinds of situation in which fascists were helped into power as we spend studying the movements themselves.

Forming Alliances

Entering seriously into a quest for power engaged mature fascist movements deeply in the process of forming alliances with the establishment. Italian and German conservatives had not created Mussolini and

Hitler, of course, though they had too often let their law breaking go unpunished. After the Fascists and the Nazis had made themselves too important to ignore, by the somewhat different mixtures of electoral appeal and violent intimidation that we saw in the last chapter, the conservatives had to decide what to do with them.

In particular, conservative leaders had to decide whether to try to coopt fascism or force it back to the margins. One crucial decision was whether the police and the courts would compel the fascists to obey the law. German chancellor Brüning attempted to curb Nazi violence in 1931–32. He banned uniformed actions by the SA on April 14, 1932. When Franz von Papen succeeded Brüning as chancellor in July 1932, however, he lifted the ban, as we saw above, and the Nazis, excited by vindication, set off the most violent period in the whole 1930–32 constitutional crisis. In Italy, although a few prefects tried to restrain Fascist lawlessness,[27] the national leaders preferred, at crucial moments, as we already know, to try to "transform" Mussolini rather than to discipline him. Conservative national leaders in both countries decided that what the fascists had to offer outweighed the disadvantages of allowing these ruffians to capture public space from the Left by violence. The nationalist press and conservative leaders in both countries consistently applied a double standard to judging fascist and left-wing violence.

When a constitutional system seizes up in deadlock and democratic institutions cease to function, the "political arena" tends to narrow. The circle of emergency decision-makers may become reduced to a few individuals, perhaps a head of state along with his immediate civil and military advisors.[28] In earlier chapters of this book, we needed to look at very broad contexts in order to understand the founding and rooting of fascism. At the stage when the breakdown of democratic regimes finally opens the way for the fascist leader to make a serious bid for power, the concentration of responsibility in the hands of a few key individuals requires something nearer a biographical perspective—with due caution, of course, about falling into the trap of attributing everything to the fascist leader alone.

Conservative complicities in the fascism's arrival in power were of several types. First of all, there was complicity in fascist violence against the Left. One of the most fateful decisions in the German case was von Papen's removal, on June 16, 1932, of the ban on SA activity. Mussolini's *squadristi* would have been powerless without the closed eyes and even the outright aid of the Italian police and army. Another form of complicity was the gift of respectability. We have seen how Giolitti helped make Mussolini respectable by including him in his electoral coalition in May 1921. Alfred Hugenberg, Krupp executive and leader of the party that competed with Hitler most directly, the German National Party (DNVP), alternately attacked the Nazi upstart and appeared at political rallies with him. One at Bad Harzburg in fall 1931 made the public believe the two had formed a "Harzburg Front." But while Hugenberg helped make Hitler look acceptable, his DNVP membership drained away to the more exciting Nazis.

We saw in chapter 3 that the Nazis received less direct financial help from business than many have assumed. Before the final deal that put Hitler in power, German big business greatly preferred a solid reassuring conservative like von Papen to the unknown Hitler with his crackpot economic advisors. In the final tense months, when Hitler was refusing all lesser offers in an all-or-nothing gamble on becoming chancellor, and when party radicalism resurfaced in the Berlin transport strike, money grew scarcer. The NSDAP was virtually broke after the disappointing election of November 1932. A relatively minor Cologne banker, Kurt von Schröder, served as go-between in negotiations between Hitler and von Papen, but business contributions did not become a major resource for Hitler until after he attained power. Then, of course, the game changed. Businessmen contributed hugely to the new Nazi authorities and set about accommodating themselves to a regime that would reward many of them richly with armaments contracts, and all of them by breaking the back of organized labor in Germany.

The financing of Italian Fascism has been less studied. When Mussolini broke with the socialists in fall 1914, nationalist newspaper publishers and industrialists and the French government paid for his new paper, *Il Popolo d'Italia*, but their purpose was to bring Italy into the war.[29] The subsequent assistance of landowners, the military, and some civil servants to *squadrismo* seems clear enough.

The more or less protracted period during which fascists and conservatives hammered out a power-sharing arrangement was a stressful time for both sides, in both Italy and Germany. These negotiations promised at best to produce a less than ideal compromise for both. Considering the alternatives, however—the Left in power, or a military dictatorship likely to exclude both the parliamentary conservatives and the fascists— both sides were willing to make the necessary adjustments and accept second-best.

The fascist parties were thus tempted into ever deeper complicity with their new allies, which risked dividing the parties and alienating some of the purists. This "normalizing" process, already evident at the earlier stage of taking root, was now intensified by the higher stakes offered as access to power became plausible. The fascist leader, engaged in a promising negotiation with conservative power holders, reshaped his party even more radically than before. He made what Wolfgang Schieder calls a *Herrschaftskompromiss*, a "compromise for rule," in which areas of agreement are located and bothersome idealists are cast aside.[30]

Hitler and Mussolini made their *Herrschaftskompromiss* from somewhat different positions of strength. The importance of *squadrismo* to Mussolini's success, and the relative unimportance of his electoral party, meant that Mussolini was also more beholden to the *ras*, his regional Fascist chieftains, than Hitler was beholden to the SA. Hitler had a somewhat freer hand in this negotiation, but even he was not free from difficulties with his party militants.

Negotiating with conservative leaders for entry into power is a time of risk for a fascist leader. While the leader bargains in secret with the political elite, his militant followers wait impatiently outside, reproaching him with sellout. Mussolini, already by late 1920 engaged in secret negotiations with party leaders, disappointed some of his militants by failing to come to the defense of D'Annunzio at Fiume at Christmas, and by joining Giolitti's electoral coalition in May 1921. In August 1921 he overcame open rebellion over his "pacification pact" with the traditional enemy, the socialists, only by resigning temporarily from the Fascist leadership and by giving up the pact.

Hitler also aroused conflicts within his party whenever he seemed to be close to striking some deal for power. Former Freikorps captain Walter Stennes, in charge of the SA in Berlin and eastern Germany, objected to Hitler's pursuit of power by legal means. Stennes's Storm Troopers were so exasperated by the deferral of gratification, by long hours with low pay, and by their subordination to nonmilitary party cadres that they occupied and wrecked Nazi Party offices in Berlin in September 1930. When they refused to obey Hitler's order to observe a ban on street violence in February 1931, Hitler kicked Stennes out of the SA. Angry SA militants occupied party headquarters again in April 1931, and it took all of Hitler's powers of persuasion to end the revolt. Five hundred SA radicals were purged. Hitler came closest to losing control of the Nazi Party at the end of 1932, as we saw earlier, as votes began to slip, money declined, and some lieutenants looked to more promising futures in coalition governments. His will and gambler's instinct intact despite a weakened bargaining position, Hitler bet all or nothing on the chancellorship.

The stakes were raised for conservatives, too, when an arrangement with a successful fascist party began to look likely: power with a mass base now became an attainable goal for them, too. There was even competition among conservatives seeking to win the support of all or part of the fascist movement (sometimes trying to detach a wing or the base). Schleicher competed with von Papen in Germany for success in harnessing the bucking Nazi horse to his wagon, as did Giolitti with Salandra in Italy.

There was nothing inevitable about the arrival of either Mussolini and Hitler in office. Looking closely at how fascist leaders became head of government is an exercise in antideterminism. It may well be that a number of factors—the shallowness of liberal traditions, late industrialization, the survival of predemocratic elites, the strength of revolutionary surges, a spasm of revolt against national humiliation—all contributed to the magnitude of the crisis and narrowed the choices available in Italy and Germany. But the conservative leaders rejected other possibilities— governing in coalition with the moderate Left, for instance, or governing under royal or presidential emergency authority (or, in the German case, continuing to do so). They chose the fascist option. The fascist leaders, for their part, accomplished the "normalization" necessary for sharing power. It did not have to turn out that way.

What Fascists Offered the Establishment

In a situation of constitutional deadlock and rising revolutionary menace, a successful fascist movement offers precious resources to a faltering elite.

Fascists could offer a mass following sufficiently numerous to permit conservatives to form parliamentary majorities capable of vigorous decisions, without having to call upon unacceptable Leftist partners. Mussolini's thirty-five deputies were not a major weight in the balance, but Hitler's potential contribution was decisive. He could offer the largest party in Germany to conservatives who had never acquired a knack for the mass politics suddenly introduced into their country by the constitution of 1919. During the 1920s, the only non-Marxist party that had successfully built a mass base in Germany was the Zentrum (Center Party), a Catholic party that enjoyed, through its roots in parish life, an actively engaged membership and multiclass recruitment. The Zentrum reached broadly into the working class through the Catholic trade unions, but, as a confessional party, it could not recruit as broadly as Hitler. Holding in his hands the largest party, Hitler permitted conservative coalition makers to escape from reliance on the president's emergency powers that had already endured nearly three years, and form a parliamentary majority that excluded the Left.

The fascists offered more than mere numbers. They offered fresh young faces to a public weary of an aging establishment that had made a mess of things. The two youngest parties in Italy and Germany were the communists and the fascists. Both nations longed for new leaders, and the fascists offered conservatives a fountain of youth. The fascists also offered another way of belonging—deeper commitment and discipline in an era when conservatives feared dissolution of the social bond.

Fascists had also found a magic formula for weaning workers away from Marxism. Long after Marx asserted that the working class had no homeland, conservatives had been unable to find any way to refute him. None of their nineteenth-century nostrums—deference, religion, schooling—had worked. On the eve of World War I, the Action Française had enjoyed some success recruiting a few industrial workers to nationalism, and the unexpectedly wide acceptance by workers of their patriotic duty to fight for their homelands when World War I began foretold that in the twentieth century Nation was going to be stronger than Class.

Fascists everywhere have built on that revelation. I mentioned the French Cercle Proudhon earlier among the precursors.[31] As for the Nazi Party, its very name proclaimed that it was a workers' party, an *Arbeiterpartei*. Mussolini expected to recruit his old socialist colleagues. Their results were not overwhelmingly successful. Every analysis of the social composition of the early fascist parties agrees: although some workers were attracted, their share of party membership was always well below their share in the general population. Perhaps those few fascist workers were enough. If the fascist parties could recruit some workers, then fascist violence would take care of the holdouts. This formula of divide and conquer was far more effective than anything the conservatives could provide on their own.

Another seductive fascist offer was a way to overcome the climate of disorder that the fascists themselves had helped cause. Having unleashed their militants in order to make democracy unworkable and discredit the constitutional state, the Nazi and Fascist leaders then posed as the only nonsocialist force that could restore order. It was not the last time that the leaders capitalized on that ambiguity: "Being in the center of the movement," Hannah Arendt wrote in one of her penetrating observations, "the leader can act as though he were above it."[32] Fascist terms for a deal were not insuperably high. Some German conservatives were uneasy about the anticapitalist rhetoric still flaunted by some Nazi intellectuals,[33] as were Italian conservatives by Fascist labor activists like Edmondo Rossoni. But Mussolini had long come around to "productivism" and admiration for the industrial hero, while Hitler made it clear in his famous speech to the Düsseldorf Industrialists' Club on January 26, 1932, as well as in in private conversations, that he was a social Darwinist in the economic sphere, too.

Even if one had to admit these uncouth outsiders to high office in order to make a bargain, conservatives were convinced that they would still control the state. It was unheard-of for such upstarts to run European governments. It was still normal in Europe, even after World War I, even in democracies, for ministers and heads of state to be educated members of the upper classes with long experience in diplomacy or administration. The first lower-class prime minister in Britain was Ramsay MacDonald, in 1924, and he soon came to look, speak, and act like a patrician, to the disgust of Labour militants, who ridiculed him as "Gentleman Mac." President Friedrich Ebert of Germany (1919–25), a saddlemaker by trade, had acquired standing in a long career as Socialist Party functionary and deputy. Hitler and Mussolini were the first lower-class adventurers to reach power in major European countries. Even to this day the French Republic has had no head of state and only a handful of prime ministers who were social outsiders of the ilk of, say, Harry Truman. But circumstances were far from normal in Italy in 1922 and in Germany in 1933. A central ingredient in the conservatives' calculation was that the Austrian corporal and the greenhorn Italian ex-socialist rabble-rouser would not have the faintest idea what to do with high office. They would be incapable of governing without the cultivated and experienced conservative leaders' savoir faire.

In sum, fascists offered a new recipe for governing with popular support but without any sharing of power with the Left, and without any threat to conservative social and economic privileges and political dominance. The conservatives, for their part, held the keys to the doors of power.

The Prefascist Crisis

Even though the two crises within which the two fascist leaders achieved office — World War I's aftershocks and the Great Depression — were different, they had common elements. Both confronted governments with problems of economic dislocation and foreign humiliation that seemed insoluble by traditional party politics; a deadlock of constitutional government (produced in part by political polarization that fascists helped abet); a militant Left growing rapidly and threatening to be the chief beneficiary of the crisis; and conservative leaders who refused to work with even the reformist elements of the Left, and who felt threatened in their capacity to continue to govern against the Left without fresh reinforcements.

It is essential to recall how real the possibility of communist revolution seemed in Italy in 1921 and Germany in 1932. Italy had just experienced the *biennio rosso*, the two "red years" following the first postwar election of November 1919, in which the Italian Socialist Party (PSI) tripled its pre-war vote to capture nearly a third of the seats in parliament and experienced a wave of "maximalist" fervor. The establishment of socialist mayors in numerous localities was accompanied by massive land seizures and strikes, culminating in a spectacular occupation of factories in Turin in September 1920. In the background loomed the example of Russia, where the world's first successful socialist revolution gave every sign of spawning others. We now know that the Italian socialist "maximalists" and the new Italian Communist Party founded in 1921 had not the slightest idea what to do next. Fear of an imagined communist revolution could mobilize conservatives as powerfully as the real thing, however. As Federico Chabod observed, middle-class fear of communism peaked in Italy after the "maximalist" wave had already subsided.[34]

In Germany after 1930 only the communists, along with the Nazis, were increasing their vote.[35] Like the Nazis, the German communists thrived on unemployment and a widespread perception that the traditional parties and constitutional system had failed. We know from Nazi Party documents captured by the German police in 1931 — the "Boxheim papers" — that Nazi strategists, like many other Germans, expected a communist revolution and planned direct action against it. The Nazi leaders seemed convinced in 1931 that forceful opposition to a communist revolution was their best route to broad national acceptance.

Under all these circumstances, democratic government functioned poorly. Although the Italian parliament was never as completely dead-locked as the German one, the incapacity of the political leadership of both countries to resolve the difficulties at hand offered fascism its indispensable opening.

Both Italian and German fascists had done their best to make democracy work badly. But the deadlock of liberal constitutions was not something the fascists alone had brought about. "The collapse of the Liberal state," says Roberto Vivarelli, "occurred independently of fascism."[36] At the time it was tempting to see the malfunction of democratic government after 1918 as a systemic crisis marking the historic terminus of liberalism. Since the revival of constitutional democracy since World War II, it has seemed more plausible to see it as a circumstantial crisis growing out of the strains of World War I, a sudden enlargement of democracy, and the Bolshevik Revolution. However we interpret the deadlock of democratic government, no fascist movement is likely to reach office without it.

Revolutions after Power: Germany and Italy

The conservatives brought Hitler and Mussolini into office quasiconstitutionally, within coalition governments that the fascist leaders did not totally control. Having achieved office quasilegally, Mussolini and Hitler had been entrusted only with the powers granted a head of government under the constitution. In more practical terms, their power was limited during their first days in office by having to govern in coalition with their conservative allies. Although the fascist parties held some vital posts in these governments, they had only a small minority of the cabinet positions.[37]

Soon, both fascist chiefs turned that toehold into outright dictatorship. Completing their grasp on the state by transforming a quasiconstitutional office into unlimited personal authority: that was the real "seizure of power." It was a different story from gaining office; its main plotline was massive illegal action by the fascist leaders. Allies were still crucial, but now they needed only to acquiesce.

Even Hitler did not become the dictator of Germany at once. At first he believed that the best device to give himself more independence from his coalition partners was one more election, hoping for the outright majority that had so far eluded him. Before the election could be held, however, a lucky break put into Hitler's hands an excuse to carry out a virtual coup d'état from within, without a breath of opposition from right or center. That lucky break was the fire that gutted the Reichstag building in Berlin on February 28, 1933.

It was long believed that the Nazis themselves set the fire and then framed a dim-witted Dutch communist youth found on the premises, Marinus van der Lubbe, in order to persuade the public to accept extreme anticommunist measures. Today most historians believe that van der Lubbe really lit the fire, and that Hitler and his associates, taken by surprise, really believed a communist coup had begun.[38] Enough Germans shared their panic to give the Nazis almost unlimited leeway.

What happened next has usually been presented as Hitler's story, as the new chancellor moved with remarkable speed and self-assurance to capitalize on the widespread fear of communist "terrorism." What needs equal emphasis is the readiness of German conservatives to give him a free hand, and of the organizations of civil society to meet him halfway. While the ruins of the Reichstag were still smoldering, President Hindenburg signed a "Decree for the Protection of People and State" on February 28, using his emergency powers under Article 48. The Reichstag Fire Decree suspended all legal protection of speech, assembly, property, and personal liberty, permitted the authorities to arrest suspected "terrorists" (i.e., communists) at will, and gave the federal government authority over the state governments' police power.

After that, few Germans were prepared to resist, in the absence of any help from the police, the judiciary, or other authorities, when Brownshirts erupted into courtrooms expelling Jewish lawyers and magistrates[39] or sacked left-wing offices and newspapers.

President Hindenburg had already authorized new elections. When they took place on March 5, however, despite Nazi terror directed against parties and voters of the Left, Hitler's party still fell short of the coveted majority. One more step would be necessary before Hitler could do his will. The Nazis proposed an Enabling Act that would empower Hitler to govern by decree for four years, without having to refer to either parliament or president, after which he promised to retire. Its official title was a splendid example of Nazi bombast, or LTI:[40] "Law to Relieve the Distress of the People and Reich." The constitution required a two-thirds vote of the parliament for such a delegation of legislative powers to the executive.

Even though a majority of Germans had still voted for other parties on March 5, Hitler assembled his two-thirds majority for the Enabling Act on March 24, 1933, aided by the arrest of communist deputies. The most decisive non-Nazi votes came from the Catholic Zentrum, together with

Hugenberg's nationalists. The Vatican agreed, reflecting Pope Pius XI's conviction that communism was worse than Nazism, and his indifference to political liberties (he thought Catholics should work in the world through schools and "Catholic Action"—grassroots youth and worker organizations—rather than through elections and political parties). Hitler paid off his debt on July 20 by signing a Concordat with the Vatican promising toleration for Catholic teaching and Catholic Action in Germany as long as these organizations kept out of politics.

Hitler was now free to dissolve all other parties (including the Catholic Zentrum) in the following weeks and establish a one-party dictatorship. His conservative accomplices were willing to turn a blind eye to the "revolution from below" carried out unofficially in spring 1933 by Nazi Party activists against Jews and Marxists, and even the establishment of the first concentration camp at Dachau, near Munich, in March 1933, for political enemies, as long as such illegalities were committed against "enemies of the people." Hitler was able to extend the Enabling Act by his own authority for another five years when it expired in 1937, almost without notice, and again indefinitely, justified by war, in 1942. He seemed to want to cover his dictatorship with the legal veneer the Enabling Act gave to the regime's arbitrary actions.

Gaining power helped a fascist leader dominate his party, but even after January 1933, Hitler's conflicts with his party were not over. Some party zealots believed that Hitler's success in establishing a Nazi dictatorship meant that they would soon have unlimited access to jobs and spoils in a "second revolution." SA leader Ernst Röhm pressured Hitler to transform the Brownshirts into a supplementary armed force, a project that alarmed the regular army. Hitler settled things once and for all on the "Night of the Long Knives," June 30, 1934, by having Röhm and other SA leaders murdered, as is well known, and also, as is less well known, recalcitrant conservatives (including several members of Vice-Chancellor von Papen's staff) and other notables who had given offense such as Gregor Strasser, General von Schleicher (along with his wife), Gustav von Kahr, the conservative Bavarian leader who had blocked Hitler's way in 1923, and thirteen Reichstag deputies. The victims totaled between 150 and 200.[41] That eye-popping lesson, along with the spoils of Nazi victories, kept doubters in line thereafter.

Mussolini's revolution after power was more gradual, and the struggle for predominance among three contenders—the leader, the party zealots, and the conservative establishment—was much less definitively settled than in Nazi Germany. For nearly two years Mussolini appeared reconciled to governing as an ordinary parliamentary prime minister, in coalition with nationalists, liberals, and a few Populari. His government pursued conventionally conservative policies in most areas, such as Finance Minister Alberto De Stefani's orthodox deflation and budget balancing.[42]

The menace of *squadristi* violence never stopped threatening to burst out of Mussolini's control, however. Many of the Blackshirts wanted a "second revolution"[43] to allocate all the jobs and all the spoils to them alone. Their anticlimactic march within Rome on October 31, 1922, spiraled into violence that caused seven deaths, seventeen injuries, and substantial damage to several opposition newspapers before the *Duce* managed to bundle them out of town the same night.[44] Thereafter, whenever they felt that Mussolini was "normalizing" too much, the frustrated *squadristi* were ready to send him a message, as in Turin on December 18–21, 1923 (at least eleven dead), and in Florence in January 1925 (several dead, including a socialist deputy and an opposition attorney).

While Mussolini sometimes tried to restrain his unruly followers, he occasionally found their pressure useful. The Acerbo election law was passed by the lower house on July 23, 1923, while Blackshirts patrolled the streets outside and Mussolini threatened "to let the revolution run its course" if the law were rejected.[45] When the senate approved it on November 18, 1923, this bizarre measure accorded two thirds of the seats to the largest party, as long as it received more than 25 percent of the votes, the other third of the seats being distributed proportionally among the other parties. In the ensuing election of April 6, 1924, with Fascist pressure on the electorate, the "National" list (Fascist plus Nationalist Parties) received 64.9 percent of the vote and thus took 374 seats. Even so, it failed to get a majority in the regions of Piedmont, Liguria, Lombardy, and Venetia. Thereafter, Mussolini had a docile parliament and the appearance of legitimacy, but his regime could hardly be considered "normal."

This quasinormal period was brought to an end by a shocking incident of renewed *squadrismo*, the murder of Giacomo Matteotti, the eloquent secretary of the reformist wing of the Italian Socialist Party. On May 30, 1924, Matteotti gave the chamber detailed evidence of Fascist corruption and illegality in the recent parliamentary elections. Ten days after this speech, the socialist leader was seized on a Rome street and bundled into a waiting car. His body was found several weeks later. When eyewitnesses made it possible to trace the car, it became clear that close personal associates of Mussolini had committed the murder. It remains uncertain whether Mussolini personally ordered the act, or whether his subordinates did it on their own. In any event, Mussolini's ultimate responsibility was clear. The murder shocked most Italians, and important conservatives who had supported Mussolini now called for a new untainted government.[46]

The outcry over Matteotti's murder offered the king and the conservative establishment their best opportunity to remove Mussolini from office. Once again, several paths were open to them. They chose not to press their doubts over Mussolini to the point of active steps to remove him, however, fearful that this would open the way to renewed chaos or to a government of the Left.

After several months of stalemate, while Mussolini's conservative allies dithered and the opposition withdrew into a self-defeating boycott of parliamentary activity,[47] the *ras* forced Mussolini's hand. On December 31, 1924, disillusioned with their leader's apparent lack of resolve, thirty-three consuls of the Fascist Militia (into which Mussolini had converted the *squadristi* in an effort at control) confronted him in his office with an ultimatum: in effect, if the *Duce* did not crush the opposition, they would act without him.

Aware of his opponents' hesitations and fearful of a revolt of the *ras*, Mussolini took the plunge. In an aggressive speech on January 3, 1925, he accepted "full political, moral and historical responsibility for all that has happened" and promised vigorous action. Mobilized Militia units had already begun closing down opposition papers and organizations and arresting members of the opposition. Over the following two years, spurred on by several attempts on Mussolini's life, the Fascist-dominated parliament passed a series of Laws for the Defense of the State that strengthened the power of the administration, replaced elected mayors with appointed officials *(podestà)*, subjected the press and radio to censorship, reinstituted the death penalty, gave Fascist unions a monopoly of labor representation, and dissolved all parties except the PNF. By early 1927 Italy had become a one-party dictatorship. Conservatives generally accepted Mussolini's coup from within because the alternatives seemed either continued deadlock or admitting the Left into government.

Comparisons and Alternatives

At this third stage, comparison acquires much greater bite than at the second. Numerous first-stage fascist movements, finding little space in which to grow, remained too weak to be interesting to allies and accomplices. A few became rooted but failed to establish the influence and elite friends necessary for plausible contention for office. Only a handful of them actually reached power. Among those that have, some became associated as junior partners within authoritarian regimes that eventually muzzled or destroyed them. Only in Germany and Italy have fascists so far fully grasped the reins.

Junior partnerships within authoritarian regimes proved disastrous for fascist movements. Playing second fiddle fit badly with fascists' extravagant claims to transform their peoples and redirect history. For their part, the authoritarian senior partners took a dim view of the fascists' impatient violence and disdain for established interests, for these cases often involved fascist movements that retained much of the social radicalism of the early movement stage.

We have already noted the bloodiest suppression of a fascist junior partner by an authoritarian dictator, the liquidation of the Legion of the Archangel Michael by the Romanian dictator Marshal Antonescu in January 1941.[48] As we will see in chapter 6, the Iberian dictators Franco and Salazar reduced fascist parties to powerlessness, though less bloodily. The Brazilian dictator Vargas tolerated a fascist movement and then crushed it.[49] In general, well-entrenched conservative regimes of all sorts have provided unfavorable terrain for fascism to reach power. Either they have repressed what they regarded as fomenters of disorder, or they have preempted fascism's issues and following for themselves.[50] If conservatives could rule alone, they did.

Another fascist route into power was to follow in the baggage train of a victorious fascist army. But this happened far less often than one might expect. Mussolini's hapless soldiers afforded him few opportunities to impose puppets elsewhere. Hitler enjoyed many such chances, but he usually put little faith in foreign fascists. Nazism, as a recipe for national unity and dynamism, was the last thing he wanted for a country he had conquered and occupied. It was the German *Volk*'s private pact with history, and Hitler had no intention of exporting it.[51] Hitler was also, for much of the time, and contrary to popular legend, a pragmatic ruler with a keen practical sense. The local fascist parties would be far less useful to him for keeping conquered peoples in line than local traditional conservative elites.

Vidkun Quisling, the Norwegian fascist leader whose name furnished the very word for a puppet government, actually had little authority in occupied Norway. Although Quisling's Nasjonal Samling (NS) had barely surpassed 2 percent of the popular vote in the 1930s, he seized the opportunity of the German invasion of April 9, 1940, and the withdrawal of the king and parliament from Oslo to declare his party in power. Although the Nazi ideologue Alfred Rosenberg supported him, more responsible German officials knew he aroused only loathing in Norway, and after only six days Hitler agreed to set him aside.

The Nazi official Joseph Terboven governed Norway as *Reichskommissar*, assisted after September 1940 by a state council in which the NS held ten of the thirteen seats, excluding Quisling himself. Terboven allowed Quisling to continue to build the NS (the only authorized party), and, on February 1, 1942, gave him the title "minister-president." Even then, however, Quisling enjoyed no independent authority, and Hitler rebuffed his repeatedly expressed wish for a more independent role for Norway in Nazi Europe. Quisling's phantom rule was met by increasing passive and active resistance.

Occupied Holland, whose Queen Wilhelmina had set up a government-in-exile in London, was governed by a civilian administration headed by the Austrian Nazi lawyer Arthur Seyss-Inquart, with the Dutch fascist leader Anton Mussert playing a very minor role. The Danish fascist movement had been almost invisible before the war. Its leader Fritz Clausen played no role after 1940. King Christian X remained in place as a symbol of national continuity while his minister Scavenius supplied the agricultural products Germany wanted and even signed the Anti-Comintern Pact.

France was the German army's most valuable conquest, and since French neutrality, products, and manpower were indispensable assets for the Reich war machine, Hitler was not about to endanger them by giving power in France to one of the petty squabbling fascist chieflings whom we met in the previous chapter. It was the *Führer's* good fortune that the defeat of May–June 1940 so discredited the Third French Republic that the French National Assembly voted full powers on July 10, 1940, to an eighty-four-year-old World War I hero, Marshal Philippe Pétain, who had stepped forward in June as the main proponent of stopping the fight. Pétain set up a provisional capital at Vichy, in the unoccupied south, and governed through authoritarian personal rule supported by the traditional French state services, the economic and social establishment, the military, and the Roman Catholic Church. He worked hard to cooperate with the Nazi occupation authorities of the northern half of France in hopes of finding a suitable place in the new German-dominated Europe, which he was convinced was permanent.

Hitler kept a number of French fascists available on the Nazi payroll in Paris, in case he needed to pressure Pétain with a rival. But only in the last days of the war, when the tide had turned and the conservative notables who had supported Vichy at the outset began to abandon it, did some pre-war fascists, such as Marcel Déat, find places in the Vichy government.[52]

The main role Hitler gave homegrown fascists in occupied countries was to recruit local volunteers to freeze and die on the Russian front. Both the Belgian Léon Degrelle[53] and the French fascist Jacques Doriot[54] rendered Hitler this service.

Hitler was equally uninterested in promoting fascist movements within satellite states. He maintained warm personal relations with Marshal Antonescu, who had crushed Romanian fascism;[55] Antonescu's thirty Romanian divisions on the Russian front helped him far more than the wild-eyed Legionaries of Horia Sima. He left Slovakia, which first came into being as an independent state when he broke up Czechoslovakia in May 1939, to Father Josef Tiso's Slovak Popular Party, even though it was more clerical authoritarian than fascist. It had received up to a third of the Slovak vote between the wars under Father Andreas Hlinka, and it was later willing to assist with the deportation of Jews.

Hitler also found it cheapest and simplest to leave Hungary unoccupied and under the rule of Admiral Horthy, who had governed the country along mostly traditional authoritarian lines since March 1, 1920. The German army entered Hungary only on March 22, 1944, when the Nazis suspected that Horthy was negotiating with the approaching Allied armies. Only in this final extremity, as Soviet troops entered Hungary, on October 16, 1944, did Hitler replace Horthy with the leader of the Hungarian Arrow-Cross movement, Ferenc Szálasi. Fascist Hungary was short-lived, for it was very soon overrun by the advancing Soviet armies.

The Nazis did allow native fascists to take power in the client state of Croatia, for this was a new creation without ruling elites already in place, and, indeed, it was in the Italian zone of influence. In May 1941, when the German army overran and split up Yugoslavia, the pre-war terrorist-nationalist Ustaša and its longtime leader Ante Pavelić were permitted to take power in the newly independent state of Croatia. Even Nazi onlookers were appalled by the disorderly slaughters in which the Ustaša massacred a soberly estimated 500,000 Serbs, 200,000 Croats, 90,000 Bosnian

Muslims, 60,000 Jews, 50,000 Montenegrins, and 30,000 Slovenes.[56] None of these puppets in satellite or occupied states could survive one moment after the defeat of their Axis protectors. In Spain and Portugal, by contrast, authoritarian regimes continued to function after 1945, carefully avoiding any hint of fascist trimmings.

That Quisling or Szálasi were brought into power in extremis depended relatively little on indigenous support, and was really a sign that Hitler had failed in his preferred policy of persuading traditional leaders of occupied countries to collaborate with Nazi authorities. Occupation fascisms are certainly interesting—defeat and collaboration brought forth all the losers of the previous governing system and exposed all the fault lines and antagonisms of the polity being occupied—but it is doubtful that we can call them authentic fascisms, if only because they are not free to pursue national grandeur and expansionism.[57]

We learn much more about fascism from other kinds of failure, such as the French radical Right movements that became quite conspicuous but remained outsiders before 1940. Here comparison puts us in a position to see real differences in the character of the setting and in the possibilities of alliances that distinguish the countries of fascist success from the others. What separated Germany and Italy, where fascism took power, from France and Britain, where fascist movements were highly visible but failed even to approach power?

We considered France in chapter 3. Radical rightist movements— some of them authentically fascist—prospered there, but most conservatives did not feel sufficiently threatened in the 1930s to call on them for help, nor did they root themselves powerfully enough to impose themselves as partners.[58] The British Union of Fascists had in Sir Oswald Mosley an articulate, energetic, and—exceptionally—socially prominent leader who won important press support at the beginning, but offended conservatives by street violence against Jews and eventually found little space available as long as the Conservative Party maintained its comfortable majority from 1931 to 1945.

In Scandinavia, social democratic parties managed to include family farmers and lower-middle-class interests in their governing coalition, denying a major constituency to the fascist parties, which remained minuscule.[59]

A comparative look at fascist access to power helps us to identify some of the approaches to fascism that seem less helpful. Agency theories, for instance, have more than one shortcoming. They reduce the story of the arrival to power of fascism to the acts of a single interest group, the capitalists. They also deny any autonomous popular backing to fascism, assuming that it is an artificial creation.

Comparison suggests that fascist success in reaching power varies less with the brilliance of fascist intellectuals and the qualities of fascist chiefs than with the depth of crisis and the desperation of potential allies. While intellectual history was indispensable for explaining the old system's loss of legitimacy in cases where fascism first managed to take root, it is of limited help to us at this stage. It offers little to explain what kinds of political space opened up in prefascist crises of deadlock, advancing Left, and conservative anxiety, and why fascism filled the opening instead of something else.

Under what conditions has the political space available for fascist growth yawned wide enough for access to power? In the previous chapter, I discussed some of the more general settings. In this chapter, I focus on more specific conditions of breakdown of democratic legitimacy and deadlock of parliamentary regimes. But why, under these circumstances, did the conservatives not simply crush the Left by armed force and install an autocracy, leaving no space for fascism's promise to attract parts of the Left as well as intimidate it?

That was indeed the way some proceeded. That is the more normal way, especially outside Europe. In Europe, Chancellor Engelbert Dollfuss of Austria set up a Catholic authoritarian regime and crushed socialist resistance by shelling a worker neighborhood of Vienna in February 1934, while holding the Austrian Nazis at bay. General Francisco Franco crushed the Spanish Left and the republic by armed insurrection and civil war, and left little room after taking power for the small Spanish Fascist party, the Falange. But that violent option amounts to giving the street and the working class and the enlightened intelligentsia back to the Left, and requires rule by overt force. German and Italian conservatives wanted to harness the fascists' power in public opinion, in the street, and in the nationalist and antisocialist sectors of the middle and working classes to their own leadership. They seem to have believed that it was too late to demobilize the public politically. It must be won over to the national and antisocialist cause, for it was too late to reduce it once more to nineteenth-century deference.

That Hitler and Mussolini reached office in alliance with powerful traditional elites was no mere quirk of German or Italian history. It is hard to believe that fascist parties could come to power any other way. It is possible to imagine other scenarios for a fascist arrival in power, but they are implausible. The Kornilov scenario—already alluded to in chapter 3—is worth considering. General Lavr Georgyevich Kornilov, appointed commander-in-chief of the Russian armies in August 1917, found the parliamentary regime of Alexander Kerensky ineffective in the face of rising revolutionary pressure—a classic setting for a fascist or authoritarian response. Kornilov sent troops marching on the capital, only to be stopped by Bolshevik forces before reaching Petrograd. If General Kornilov had succeeded in his mission, the most likely outcome would have been simple military dictatorship, for democracy was still too new in Russia to furnish the mass counterrevolutionary mobilization characteristic of a fascist response to a weak social democracy about to be overwhelmed by Bolshevism.

We are not required to believe that fascist movements can only come to power in an exact replay of the scenario of Mussolini and Hitler. All that is required to fit our model is polarization, deadlock, mass mobilization against internal and external enemies, and complicity by existing elites. In the Balkans in the 1990s something that looks very much like fascism was produced by a very different scenario, a change of course by leaders already in power. Postcommunist dictators learned to play the card of expansionist nationalism as a substitute for discredited communism. When the Serbian dictator Slobodan Milosevic mobilized the patriotism of his people first against Serbia's neighbors and next against Allied air attack, with dancing and singing and slogans, he was successfully rallying a population against enemies internal and external and in favor of a policy of ethnic cleansing of a ruthlessness that Europe had not seen since 1945.

It is of course also conceivable that a fascist party could be elected to power in free, competitive elections, though, as we saw at the beginning of this chapter, even the Nazi Party, by far the most successful electorally of all fascist parties, never exceeded 37 percent in a free election. The Italian Fascist Party received far fewer votes than the Nazis. Most fascist parties won little or no electoral success, and consequently had no bargaining power in the parliamentary game. What they could try to do was to discredit the parliamentary system by making orderly government impossible. But that could backfire. If the fascists seemed to be more evidently making disorder than blocking communism, they lost the support of conservatives. Most fascist movements were thus reduced to propaganda and symbolic gestures. That is how most of them remained at the margins when no space opened up.

On closer inspection, of course, electoral success was not the most important precondition of fascist arrival in power. The deadlock or collapse of an existing liberal state was more crucial. It is vital to remember that in both Germany and Italy, the constitutional state had ceased to function normally well before the fascists were brought into power. It was not the fascist parties that had overthrown it, though they had helped bring it to deadlock. It had ceased to function because it had been unable to deal with the problems at hand—including, to be sure, the problem of an aggressive fascist opposition. The collapse of the liberal state is to some degree a separate issue from the rise of fascism. Fascism exploits the opening, but it is not the sole cause of it.

At the stage of attaining power, when the elites chose to coopt fascism, the functions of mature fascism became even clearer: in immediate terms, its role was to break a logjam in national politics by a solution that excluded socialists. In a longer term, it was to enlist mass support behind national, social defense, to unify, regenerate and rejuvenate, "moralize," and purify the nation that many saw as weak, decadent, and unclean.

The transformation that we glimpsed in stage 2 as fascist parties mutated to fit the available space was now further developed and completed in the shift from the local level to the national stage. The fascists and the allies negotiated a common ground—the *Herrschaftskompromiss* that Wolfgang Schieder refers to.[60] At this stage, as in the stage of rooting, purges and secessions thrust aside the party purists from the early days who wanted to retain some of the old social radicalism.

It is a worthwhile exercise of the historical imagination to recall the other options open to the fascists' principal allies and accomplices. In that way, we can do what historians are supposed to do: restore the openness of the historical moment with all its uncertainties. What else could the political elite of Germany and Italy do? In Italy, a coalition of the social-Catholic Popolari and the reformist socialists would have assured a parliamentary majority. It would have taken a lot of persuasion and cajolery, since issues of Church-state relations and religious education separated the two. We know that it was not tried, and it was not wanted. In Germany, a parliamentary government with the social democrats and the centrist parties was an arithmetic possibility, but a real possibility only with strong presidential leadership. A workable alternative in both countries might have been a government of technicians and nonparty experts, to deal in a nonpartisan way with the crisis of government authority and of institutions. This, too, was never tried. If constitutional government had to be abandoned, we know today that we would prefer a military authoritarian government to Hitler. But the army did not want to do that (unlike in Spain), and chose to support the fascist alternative. The Italian army would not oppose fascism in Italy because its leaders feared the Left more.

In each case, it helps to see that political elites make choices that might not be their first preferences. They proceed, from choice to choice, along a path of narrowing options. At each fork in the road, they choose the antisocialist solution.

It works better to see the fascist seizure of power as a process: alliances are formed, choices made, alternatives closed off.[61] High officials, possessing some freedom of maneuver, choose the fascist option over others. Neither Hitler's nor Mussolini's arrival in power was inevitable.[62] Our explanatory model must also leave room for luck—good or bad, depending on one's point of view. Mussolini could have been turned back in October 1922 or removed in June 1924 if the king, Establishment political leaders, and the army had resolutely taken actions within their legal competence. Mussolini's luck was that the king exercised a choice in his favor. Hitler also had some lucky breaks. The *Führer* benefitted from the rivalry for office of von Papen and Schleicher, and the refusal of German conservatives to accept reformist socialists as fellow citizens. It was von Papen who took the decision to make Hitler chancellor, as the best way to form a majority that would exclude both his rival Schleicher and the moderate Left. Crises of the political and economic system made a space available to fascism, but it was the unfortunate choices by a few powerful Establishment leaders that actually put the fascists into that space.

CHAPTER 5

Exercising Power

The Nature of Fascist Rule:
"Dual State" and Dynamic Shapelessness

Fascist propagandists wanted us to see the leader alone on his pinnacle, and they had remarkable success. Their image of monolithic power was later reinforced by the Allies' wartime awe of the Nazi juggernaut, as well as by postwar claims by German and Italian conservative elites that they had been the fascists' victims rather than their accomplices. It lingers on today in most people's idea of fascist rule.

Perspicacious observers soon perceived, however, that fascist dictatorships were neither monolithic nor static. No dictator rules by himself. He must obtain the cooperation, or at least the acquiescence, of the decisive agencies of rule—the military, the police, the judiciary, senior civil servants—and of powerful social and economic forces. In the special case of fascism, having depended upon conservative elites to open the gates to him, the new leaders could not shunt them casually aside. Some degree, at least, of obligatory power sharing with the preexisting conservative establishment made fascist dictatorships fundamentally different in their origins, development, and practice from that of Stalin.

Consequently we have never known an ideologically pure fascist regime. Indeed, the thing hardly seems possible. Each generation of scholars of fascism has noted that the regimes rested upon some kind of pact or alliance between the fascist party and powerful conservative forces. In the early 1940s the social democratic refugee Franz Neumann argued in his classic *Behemoth* that a "cartel" of party, industry, army, and bureaucracy ruled Nazi Germany, held together only by "profit, power, prestige, and especially fear."[1] At the end of the 1960s, the moderate liberal Karl Dietrich Bracher found that "National Socialism came into being and into power under conditions that permitted an alliance between conservative-authoritarian and technicistic, nationalistic, and revolutionary-dictatorial forces."[2] Martin Broszat referred to the conservatives and nationalists in Hitler's cabinet as his "coalition partners."[3] In the late 1970s, Hans Mommsen described the National Socialist "governing system" as an "alliance" between "ascending fascist elites and members of traditional leadership groups" "interlocked . . . despite differences" in a common project to set aside parliamentary government, reestablish strong government, and crush "Marxism."[4]

The composite nature of Fascist rule in Italy was even more flagrant. The historian Gaetano Salvemini, home from exile, recalled the "dualistic dictatorship" of *Duce* and king.[5] Alberto Aquarone, the preeminent scholar of the Fascist state, emphasized the "centrifugal forces" and "tensions" Mussolini confronted in a regime that still, "fifteen years after the March on Rome," had "many features derived directly from the Liberal State."[6] The prominent German scholars of Italian Fascism Wolfgang Schieder and Jens Petersen speak of "opposing forces" and "counterweights"[7] and Massimo Legnani of the "conditions of cohabitation/cooperation" among the regime's components.[8] Even Emilio Gentile, most eager to demonstrate the power and success of the totalitarian impulse in Fascist Italy, concedes that the regime was a "composite" reality in which Mussolini's "ambition of personal power" struggled in "constant tension" with both "traditional forces" and "Fascist Party intransigents," themselves divided by "muffled conflict" (*sorda lotta*) among factions.[9]

Composite makeup also means that fascist regimes have not been static. It is a mistake to suppose that once the leader reached power history ended and was replaced by pageantry.[10] On the contrary, the history of the fascist regimes we have known has been filled with conflict and tension. The conflicts we have already observed at the stage of taking root sharpen when the moment arrives to distribute the spoils of office and to choose among courses of action. The stakes grow as policy differences play out into tangible gains and losses. Conservatives tend to pull back toward a more cautious traditional authoritarianism, respectful of property and social hierarchy; fascists pull forward toward dynamic, leveling, populist dictatorship, prepared to subordinate every private interest to the imperatives of national aggrandizement and purification. Traditional elites try to retain strategic positions; the parties want to fill them with new men or bypass the conservative power bases with "parallel structures"; the leaders resist challenges from both elites and party zealots.

These struggles waxed and waned in Italy and Germany, with varying outcomes. While the Italian Fascist regime decayed toward conservative authoritarian rule, Nazi Germany radicalized toward unbridled party license. But fascist regimes have never been static. We must see fascist rule as a never-ending struggle for preeminence within a coalition, exacerbated by the collapse of constitutional restraints and the rule of law, and by a prevailing climate of social Darwinism.

Some commentators have reduced this struggle to a conflict between party and state. One of the earliest and most suggestive interpretations of party-state conflict was the refugee scholar Ernst Fraenkel's portrayal of Nazi Germany as a "dual state." In Hitler's regime, Fraenkel wrote, a "normative state," composed of the legally constituted authorities and the traditional civil service, jostled for power with a "prerogative state" formed by the party's parallel organizations.[11] Fraenkel's perception was a fruitful one, and I will draw on it.

According to Fraenkel's model of Nazi governance, the "normative" segment of a fascist regime continued to apply the law according to due process, and officials in that sector were recruited and promoted according to bureaucratic norms of competence and seniority. In the "prerogative" sector, by contrast, no rules applied except the whim of the ruler, the gratification of party militants, and the supposed "destiny" of the *Volk*, the *razza*, or other "chosen people." The normative state and the prerogative state coexisted in conflict-ridden but more or less workmanlike cooperation, giving the regime its bizarre mixture of legalism[12] and arbitrary violence.

Hitler never formally abolished the constitution drafted in 1919 for the Weimar Republic, and never totally dismantled the normative state in Germany, though he himself refused to be bound by it—refusing, for example, to have a euthanasia law drafted for fear of having his hands tied by rules and bureaucracy.[13] After the Reichstag fire, as we saw in the last chapter, Hitler was given the authority to set aside any existing law or right as needed to cope with a perceived national emergency of Marxist "terror." After spring 1933, unlimited police and judicial repression were permissible in Germany if national security seemed to demand it, despite the continued existence of a normative state.

Over time the Nazi prerogative state steadily encroached upon the normative state and contaminated its work,[14] so that even within it the perception of national emergency allowed the regime to override individual rights and due process.[15] After the war began, the Nazi prerogative state achieved something approaching total dominance. Normative institutions atrophied at home and functioned hardly at all in the occupied territories of former Poland and the Soviet Union, as we shall see more fully in the next chapter.

Fascist Italy can also be fruitfully interpreted as a dual state, as we already know. Mussolini, however, accorded far more power to the normative state than Hitler did.[16] Fascist propaganda put the state, not the party, at the center of its message. We are not quite sure why Mussolini subordinated his party to the state, but there are several possible explanations. He had less leeway, less drive, and less luck than Hitler. President Hindenburg died in August 1934, leaving Hitler alone at the helm. Mussolini was burdened with King Victor Emmanuel III to the end, and it was the king who eventually deposed him in July 1943. Mussolini may also have feared the rivalry of his freewheeling party chieftains.

Even so, the Italian Fascist state contained important prerogative elements: its secret police (the OVRA);[17] its controlled press; its economic baronies (the IRI,[18] for example); and its African fiefdoms, where party chiefs like Italo Balbo could strut and command the life and death of indigenous peoples. And in the late 1930s, involvement in war strengthened the Italian prerogative state.[19]

The struggle for dominance within fascist dictatorships involves more than party and state, however, or prerogative and normative states. Fraenkel's dual state image is incomplete. Elements outside the state also participate in the tug-of-war for power within fascist regimes. The German and Italian fascist regimes replaced with their own organizations traditionally independent power centers such as labor unions, youth clubs, and associations of professions and producers. The Nazis even attempted to impose a "German Christian" bishop and doctrine on the Protestant churches.[20] Fascist regimes could not always succeed in swallowing up civil society, however.

Carl Friedrich and Zbigniew Brzezinski, the founding scholars of the "totalitarian" model, coined the term "islands of separateness" to describe elements of civil society that survive within a totalitarian dictatorship.[21] Such islands of separateness as Catholic parishes—however little inclined they might be to oppose the regime fundamentally, beyond objecting to specific actions[22]—could possess sufficient organizational resiliency and emotional loyalty to withstand party infiltration.[23] One does not have to accept the totalitarian model integrally to find the islands of separateness metaphor useful.

Hitler and the Nazi Party gradually overcame most of the islands of separateness within the German state and society in a process called euphemistically by party propagandists *Gleichschaltung*: coordination, or leveling. A common oversimplification makes this process seem both inevitable and unilinear. Well-rooted economic and social associations could not be swept away so casually, however, even in Nazi Germany. *Gleichschaltung* could involve two-way negotiation as well as force. Some groups and organizations were able to subvert Nazi institutions from within or "appropriate" them for their own aims.[24] Others quietly but stubbornly defended partial autonomy, even while accepting some of the regime's aims.

German citizens could turn even the dread Gestapo to their own personal ends by denouncing a rival, a creditor, a parent, or an unsatisfactory spouse to the secret police.[25] Fraternities in German universities are a good example of survival. Nazism was so attractive to students that even before 1933 their national organization had been taken over by party activists. One would therefore have expected fraternities to disappear into *Gleichschaltung* without a murmur after January 1933. Despite the Nazi regime's efforts to transform the "reactionary" dueling clubs into party *Kameradschaften* (social and training centers), however, fraternities persisted unofficially, partly because powerful Nazi officials among the "old boy" networks and alumni associations defended them, partly because students grew increasingly apathetic toward party propaganda.[26]

In the much slower process of consolidating Fascist rule in Italy, only the labor unions, the political parties, and the media were fully "brought into line." The Catholic Church was the most important island of separateness in Fascist Italy, and although the regime encroached briefly in 1931 on the Church's youth movements and schools, it ultimately lost that battle.[27] The Italian Fascist student clubs, the Gruppi Universitaria Fascista (GUF), were quietly "appropriated" by their members for their own extra-Fascist or even anti-Fascist enjoyment,[28] as was the leisure-time organization, the Dopolavoro.[29]

All these enduring tensions within fascist regimes pitted against each other four elements that together forged these dictatorships out of their quarrelsome collaboration: the fascist leader; his party (whose militants clamored for jobs, perquisites, expansionist adventures, and the fulfillment of some elements of their early radical program); the state apparatus (functionaries such as police and military commanders, magistrates, and local governors); and, finally, civil society (holders of social, economic, political, and cultural power such as professional associations, leaders of big business and big agriculture, churches, and conservative political leaders).[30] This four-way tension gave these regimes their characteristic blend of febrile activism and shapelessness.[31]

Tension was permanent within fascist regimes because none of the contending groups could dispense completely with the others. Conservatives hesitated to get rid of the fascist leader, for fear of letting the Left or the liberals regain power.[32] Hitler and Mussolini, for their part, needed the economic and military resources that the conservatives controlled. At the same time, the dictators could not afford to weaken their obstreperous parties too much, lest they undermine their own independent power base. No contender could destroy the others outright, for fear of upsetting the balance of forces that kept the tandem in power and the Left at bay.[33]

In their protracted struggles for supremacy within fascist rule, the parallel organizations that fascist parties developed during the period of taking root played complex and ambiguous roles. They were an asset for a fascist leader who wished to outflank the conservative bastions instead of attacking them frontally. At the same time, however, they offered ambitious radical militants an autonomous power base to challenge the leader's preeminence.

In Italy, the Fascist Party at first duplicated every level of public authority with a party agency: the local party chief flanked the appointed mayor (*podestà*), the regional party secretary (*federale*) flanked the prefect, the Fascist militia flanked the army, and so on. As soon as his power was consolidated, however, Mussolini declared that the "revolution is over" and explicitly made the prefect "the highest authority of the state," to whom party leaders were subordinated.[34] The *Duce* had no intention of letting the *ras* push him around again.

Italian Fascism's most successful parallel organization did not challenge the state but invaded the realm of leisure-time recreation, an area heretofore left to individual choice, private clubs, or Catholic parishes. In practice, the Fascist Dopolavoro fell far short of its announced aims of building the nation and creating the Fascist "new man" (and woman). It was substantially appropriated from within by ordinary Italians who just wanted to see movies or play sports. It was, nonetheless, the Fascist regime's most ambitious attempt to penetrate Italian society down to the country towns and compete with the local boss and the priest for social authority there.[35]

The Nazi Party competed with traditional agencies by a similar array of parallel organizations. The party had its own paramilitary force (the SA), its own party court, party police, and youth movement. The party's foreign policy branch, first under Alfred Rosenberg but later part of Joachim von Ribbentrop's personal staff (the Dienststelle Ribbentrop), intervened actively among German-speaking foreign populations in Austria and the Czech Sudetenland.[36] After the Nazi Party attained power, the parallel organizations threatened to usurp the functions of the army, the Foreign Office, and other agencies. In a separate and sinister development, the political police was detached from the Interior Ministries of the German states and centralized, step by step, as the notorious Gestapo (Geheime Staatspolizei), under the command of fanatical Nazi Heinrich Himmler. Duplication of traditional power centers by parallel party organizations was a principal reason for the already noted "shapelessness" and the chaotic lines of authority that characterized fascist rule and set it apart from military dictatorship or authoritarian rule.

In a further complication, fascist regimes allowed opportunists to flood into the parties, which thereby ceased to be the private clubs of "old fighters." The Italian Partito Nazionale Fascista (PNF) opened its rolls in 1933 in an effort to fascistize the whole population. Thereafter party membership was required for civil-service jobs, including teaching. Mussolini hoped that party membership would fortify the casual Italian civic spirit that so annoyed him,[37] but the opposite seems to have happened. As party membership became a good career move, cynics said that the initials PNF stood for *"per necessità famigliari."*[38] Nazi Party membership ballooned by 1.6 million between January and May 1933. Even though party rolls were then closed to preserve the party's identity as a select elite, many opportunist officials were given dispensations to join.[39]

In the endless contest for predominance within fascist regimes, the fascist leader sometimes managed to subject his allies to unwanted policies, as Hitler did to a significant degree. In other cases, conservative forces and bureaucrats might retain substantial independent power, as they did in Fascist Italy—enough to persuade the atheist Mussolini to give the Catholic Church its most favorable treatment since Italian unification, to force him to sacrifice his syndicalist friends to businessmen's desires for autonomy and privilege,[40] and, ultimately, to remove him from power in July 1943 when the approach of Allied armies convinced them that Fascism was no longer serving national ends.[41] Even Hitler, however easily he seemed to override many conservative preferences, never freed himself, until war became total in 1942, from the need to placate owners of munitions plants, army officers, professional experts, and religious leaders—and even public opinion.

Nevertheless, fascist leaders enjoyed a kind of supremacy that was not quite like leadership in other kinds of regime. The *Führer* and the *Duce* could claim legitimacy neither by election nor conquest. It rested on *charisma*,[42] a mysterious direct communication with the *Volk* or *razza* that needs no mediation by priests or party chieftains. Their *charisma* resembled media-era celebrity "stardom," raised to a higher power by its say over war and death. It rested on a claim to a unique and mystical status as the incarnation of the people's will and the bearer of the people's destiny. A whiff of *charisma* is not unknown among traditional dictators, of course, and even some democratically elected leaders, such as Churchill, de Gaulle, and the two Roosevelts, had it. Stalin surely had *charisma*, as the public hysteria at his funeral showed. But Stalin shared his role as the bearer of historical destiny with the Communist Party, which made succession possible even if palace intrigues and murders multiplied before the successor could emerge. But fascist rule is more nakedly dependent on *charisma* than any other kind, which may help explain why no fascist regime has so far managed to pass power to a successor.[43] Both Hitler and Mussolini had *charisma*, though Mussolini's declining vitality in middle age and his tawdry end made most people forget the magnetism he had once exerted, even outside Italy.[44]

Charisma helps us understand several curious features of fascist leadership. The notorious indolence of Hitler,[45] far from making Nazism more tepid, freed his subordinates to compete in driving the regime toward ever more extreme radicalization. A charismatic leader is also immune from the surprisingly widespread grumbling against the administration that quickly arose in both Germany and Italy.[46] At the same time, charismatic leadership is brittle. It promises to the *Volk* or the *razza*, as Adrian Lyttelton once noted, "a privileged relation with history."[47] Having raised expectations so high, a fascist leader unable to deliver the promised triumphs risks losing his magic even faster than an elected president or prime minister, of whom less is expected. Mussolini discovered this rule to his sorrow in July 1943.

Studying the fascist exercise of power, therefore, is not simply a matter of laying out the dictator's will (as the propagandists claimed, and as unreflective "intentionalists" seem to believe). It means examining the never-ending tensions within fascist regimes among the leader, his party, the state, and traditional holders of social, economic, political, or cultural power. This reality has produced an influential interpretation of fascist governance as "polyocracy," or rule by multiple relatively autonomous power centers, in unending rivalry and tension with each other.[48] In polyocracy the famous "leadership principle" cascades down through the social and political pyramid, creating a host of petty *Führers* and *Duces* in a state of Hobbesian war of all against all.

This effort to understand the complex character of fascist dictatorship and its interaction with society, entirely worthy in itself, entails two risks. It makes it hard to account for the demonic energy unleashed by fascism: Why did "polyocracy" not simply tie everyone's hands in stalemate? Furthermore, in extreme versions, it may make us lose sight of the leader's supremacy. In an energetic debate in the 1980s, "intentionalists" defended the centrality of the dictator's will, while "structuralists" or "functionalists" asserted that the dictator's will could not be applied without multiple links with state and society. Both views were easy to caricature, and were sometimes taken to extremes. Intentionalism worked best for foreign and military policy, where Hitler and Mussolini both played hands-on roles. The most emotionally charged issue within the intentionalist-structuralist debate was the Holocaust, where the enormity of the outcome seemed to demand the presence of a correspondingly enormous criminal will. I will look at this issue more closely in the next chapter.

A major problem for intentionalists was Hitler's personal style of rule. While Mussolini toiled long hours at his desk, Hitler continued to indulge in the lazy bohemian dilettantism of his art-student days. When aides sought his attention for urgent matters, Hitler was often inaccessible. He spent much time at his Bavarian retreat; even in Berlin he often neglected pressing business. He subjected his dinner guests to midnight monologues, rose at midday, and devoted his afternoons to personal passions such as plans by his young protégé Albert Speer to reconstruct his hometown of Linz and the center of Berlin in a monumental style befitting the Thousand-Year Reich. After February 1938 the cabinet ceased to meet; some cabinet ministers never managed to see the *Führer* at all. Hans Mommsen went so far as to call him a "weak dictator." Mommsen never meant to deny the unlimited nature of Hitler's vaguely defined and haphazardly exercised power, but he observed that the Nazi regime was not organized on rational principles of bureaucratic efficiency, and that its astonishing burst of murderous energy was not produced by Hitler's diligence.[49] I will consider further the mystery of fascist radicalization in chapter 6.

Neither an extreme intentionalist view of the all-powerful leader ruling alone nor an extreme structuralist view that initiatives from below are the main motor of fascist dynamism is tenable. In the 1990s, the most convincing work established two-way explanations in which competition among midlevel officials to anticipate the leader's intimate wishes and "work toward" them are given due place, while the leader's role in establishing goals and removing limits and rewarding zealous associates plays its indispensable role.[50]

The Tug-of-War between Fascists and Conservatives

When Adolf Hitler became chancellor of Germany on January 30, 1933, his conservative allies, headed by Deputy Chancellor Franz von Papen, along with those conservative and nationalist leaders who supported von Papen's Hitler experiment, expected to manage the untrained new head of government without difficulty. They were confident that their university degrees, experience in public affairs, and worldly polish would give them easy superiority over the uncouth Nazis. Chancellor Hitler would spellbind the crowds, they imagined, while Deputy Chancellor von Papen ran the state.

Hitler's conservative allies were not the only ones to suppose that Nazism was a flash in the pan. The Communist International was certain that the German swing to the Right under Hitler would produce a counterswing to the Left as soon as German workers understood that democracy was an illusion and turned away from the reformist social democrats. "The current calm after the victory of Fascism is only temporary. Inevitably, despite Fascist terrorism, the revolutionary tide in Germany will grow. . . . The establishment of open Fascist dictatorship, which is destroying all democratic illusions among the masses and is freeing them from the influence of the Social Democrats, will speed up Germany's progress toward the proletarian revolution."[51]

Against the expectations of both Right and Left, Hitler quickly established full personal authority. The first period of Nazi rule saw the *Gleichschaltung*, the bringing into line, not only of potential enemies but also of conservative colleagues. The keys to Hitler's success were his superior audacity, drive, and tactical agility; his skillful manipulation (as we saw in the previous chapter) of the idea that imminent communist "terror" justified the suspension of due process and the rule of law; and a willingness to commit murder.

Hitler's dominance over his conservative allies had clearly been established by the early summer of 1933. By July 14, with the law establishing a one-party state, "an open 'legal' struggle against national-socialist domination was now no longer possible."[52] Thereafter conservatives fought a rearguard action to defend the autonomy of their remaining centers of power from the encroachment by the Nazi Party's parallel organizations. This meant defending the army from the SA, state *(Land)* governments from regional party leaders *(Gauleiter)*, the civil service and professional corps from party novices, the churches from Nazi efforts to create a "German Christianity," and business concerns from SS enterprises.

The conservatives' main hopes for keeping Hitler in check were President Hindenburg and Deputy Chancellor von Papen.[53] Hindenburg's great age and failing health weakened him, however, and von Papen lacked sufficient personal drive as well as the necessary independent administrative staff to block Nazi penetration of state agencies, especially after he had been replaced by Goering as minister-president of Prussia, the largest German state, on April 7, 1933. When von Papen attacked Nazi arbitrariness openly in a speech at the University of Marburg on June 17, 1934, the text circulated rapidly through the country. Hitler had von Papen's speechwriter, Edgar Jung, arrested, banned publication of the speech, and closed down the deputy chancellor's offices. Jung and other von Papen intimates were among those murdered in the Night of the Long Knives two weeks later, on June 30, 1934. The cautious and the ambitious stepped around the bloodstains and went on about their business.[54] Von Papen himself departed meekly in July to assume the relatively modest post of ambassador to Austria. The conservatives' game was up when President Hindenburg died on August 2.

The conservatives' defensive wrigglings surfaced again in early 1938, when some of them disagreed with the pace and risk of Hitler's increasingly aggressive foreign policy. This conflict ended in February 1938 with the removal under humiliating circumstances of the commanding officers of the General Staff and the Army Staff (Generals Blomberg and Fritsch), falsely accused of sexual improprieties. The former corporal took over the military high command (Oberkommando der Wehrmacht, OKW) in person, and demanded a personal oath from his generals, like the kaiser before him. A number of senior officers wanted to resist the army's loss of independence, but they would not act without the support of the top commanders.[55] The subordination of the army to Hitler was even more complete than it had been to the kaiser.

Simultaneously the Foreign Office was brought under party control. The career diplomat Konstantin von Neurath was removed as foreign minister on February 5, 1938, and German diplomats had the humiliation of seeing their proud corporation pass under the control of the leader of the party's parallel organization, Joachim von Ribbentrop, a man whose main international experience before 1933 had been selling German fake champagne in Britain. Under Ribbentrop, old SA men tended to fill diplomatic posts abroad.[56]

Since Nazism's defeat in 1945, German conservatives have made much of their opposition to Hitler and of his hostility to them. As we have seen, Nazis and conservatives had authentic differences, marked by very real conservative defeats. At every crucial moment of decision, however—at each ratcheting up of anti-Jewish repression, at each new abridgment of civil liberties and infringement of legal norms, at each new aggressive move in foreign policy, at each further subordination of the economy to the needs of autarky and hasty rearmament—most German conservatives (with some honorable exceptions) swallowed their doubts about the Nazis in favor of their overriding common interests.

Conservatives did manage to hamper one Nazi policy: the euthanasia of so-called useless persons, a matter I will discuss more fully in the next chapter. For the rest, while conservative institutions and organizations sought to safeguard their class and personal interests, they rarely challenged the regime itself. Some individual conservatives, such as those who gathered around Helmut von Moltke at his country estate at Kreisau, opposed the regime morally and intellectually and pondered about what form a new Germany should take after the war. Toward the end, when they had finally understood that Hitler was leading Germany to annihilation, some conservative senior officers and civil servants came closest to forming an effective resistance to the Nazi regime and nearly succeeding in assassinating Hitler himself on July 20, 1944.

Since Mussolini's regime failed to develop the total reach of Hitler's, it is often considered less than totalitarian.[57] But the same elements vied for power within Fascist Italy as in Nazi Germany: the leader, the party, the state bureaucracy, and civil society. It was the outcome that differed, for power was apportioned among them in rather different ways. Distrustful of his party activists, Mussolini worked to subordinate them to an all-powerful state. At the same time, he was forced by circumstances to share the summit with the king and to placate the much stronger Catholic Church. Party activists fought back with accusations that the *Duce* was allowing the conservative fellow travelers (*fiancheggiattori*, literally "flankers") to dilute the movement.[58]

The final result in Italy was what some have called "a tougher version of Liberal Italy."[59] This view underestimates both the party's innovations in state organization and propaganda, especially in its dealings with youth and especially during the Ethiopian War, Mussolini's capacity for arbitrary action, and the degree of latent tension among *Duce*, party, and conservative elites in the Italian version of the dual state.

The Tug-of-War between Leader and Party

In fascist propaganda, and in most people's image of fascist regimes, leader and party are fused into a single expression of the national will. In reality, there is permanent tension between them, too. The fascist leader inevitably neglects some early campaign promises in his quest for the alliances necessary for power, and thus disappoints some of his radical followers.

Mussolini had to face down both the partisans of radical *squadrismo*, like Farinacci, and enthusiasts for "integral syndicalism," like Edmondo Rossoni. Although Hitler always controlled his party more fully than Mussolini, even he confronted dissent many times until he drowned it in blood in June 1934. Before power, the partisans of an authentic "German socialism," a "third way" intermediate between capitalism and Marxism, whom we have already met,[60] created embarrassments for him with businessmen whom he wanted to court. There were also those impatient with his all-or-nothing strategy like Walter Stennes and Gregor Strasser. As we have already seen, he did not hesitate to expel the latter two from the party.[61]

In the first days of Hitler's rule, conflict erupted over the "second revolution," a further wave of radical change that would give the spoils of place and position to the "old fighters." In the spring of 1933, party militants celebrated their arrival in power by continuing their street actions against the Left, against the moderate bourgeoisie, and against the Jews. The boycott of Jewish businesses organized by the militant Fighting League of the Commercial Middle Classs in spring 1933 was only one of the more conspicuous examples of "revolution from below." Hitler, however, needed calm and order then instead of challenges to the state's monopoly of violence, and party leaders announced "the end of the revolution" in the summer of 1933.

Aspirations for continued "revolution" still percolated within the SA, however, arousing concern in the business community. The SA's wish to become the armed force of the new regime made the army high command uneasy. Hitler settled these matters far more brutally and decisively than Mussolini in the Night of the Long Knives. The lesson was not lost on other would-be opponents.

The problem for fascist regimes—a problem traditional dictators never had to face—was how to keep the party's energy boiling without troubling public order and upsetting conservative allies. Most Nazi Party radicals were kept from troubling the regime by Hitler's personal control, by the regime's domestic and foreign successes, and, eventually, by the outlets of war and the murder of the Jews. The occupation of western Europe provided gratifying opportunities for spoliation.[62] Things went much further on the eastern front: there the party ran amok with occupation policy, as we will see in the next chapter.

Mussolini dominated his party, too, but in the face of much more open and durable challenges. The Fascist Party leaders, particularly the local *ras*, whose exploits during the period of *squadrismo* gave them a certain autonomous power, often expressed dissatisfaction with Mussolini. There were two sources to these tensions: a functional one, in that Mussolini had different responsibilities as party leader than the local *ras* and therefore saw things differently; and a personal one, in that Mussolini was more inclined to "normalize" relations with traditional conservatives than were some of his hotheaded followers. As we saw, movement and leader quarreled in 1921 over the transformation of the movement into a party, and in August 1921 the *ras* forced Mussolini to give up his intended pact of pacification with the socialists.

After power, those divergences became even sharper. Party militants were frustrated by Mussolini's first two years of moderate coalition government in 1922–24. We saw in chapter 4 how in December 1924 party militants prodded Mussolini to end his six months of indecision after the Matteotti murder and to choose the aggressive way out by establishing one-party rule.[63]

In need of strong party support as he set up his new dictatorship, Mussolini named in February 1925 the most uncompromising partisan of violent *squadrismo*, Roberto Farinacci, *ras* of Cremona, to be secretary of the Fascist Party. Farinacci's appointment looked like a signal of renewed violence against opponents, of party encroachment on the civil service, and of radical social, economic, and foreign policies.[64] Farinacci was dismissed, however, after only a year. Renewed eruptions of violence, such as eight more killings in Florence in October 1925 "in front of the tourists" were intolerable, and it was revealed that Farinacci's law thesis had been plagiarized. A series of more pliable party secretaries followed who, while increasing the party's size and reach, subordinated it unquestioningly to the *Duce* and to the state bureaucracy. In the next chapter, I will take up the continued tension between Mussolini's instinct for normalization and his periodic episodes of radicalization.

The Tug-of-War between Party and State

Both Hitler and Mussolini had to make the machinery of the state work for them, by persuasion or by force. Party militants wanted to sweep away career bureaucrats and take all the places themselves. The leaders almost never gave in to this demand. We have already seen how Hitler sacrificed the SA to the army in June 1934. Similarly, Mussolini prevented the *Milizia* from invading the professional sphere of the Italian army, except for service in the colonies.

In general, the Fascist and Nazi regimes had no serious difficulty establishing control over public services. They largely protected civil servants' turf from party intrusion and left their professional identity intact. Civil servants were frequently in broad sympathy with fascist regimes' biases for authority and order against parliament and the Left, and they appreciated enhanced freedom from legal restraint.[65] Eliminating Jews sometimes opened up career advancement.

The police were the key agency, of course. The German police were very quickly removed from the normative state and brought under Nazi Party control via the SS. Himmler, supported by Hitler against rivals and the Ministry of the Interior, which traditionally controlled the police, ascended in April 1933 from political police commander of Bavaria (where he set up the first concentration camp at Dachau) to chief of the whole German police system in June 1936.[66]

This process was facilitated by the disgruntlement many German police had felt for the Weimar Republic and its "coddling of criminals,"[67] and by the regime's efforts to enhance police prestige in the eyes of the public. By 1937, the annual congratulatory "Police Day" had expanded from one day to seven.[68] Initially the SA were deputized as auxiliary police in Prussia, but this practice was ended on August 2, 1933,[69] and the police faced no further threat of dilution from party militants. They enjoyed a privileged role above the law as the final arbiters of their own form of unlimited "police justice."

While the German police were run more directly by Nazi Party chiefs than any other traditional state agency, the Italian police remained headed by a civil servant, and their behavior was little more unprofessional or partisan than under previous governments. This is one of the most profound differences between the Nazi and Fascist regimes. The head of the Italian police for most of the Fascist period was the professional civil servant Arturo Bocchini. There was a political police, the OVRA, but the regime executed relatively few political enemies.

Another crucial instrument of rule was the judiciary. Although very few judges were Nazi Party members in 1933,[70] the German magistracy was already overwhelmingly conservative. It had established a solid track record of harsher penalties against communists than against Nazis during the 1920s. In exchange for a relatively limited invasion of their professional sphere by the party's Special Courts and People's Court, the judges willingly submerged their associations in a Nazi organization and happily accepted the powerful role the new regime gave them.[71] The Italian judiciary was little changed, since political interference had already been the norm under the liberal monarchy. Italian judges felt general sympathy for the Fascist regime's commitment to public order and national grandeur.[72]

Medical professionals—not strictly part of the state but essential to the regime's smooth functioning—cooperated with the Nazi regime with surprising alacrity. The Nazis' determination to improve the biological purity of the "race" (Italian culture was quite different on this point) contained a public health component that gratified many medical professionals. For a long time, the cruel experiments performed on prisoners by Dr. Josef Mengele gave a distorted impression of Nazi medicine. Nazi medicine was not mere sadism, though it did cause much suffering. It embarked on extensive basic public health research. German scientists were the first to link smoking and asbestos conclusively with cancer, for example.[73] Improving the "race" also meant encouraging large families, and fascist regimes were particularly active in the development of demographic science in the service of pronatalism. We will see in the next chapter how in Germany, under the pressure of war, improving the race turned into the sterilization of the "unfit" and the elimination of "useless mouths"—the mentally and incurably ill—and from there to ethnic genocide. Nazi administrators were proud of the scientific and bureau-cratic care with which they approached these matters, so unlike the Slavs' disorderly pogroms, and they rewarded doctors and public health profes-sionals with extensive authority over them. Many participated willingly in "medicalized killing."[74]

An "astonishing number" of child welfare professionals, weary of the ideological bickering between public and private and between reli-gious and secular agencies that had nearly paralyzed this field under Weimar, and already turning back toward parental authority and disci-pline after Weimar's experimentation, welcomed Nazism in 1933 as a new beginning.[75]

The party-state conflict was the most easily and most definitively set-tled of all the tensions within fascist rule. The Nazi state, in particular, ran vigorously right up to the end, in conscious and determined rejection of any hint of the breakdown of public authority that had occurred in 1918.

Accommodation, Enthusiasm, Terror

The dual state model is incomplete in yet one more crucial dimension: it leaves out public opinion. It is not enough to study the way a fascist regime exerted its authority from above; one must also explore how it interacted with its public. Did a majority of the population support fascist regimes consensually, even with enthusiasm, or were they bent to submis-sion by force and terror? The terror model has prevailed, partly because it serves as an alibi for the peoples concerned. But recent scholarship has tended to show that terror was selective and that consensus was high in both Nazi Germany and Fascist Italy.

Neither regime was conceivable without terror. Nazi violence was omnipresent and highly visible after 1933. The concentration camps were not hidden, and executions of dissidents were meant to be known.[76] The publicity of Nazi violence does not mean that support for the regime was coerced, however. Since the violence was directed at Jews, Marxists, and "asocial" outsiders (homosexuals, Gypsies, pacifists, the congenitally insane or crippled, and habitual criminals—groups that many Germans were often happy to see the last of), Germans often felt more gratified than threatened by it. The rest soon learned to keep silent. Only at the end, as the Allies and the Russians closed in, when the authorities attacked anyone accused of giving in, did the Nazi regime turn its violence upon ordinary Germans.[77]

The Italian Fascist pattern of violence was the opposite of the Nazi one. Mussolini spilled more blood coming to power than Hitler did,[78] but his dictatorship was relatively mild after that. The main form of punishment for political dissidents was forced residence in remote southern hill villages.[79] About ten thousand serious opponents of the regime were imprisoned in camps or on offshore islands. The regime sentenced to death a mere nine opponents between 1926 and 1940.[80]

But we must avoid the commonplace assumption that Mussolini's dictatorship was more comic than tragic. His order to assassinate the Rosselli brothers in France in 1937, the articulate leaders of the most important democratic resistance movement, Giustizia e Libertà, along with the notorious murder of the socialist deputy Giacomo Matteotti in June 1924, put indelible bloodstains on his regime. Fascist justice, while several orders of magnitude less vicious than Nazi justice, proclaimed no less boldly the "subordination of individual interests to collective [interests],"[81] and one must not forget the spectacular ruthlessness of Italian colonial conquest.[82]

As with the Third Reich, Fascist violence was directed selectively against "enemies of the nation"—socialists, or South Slavic or African peoples who stood in the way of Italian hegemony around the Mediterranean. So it could inspire more approval than fear.

The popularity-terror dichotomy is obviously much too rigid. Even Nazism did not depend on brute force alone. One remarkable discovery of recent scholarship is how small a police apparatus sufficed to enforce its will. The Gestapo was so well supplied with denunciations from zealous (or jealous) citizens that it could get along with a ratio of about one police officer for ten thousand to fifteen thousand citizens,[83] far fewer than the STASI required in the postwar German Democratic Republic.

The most interesting aspects of the story lie between the two extremes of coercion and popularity. It might be instructive to consider fascist regimes' management of workers, who were surely the most recalcitrant part of the population. It is clear that both Fascism and Nazism enjoyed some success in this domain. According to Tim Mason, the ultimate authority on German workers under Nazism, the Third Reich "contained" German workers by four means: terror, division, some concessions, and integration devices such as the famous Strength Through Joy (Kraft durch Freude) leisure-time organization.[84]

Let there be no doubt that terror awaited workers who resisted directly. It was the cadres of the German Socialist and Communist parties who filled the first concentration camps in 1933, before the Jews. Since socialists and communists were already divided, it was not hard for the Nazis to create another division between those workers who continued to resist and those who decided to try to live normal lives. The suppression of autonomous worker organizations allowed fascist regimes to address workers individually rather than collectively.[85] Soon, demoralized by the defeat of their unions and parties, workers were atomized, deprived of their usual places of sociability, and afraid to confide in anyone.

Both regimes made some concessions to workers—Mason's third device for worker "containment." They did not simply silence them, as in traditional dictatorships. After power, official unions enjoyed a monopoly of labor representation. The Nazi Labor Front had to preserve its credibility by actually paying some attention to working conditions. Mindful of the 1918 revolution, the Third Reich was willing to do absolutely anything to avoid unemployment or food shortages. As the German economy heated up in rearmament, there was even some wage creep. Later in the war, the arrival of slave labor, which promoted many German workers to the status of masters, provided additional satisfactions.

Mussolini was particularly proud of how workers would fare under his corporatist constitution. The Labor Charter (1927) promised that workers and employers would sit down together in a "corporation" for each branch of the economy, and submerge class struggle in the discovery of their common interests. It looked very imposing by 1939 when a Chamber of Corporations replaced parliament. In practice, however, the corporative bodies were run by businessmen, while the workers' sections were set apart and excluded from the factory floor.[86]

Mason's fourth form of "containment"—integrative devices—was a specialty of fascist regimes. Fascists were past masters at manipulating group dynamics: the youth group, the leisure-time association, party rallies. Peer pressure was particularly powerful in small groups. There the patriotic majority shamed or intimidated nonconformists into at least keeping their mouths shut. Sebastian Haffner recalled how his group of apprentice magistrates was sent in summer 1933 on a retreat, where these highly educated young men, mostly non-Nazis, were bonded into a group by marching, singing, uniforms, and drill. To resist seemed pointless, certain to lead nowhere but to prison and an end to the dreamed-of career. Finally, with astonishment, he observed himself raising his arm, fitted with a swastika armband, in the Nazi salute.[87]

These various techniques of social control were successful. Mussolini was broadly supported from 1929 at least up through his victory in

Ethiopia in 1936.[88] Accommodation with the Catholic Church was central to this support. The Lateran Treaties concluded by Mussolini and Pope Pius XI in February 1929 ended nearly sixty years of conflict between the Italian state and the Vatican with mutual recognition and the payment by Italy of a substantial indemnity for its seizure of papal lands in 1870. Italy recognized Roman Catholicism as "the religion of most Italians." The once anticlerical Mussolini, who had written a youthful novel called *The Cardinal's Mistress* and, at twenty-one, in a debate with a Swiss pastor, had given God—if He existed—five minutes to strike him dead,[89] had submitted in 1925 to a belated church marriage to his longtime common-law companion Rachele Guidi and to the baptism of their children. In elections on March 24, 1929, the Church's explicit support helped produce a vote of 98 percent in favor of the Fascist list of candidates (there were no others) for parliament.[90] Fascism paid a high price in the long term for the Church's aid to consensus: as the hare of Fascist dynamism wore itself out, the tortoise of Catholic parish life and culture plodded along to become the basis of Christian democratic rule in Italy after 1945.

The other ingredient of Mussolini's popularity in the middle years was his victory over Ethiopia in summer 1936, the last—it turned out—of his military successes. Popular approval of the Italian Fascist regime declined only when Mussolini's expansionist foreign policy began to produce defeats. The *Duce*'s need to demonstrate a "special relation with history" required him to mount a dynamic foreign policy. Beginning with the defeat of his "volunteer" armored force by Spanish Republicans and international volunteers at Guadalajara, in the hills northeast of Madrid, in March 1937, however, foreign policy provided more humiliation than reinforcement for Mussolini's regime.[91]

The Nazi regime, too, aroused considerable popular enthusiasm within Germany by the mid-1930s. Full employment plus a long string of bloodless foreign policy victories raised approval far above the Nazis' initial 44 percent in the March 1933 elections. Although Germans grumbled a lot about restrictions and shortages, and although the outbreak of war in September 1939 was received glumly,[92] the Hitler cult was exempt from the criticism reserved for party officials and bureaucrats.

Fascist regimes were particularly successful with young people. Fascist arrival in power sent a shock wave down through society to each neighborhood and village. Young Italians and Germans had to face the destruction of their social organizations (if they came from socialist or communist families) as well as the attraction of new forms of sociability. The temptation to conform, to belong, and to achieve rank in the new fascist youth and leisure organizations (which I will discuss more fully below) was very powerful.[93] Especially when fascism was still new, joining in its marching and uniformed squads was a way to declare one's independence from smothering bourgeois homes and boring parents.[94] Some young Germans and Italians of otherwise modest attainments found satisfaction in pushing other people around.[95] Fascism was more fully than any other political movement a declaration of youthful rebellion, though it was far more than that.

Women and men could hardly be expected to react in the same way to regimes that put a high priority on restoring women to the traditional spheres of homemaking and motherhood. Some conservative women approved. The female vote for Hitler was substantial (though impossible to measure precisely), and scholars have argued sharply about whether women should be considered accomplices or victims of his regime.[96] In the end, women escaped from the roles Fascism and Nazism projected for them, less by direct resistance than simply by being themselves, aided by modern consumer society. Jazz Age lifestyles proved more powerful than party propaganda. In Fascist Italy, Edda Mussolini and other modern young women smoked and asserted an independent lifestyle like young women everywhere after World War I, while also participating in the regime's institutions.[97] The Italian birth rate did not rise on the *Duce's* command. Hitler could not keep his promise to remove women from the workforce when the time came to mobilize fully for war.

Intellectuals found their relationship with fascist regimes more strained than with early fascist movements. They had good reason to feel uncomfortable under the rule of former street fighters contemptuous of "professors examining things behind their glasses, idiots who raise unrealistic objections to every affirmation of doctrine."[98] All the more so since these regimes regarded the arts and sciences not as a domain of free creativity but as a national resource subject to tight state control. Since leaders supposedly had superhuman mental powers, fascist militants preferred to settle intellectual matters by a *reductio ad ducem*.[99]

Fascist regimes also had the power to reward tractable and celebrated intellectuals with positions and honors. Where the regime was ready to leave a fair amount of leeway to intellectuals, as in Fascist Italy, a wide range of responses was possible. Some liberal and socialist critics rejected the regime totally, in the face of arrest[100] or even death,[101] joined soon by the untouchable liberal eminence Benedetto Croce; at the other extreme, a few authentically distinguished intellectuals like the philosopher Giovanni Gentile,[102] the historian Gioacchino Volpe, and the statistician/demographer Corrado Gini[103] offered enthusiastic support.

Mussolini never needed to crack down severely on cultural life because most intellectuals accepted some degree of accommodation with his regime, if only partially and occasionally. Of the signers of Croce's *Manifesto of the Intellectuals* of 1925, ninety could be found in 1931 writing for the very official *Enciclopedia italiana*.[104] When university professors were required to take an oath to the regime during the academic year 1931–32, only 11 out of 1,200 refused.[105] Only after the racial legislation of 1938, about which I talk more in the next chapter, did a significant number of Italian intellectuals emigrate.

Intellectuals faced more intense pressure in Nazi Germany. Nazi ideologues attempted to transform thought, as in the German physics that was supposed to supplant the "Jewish physics" of Einstein[106] and the "German Christianity" that was supposed to purge Christian doctrine of its Jewish influences. Substantial numbers of intellectual emigrants included some non-Jews (Thomas Mann was only the most celebrated). The physicist Max Planck managed to remain active in Germany, defend some measure of independence and that of some of his colleagues, and retain the respect of the international scientific community.[107] Still other prominent intellectuals—among them the philosopher Martin Heidegger, the sociologist Hans Freyer,[108] and the legal scholar Carl Schmitt[109]—found sufficient common ground with Nazism to accept official assignments. Within the range of compromise, accommodation, and quiet reticence adopted by most intellectuals, some positions remain obscure even today: Did the Nobel Prize physicist Werner Heisenberg weaken the German atomic energy program from within, as he claimed, or did it fail because of inadequate funding, changed priorities, the departure of important Jewish colleagues like Lise Meitner, and Heisenberg's own erroneous overestimate of the amount of plutonium required to operate an atomic pile?[110]

Even if public enthusiasm was never as total as fascists promised their conservative allies, most citizens of fascist regimes accepted things as they were. The most interesting cases are people who never joined the party, and who even objected to certain aspects of the regime, but who accommodated because its accomplishments overlapped with some of the things they wanted, while the alternatives all seemed worse. The eminent

German orchestral conductor Wilhelm Furtwängler was penalized after the war for having been photographed with a beaming Hitler, but in fact his relations with the Nazi regime were complicated. Furtwängler never joined the party. He tried in two tense face-to-face meetings to persuade the *Führer* to relax his ban on Jewish music and musicians. He was removed from some of his conducting posts for persisting in playing the atonal music of Hindemith. But he shared the Nazis' assumptions that "music arises from deep and secret forces which are rooted in the people of the nation"[111]—especially the German nation. It was unthinkable for him to leave Germany or cease his musical activity. He was indeed a privileged person under Nazism, for even though Hitler knew of Furtwängler's reservations, he also understood enough about music to realize that Furtwängler was the best conductor in Germany.[112]

By accepting accommodations of this sort, fascist regimes were able to retain the loyalty of nationalists and conservatives who did not agree with everything the party was doing.

The Fascist "Revolution"

The radical rhetoric of the early fascist movements led many observers, then and since, to suppose that once in power the fascist regimes would make sweeping and fundamental changes in the very bases of national life. In practice, although fascist regimes did indeed make some breathtaking changes, they left the distribution of property and the economic and social hierarchy largely intact (differing fundamentally from what the word *revolution* had usually meant since 1789).

The reach of the fascist "revolution" was restricted by two factors. For one thing, even at their most radical, early fascist programs and rhetoric had never attacked wealth and capitalism as directly as a hasty reading might suggest.[113] As for social hierarchy, fascism's leadership principle effectively reinforced it, though fascists posed some threat to inherited position by advocating the replacement of the tired bourgeois elite by fascist "new men." The handful of real fascist outsiders, however, went mostly into the parallel organizations.

The scope of fascist change was further limited by the disappearance of many radicals during the period of taking root and coming to power. As fascist movements passed from protest and the harnessing of disparate resentments to the conquest of power, with its attendant alliances and compromises, their priorities changed, along with their functions. They became far less interested in assembling the discontented than in mobilizing and unifying national energies for national revival and aggrandizement. This obliged them to break many promises made to the socially and economically discontented during the first years of fascist recruitment. The Nazis in particular broke promises to the small peasants and artisans who had been the mainstay of their electoral following, and to favor urbanization and industrial production.[114]

Despite their frequent talk about "revolution," fascists did not want a socioeconomic revolution. They wanted a "revolution of the soul," and a revolution in the world power position of their people. They meant to unify and invigorate and empower their decadent nation—to reassert the prestige of *Romanità* or the German *Volk* or Hungarism or other group destiny. For that purpose they believed they needed armies, productive capacity, order, and property. Force their country's traditional productive elements into subjection, perhaps; transform them, no doubt; but not abolish them. The fascists needed the muscle of these bastions of established power to express their people's renewed unity and vitality at home and on the world stage. Fascists wanted to revolutionize their national institutions in the sense that they wanted to pervade them with energy, unity, and willpower, but they never dreamed of abolishing property or social hierarchy.

The fascist mission of national aggrandizement and purification required the most fundamental changes in the nature of citizenship and in the relation of citizens to the state since the democratic revolutions of the eighteenth and nineteenth centuries. The first giant step was to subordinate the individual to the community. Whereas the liberal state rested on a compact among its citizens to protect individual rights and freedoms, the fascist state embodied the national destiny, in service to which all the members of the national group found their highest fulfillment. We have seen that both regimes found some distinguished nonfascist intellectuals ready to support this position.

In fascist states, individual rights had no autonomous existence. The State of Law—the *Rechtsstaat*, the *état de droit*—vanished, along with the principles of due process by which citizens were guaranteed equitable treatment by courts and state agencies. A suspect acquitted in a German court of law could be rearrested by agents of the regime at the courthouse door and put in a concentration camp without any further legal procedure.[115] A fascist regime could imprison, despoil, and even kill its inhabitants at will and without limitation. All else pales before that radical transformation in the relation of citizens to public power.

It follows almost as an anticlimax that fascist regimes contained no mechanisms by which citizens could choose representatives or otherwise influence policy. Parliaments lost power, elections were replaced by yes-no plebiscites and ceremonies of affirmation, and leaders were given almost unlimited dictatorial powers.

Fascists claimed that the division and decline of their communities had been caused by electoral politics and especially by the Left's preparations for class warfare and proletarian dictatorship. Communities so afflicted, the fascists taught, could not be unified by the play of naturally harmonious human interests, as the liberals had believed. They had to be unified by state action, using persuasion and organization if possible, using force if necessary. The job required what the French sociologist Émile Durkheim called "mechanical solidarity" rather than "organic solidarity." Fascist regimes thus contained multiple agencies for shaping and molding the citizenry into an integrated community of disciplined, hardened fighters. The fascist state was particularly attentive to the formation of youth, jealously attempting to retain a monopoly of this function (a matter that brought fascist regimes and the Catholic Church into frequent conflict).

Fascist regimes set out to make the new man and the new woman (each in his or her proper sphere). It was the challenging task of fascist educational systems to manufacture "new" men and women who were simultaneously fighters and obedient subjects. Educational systems in liberal states, alongside their mission to help individuals realize their intellectual potential, were already committed to shaping citizens. Fascist states were able to use existing educational personnel and structures with only a shift of emphasis toward sports and physical and military training. Some of the schools' traditional functions were absorbed, to be sure, by party parallel organizations like the obligatory youth movements. All children in fascist states were supposed to be enrolled automatically in party organizations that structured their lives from childhood through university. Close to 70 percent of Italians aged six to twenty-one in the northern cities of Turin, Genoa, and Milan belonged to Fascist youth organizations, though the proportion was much lower in the undeveloped south.[116] Hitler was even more determined to take young Germans away from their traditional socializers—parents, schoolteachers, churches—and their traditional spontaneous amusements. "These boys," he told the Reichstag on December 4, 1938, "join our organization at the age of ten and get a breath of fresh air for the first time; then, four years later, they move from the *Jungvolk* to the Hitler Youth and there we keep them for another four years. And then we are even less prepared to give them back into the hands of those who create our class and status barriers, rather we take them immediately into the Party, into the Labor Front, into the SA or the SS . . . and so on."[117] Between the end of 1932 and the beginning of 1939, the Hitlerjugend expanded its share of the ten-to-eighteen age group from 1 percent to 87 percent.[118] Once out in the world, the citizens of a fascist state found the regime watching over their leisure-time activities as well: the Dopolavoro in Italy and the Kraft durch Freude in Germany.

Indeed, fascist regimes tried to redraw so radically the boundaries between private and public that the private sphere almost disappeared. Robert Ley, head of the Nazi Labor Office, said that in the Nazi state the only private individual was someone asleep.[119] For some observers, this effort to have the public sphere swallow up the private sphere entirely is indeed the very essence of fascism.[120] It is certainly a fundamental point on which fascist regimes differed most profoundly from authoritarian conservatism, and even more profoundly from classical liberalism.

There was no room in this vision of obligatory national unity for either free-thinking persons or for independent, autonomous subcommunities. Churches, Freemasonry, class-based unions or syndicates, political parties— all were suspect as subtracting something from the national will.[121] Here were grounds for infinite conflict with conservatives as well as the Left.

In pursuit of their mission to unify the community within an all-consuming public sphere, fascist regimes dissolved unions and socialist parties. This radical amputation of what had been normal worker representation, encased as it was in a project of national fulfillment and managed economy, alienated public opinion less than pure military or police repression, as in traditional dictatorships. And indeed the fascists had some success in reconciling some workers to a world without unions or socialist parties, those for whom proletarian solidarity against capitalist bosses was willingly replaced by national identity against other peoples.

Brooding about cultural degeneracy was so important a fascist issue that some authors have put it at the center. Every fascist regime sought to control the national culture from the top, to purify it of foreign influences, and make it help carry the message of national unity and revival. Decoding the cultural messages of fascist ceremonies, films, performances, and visual arts has today become the most active field of research on fascism.[122] The "reading" of fascist stagecraft, however ingenious, should not mislead us into thinking that fascist regimes succeeded in establishing monolithic cultural homogeneity. Cultural life in fascist regimes remained a complex patchwork of official activities, spontaneous activities that the regimes tolerated, and even some illicit ones. Ninety percent of the films produced under the Nazi regime were light entertainment without overt propaganda content (not that it was innocent, of course).[123] A few protected Jewish artists hung on remarkably late in Nazi Germany, and the openly homosexual actor and director Gustav Gründgens remained active to the end.[124]

In no domain did the proposals of early fascism differ more from what fascist regimes did in practice than in economic policy. This was the area where both fascist leaders conceded the most to their conservative allies. Indeed, most fascists—above all after they were in power—considered economic policy as only a means to achieving the more important fascist ends of unifying, energizing, and expanding the community.[125] Economic policy tended to be driven by the need to prepare and wage war. Politics trumped economics.[126]

Much ink has been spilled over whether fascism represented an emergency form of capitalism, a mechanism devised by capitalists by which the fascist state—their agent—disciplined the workforce in a way no traditional dictatorship could do. Today it is quite clear that businessmen often objected to specific aspects of fascist economic policies, sometimes with success. But fascist economic policy responded to political priorities, and not to economic rationale. Both Mussolini and Hitler tended to think that economics was amenable to a ruler's will. Mussolini returned to the gold standard and revalued the lira at 90 to the British pound in December 1927 for reasons of national prestige, and over the objections of his own finance minister.[127]

Fascism was not the first choice of most businessmen, but most of them preferred it to the alternatives that seemed likely in the special conditions of 1922 and 1933—socialism or a dysfunctional market system. So they mostly acquiesced in the formation of a fascist regime and accommodated to its requirements of removing Jews from management and accepting onerous economic controls. In time, most German and Italian businessmen adapted well to working with fascist regimes, at least those gratified by the fruits of rearmament and labor discipline and the considerable role given to them in economic management. Mussolini's famous corporatist economic organization, in particular, was run in practice by leading businessmen.

Peter Hayes puts it succinctly: the Nazi regime and business had "converging but not identical interests."[128] Areas of agreement included disciplining workers, lucrative armaments contracts, and job-creation stimuli. Important areas of conflict involved government economic controls, limits on trade, and the high cost of autarky—the economic self-sufficiency by which the Nazis hoped to overcome the shortages that had lost Germany World War I. Autarky required costly substitutes—*Ersatz*—for such previously imported products as oil and rubber.

Economic controls damaged smaller companies and those not involved in rearmament. Limits on trade created problems for companies that had formerly derived important profits from exports. The great chemical combine I. G. Farben is an excellent example: before 1933, Farben had prospered in international trade. After 1933, the company's directors adapted to the regime's autarky and learned to prosper mightily as the suppliers of German rearmament.[129]

The best example of the expense of import substitution was the Hermann Goering Werke, set up to make steel from the inferior ores and brown coal of Silesia. The steel manufacturers were forced to help finance this operation, to which they raised vigorous objections.[130]

The businessmen may not have gotten everything they wanted from the Nazi command economy, but they got far more than the Nazi Party radicals did. In June 1933, Otto Wagener, an "old fighter" who had become head of the economic policy branch of the party and who took his National Socialism seriously enough to want to replace the "egoistic spirit of profit of the individual person with common striving in the interest of the community," seemed likely to become minister of the economy. Hermann Goering, the Nazi leader closest to business, skillfully eliminated Wagener by showing Hitler that Wagener had been campaigning within the Nazi leadership for this appointment. Hitler, enraged at the slightest encroachment on his authority to name ministers, expelled Wagener from the party and named to the post Dr. Kurt Schmitt, head of Allianz, Germany's biggest insurance company.

Nazi economic radicalism did not disappear, however. Private insurance executives never stopped fighting attempts by Nazi radicals to replace them with nonprofit mutual funds organized within each economic sector—"*völkisch*" insurance. While the radicals found some niches for public insurance companies in SS enterprises in the conquered territories and in the Labor Front, the private insurers maneuvered so skillfully within a regime for which some of them felt distaste that they ended up with 85 percent of the business, including policies on Hitler's *Berghof*, Göring's *Karinhall*, and slave-labor factories in Auschwitz and elsewhere.[131]

Generally, economic radicals in the Nazi movement resigned (like Otto Strasser) or lost influence (like Wagener) or were murdered (like Gregor Strasser). Italian "integral syndicalists" either lost their influence (like Rossoni) or left the party (like Alceste De Ambris).

In the short term, as liberal economies floundered in the early 1930s, fascist economies could look more capable than democracies of performing the harsh task of reconciling populations to diminished personal consumption in order to permit a higher rate of savings and investment, particularly in the military. But we know now that they never achieved the growth rates of postwar Europe, or even of pre-1914 Europe, or even the total mobilization for war achieved voluntarily and belatedly by some of the democracies. This makes it difficult to accept the definition of fascism as a "developmental dictatorship" appropriate for latecomer industrial nations.[132] Fascists did not wish to develop the economy but to prepare for war, even though they needed accelerated arms production for that.

Fascists had to do something about the welfare state. In Germany, the welfare experiments of the Weimar Republic had proved too expensive after the Depression struck in 1929. The Nazis trimmed them and perverted them by racial forms of exclusion. But neither fascist regime tried to dismantle the welfare state (as mere reactionaries might have done).

Fascism was revolutionary in its radically new conceptions of citizenship, of the way individuals participated in the life of the community. It was counterrevolutionary, however, with respect to such traditional projects of the Left as individual liberties, human rights, due process, and international peace.

In sum, the fascist exercise of power involved a coalition composed of the same elements in Mussolini's Italy as in Nazi Germany. It was the relative weight among leader, party, and traditional institutions that distinguished one case from the other. In Italy, the traditional state wound up with supremacy over the party, largely because Mussolini feared his own most militant followers, the local *ras* and their *squadristi*. In Nazi Germany, the party came to dominate the state and civil society, especially after war began.

Fascist regimes functioned like an epoxy: an amalgam of two very different agents, fascist dynamism and conservative order, bonded by shared enmity toward liberalism and the Left, and a shared willingness to stop at nothing to destroy their common enemies.

CHAPTER 6

The Long Term: Radicalization or Entropy?

Fascist regimes could not settle down into a comfortable enjoyment of power. The charismatic leader had made dramatic promises: to unify, purify, and energize his community; to save it from the flabbiness of bourgeois materialism, the confusion and corruption of democratic politics, and the contamination of alien people and cultures; to head off the threatened revolution of property with a revolution of values; to rescue the community from decadence and decline. He had offered sweeping solutions to these menaces: violence against enemies, both inside and out; the individual's total immersion in the community; the purification of blood and culture; the galvanizing enterprises of rearmament and expansionist war. He had assured his people a "privileged relation with history."[1]

Fascist regimes had to produce an impression of driving momentum— "permanent revolution"[2]—in order to fulfill these promises. They could not survive without that headlong, inebriating rush forward. Without an ever-mounting spiral of ever more daring challenges, fascist regimes risked decaying into something resembling a tepid authoritarianism.[3] With it, they drove toward a final paroxysm of self-destruction.

Fascist or partly fascist regimes do not inevitably succeed in maintaining momentum. Several regimes sometimes considered fascist deliberately took the opposite tack of damping down excitement. They "normalized" themselves—and thereby became more authoritarian than fascist.

The Spanish dictator General Francisco Franco, for example, is often considered fascist because of his armed conquest of power in the Spanish Civil War with the overt aid of Mussolini and Hitler. Indeed, helping the Spanish Republicans defend themselves against Franco's rebellion after July 1936 was the first and most emblematic antifascist crusade. After his victory in March 1939, Franco unleashed a bloody repression that may have killed as many as two hundred thousand people, and attempted to seal off his regime from both economic exchange and cultural contamination from the democratic world.[4] Virulently hostile to democracy, liberalism, secularism, Marxism, and especially Freemasonry, Franco joined Hitler and Mussolini in April 1939 as a signatory of the Anti-Comintern Pact. During the battle for France in 1940, he seized Tangiers. He seemed eager to expand further at the expense of Britain and France, and to become a "full-scale military partner of the Axis."[5]

Whenever Hitler pressed him to act, however, the cautious *Caudillo* always set his price for full belligerency on the Axis side unattainably high. A few days after meeting Franco at Hendaye, on the French-Spanish border, on October 23, 1940, Hitler told Mussolini that he would rather have three or four teeth pulled than spend another nine hours bargaining with that "Jesuit swine."[6] After the terrible bloodletting of 1936–39, Franco wanted order and quiet; fascist dynamism fit badly with his reserved temperament.

Franco's regime did have a single party—the Falange—but without "parallel structures" it lacked autonomous power. Although it grew to nearly a million members during the period of German victories in 1941–42, and gave the dictatorship useful support with its ceremonies, the *Caudillo* allowed it no share in policy-making or administration.

The elimination of the Falange's charismatic leader José Antonio Primo de Rivera at the beginning in the Civil War, as we recall from chapter 3, helped Franco to establish the preeminence of the established elites and the normative state. Thereafter he was able to exploit the multiplicity of extreme Right parties and the inexperience of José Antonio's successor, Manuel Hedilla, to reduce fascist influence further. He cleverly submerged the Falange within an amorphous umbrella organization that included both fascists and traditional monarchists, the Falange Española Tradicionalista y de las Juntas de Ofensiva Nacional Sindicalista. Its leader was condemned to "impotence as a decorative part of Franco's entourage."[7] When Hedilla tried to reassert independent authority in April 1937, Franco had him arrested. The domestication of the Falange made it easier for Franco to give his dictatorship the traditional form, with a minimum of fascist excitement, that was clearly his preference, certainly after 1942, and probably before.

After 1945 the Falange became a colorless civic solidarity association, normally referred to simply as the Movimiento. In 1970 its very name was abolished. By then Franquist Spain had long become an authoritarian regime dominated by the army, state officials, businessmen, landowners, and the Church, with almost no visible fascist coloration.[8]

Portugal, whose malfunctioning parliamentary regime had been overthrown by a military coup in 1926, was governed after the early 1930s by a reclusive economics professor of integrist Catholic views, Antonio de Oliveira Salazar. Dr. Salazar leaned even more than Franco toward cautious quietism. Where Franco subjected Spain's fascist party to his personal control, Salazar abolished outright in July 1934 the nearest thing Portugal had to an authentic fascist movement, Rolão Preto's blue-shirted National Syndicalists. The Portuguese fascists, Salazar complained, were "always feverish, excited and discontented . . . shouting, faced with the impossible: More! More!"[9] Salazar preferred to control his population through such "organic" institutions traditionally powerful in Portugal as the Church.

When civil war broke out in neighboring Spain in 1936, "organic" authority was no longer enough. Dr. Salazar experimented with a "New State" (Estado Novo) fortified with devices borrowed from fascism, including corporatist labor organization, a youth movement (Portuguese Youth, or Mocidade Portuguesa), and a powerless "single party" clad in blue shirts, the Portuguese Legion.[10] Rejecting fascist expansionism, Portugal remained neutral in World War II and all subsequent conflicts until it decided to fight the Angolan independence movement in 1961. Hoping to spare Portugal the pains of class conflict, Dr. Salazar even opposed the industrial development of his country until the 1960s. His regime was not only nonfascist, but "voluntarily nontotalitarian," preferring to let those of its citizens who kept out of politics "live by habit."[11]

At the other extreme, Nazi Germany alone experienced full radicalization. A victorious war of extermination in the east offered almost limitless freedom of action to the "prerogative state" and its "parallel institutions," released from the remaining constraints of the "normative state," such as they were. In a "no-man's-land" composed of conquered territories in what had been Poland and the western parts of the Soviet Union, Nazi Party radicals felt free to carry out their ultimate fantasies of racial cleansing. Extreme radicalization remains latent in all fascisms, but the circumstances of war, and particularly of victorious wars of conquest, gave it the fullest means of expression.

Radicalizing impulses were not absent from Mussolini's Italy. Torn between periodic urges to reinvigorate the aging Blackshirts and the normalizing drag of conservative fellow travelers, the Fascist regime followed an irregular trajectory. Mussolini had popularized the term "totalitarianism," and he continued to lace his orations with bombastic appeals to action and promises of revolution. In practice, however, he shifted back and forth, unleashing party radicals on occasion when his power position would benefit, but more often reining them in when his rule needed stable conditions and an unchallenged state.

Having been a daring gambler during the "seizure of power," Mussolini turned out as prime minister to prefer stability to adventure. The penchant for normalization that had first appeared in 1921 with his proposed pact of pacification with the socialists was to grow with age, through the force of circumstances as well as by personal predilection. As we saw in chapter 4, he sought during the first two years after taking office in 1922 to curb the party's adventurism and the rival power of the *ras* by asserting the primacy of the state. He declined to challenge the extensive powers held by the monarchy, the Church, and his conservative partners. Mussolini's economic policy conformed during those early years to the laissez-faire policies of liberal regimes. His first minister of finance (1922–25) was the professor of economics (and party activist) Alberto De Stefani, who reduced state intervention in the economy, cut and simplified taxes, diminished government spending, and balanced the budget. It is true that De Stefani, committed not only to free trade but also to the fascist ideal of stimulating productive energy, made some businessmen angry by cutting such import duties as the one protecting expensive locally produced beet sugar. In general, however, he displayed "an unmistakable pro-business bias."[12]

Another cycle of radicalization and normalization followed the murder of the socialist leader Giacomo Matteotti.[13] Mussolini's first response to the ensuing firestorm of criticism was further "normalization": He gave the crucial Ministry of the Interior, with its supervision over the police, to Luigi Federzoni, head of the Nationalist Party, which had merged with the Fascist Party in 1923. After hunkering down for six months against attacks not only from the democratic opposition but from some of his conservative allies, seemingly paralyzed by uncertainty, the *Duce* was forced by pressure from party radicals—as we saw in chapter 4—to carry out what amounted to a preemptive coup d'état on January 3, 1925, and to begin the long process that, by fits and starts, replaced the parliamentary regime with what he called (with some exaggeration) a "totalitarian" state. His appointment of one of the most intransigent Fascist militants, Roberto Farinacci, as secretary of the Fascist Party seemed to confirm his intention to let the party set the pace, infiltrate the bureaucracy, and dominate national policy-making.

When Mussolini sacked Farinacci a little more than a year later, however, in April 1926,[14] and replaced him with the less headstrong Augusto Turati (1926–29), he was again strengthening the normative state at the expense of the party. It was at this point, most significantly, that he entrusted the Italian police to a professional civil servant, Arturo Bocchini, rather than to a party zealot on the Himmler model. Operating the all-important police force on bureaucratic principles (promotion of trained professionals by seniority, respect for legal procedures at least in nonpolitical cases) rather than as part of a prerogative state of unlimited arbitrary power was Italian Fascism's most important divergence from Nazi practice.

In 1928, Mussolini removed the old syndicalist militant Edmondo Rossoni from leadership of the Fascist trade unions, putting an end to Rossoni's efforts to give them a real share in economic policy and equal representation alongside management in a single set of corporatist organizations. After Rossoni's departure, the Fascist unions' monopoly of labor representation was all that remained of "Fascist syndicalism." Labor and management faced each other in separate organizations, and union representatives were banished from the shop floor. The form in which Mussolini's much-vaunted "Corporate State" developed henceforth amounted, in effect, to the reinforcement under state authority of employers' "private power."[15]

Mussolini's most decisive step toward normalization was the 1929 Lateran Pact with the papacy.[16] Though this treaty had forbidden any Catholic political activity in Italy, its long-term effects were favorable to the Church. Pope Pius XI, no democrat, had little taste for Catholic political parties anyway, much preferring to nurture schools and Catholic Action—the network of youth and worker associations that would transform society from within.[17] Thereafter (despite a bout with Fascist zealots who harassed Catholic youth programs in 1931), the Church's grassroots organizations were to outlast Fascism and sustain the long postwar rule of the Christian Democratic Party.[18] Mussolini had retreated far toward traditional authoritarian rule, in which the monarchy, organized business, the army, and the Catholic Church possessed large spheres of autonomous responsibility independent of either the Fascist Party or the Italian state.

Mussolini probably preferred to rule that way as he grew older, but he knew the younger generation was impatient with his aging regime. "We were spiritually equipped to be assault squads," complained the young Fascist Indro Montanelli in 1933, "but fate has given us the role of Swiss Guards of the constituted order."[19] That was one reason why in 1935 he took the classic way "forward" for a Fascist regime: a war of aggression in Ethiopia. I will examine in more detail below[20] the downward spiral of radicalizing adventure that followed: the "cultural revolution" of 1936–38, European war in 1940, and the puppet republic of Salò under Nazi occupation in 1943–45.

What Drives Radicalization?

This brief review of Mussolini's vacillation between normalization and radicalization suggests that the leader alone drives things along, a position that came to be known and debated in the 1980s as "intentionalism."[21] Obviously, however, the leader's intentions mean little unless police officers, army commanders, magistrates, and civil servants are willing to obey his orders. Contemplating the notoriously indolent Hitler, some scholars were led to propose that the impulses to radicalization must have erupted from below, in the initiatives taken by underlings frustrated by local emergencies and confident that the *Führer* would cover their excesses, as he had done with the Potempa murderers. This position was known in the debates of the 1980s as "structuralism."

We do not need to accept the absurdity of pure "structuralism" to recognize that, in addition to the leader's actions or words, fascist regimes embrace radicalizing impulses from below that distinguish them sharply from traditional authoritarian dictatorships. I have already alluded to the deliberate arousal of expectations of dynamism, excitement, momentum, and risk that were inherent to fascism's appeal, and which it was dangerous to abandon completely for fear of undermining the leader's principal source of power independent of the old elites.

The party and its militants were themselves a powerful force for continued radicalization. No regime was authentically fascist without a popular movement that helped it achieve power, monopolized political activity, and played a major role in public life after power with its parallel organizations. We know already what serious problems the party could pose for the leader. Its battle-scarred militants thirsted after immediate rewards—jobs, power, money—in ways that troubled the leader's necessary cooperation with the Establishment. Old party comrades could easily turn into rivals for the supreme role if the leader falters.

No fascist leader, not even Hitler, failed to have problems with his party, as we saw in the previous chapter. He needed to keep it in line, but he could hardly dispense with it, for it was his chief weapon in his permanent rivalry with the old elites. Hitler solved his conflicts with the Nazi Party with characteristic speed and brutality—but it must not be imagined that even he did so without strain, or that he was always entirely in perfect control.

Mussolini, too, was not unwilling to shed blood, as the murders of the Rosselli brothers and Matteotti witnessed. But he dared execute his unruly party lieutenants only under the German boot in 1944.[22] Sometimes he gave in to them (for example, when he abandoned his proposed pact of pacification with the socialists, after four months of raucous party debate, in November 1921, and when he assumed dictatorial power in January 1925). Often he tried to channel them, as when he named Farinacci party secretary in 1925, or when he diverted the energies of another powerful *ras*, Italo Balbo, into the air force and the African empire.

Not unlike Mussolini in his early laissez-faire period with Alberto De Stefani, Hitler named as his first minister of finance the conservative Lutz Graf Schwerin von Krosigk.[23] For a time, the *Führer* left foreign policy in the hands of professional diplomats (with the aristocratic Constantin von Neurath as foreign minister) and the army in the hands of professional soldiers. But Hitler's drive to shrink the normative state and expand the prerogative state was much more sustained than Mussolini's. Total master of his party, Hitler exploited its radical impulses for his own aggrandizement against the old elites and rarely (after the exemplary bloodbath of June 1934) needed to rein it in. Another suggested key to radicalization is the chaotic nature of fascist rule. Contrary to wartime propaganda and to an enduring popular image, Nazi Germany was not a purring, well-oiled machine. Hitler allowed party agencies to compete with more traditional state offices, and he named loyal lieutenants to overlapping jobs that pitted them against each other. The ensuing "feudal"[24] struggles for supremacy within and between party and state shocked those Germans proud of their country's traditional superbly trained and independent civil service. Fritz-Dietlof Count von der Schulenburg, a young Prussian official initially attracted to Nazism, lamented in 1937 that "the formerly unified State power has been split into a number of separate authorities; Party and professional organizations work in the same areas and overlap with no clear divisions of responsibility." He feared "the end of a true Civil Service and the emergence of a subservient bureaucracy."[25]

We saw in the previous chapter how the self-indulgently bohemian Hitler spent as little time as possible on the labors of government, at least until the war. He proclaimed his visions and hatreds in speeches and ceremonies, and allowed his ambitious underlings to search for the most radical way to fulfill them in a Darwinian competition for attention and reward. His lieutenants, fully aware of his fanatical views, "worked toward the Führer,"[26] who needed mainly to arbitrate among them. Mussolini, quite unlike Hitler in his commitment to the drudgery of government, refused to delegate and remained suspicious of competent associates—a governing style that produced more inertia than radicalization.

War provided fascism's clearest radicalizing impulse. It would be more accurate to say that war played a circular role in fascist regimes. Early fascist movements were rooted in an exaltation of violence sharpened by World War I, and war making proved essential to the cohesion, discipline, and explosive energy of fascist regimes. Once undertaken, war generated both the need for more extreme measures, and popular acceptance of them. It seems a general rule that war is indispensable for the maintenance of fascist muscle tone (and, in the cases we know, the occasion for its demise).

It seems clear that both Hitler and Mussolini deliberately chose war as a necessary step in realizing the full potential of their regimes. They wanted to use war to harden internal society as well as to conquer vital space. Hitler told Goebbels, "the war . . . made possible for us the solution of a whole series of problems that could never have been solved in normal times."[27]

Hitler deliberately sought confrontation. Did he want war? A. J. P. Taylor argued in 1962 that Hitler stumbled into a war he did not want in September 1939, and that it was British Prime Minister Neville Chamberlain who made the fatal decision for war by extending a military guarantee to Poland in March 1939.[28] Taylor's revisionism was useful, for it forced a closer look at the archives. The most convincing conclusion, however, is that while Hitler may indeed not have wanted the long war of attrition on two fronts that he eventually got, he probably did want a local, short, victorious war in Poland—or at least the public impression of having got his way by a show of force. Every fiber of the Nazi regime had been bent to the business of preparing Germany materially and psychologically for war, and not to use that force, sooner or later, would produce a potentially fatal loss of credibility.

Mussolini was no less clearly drawn to war. "When Spain is finished, I will think of something else," he told his son-in-law and Foreign Minister Galeazzo Ciano. "The character of the Italian people must be molded by fighting."[29] He acclaimed war as the sole source of human advance. "War is to men as maternity is to women."[30]

Less than a year after becoming prime minister, in August 1923, Mussolini made his foreign policy debut with the Corfu incident, a spectacular piece of Fascist bravado. After an Italian general and other members of an Italian commission trying to settle a border dispute between Albania and Greece were murdered, apparently by Greek bandits, Mussolini sent the Greek government a list of exorbitant demands. When the Greek authorities hesitated, Italian forces bombarded and occupied the island of Corfu.

The *Duce* began preparations to invade Ethiopia in 1933–34. That fateful decision—it aligned him irrevocably with Hitler against Britain and France—grew as much out of a need to revive Fascist dynamism as out of traditional nationalist imperial dreams and vengeance for Italy's defeat by Ethiopia at Adwa in 1896. In the early 1930s, the Italian Fascist regime faced a crisis of identity. It had been in power for a decade. The Blackshirts were growing complacent, and party ranks had been opened up to all comers. Many young people were coming of age unaware of Fascism's heroic early days, perceiving Fascists only as comfortable careerists.

Later, when European war approached, although Mussolini (unlike Hitler) clearly wanted a negotiated settlement of the Czech crisis in 1938 and the Polish crisis in August 1939, he could not afford to stand aside forever. When Germany appeared to be on the point of definitive victory, he rushed into war against France, on June 10, 1940, despite the poor state of his armed forces. Possibly sharing some of his radical lieutenants' conviction that war would restore Fascism's original spirit,[31] he may also have thought it would strengthen his control. Above all, he had preached the martial virtues too long to stand aside without ridicule from an apparently easy victory.[32] Mussolini's attacks on Albania and Greece in the fall of 1940, similarly, were necessary for reasons of prestige and to maintain the fiction that he was waging his own war "parallel" to Hitler's. No vital economic or strategic stakes were involved in any of these campaigns.

Even nonradicalized authoritarian regimes glorified the military. For all his desire to stay out of the war, Franco seized the opportunity offered by the defeat of France in 1940 to occupy Tangiers, as we saw earlier. Military parades were a major form of public ritual for Franquist Spain. Defeated France, under the Vichy regime of World War I hero Marshal Pétain, put much energy into military pomp and patriotic display. It never stopped asking the Nazi occupation authorities to allow the tiny Vichy Armistice Army to play a greater role in the defense of French soil from an Allied invasion.[33] Even the quietist Portuguese dictator Salazar could not neglect the African empire that provided major emotional and economic support for his authoritarian state.

But there is a difference between authoritarian dictatorships' glorification of the military and the emotional commitment of fascist regimes to war. Authoritarians used military pomp, but little actual fighting, to help prop up regimes dedicated to preserving the status quo. Fascist regimes could not survive without the active acquisition of new territory for their "race"—*Lebensraum, spazio vitale*—and they deliberately chose aggressive war to achieve it, clearly intending to wind the spring of their people to still higher tension.

Fascist radicalization was not simply war government, moreover. Making war radicalizes all regimes, fascist or not, of course. All states demand more of their citizens in wartime, and citizens become more willing, if they believe the war is a legitimate one, to make exceptional sacrifices for the community, and even to set aside some of their liberties. Increased state authority seems legitimate when the enemy is at the gate. During World War II, citizens of the democracies accepted not only material sacrifices, like rationing and the draft, but also major limitations on freedom, such as censorship. In the United States during the cold war an insistent current of opinion wanted to limit liberties again, in the interest of defeating the communist enemy.

War government under fascism is not the same as the democracies' willing and temporary suspension of liberties, however. In fascist regimes at war, a fanatical minority within the party or movement may find itself freed to express a furor far beyond any rational calculation of interest. In this way, we return to Hannah Arendt's idea that fascist regimes build on the fragmentation of their societies and the atomization of their populations. Arendt has been sharply criticized for making atomization one of the prerequisites for Nazi success.[34] But her *Origins of Totalitarianism*, though cast in historical terms, is more a philosophical meditation on fascism's ultimate radicalization than a history of origins. Even if the fragmentation and atomization of society work poorly as explanations for fascism's taking root and arriving in power, the fragmentation and atomization of government were characteristic of the last phase of fascism, the radicalization process. In the newly conquered territories, ordinary civil servants, agents of the normative state, were replaced by party radicals, agents of the prerogative state. The orderly procedures of bureaucracy gave way to the wild unstructured improvisations of inexperienced party militants thrust into ill-defined positions of authority over conquered peoples.

Trying to Account for the Holocaust

The outermost reach of fascist radicalization was the Nazi murder of the Jews. No mere prose can do justice to the Holocaust, but the most convincing accounts have two qualities. For one, they take into account not only Hitler's obsessive hatred of Jews but also the thousands of subordinates whose participation in the increasingly harsh actions against them that made the mechanism function. Without them, Hitler's murderous fantasy would have remained only a fantasy.

The other quality is the recognition that the Holocaust developed step by step, from lesser acts to more heinous ones.[35] Most scholars accept today that the Nazi assault upon the Jews developed incrementally. It grew neither entirely out of the disorderly local violence of a popular pogrom, nor entirely from the imposition from above of a murderous state policy. Both impulses ratcheted each other up in an ascending spiral, in a way appropriate to a "dual state." Local eruptions of vigilantism by party militants were encouraged by the language of Nazi leaders and the climate of toleration for violence they established. The Nazi state, in turn, kept channeling the undisciplined initiatives of party militants into official policies applied in an orderly fashion.

The first phase was segregation: marking the internal enemies, setting them apart from the nation, and suppressing their rights as citizens. This began in spring 1933 as street actions by party militants, the so-called revolution from below that followed immediately upon Hitler's assumption of office. The new regime tried to channel and control these chaotic incidents of marking and smashing Jewish shops with an official one-day boy-

cott on April 1, 1933. The Nuremberg laws of September 15, 1935, pro-
hibiting intermarriage and annulling Jewish citizenship elevated segregation into state policy.[36] A pause followed, partly motivated by the regime's
desire to present a positive face during the Berlin Olympics of 1936.

When street violence erupted again in November 1938 in the synagogue burnings and shop smashings of *Kristallnacht*, fanned by Goebbels,[37]
other Nazi authorities sought to channel this grassroots action into a more
orderly state policy of "Aryanizing" Jewish businesses. "I have had enough
of these demonstrations," Goering complained two days after *Kristallnacht*. "It is not the Jew they harm but me, as the final authority for coor-
dinating the German economy. . . . The insurance company will pay for
the damage, which does not even touch the Jew; and furthermore
the goods destroyed come from the consumer goods belonging to the
people. . . . We have not come together simply for more talk but to make
decisions . . . to eliminate the Jew from the German economy."[38] Segregation reached its climax with the marking of the Jewish population. First
in occupied Poland in late 1939 and then in the Reich in August 1941, all
Jews had to wear a yellow Star of David sewn to the chest of their external
garments. By this time, the next phase—expulsion—had already begun.

The policy of expulsion germinated in the mixture of challenge and
opportunity presented by the annexation of Austria in March 1938. This
increased the number of Jews in the Reich, and, at the same time, gave
the Nazis more freedom to deal harshly with them. The SS officer Adolf
Eichmann worked out in Vienna the system whereby wealthy Jews, terrorized by Nazi thugs, would pay well for exit permits, generating funds
that could be applied to the expulsion of the others.

German conquest of the western half of Poland in September 1939
brought further millions of Jews, and an even freer hand in dealing with
them. The murder of large numbers of the Polish and Jewish male elite by
special military units—the *Einsatzgruppen*—was an integral part of the
Polish campaign, but, for the Jewish population in general, expulsion
remained the ultimate aim.

Trouble arose, however, when individual Nazi satraps tried to expel
their Jews into territory governed by another. Many Nazi officials thought
of the Nazi-occupied area of former Poland as an ideal dumping ground
for Jews, but its governor, Hans Frank, wanted to make his territory a
"model colony" by expelling Polish Jews eastward. It was Frank who won
the race to Hitler's ear and stopped the expulsion of German Jews into
Poland.[39]

The situation was further complicated by Himmler's project to resettle some five hundred thousand ethnic Germans from eastern Europe and northern Italy on lands vacated by expelled Jews and Poles.[40] This "domino game" of interlocking population movements soon produced a "traffic jam" that some Nazi racial planners thought of relieving in spring and summer 1940 by sending European Jews to the French colony of Madagascar.[41]

The Nazis hoped that invading the Soviet Union in June 1941 would make expulsion easier again. Although the anticipated rapid conquest of Soviet territory would bring millions more Jews into Nazi hands, it would also open up the vast Russian hinterland into which to expel them. These hopes maintained expulsion as the official Nazi solution to the "Jewish Problem" until late in 1941.

Close studies of Nazi-occupied territories in Poland and the Soviet Union between September 1939 and late 1941, however, show surprising amounts of individual leeway and local variation among Nazi administrators in their treatment of Jews. Left to cope on their own with unexpectedly severe problems of security, supply, land tenure, and disease, they experimented with all sorts of local initiatives—ghettoization, forced labor, resettlements.[42] In the newly occupied Baltic States and eastern Poland some Nazi administrators crossed the line from killing Jewish men for "security" reasons to the mass murder of whole Jewish populations, including women and children, as early as August–September 1941, apparently on local initiative (confident, of course, of Berlin's approval).[43] Seen from this perspective, the famous meeting of high-level Nazi leaders under the chairmanship of Himmler's deputy Reinhard Heydrich on January 20, 1942 (the Wannsee Conference), looks more like further state coordination of local extermination initiatives than the initiation of a new policy from above.

Exactly when and why the old policy of expulsion, punctuated by the murder of many Jewish men for "security" reasons, gave way in Nazi-occupied eastern Europe to a new policy of total extermination of all Jews, including women and children, remains one of the most hotly debated issues in interpreting the Holocaust. It is not even certain whether we should focus on Hitler or on his underlings in the field. If we focus on Hitler, the absence of any trace of an explicit *Führer* order for the final stage of annihilation has caused trouble to the "intentionalists," probably unnecessarily. No serious scholar doubts Hitler's central responsibility.[44] The *Führer's* unswerving hatred of Jews was known to all, and he was briefed regularly on what was going on.[45] Local administrators knew he would "cover" their most extreme actions. It is likely that he issued some kind of verbal order in fall 1941 in response to the ongoing campaign against Soviet Russia: either in the euphoria of the first advance,[46] or, more likely, in rage as he failed to take Moscow before winter and achieve the Blitzkrieg victory upon which the whole operation depended.[47] A recent plausible theory locates Hitler's order in a secret speech to high party officials on December 12, 1941, in reaction to the entry of the United States into the war and its transformation into a truly worldwide conflict. Hitler would thus be fulfilling the threat he made in a speech on January 30, 1939—that if the war became worldwide, the Jews were to blame and would pay (Hitler believed Jews controlled American policy).[48]

If we shift our focus to the administrators in the field, we have seen how some of them had already crossed the line in late summer 1941 between the selective killing of adult males and the total extermination of the whole Jewish population. This would not have been possible without widespread, murderous Jew-hatred, one point on which Daniel Goldhagen's celebrated and controversial *Hitler's Willing Executioners* is right. But the existence of widespread, murderous Jew-hatred does not tell us why the line was crossed in certain places at certain times, and not others. The most convincing studies present a dynamic process of "cumulative radicalization" in which problems magnify, pressures build, inhibitions fall away, and legitimating arguments are found.

Two kinds of development help explain how a readiness built up to kill all Jews, including women and children. One is a series of "dress rehearsals" that served to lower inhibitions and provided trained personnel hardened for anything. First came the euthanasia of incurably ill and insane Germans, begun on the day when World War II began. Nazi eugenics theory had long provided a racial justification for getting rid of "inferior" persons. War provided a broader justification for reducing the drain of "useless mouths" on scarce resources. The "T-4" program killed more than seventy thousand people between September 1939 and 1941, when, in response to protests from the victims' families and Catholic clergy, the matter was left to local authorities.[49] Some of the experts trained in this program were subsequently transferred to the occupied east, where they applied their mass killing techniques to Jews. This time, there was less opposition.

The second "dress rehearsal" was the work of the *Einsatzgruppen*, the intervention squads specially charged with executing the political and cultural elite of invaded countries. In the Polish campaign of September 1939 they helped wipe out the Polish intelligentsia and high civil service, evoking some opposition within the military command. In the Soviet campaign the *Einsatzgruppen* received the notorious "Commissar Order" to kill all Communist Party cadres as well as the Jewish leadership (seen as identical in Nazi eyes), along with Gypsies. This time the army raised no objections.[50] The *Einsatzgruppen* subsequently played a major role, though they were far from alone, in the mass killings of Jewish women and children that began in some occupied areas in fall 1941.

A third "dress rehearsal" was the intentional death of millions of Soviet prisoners of war. It was on six hundred of them that the Nazi occupation authorities first tested the mass killing potential of the commercial insecticide Zyklon-B at Auschwitz on September 3, 1941.[51] Most Soviet prisoners of war, however, were simply worked or starved to death.

The second category of developments that helped prepare a "willingness to murder" consisted of blockages, emergencies, and crises that made the Jews become a seemingly unbearable burden to the administrators of conquered territories. A major blockage was the failure to capture Moscow that choked off the anticipated expulsion of all the Jews of conquered eastern Europe far into the Soviet interior. A major emergency was shortages of food supplies for the German invasion force. German military planners had chosen to feed the invasion force with the resources of the invaded areas, in full knowledge that this meant starvation for local populations. When local supplies fell below expectations, the search for "useless mouths" began. In the twisted mentality of the Nazi administrators, Jews and Gypsies also posed a security threat to German forces. Another emergency was created by the arrival of trainloads of ethnic Germans awaiting resettlement, for whom space had to be made available.

Faced with these accumulating problems, Nazi administrators developed a series of "intermediary solutions."[52] One was ghettos, but these proved to be incubators for disease (an obsession with the cleanly Nazis), and a drain on the budget. The attempt to make the ghettos work for German war production yielded little except another category of useless mouths: those incapable of work. Another "intermediary solution" was the stillborn plan, already mentioned, to settle European Jews en masse in some remote area such as Madagascar, East Africa, or the Russian hinterland. The failure of all the "intermediary solutions" helped open the way for a "final solution": extermination.

The first mass executions were accomplished by gunfire, a process that was slow, messy, and psychologically stressful for the killers (though many became inured to it). The search for more-efficient killing techniques led to the development of specially prepared vans, *Gaswagen*, into which exhaust fumes were piped, an idea derived from the trailers in which the mentally ill had been gassed by carbon monoxide in Poland in 1940. In fall 1941 thirty such vans were constructed for the wholesale liquidation of Jewish populations in occupied Russia.[53] Even faster technology was adopted in spring 1942 when fixed killing installations were constructed at six camps on former Polish territory. Most of these continued to use carbon monoxide, but some, notably Auschwitz, used the quicker and more easily handled Zyklon-B. The death factories eventually accounted for 60 percent of the Jews murdered by the Nazis during World War II.

The new centers for industrialized mass killing were constructed outside the reach of the German normative state and of German law. Two (Auschwitz and Chelmno) were in territory annexed from Poland in 1939, and the other four (Treblinka, Sobibor, Majdanek, and Belzec) were located in the former Polish lands now known as the "*Generalgouvernement.*"[54] There military authorities shared power with civilian officials largely composed of party militants.

In captured areas of Poland and the Soviet Union, parallel organizations like the party's agency that seized land for redistribution to German peasants (the *Rasse- und Siedlungshauptamt*) had more freedom than in the Reich. The SS set up its own military-economic empire there where the normative state played hardly any role at all.[55] In that no-man's-land, both bureaucratic regularity and moral principles were easily set aside, and the needs of the master race became the only criteria for action. The traditional contempt of German nationalists for Slavic *Untermenschen* aggravated the permissive climate. In that nameless nonstate, Nazi zealots had free rein to fulfill their wildest fantasies of racial purification without interference from a distant normative state.

The fragmented Nazi administrative system left the radicals unaccountable, and able to enact their darkest impulses. The *Führer*, standing above and outside the state, was ready to reward initiative in the jungle of Nazi administration of the eastern occupied territories.

We can dismiss any notion that the Nazi regime murdered Jews in order to gratify German public opinion. It took elaborate precautions to hide these actions from the German people and from foreign observers. In official documents the responsible authorities referred to the killings

THE ANATOMY OF FASCISM

with euphemisms like *Sonderbehandlung* ("special handling"), and under-
took major operations to eliminate all traces of them, at a time when men
and materiel could hardly be spared from the fighting.[56] At the same time,
there was no particular effort to keep the secret from German troops on
the eastern front, many of whom were regularly assigned to participate.
Some soldiers and officials photographed the mass executions and sent
pictures home to their families and girlfriends.[57] Many thousands of soldiers, civil administrators, and technicians stationed in the eastern occupied territories were eyewitnesses to mass killings. Many more thousands
heard about them from participants. The knowledge inside Germany that
dreadful things were being done to Jews in the east was "fairly widespread."[58] As long as disorderly destruction such as the shop-front smashings, beatings, and murders of *Kristallnacht* did not take place under their
windows, most of them let distance, indifference, fear of denunciation,
and their own sufferings under Allied bombing stifle any objections.

In the end, radicalized Nazism lost even its nationalist moorings. As
he prepared to commit suicide in his Berlin bunker in April 1945, Hitler
wanted to pull the German nation down with him in a final frenzy. This
was partly a sign of his character—a compromise peace was as unthinkable for Hitler as it was for the Allies. But it also had a basis within the
nature of the regime: not to push forward was to perish. Anything was better than softness.[59]

Italian Radicalization: Internal Order, Ethiopia, Salò

Nazi Germany in its final paroxysm is the only authentic example so far of
the ultimate stage of fascist radicalization. Italian Fascism, too, displayed
some signs of the forces that drive all fascisms toward the extreme.

We saw earlier in this chapter how Mussolini was torn between the
radical wishes of the *ras* and the *squadristi* and his own preference for
order and state predominance over the party. But he could not escape
from his self-promoted image as activist hero, and his language remained
colored with revolutionary imagery. He could not ignore entirely his followers' need for fulfillment and the public's expectation of dramatic
achievements that he had himself encouraged.

In the 1930s, perhaps with the already mentioned aim of rejuvenat-
ing his paunchy Blackshirts, perhaps also under pressure to divert his people's attention from Italy's mediocre economic performance during the

Depression, Mussolini embarked on a farther-reaching period of radicalization. After 1930 he had already adopted a more aggressive tone in foreign policy, calling for rearmament and predicting that "the twentieth century will be the century of Fascism."[60] He took back into his own hands in 1932 the Ministry of Foreign Affairs, and in 1933 the Ministries of War, the Navy, and Air. By 1934 he was secretly preparing a military operation in Ethiopia. Taking as a pretext a minor skirmish in December 1934 at Wal-wal, a remote desert waterhole near the unmarked frontier between Ethiopia and Italian Somaliland (now Eritrea), Mussolini launched his armies against Ethiopia on October 3, 1935.

After a one-sided campaign that required more Italian effort than foreseen, Mussolini was able to proclaim victory and declare King Victor Emmanuel III emperor of Ethiopia on May 9, 1936. From the balcony of his offices in the Palazzo Venezia in Rome, Mussolini engaged in a triumphal dialogue with the excited crowd:

> Officers, non-commissioned officers, soldiers of all the armed forces of the State in Africa and Italy, Blackshirts of the Revolution, Italian men and women in the fatherland and throughout the world, listen!
>
> Our gleaming sword has cut all the knots, and the African victory will remain in the history of the fatherland complete and pure, a victory such as the legionaries who have fallen and those who have survived dreamed of and willed. . . .
>
> The Italian people has created the empire with its blood. It will fertilize it with its labor and defend it with its arms against anybody whomsoever. Will you be worthy of it?
>
> Crowd: Yes![61]

The Ethiopian War gave the Fascist Party a "new impulse."[62] At home, it was the occasion for a masterly bit of nationalist theater: the collection of gold wedding rings from the women of Italy, from Queen Elena on down, to help pay for the campaign. Officially it was the Fascist Militia (MVSN) that went to fight in Ethiopia. The party presence was strong in the conquered territory. The party Federale shared power with the prefect and the army commander, and attempted to regiment both the settler population and young Ethiopians through Fascist youth and leisure organizations. Colonial rule even permitted a revival of *squadrismo*, long shut down at home. In 1937, after an assassination attempt on General Graziani, governor-general and viceroy, party activists terrorized the inhabitants of Addis Ababa for three days and killed hundreds of them.[63]

The excitement and effort of war were accompanied by a "cultural revolution" and a "totalitarian leap" *(svolta totalitaria)* at home.[64] Another activist party secretary, Achille Starace (1931–39), led a campaign to shape the Fascist "new man" by instituting "Fascist customs," "Fascist language," and racial legislation. The "reform of custom" replaced the deferential and formal way of saying "you" in the third person *("lei")*, used by proper bourgeois, by the more familiar and comradely second person *("tu"* in the singular, *"voi"* in the plural).[65] The Fascist salute replaced the bourgeois handshake. Civil servants were dressed in uniform, and the army began to march with the exaggerated high step that the regime called *passo romano* to make clear that it was not copied from the Nazi goose step.

The most striking step in the Fascist radicalization of the 1930s was discriminatory legislation against Jews. In July 1938, a "Manifesto of Fascist Racism" announced the new policy, and it was soon followed up by laws in September and November that forbade racial intermarriage, along the lines of the Nazi Nuremberg laws, and excluded Jews from government service and the professions. One out of twelve university professors had to abandon their chairs. The Nobel Prize–winnning physicist Enrico Fermi, not Jewish himself, left voluntarily for the United States because he was deprived of many of his research associates.

The Fascists are usually assumed to have copied Nazi racial laws to please Hitler during the period of Italian foreign policy alignment with the Axis.[66] Italy had been largely devoid of anti-Semitism, and its small and ancient Jewish community had been exceptionally well integrated. As we saw in chapter 1, Mussolini had had Jewish backers and even close associates in the early days. In 1933 he was listed by American Jewish publishers among the world's "twelve greatest Christian champions" of the Jews.[67]

On closer inspection, one can find Italian stems upon which a native anti-Semitism could be grafted. Policies of racial discrimination had already become acceptable to Italians in the colonies. First in Libya and then in Ethiopia, the Italian military adopted tactics of separating nomads from their animals and from food and water. Their mass internment seemed to prefigure their elimination. In Ethiopia, laws forbade racial mixing (though they were widely flaunted). Angelo Del Boca can even use the word *apartheid* for what Fascism tried to institute in Ethiopia.[68]

Another stem was the ambiguity of Catholic attitudes about Jews. To its credit, Catholic tradition was hostile to biological racism—the Church insisted, for example, that the sacrament of baptism prevented a convert from being henceforth considered Jewish, regardless of who his or her parents had been. Pope Pius XI had been trying to decide whether to issue an encyclical denouncing Nazi biological racism when he died in 1939. On the other hand, the language of the mass for Good Friday identified the Jews as the "deicide people" who had killed Christ. Church publications continued for a shockingly long time to express the coarsest forms of anti-Semitism, including accrediting the ancient legend of Jewish ritual murder.[69] The Church raised no objection to nonbiological forms of discrimination against Jews in Catholic countries, such as quotas in universities and limitations on economic activity.[70] As for secular Fascists, there had always been anti-Semites among them. Some of them, like Telesio Interlandi, were given prominent space in the party press from the middle 1930s on, even before the formation of the Axis.

It is true that the new legislation was generally unpopular, and that in Italian-occupied Croatia and southeastern France Italian authorities actually protected Jews.[71] When the Germans began deporting Jews from Italy in 1943, few Italians joined in that undertaking. There had been enough support for the 1938 legislation, however, for it to be applied quite firmly. After 1938, Mussolini's regime subsided once more into business as usual. When war began in September 1939, he told Hitler he was not ready. When he finally entered World War II, at the last possible moment, it brought Mussolini neither the spoils of victory nor the heightened popular enthusiasm he had hoped for.[72] Mussolini's "parallel war" after June 1940, intended to assert equality with Hitler, led only to defeats and humiliations that ended Fascism's "privileged relation with history" and snapped the last links of affection between the Italian people and the Duce.

The Germans, too, received with gloom the news that World War II had begun. Hitler's successes, however, charged them with zeal. They made war longer and with more determination in 1939–45, despite greater civilian suffering, than in 1914–18. In Italy, by contrast, the balloon of fascist excitement burst quickly. In retrospect, Fascist mobilization turned out to be more fragile than democratic mobilization. Churchill could move the British people by an honest promise of nothing but blood, sweat, toil, and tears.

Mussolini's final days offer another case of radicalization, though it was geographically limited to northern Italy. When it became clear that Italy's participation in World War II on Hitler's side was turning into a disaster, parts of the Establishment—senior military officers, advisors to the king, even some dissident fascists—wanted to get rid of Mussolini and make a separate peace with the Allies. Soon after the Allies landed in Sicily on July 10, 1943, in the predawn hours of July 25, the Fascist Grand Council voted a resolution to restore full authority to the king. The same afternoon, Victor Emmanuel dismissed the deflated *Duce* from office and had him arrested.

That ignominious arrest should have put an end to Mussolini's charisma. On September 12, however, a daring German commando raid led by SS captain Otto Skorzeny liberated him from his captivity atop the Gran Sasso ski resort, east of Rome. Hitler reinstated the *Duce* as the dictator of a Fascist republic whose capital was at Salò, on Lake Garda, handy to the main road to Germany via the Brenner Pass. The Italian Social Republic was never more than a German puppet, and deserves little more than a footnote in history.[73] It interests us here, however, for, freed from the need to mollify the Church, the king, and the financial and industrial leadership of Italy, the Salò republic reverted to the radical impulses of fascism's first days.

At Salò, Mussolini surrounded himself with some remaining party fanatics and a few pro-Nazi officers. They played the one card left to them: a populist national socialism. The new Fascist Republican Party program of November 1943 called for the "socialization" of those sectors of the economy necessary for self-sufficiency (energy, raw materials, indispensable services), and leaving in private hands only property that was the fruit of personal effort and savings. The public sector was to be run by management committees in which the workers would have a voice. Unproductive or uncultivated farms would be taken over by their hired hands. Roman Catholicism remained the religion of the Fascist republic, but many of the new leaders were irreligious. The new republic promised to govern through an assembly which would be chosen by unions, professional groups, and soldiers. The Italian Social Republic at Salò never had the power to put these measures into effect, however. Its radicalization's main effect was to make its police and armed squads murderous in the Italian civil war of 1944–45.

The Salò republic also tried to remedy the slackness that had overcome established Fascism in Italy. It raised new armed forces of committed Fascists to carry on the war against the Allies. These consisted mainly of volunteer groups like Prince Borghese's Tenth Torpedo Boat Squadron, which fought on dry land, and mostly against the Resistance.[74] The agents of the Salò republic also tried to remedy most Italians' refusal to take anti-Semitism seriously. It was at this point that Fascist activists rounded up Jews and put them in camps where the Nazis had easy access to them. This is how the chemist (and later celebrated author) Primo Levi was taken prisoner in December 1943, to end up in Auschwitz.[75]

The Salò republic sought revenge against the traitors to Mussolini within Fascism. The republic had its hands on only a few members of the Fascist Grand Council who had voted against Mussolini on July 25, but it executed five of them—including Mussolini's own son-in-law Count Ciano, the Fascist regime's former foreign minister—at Verona in January 1944. Even so, all the blood shed by the republic of Salò was only a few drops compared to that spilled by Nazism's final days.

As the Allied armies approached in April 1945, Mussolini's few remaining supporters melted away. Italian Partisans found him on April 28 hidden in the back of a German army truck withdrawing up the western shore of Lake Como, and killed him along with his steadfast young mistress, Clara Petacci, and several Fascist notables. They strung up the bodies in a Milan filling station, after a bitter crowd had mutilated the *Duce*'s corpse. Only a generation later would Mussolini's remains, restored to the family in 1957 and buried in his home village of Predappio, become an object of pilgrimage.[76]

Final Thoughts

The radicalization stage shows us fascism at its most distinctive. While any regime can radicalize, the depth and force of the fascist impulse to unleash destructive violence, even to the point of self-destruction, sets it apart.

At this ultimate stage, comparison is hardly possible: only one fascist regime really reached it. A tempting candidate for comparison has been Stalin's radicalization of the Soviet dictatorship. The Nazi and Soviet cases shared a rejection of the state of law and due process; both subordinated them to the imperatives of History. In other respects, however, fascist radicalization was not identical to the Stalinist form. Fascism idealized violence in a distinctive way, as a virtue proper to a master race. And while the agents of Stalin's purges knew that they would be covered by the dictator, the Soviet system lacked Nazism's ingrained competition between party parallel organizations and established elites for the leader's favor.

Expansionist war lies at the heart of radicalization. Insofar as Fascist Italy radicalized, it did so most fully in conquered East Africa and in the final paroxysm of the Italian campaign. The Nazi regime reached the outer limits of radicalization with its war of extermination against the Soviet Union. In that specially charged situation Nazi officials felt free to take more violent action than they had done in the western campaigns of 1940, first against the enemies of the regime, then against fascism's conservative allies, and eventually against the German people themselves, in an ecstasy of terminal destruction.[77]

Whereas in traditional authoritarian war regimes, the army tends to extend its control, as it did in the German Reich during 1917–18 and in Franco's Spain, the German army lost control of occupation policy in the east after 1941, as we have seen, to the Nazi Party's parallel organizations.[78] Party radicals felt free to express their hatreds and obsessions in ways that were foreign to the traditions of the state services. The issue here is not simply one of moral sensitivity; some officers and civil servants were appalled by SS actions in the conquered territories, while others went along because of group solidarity or because they had become hardened.[79] It was to some degree an issue of turf. It would be unthinkable for a traditional military dictatorship to tolerate the incursions of amateurish party militias into military spheres that Hitler—and even, in Ethiopia, Mussolini—permitted.

Hannah Arendt's *Origins of Totalitarianism*, so problematical for the earlier stages of fascism, fits here. For here we enter a realm where the calculations of interest that arguably governed the behavior of both the Nazis and their allies under more ordinary circumstances in the exercise of power no longer determined policy. At this ultimate stage an obsessed minority is able to carry out its most passionate hatreds implacably and to the ultimate limit of human experience.

Liberation from constraints permitted a hard core of the movement's fanatics to regain the upper hand over their bourgeois allies and carry out some of the initial radical projects. At the outposts of empire, fascism recovered the face-to-face violence of the early days of *squadrismo* and SA street brawling. One must resist the temptation at this final stage to revert to a highly personalized way of looking at the exercise of power in fascist regimes, with its discredited notions of hoodlums kidnapping the state. The Nazi regime was able to pursue the war with ever mounting intensity only with the continued complicity of the state services and large sectors of the socially powerful.

Fascist radicalization, finally, cannot be understood as a rational way to persuade a people to give their all to a war effort. It led Nazi Germany into a runaway spiral that ultimately prevented rational war making, as vital resources were diverted from military operations to the murder of the Jews. Finally radicalization denies even the nation that is supposed to be at fascism's heart. At the end, fanatical fascists prefer to destroy everything in a final paroxysm, even their own country, rather than admit defeat.

Prolonged fascist radicalization over a very long period has never been witnessed. It is even hard to imagine. Can one suppose that even Hitler could keep up the tension into old age? Arranging the succession to a senescent fascist leader is another intriguing but, so far, hypothetical problem.[80] The more normal form of succession to a fascist regime is likely to be decay into a traditional authoritarianism. At that point, there can be progressive liberalization as in post-Franco Spain or perhaps revolution (as in post-Salazar Portugal). But orderly succession is clearly far more of a problem with fascism than with other forms of rule, even communism. Fascism is, in the last analysis, destabilizing. In the long run, therefore, it was not really a solution to the problems of frightened conservatives or liberals.

The final outcome was that the Italian and German fascist regimes drove themselves off a cliff in their quest for ever headier successes. Mussolini had to take his fatal step into war in June 1940 because Fascist absence from Hitler's victory over France might well fatally loosen his grip on his people. Hitler never stopped imagining further conquests—India, the Americas—until he committed suicide in his besieged bunker in Berlin on April 30, 1945. The fascisms we know seem doomed to destroy themselves in their headlong, obsessive rush to fulfill the "privileged relation with history" they promised their people.

CHAPTER 7

Other Times, Other Places

Is Fascism Still Possible?

In chapter 2, I traced the early boundary of fascism easily enough at the moment when mass democracy was entering into full operation and encountering its first heavy weather. Although precursors can be identified before 1914 (we discussed some in chapter 2), adequate space was not available for fascism until after World War I and the Bolshevik Revolution. Fascist movements could first reach full development only in the outwash from those two tidal waves.

The outer time limit to fascism is harder to locate. Is fascism over? Is a Fourth Reich or some equivalent in the offing? More modestly, are there conditions under which some kind of neofascism might become a sufficiently powerful player in a political system to influence policy? There is no more insistent or haunting question posed to a world that still aches from wounds that fascisms inflicted on it during 1922–45.

Important scholars have argued that the fascist period ended in 1945. In 1963 the German philosopher Ernst Nolte wrote in a celebrated book about "fascism in its era" that although fascism still existed after 1945 it had been stripped of real significance.[1] Many have agreed with him that fascism was a product of a particular and unique crisis growing out of the cultural pessimism of the 1890s, the turmoil of the first "nationalization of the masses,"[2] the strains of World War I, and the incapacity of liberal Democratic regimes to cope with that war's aftermath, and in particular with the spread of the Bolshevik Revolution.

The greatest obstacle to the revival of classical fascism after 1945 was the repugnance it had come to inspire. Hitler aroused nausea as gruesome pictures of the liberated camps were released. Mussolini inspired derision. Devastated landscapes testified to the failure of both of them. Hitler's charred body in the ruins of his Berlin bunker and Mussolini's corpse strung up by the heels in a seedy Milan filling station marked the extinction by squalor of their charisma.[3]

A revival of fascism faced additional obstacles after 1945: the increasing prosperity and seemingly irreversible globalization of the world economy, the triumph of individualistic consumerism,[4] the declining availability of war as an instrument of national policy for large nations in the nuclear age, the diminishing credibility of a revolutionary threat. All these postwar developments have suggested to many that fascism as it flourished in Europe between the two world wars could not exist after 1945, at least not in the same form.[5]

The end of fascism was opened to doubt in the 1990s by a series of sobering developments: ethnic cleansing in the Balkans; the sharpening of exclusionary nationalisms in postcommunist eastern Europe; spreading "skinhead" violence against immigrants in Britain, Germany, Scandinavia, and Italy; the first participation of a neofascist party in a European government in 1994, when the Italian Alleanza Nazionale, direct descendant of the principal Italian neofascist party, the Movimento Sociale Italiano (MSI), joined the first government of Silvio Berlusconi;[6] the entry of Jörg Haider's Freiheitspartei (Freedom Party), with its winks of approval at Nazi veterans, into the Austrian government in February 2000; the astonishing arrival of the leader of the French far Right, Jean-Marie Le Pen, in second place in the first round of the French presidential elections in May 2002; and the meteoric rise of an anti-immigrant but nonconformist outsider, Pym Fortuyn, in the Netherlands in the same month. Finally, a whole universe of fragmented radical Right "grouplets" proliferated, keeping alive a great variety of far Right themes and practices.[7]

Whether or not one believes that fascism can recur depends, of course, on one's understanding of fascism. Those who warn that fascism is returning tend to present it rather loosely as overtly violent racism and nationalism.[8] The author who announced most categorically the death of fascism in 1945 argues that its defining elements—unlimited particular sovereignty, a relish for war, and a society based on violent exclusion— simply have no place in the complex, interdependent post–World War II world.[9] The commonest position is that although fascists are still around, the conditions of interwar Europe that permitted them to found major movements and even take power no longer exist.[10]

The issue of fascism since 1945 is further clouded by polemical name-calling. The far Right in Europe after 1945 is loudly and regularly accused of reviving fascism; its leaders deny the charges no less adamantly. The postwar movements and parties themselves have been no less broad than interwar fascisms, capable of bringing authentic admirers of Mussolini and Hitler into the same tent with one-issue voters and floating protesters. Their leaders have become adept at presenting a moderate face to the general public while privately welcoming outright fascist sympathizers with coded words about accepting one's history, restoring national pride, or recognizing the valor of combatants on all sides.

The inoculation of most Europeans against the original fascism by its public shaming in 1945 is inherently temporary. The taboos of 1945 have inevitably faded with the disappearance of the eyewitness generation. In any event, a fascism of the future—an emergency response to some still unimagined crisis—need not resemble classical fascism perfectly in its outward signs and symbols. Some future movement that would "give up free institutions"[11] in order to perform the same functions of mass mobilization for the reunification, purification, and regeneration of some troubled group would undoubtedly call itself something else and draw on fresh symbols. That would not make it any less dangerous.

For example, while a new fascism would necessarily diabolize some enemy, both internal and external, the enemy would not necessarily be Jews. An authentically popular American fascism would be pious, antiblack, and, since September 11, 2001, anti-Islamic as well; in western Europe, secular and, these days, more likely anti-Islamic than anti-Semitic; in Russia and eastern Europe, religious, anti-Semitic, Slavophile, and anti-Western. New fascisms would probably prefer the mainstream patriotic dress of their own place and time to alien swastikas or *fasces*. The British moralist George Orwell noted in the 1930s that an authentic British fascism would come reassuringly clad in sober English dress.[12] There is no sartorial litmus test for fascism.

The stages around which I have structured this book can offer further help with deciding whether fascism is still possible. It is relatively easy to admit the widespread continuation of Stage One—the founding stage— of radical Right movements with some explicit or implicit link to fascism. Examples have existed since World War II in every industrial, urbanized society with mass politics. Stage Two, however, where such movements become rooted in political systems as significant players and the bearers of important interests, imposes a much more stringent historical test. The test does not require us, however, to find exact replicas of the rhetoric, the programs, or the aesthetic preferences of the first fascist movements of the 1920s. The historic fascisms were shaped by the political space into which they grew, and by the alliances that were essential for growth into Stages Two or Three, and new versions will be similarly affected. Carbon copies of classical fascism have usually seemed too exotic or too shocking since 1945 to win allies. The skinheads, for example, would become functional equivalents of Hitler's SA and Mussolini's *squadristi* only if they aroused support instead of revulsion. If important elements of the conservative elite begin to cultivate or even tolerate them as weapons against some internal enemy, such as immigrants, we are approaching Stage Two.

By every evidence, Stage Two has been reached since 1945, if at all, at least outside the areas once controlled by the Soviet Union, only by radical Right movements and parties that have taken pains to "normalize" themselves into outwardly moderate parties distinguishable from the center Right only by their tolerance for some awkward friends and occasional verbal excesses. In the unstable new world created by the demise of Soviet communism, however, movements abound that sound all too much like fascism. If we understand the revival of an updated fascism as the appearance of some functional equivalent and not as an exact repetition, recurrence is possible. But we must understand it by an intelligent comparison of how it works and not by superficial attention to external symbols.

Western Europe is the area with the strongest fascist legacy since 1945.

Western Europe since 1945

Even after Nazism and Fascism had been humiliated and exposed as odious in 1945, some of their followers kept the faith. Unreconstructed former Nazis and fascists created legacy movements in every European country for a generation after World War II.

Germany naturally raised the most concern.[13] Soon after the Allied occupation began, a survey of opinion in the American zone reported that 15–18 percent of the population remained committed to Nazism. Those figures dropped sharply, however, to about 3 percent in the early 1950s.[14] The ranks of potential neo-Nazis were swollen by over ten million refugees of German national origin expelled in 1945 from central Europe into what would become the Federal Republic of Germany (West Germany). Under those conditions, it was remarkable how weak the radical Right remained after political life revived in the Federal Republic in the late 1940s.

The West German radical Right was further weakened by division. The largest radical Right party of the founding years of the Federal Republic, the Socialist Reich Party (Sozialistische Reichspartei, SRP), gained 11 percent of the popular vote in Lower Saxony, one of the ten federal states, in 1951, but was banned in 1952 for being too overtly neo-Nazi. Its main surviving rival, the German Reich Party (Deutsche Reichspartei, DRP), received only about 1 percent of the vote for most of the 1950s as West Germany prospered under conservative chancellor Konrad Adenauer. The DRP's one momentary success came in provincial elections in Rhineland Palatinate in 1959 when it just passed the 5 percent minimum needed to enter a German provincial *(Land)* parliament for the first and only time.

When DRP leaders and other radical Right groups combined to form the National Democratic Party (Nationaldemokratische Partei Deutschlands, NPD) in 1964, this new formation was soon buoyed by the backlash to student radicalism, to West Germany's first serious economic downturn, in 1966–67, and to the wider space opened up on the right when the Christian Democrats brought the Social Democrats into a "Great Coalition" government in 1966. But although the NPD attained the necessary threshold of 5 percent in some local elections and entered seven of the ten state parliaments during the troubled years of 1966–68, it never reached the 5 percent minimum in federal elections required to form a national parliamentary group. It came closest in 1969, with 4.3 percent. Following a low ebb in the 1970s, radical Right activity increased again in the 1980s for reasons that will be discussed below. A new far Right formation, the Republican Party, reached 7.5 percent in a municipal election in Berlin in 1989, but thereafter slipped to 2 percent and below in national elections.

The Italian Movimento Sociale Italiano (MSI) had a more substantial existence as Mussolini's sole direct heir. It was founded in 1946 by Giorgio Almirante, who had been editorial secretary of the anti-Semitic review *La difesa della razza* after 1938 and chief of staff to the minister of propaganda in Mussolini's Italian Social Republic at Salò in 1943–45. After a feeble 1.9 percent of the vote in 1948, the MSI averaged 4–5 percent in national elections thereafter and reached a peak of 8.7 percent in 1972, benefitting from a merger with monarchists and a backlash against the "hot autumn" of 1969. Most of the time it was a distant fourth among Italian parties.

The MSI earned its best scores following "red scares": in 1972 it tied neck and neck with the socialists for third place among national parties with 2.8 million votes, and in 1983 its total vote reached nearly as high again after the Christian Democrats accepted communist votes in 1979 in an "opening to the left" that they hoped would bolster their increasingly slender majorities. It remained in political isolation, however. When the weak government of Fernando Tambroni counted MSI votes to complete its majority in 1960, veterans of the anti-Fascist Resistance demonstrated until Tambroni resigned. No mainstream Italian politician dared for thirty years after that to break the MSI's quarantine.

The MSI drew best in the south, where memories of fascist public works were positive and where the population had not experienced the civil war of 1944–45 in the north between the Resistance and the Salò republic. Alessandra Mussolini, the *Duce's* granddaughter as well as a medical school graduate, sometime film actress, and pornography pinup star, represented Naples in parliament after 1992 as an MSI deputy. As a candidate for mayor of Naples in 1993 she won 43 percent of the vote. Outside the south, the MSI did well among alienated young males everywhere except in the north, where a regional separatist movement— Umberto Bossi's Lega Nord[15]—occupied the far Right terrain. MSI leader Gianfranco Fini won 47 percent of the vote for mayor of Rome in 1993.[16]

Legacy neofascism was not limited to Germany and Italy. Britain and France, victorious but exhausted after World War II, endured the humiliation of losing their empires and their status as Great Powers. To make matters worse, their final efforts to win more time for their empires entailed accepting massive immigration from Africa, south Asia, and the Caribbean. Although the radical Right had little electoral success in these two countries for thirty years after the war, it kept the racial issue before the public and succeeded in influencing national policy.

France emerged from World War II bitterly divided. The purged collaborators of Vichy France joined virulent anticommunists and those disillusioned by the weakness of the Fourth Republic (1945–58) to form a ready clientele for antisystem nationalist movements. The principal impetus for the radical Right in postwar France was seventeen years of unsuccessful colonial war, first in Indochina (1945–54) and especially in Algeria (1954–62). As the French republic floundered in its attempt to hold on to its colonies, the Jeune Nation movement (JN) called for its replacement by a corporatist and plebiscitary state freed of "stateless" (i.e., Jewish) elements and capable of all-out military effort. In the later phases of the Algerian War, the JN kept Paris on edge by setting off plastic bombs at the doors of leaders of the Left and by daubing city walls with its Celtic Cross symbol.

A second impetus was the bitterness of small shopkeepers and peasants who were losing out in the industrial and urban modernization of France in the 1950s. A southern stationery shop owner, Pierre Poujade, set up a mass movement in 1955 calling for tax cuts, the protection of small business against chain stores, and a cleanup of public life. Poujadism had more than a whiff of antiparliamentarism and xenophobia about it. In the parliamentary election of January 1956, the movement won about 2.5 million votes (12 percent)[17] and helped shake the Fourth Republic, which ended unmourned two years later with an army officers' revolt in Algeria.

The French loss of Algeria provoked the creation of an underground terrorist movement, the Secret Army (L'Organisation de l'Armée Secrète, OAS), devoted to destroying the "internal enemies" on the Left whom they accused of stabbing the French army in the back while it was defending the French empire from the communists. Following the suppression of the OAS, the far Right regrouped in a series of movements such as Occident and Ordre Nouveau that fought with communists and students in the streets. Backlash from the student rising of May 1968 gave them a second wind.

A million European settlers were hastily uprooted from Algeria and repatriated to France, even though not all were of French ancestry, plus many thousands of Algerians who had collaborated with the French and had to be rescued, such as supplementary policemen (harkis). The former threatened to fuel a powerful antidemocratic movement in France. The harkis's children, plus later immigrants, formed the core of a settled but only partially assimilated Muslim population in France that provoked the anti-immigrant feelings later exploited by the most successful French radical Right party, the Front National (FN). The FN, formed in 1972 in an effort to assemble under a single umbrella all the various components of the French far Right, electoral parties as well as street-fighting activists, began to win local elections in the 1980s.[18]

The British extreme Right also mobilized resentment against colonial immigration, starting in the 1950s with the White Defence League. Veterans of interwar fascism played leading roles in this and the National Socialist Movement, dissolved for paramilitary activity in the 1960s. They were supplanted in 1967 by the National Front, a blatantly racialist anti-immigrant formation. The British radical Right was much more openly extreme than most continental parties, and consequently had almost no electoral success. But it forced the traditional parties to take the immigrant issue seriously, and restrict entry into Britain for the populations of the former colonies.[19]

It could be expected that legacy neofascisms would diminish as Hitler's and Mussolini's generation, mostly born in the 1880s, and the generation formed by them, mostly born in the 1900s, died off. Unexpectedly, however, radical Right movements and parties entered a new period of growth in the 1980s and 1990s. While some children carried on their parents' cause,[20] new recruits voicing new grievances gave the European radical Right a renewed impetus. Something akin to fascism was far from dead in Europe as the twenty-first century opened.

A decade of transition began around 1973. Many first-generation postwar far Right parties, such as the NPD in Germany and the British National Front, declined during the 1970s, and the French Ordre Nouveau was dissolved in 1973. Fundamental social, economic, and cultural changes were underway, however, further exacerbated by the oil crisis and economic contraction that began in 1973. These changes were raising new issues and preparing a new public for fresh radical Right movements and parties that would enjoy greater success in the 1980s and 1990s than the legacy neofascisms had achieved in the three decades following the war.

One set of changes was an economic shift with profound social consequences. The decline of traditional smokestack industries was a long process, but it assumed crisis proportions after the first and second "oil shocks" of 1973 and 1979. Faced with competition from Asian "tigers" with cheaper labor costs, burdened with expensive welfare systems and short of increasingly costly energy supplies, Europe faced long-term structural unemployment for the first time since the 1930s.

This was no ordinary cyclical downturn. In what was now called "postindustrial society," the conditions for finding work had changed. More education was required for the service, communication, high technology, and entertainment industries that emerged as the most remunerative forms of work for high-cost economies in a global marketplace. This seismic shift in the job market tended to produce two-tier societies: the better-educated part of the population succeeded very well in the new economy, while those without the necessary training—including once-proud skilled artisans and industrial craftsmen—appeared doomed to permanent underclass status. To make matters worse, the traditional communities that had once supported these skilled artisans and industrial craftsmen—trade unions, Marxist parties, and proletarian neighborhoods—lost much of their power to defend and console after the 1970s. Some orphans of the new economy who might earlier have turned to communism rallied to the radical Right instead after the collapse of the Soviet Union completed the discredit of communism.[21]

The collapse of solidarity and security for many western European working people after the 1970s was compounded by the postwar flood of Third World immigrants into western Europe. When times were good, the immigrants were welcome to do the dirty jobs that the national labor force now spurned. When Europeans began to face long-term structural unemployment for the first time since the Great Depression, however, immigrants became unwelcome.

Moreover, European immigration had changed. Whereas earlier immigrants had come from southern or eastern Europe and differed only slightly from their new hosts (with the notable and significant exception of Jews from eastern Europe in the 1880s and the 1930s), the new immigrants came from former colonial territories: North and sub-Saharan Africa, the Caribbean, India, Pakistan, and Turkey. And whereas earlier immigrants (some Jews again excepted) had tended to assimilate quickly and disappear, the new immigrants often clung to visibly different customs and religions. Europeans had to learn to coexist with permanent African, Indian, and Islamic communities that flaunted their separate identities.

The immigrant threat was not only economic and social. The immigrants were seen increasingly as undermining national identity with their alien customs, languages, and religions. A global youth culture, mostly marketed by Americans and often associated with black performers, did to local cultural traditions what the global economy had done to local smokestack industry.

Anti-immigrant resentment was pay dirt for radical Right movements in western Europe after the 1970s. It was the main force behind the British National Front. The most successful of them—Jean-Marie Le Pen's Front National in France and Jörg Haider's Freiheitspartei in Austria—were almost entirely devoted to exploiting anti-immigrant fears, fighting multiculturalism and an alleged immigrant criminal propensity, and proposing the expulsion of the alien poor.

The most disturbing new component of the radical Right after the 1980s was the "skinhead" phenomenon. Disaffected, idle, and resentful youths developed a cult of action and violence expressed by shaved skulls, Nazi insignia, aggressive "oi" music,[22] and murderous assaults upon immigrants—especially Muslims and Africans—and gays. While the more mainstream elements of the new Right carefully avoided open reference to the symbols and paraphernalia of fascism, the skinheads reveled in them. Nazi emblems triumphed even in Italy, where homegrown Fascist precursors like the Salò militias were forgotten. In Germany a surge of arson, beatings, and murders peaked at 2,639 incidents in 1992.[23] The violence declined a bit in the following years, but in March 1994 the Lübeck synagogue was firebombed, and the Dresden synagogue in October 2000.[24]

Governments and mainstream parties coped badly with the new problems faced by western Europe after the 1970s. They could not solve unemployment, because the Keynesian job-creation measures that had worked during the postwar boom now triggered dangerous levels of inflation, and because governments felt unable to opt out of the emerging European and global marketplaces with their powerful competitive pressures. The state, the traditional source of support in difficult times, was losing part of its authority, whether to the European Union or to the global marketplace, forces beyond the control of ordinary European citizens. Welfare programs now came under serious strain, for tax revenues were falling just as the need was growing to pay increased benefits to the new unemployed. And should the welfare state also take care of foreigners?[25] An interlocking set of new enemies was emerging: globalization, foreigners, multiculturalism, environmental regulation, high taxes, and the incompetent politicians who could not cope with these challenges. A widening public disaffection for the political Establishment opened the way for an "antipolitics" that the extreme Right could satisfy better than the far Left after 1989. After the Marxist Left lost credibility as a plausible protest vehicle when the Soviet Union collapsed, the radical Right had no serious rivals as the mouthpiece for the angry "losers" of the new postindustrial, globalized, multiethnic Europe.[26]

These new opportunities permitted a new generation[27] of extreme Right movements to emerge in Europe in the 1980s, and then, in the 1990s, to move "from the margins to the mainstream."[28] Jean-Marie Le Pen's Front National was the first extreme Right party in Europe to find the appropriate formula for post-1970s conditions. The FN reached 11 percent of the vote in French municipal elections in 1983 and European elections in 1984, unprecedented for any extreme Right party in Europe since 1945. It climbed even further, to 14.4 percent, in the presidential elections of 1988.[29] And unlike some "flash" movements that surge and then quickly decline, the FN maintained or exceeded these levels for the next decade.

Le Pen's recipe for success was closely watched by fearful French democrats as well as by his emulators abroad. The FN focused intensely on the immigrant issue, and its ramifying related issues of employment, law and order, and cultural defense. It managed to bundle together a variety of constituencies and positioned itself to become a broad catch-all party of protest.[30] It refrained from appearing to threaten democracy directly.[31] When it won control of three important cities in southern France in 1995 and another in 1997, as well as 273 seats in regional legislatures in 1998,[32] it acquired a capacity to reward its militants with office and force mainstream parties to treat with it. While there seemed little likelihood of its winning a national majority, the FN forced mainstream conservative parties to adopt some of its positions in order to hold on to crucial voters. The FN's strategic leverage became so important in some southern and eastern localities that some conservatives with narrow margins allied with it in the local elections of 1995 and 2001 as the only way to defeat the Left.

These successes at bundling constituencies, gratifying the ambitious, and forcing mainstream politicians into alliances moved the FN firmly into the process of taking root—Stage Two. In December 1998, however, a quarrel between Le Pen and his heir apparent, Bruno Mégret, divided the movement and drove its vote back down below 10 percent. Despite this setback, Le Pen rode a groundswell of resentment against immigrants, street crime, and globalization back to a shocking second-place 17 percent in the first round of the presidential elections of April 2002. In the runoff with incumbent president Jacques Chirac, however, Le Pen was held to 19 percent by a groundswell of French revulsion.

Two other extreme Right parties—the Italian MSI and the Austrian Freedom Party—put Le Pen's lessons to such good use in the 1990s that they actually participated in national governments. The major element in their success was an available space opened up not only by the disrepute into which governing parties had fallen, but also by the absence in both Italy and Austria of a credible mainstream political opposition.

In Italy, the Christian Democrats (CD) had enjoyed uninterrupted rule since 1948. For forty years no serious alternative had presented itself to the Italian electorate. The communist-socialist split had so weakened the Left that all noncommunist opposition parties preferred to seek a share in CD hegemony rather than pursue the hopeless task of forming an alternate majority.

When the Christian Democrats and some of their smaller coalition partners became tarnished by scandal in the 1990s, no alternate majority existed among the disparate opposition parties. New personalities filled the void, claiming to be "nonparty outsiders." The most successful of these was the media tycoon Silvio Berlusconi, the richest man in Italy, who quickly mounted a new party named after a soccer cheer, Forza Italia.[33] Berlusconi put together a coalition with two other outsider movements: Umberto Bossi's separatist Northern League and the MSI (now calling itself the Alleanza Nazionale and proclaiming itself "postfascist"). Together they won the parliamentary election of 1994, having successfully filled the unoccupied niche of plausible alternative to the discredited Christian Democrats. The ex-MSI, with 13 percent of the vote, was rewarded with five ministerial portfolios. It was the first time that a party descended directly from fascism had participated in a European government since 1945. Berlusconi's Forza Italia won elections again in 2001, and this time the head of the Alleanza Nazionale, Gianfranco Fini, was vice-premier.

A similar opportunity opened up in Austria after twenty years in which the socialists and the People's Party (moderate centrist Catholics) parceled out offices and favors in a power-sharing arrangement that came to be known as the *Proporz*. Electors fed up with an immovable political monopoly had no place to turn except to Haider's Freedom Party, which succeeded brilliantly under its photogenic leader in offering the only noncommunist alternative to the *Proporz*. In elections on October 3, 1999, the Freedom Party won 27 percent of the national vote, second only to the Socialists' 33 percent, and received six out of twelve ministerial portfolios in a coalition government with the People's Party in February 2000.

The same mix of anti-immigrant feeling and frustration with conventional politics propelled the meteoric rise of a total outsider, the flamboyantly wealthy and openly gay Pym Fortuyn, to political prominence in the Netherlands in 2002. Fortuyn's views were really libertarian, though his vilification of European bureaucracy and Islamic immigrants (a mullah had called him lower than a pig for his homosexuality) tended to align him with the far Right. After he was assassinated by an animal-rights activist on May 6, 2002, his new party—the Pym Fortuyn List—still drew

17 percent of the votes from across the political spectrum in parliamentary elections a week later, and held ministries for three months in the new government.

By themselves, these raw electoral statistics tell us little about the second generation of far Right movements in Europe after 1980. We need to know what kind of movements and parties these were, and how they related to the European societies in which they operated. In other words, we need to ask about them the kinds of questions raised by Stage Two: Did any of them become bearers of important interests and grievances? Did significant spaces become available to them in the political system, and were any of them able to acquire the kinds of alliances and complicities among frightened elites that would make Stage Three, an approach to power, conceivable? A final question governs all the others: Does anything justify our calling these second-generation movements fascist or even neofascist, in the face of their vehement denials? An inverse relationship exists in contemporary western Europe between an overtly fascist "look" and succeeding at the ballot box.[34] So the leaders of the most successful extreme Right movements and parties have labored to distance themselves from the language and images of fascism.

The successful efforts of the Italian MSI to "normalize" itself make this point most eloquently. Until the death of Giorgio Almirante in 1988, the MSI proclaimed its loyalty to Mussolini's legacy. Almirante's successor, Gianfranco Fini, willing as late as 1994 to praise Mussolini as the greatest statesman of the century,[35] began to move his party toward the center space opened up by the collapse of Christian Democratic rule in the elections of 1992. In January 1994 the MSI changed its name to Alleanza Nazionale (AN). The AN's founding congress in 1995 proclaimed that Europe had entered a "postfascist" era in which the party members' unabashed Mussolinian nostalgia[36] had become simply irrelevant. Thus Fini could participate in the Berlusconi government after the elections of 1994 had ended nearly fifty years of Christian Democratic rule, and again in the second Berlusconi government (2001–). The diehard Mussolinians followed the unreconstructed neofascist Pino Rauti into a splinter movement, the MSI–Fiamma Tricolore, a secession that helped substantiate Fini's new moderate credentials.

Not all western European far Right movements followed the normalization strategy. Colin Jordan's National Socialist Movement in Britain, preferring doctrinal purity to a probably unattainable growth, made no effort to conceal its overt fascism. The later National Front in Britain was among the most overtly racialist and violently antisystem of any European radical Right party. The potential space for a normalized British far Right, always small, was further reduced in the 1980s when Margaret Thatcher turned the Conservative Party rightward. Even so, following episodes of racial violence in some Midlands cities in summer 2001, a successor party, the British National Party (BNP), drew up to 20 percent of the vote in Oldham and won three city council seats in Burnley, two depressed Lancashire industrial towns, in municipal elections in May 2002.

The temptations of normalization were greater in France, Italy, and Austria than in Britain and Belgium because there was more chance of success. Le Pen and Haider, the two most successful extreme Right leaders in western Europe, had more to gain than many others from professing "normalcy." They also had less distance to travel than Fini to become "normal," never having openly admitted any links with fascism.

It was little phrases that slipped out between the lines or at the microphone in private meetings, and the lineage of some of their supporters, that a watchful press seized upon to accuse Le Pen, Haider, and Fini of cryptofascism. Le Pen, who knew that his gruff manner formed part of his appeal, often made remarks readily interpreted as anti-Semitic. He was fined for belittling Hitler's murder of the Jews as a "detail of history" in a September 1987 television interview and again in a speech in Germany in 1996, and lost his eligibility for a year in 1997 for striking a female candidate in an election rally. Haider openly praised the full-employment policies of the Nazis (though no other aspects of Nazism), and he appeared at private rallies of SS veterans and told them that they were models for the young and had nothing to be ashamed of.

All of these radical Right parties were havens for veterans of Nazism and Fascism. The leader of the German Republikaner after 1983, Franz Schönhuber, was a former SS officer. He and his like did not want to reject potential recruits from among the old fascists and their sympathizers, but at the same time they wanted to extend their reach toward moderate conservatives, the formerly apolitical, or even fed-up socialists. Since the old fascist clientele had nowhere else to go, it could be satisfied by subliminal hints followed by the ritual public disavowals. For in order to move toward Stage Two in the France, Italy, or Austria of the 1990s, one must be firmly recentered on the moderate Right. (This had also been true in 1930s France, as shown by the success of La Rocque's more centrist tactics after 1936.)[37]

In the programs and statements of these parties one hears echoes of classical fascist themes: fears of decadence and decline; assertion of national and cultural identity; a threat by unassimilable foreigners to national identity and good social order; and the need for greater authority to deal with these problems. Even though some of the European radical Right parties have full authoritarian-nationalist programs (such as the Belgian Vlaams Blok's "seventy points" and Le Pen's "Three Hundred Measures for French Revival" of 1993), most of them are perceived as single-issue movements devoted to sending unwanted immigrants home and cracking down on immigrant delinquency, and that is why most of their voters chose them.

Other classical fascist themes, however, are missing from the programmatic statements of the most successful postwar European radical Right parties. The element most totally absent is classical fascism's attack on the liberty of the market and economic individualism, to be remedied by corporatism and regulated markets. In a continental Europe where state economic intervention is the norm, the radical Right has been largely committed to reducing it and letting the market decide.[38]

Another element of classical fascist programs mostly missing from the postwar European radical Right is a fundamental attack on democratic constitutions and the rule of law. None of the more sucessful European far Right parties now proposes to replace democracy by a single-party dictatorship. At most they advocate a stronger executive, less inhibited forces of order, and the replacement of stale traditional parties with a fresh, pure national movement. They leave to the skinheads open expressions of the beauty of violence and murderous racial hatred. The successful radical Right parties wish to avoid public association with them, although they may quietly share overlapping membership with some ultraright action squads and tolerate a certain amount of overheated language praising violent action among their student branches.[39]

No western European radical Right movement or party now proposes national expansion by war—a defining aim for Hitler and Mussolini. Indeed the advocates of border changes in postwar Europe have mostly been secessionist rather than expansionist, such as the Vlaams Blok in Belgium and (for a time) Umberto Bossi's secessionist Northern League (Lega Nord) in northern Italy. The principal exceptions have been the expansionist Balkan nationalisms that sought to create Greater Serbia, Greater Croatia, and Greater Albania.

Bilingual Belgium, whose northern Flemish-speaking population has long resented its relative poverty and subordinate status, spawned the most important secessionist far Right movement in continental western Europe. Flemish nationalists had already collaborated with the Nazi occupiers during 1940–44. Their remnants, embittered by a forceful purge in 1945, were ready after the war to support antisystem activism.[40] After a period of dormancy, Flemish nationalism emerged into political activity again in 1977, following the adoption of a federal system for Belgium (the Egmont Agreement) that did not go far enough to satisfy separatists. The Vlaams Blok combined Flemish separatism with violent anti-immigrant feeling and an "antipolitics" for all those alienated by the political establishment. It became in the 1990s one of the most successful radical Right parties in western Europe. In the national elections of 1991, it surpassed 10 percent of the national vote, and won 25.5 percent in Antwerp, the largest Flemish-speaking city in Belgium. In local elections in 1994, it emerged as the largest party in Antwerp, with 28 percent. It was excluded from power only by a coalition of all other parties.[41] The Vlaams Blok became "the most blatantly xenophobic (if not overtly racist) among the major radical right-wing populist parties in western Europe" and "attained a level of viciousness that surpassed even that of the [French] *Front National.*"[42]

One new space opened up for the western European radical Right after the 1970s: a taxpayers' revolt against the welfare state. Most striking were the Scandinavian Progress parties that brought to an end after the 1970s the broad consensus that social benefits had enjoyed there since the 1930s. These movements had no hint of fascist style or language, though they were the place where the handful of extreme Right Scandinavians felt most at home, and where expressions of anti-immigrant feeling and even violence against immigrants became legitimate. These parties also recruited opponents of European integration and economic and cultural globalization.

While comparing programs and rhetoric may reveal some points of contact with classical fascism, partly disguised because of fascism's ignominy and the moderation tactics of the post-1970s western European radical Right, programs and rhetoric are not the only thing we should be comparing. Much greater contrast appears when one compares the circumstances of today with those of interwar Europe.[43] Except for post-communist central and eastern Europe since 1989, most Europeans have known peace, prosperity, functioning democracy, and domestic order since 1945. Mass democracy is no longer taking its shaky first steps as in Germany and Italy in 1919. Bolshevik revolution poses not even the ghost of a threat. The global competition and Americanized popular culture that still upset many Europeans seem manageable today within existing constitutional systems, without needing to "give up free institutions."

To sum up, while western Europe has had "legacy fascisms" since 1945, and while, since 1980, a new generation of normalized but racist extreme Right parties has even entered local and national governments there as minority partners, the circumstances are so vastly different in postwar Europe that no significant opening exists for parties overtly affiliated with classical fascism.

Post-Soviet Eastern Europe

No place on earth has harbored a more virulent collection of radical Right movements in recent years than post-Soviet eastern Europe and the Balkans.

Russia had been insulated from the "magnetic field" of classical fascism during the Soviet years (whatever parallels some have wished to draw), but the Russian Slavophile tradition contained the most powerful currents of antiliberal, anti-Western, anti-individualistic communitarian nationalism in all of Europe before 1914. In the backlash from the Russian defeat by Japan and the ensuing revolutionary rising of 1905, the Union of Russian People (URP) became "the strongest, the best organized, and the largest of the right-wing parties" in imperial Russia.[44] The URP was an "all-class" movement of national revival and unification that sought to save Russia from the contamination of Western individualism and democracy, if necessary against the tsar himself and the liberal aristocracy, whom they considered too cosmopolitan and too soft on parliamentarism. Its Black Hundreds killed three hundred Jews in Odessa in October 1905.[45] It deserves a prominent place among the precursors I discussed in chapter 2.

When the post-Soviet experiment in electoral democracy and market economics turned out disastrously for Russia after 1991, movements like Pamyat ("memory") revived this rich Slavophile tradition, now updated by open praise for the Nazi experiment. The most successful of a number of antiliberal, anti-Western, anti-Semitic parties in Russia was Vladimir Zhirinovsky's badly misnamed Liberal Democratic Party (LDP), founded at the end of 1989, with a program of national revival and unification under strong authority combined with wild-eyed proposals for the reconquest of Russia's lost territories (including Alaska). Zhirinovsky came in third in the Russian presidential election of June 1991, with more than

6 million votes, and his LDP became the largest party in Russia in parliamentary elections in December 1993, with nearly 23 percent of the total vote.[46] Zhirinovsky's star faded thereafter, partly because of erratic behavior and bizarre statements (plus the revelation that his father was Jewish), but mainly because President Boris Yeltsin held the reins and ignored parliament. For the moment Russia limped along as a quasi democracy under Yeltsin and his handpicked successor, the former KGB agent Vladimir Putin. If the Russian president were to lose credibility, however, some extreme Right leader more competent than Zhirinovsky would be a much more plausible outcome than any kind of return to Marxist collectivism.

All the eastern European successor states have contained radical Right movements since 1989, but most of these have remained gratifyingly weak.[47] Messy democracy and economic strains, along with the persistence of contested frontiers and discontented ethnic minorities, offer them fertile soil. For the moment, however, the appeal of joining the European Union is such that most eastern Europeans accept imperfect democracy and market economics as its necessary precondition, while the integral nationalist alternative (whose horrors are clearly revealed in the former territories of Yugoslavia) appeals only to a marginal fringe.

It was in postcommunist Yugoslavia that Europe's nearest postwar equivalent to Nazi extermination policies appeared. After Tito's death in 1980, faced with the problem of distributing a declining economic product among fractious competing regions, the Yugoslav federal state gradually lost its legitimacy. Serbia, which once had been the federation's dominant member, now led in its destruction. Serbia's president, Slobodan Milosevic, a heretofore colorless communist bureaucrat, discovered on April 24, 1987, that he had a talent for exciting crowds while addressing the Serbs of Kosovo on the six hundredth anniversary of the Serbian defeat by the Muslims in the battle of Kosovo Polje, a day rich in meaning for Serbs. The Serbs were by then massively outnumbered by Albanians in the Kosovo region, and Milosevic aroused a frenzy of excitement by playing on the themes of victimhood and justified revenge. He had discovered in Serbian nationalism a substitute for the dwindling faith in communism as a source of legitimacy and discipline. At the end of 1988, he increased central control within Serbia by abolishing local autonomy in two regions, Kosovo with its Albanians, and the Voivodina with its Hungarians.

Milosevic's efforts to increase Serbian power within the Yugoslav federation provoked separatism among other nationalities. When Slovenia and Croatia declared their independence from the federation in 1991, the Serb-dominated districts (15 percent of the population) seceded from Croatia, with the support of the federal Yugoslav army (mainly Serb). The war in Croatia involved efforts by both Croats and Serbs to expel each other from the territories they controlled by the tactics of arson, murder, and gang rape that the West came to call "ethnic cleansing" (though the differences were historical, cultural, and religious rather than ethnic).

When Bosnia declared its independence in 1992, its Serb areas likewise broke away and called in the federal Yugoslav army. Ethnic cleansing was even more gruesome in Bosnia, which had been the most integrated region of Yugoslavia, with mingled neighborhoods and frequent intermarriages. Milosevic aimed to enfold the Serb areas of Croatia and Bosnia into a Greater Serbia. He failed. Croatian armies, backed by the West, brutally expelled most Serbs from the Krajina, the main Serbian region of Croatia. In Bosnia, NATO military intervention forced Milosevic to accept a bargain (the Dayton Agreement of November 1995) in which he remained in power in Serbia but abandoned his Serbian cousins in Bosnia, who were fobbed off with a separate region within a Bosnian federal state. When Milosevic tried to expel Albanians from the province of Kosovo in 1999, NATO air strikes forced him to withdraw. His rule ended in September 2000 after the Serbs themselves chose the opposition candidate in federal elections. The new Serbian government eventually turned him over to the United Nations War Crimes Tribunal in The Hague.

It must be admitted that Serbian nationalism displayed none of the outward trappings of fascism except brutality, and that Serbia permitted relatively free electoral competition by multiple parties. Milosevic's regime did not come to power by the rooting of a militant party that then allied with the establishment to reach office. Instead, a sitting president adopted expansionist nationalism as a device to consolidate an already existing personal rule, and was supported by a passionately enthusiastic public. On that improvised basis, Milosevic's Serbia was able to present the world with a spectacle not seen in Europe since 1945: a de facto dictatorship with fervent mass support engaged in the killing of men, women, and children in order to avenge alleged historic national humiliations and to create an ethnically pure and expanded nation-state. While pinning the epithet of *fascist* upon the odious Milosevic adds nothing to an explanation of how his rule was established and maintained, it seems appropriate to recognize a functional equivalent when it appears.

The horror aroused by Milosevic was such that the Greater Croatia project of President Franjo Tudjman (1991–99) received less notice outside. Tudjman, a retired army officer and history professor, built his own regime of personal rule upon the no less cruel expulsions of Serbs from Croatia, and he reached more of his goals than did Milosevic. While Serbian patriotic themes included its anti-Nazi role in World War II, Croatian patriotic themes included Ante Pavelić's Ustaša, the terrorist nationalist sect that had governed Hitler's puppet state of Croatia during 1941–44 and had carried out mass murders of Serbs and Jews there. Tudjman's newly independent Croatia resurrected Ustaša emblems and honored the memory of one of the most sanguinary fascist regimes in Nazi-occupied Europe.

Fascism Outside Europe

Some observers doubt that fascism can exist outside Europe. They contend that specific historic fascism required the specific European preconditions of the fin de siècle cultural revolution, intense rivalry among newly formed claimants to Great Power status, mass nationalism, and contentions over the control of new democratic institutions.[48] Those who relate fascism more closely to replicable social or political crises are readier to entertain the possibility of a fascist equivalent in a non-European culture. If we hold firmly to Gaetano Salvemini's position that fascism means "giving up free institutions," and hence is a malady of sick democracies,[49] then of course our field is limited to countries outside Europe that have functioned as democracies or at least have attempted to install representative government. This essential criterion excludes all sorts of Third World dictatorships. Simply being murderous is not enough in itself to make Idi Amin Dada, for example, the bloodthirsty tyrant of Uganda from 1971 to 1979, a fascist.

European colonies of settlement constituted the most likely setting for fascism outside Europe, at least during the period of fascist ascendancy in Europe. During the 1930s, South African white-protection movements powerfully influenced by Nazism grew strong among Boer planters. The most unabashedly fascist were Louis Weichardt's South African Gentile National Socialist Movement, with its Greyshirt militia, and J. S. von Moltke's South African Fascists, whose Junior Nationalists wore orange shirts. The most successful far Right movement in pre-war South Africa was the Ossebrandwag (OB, Ox-Wagon Sentinel) of 1939.[50] It adopted

Boer folklore about their "great trek" inland to the Transvaal in covered wagons in 1835–37, to protect their way of life from the contamination of British liberalism. The OB's authentic local garb and its ties to the Calvinist Church appealed to the Boer elite more than borrowed imitations of European fascisms, though its Nazi sympathies were unconcealed. Even today one can see the movement's covered-wagon symbols on South African hillsides.

After 1945, fascist references became more discreet in white South Africa, but an appeal to white Anglo-Boer racial unity against the black majority offered what seemed an almost chemically pure potential setting for fascism. Many observers of South Africa expected the apartheid (segregation) system installed in 1948 to harden under pressure into something close to fascism. Its eventual dismantling under the inspired leadership of Nelson Mandela and the grudging acquiescence of President P. W. Botha turned out to be one of the most breathtaking happy endings of history (at least for the moment), to the relief of even many Boers. Things could still turn sour, of course. The black majority's frustrated yearning for faster improvement in living standards, especially if accompanied by violence, could produce defensive white protective associations eager to "give up free institutions" that threatened not only their way of life but their lives.

Latin America came closest of any continent outside Europe to establishing something approaching genuine fascist regimes between the 1930s and the early 1950s. We must tread warily here, however, for a high degree of mimicry was involved during the period of fascist ascendancy in Europe. Local dictators tended to adopt the fascist decor that was the fashion of the 1930s, while drawing Depression remedies as much from Roosevelt's New Deal as from Mussolini's corporatism.

The closest thing to an indigenous mass fascist party in Latin America was the Ação Integralista Brasileira (AIB), founded by the writer Plinio Salgado after he returned from a trip to Europe where, upon meeting Mussolini, "a sacred fire had entered his existence."[51] The Integralists were much more solidly implanted in Brazilian society than the Nazi and Fascist clubs that spread among German and Italian immigrants there, and Salgado successfully merged indigenous Brazilian historical imagery (including the Tupi Indian culture) with the more overtly fascist aspects of his program, such as dictatorship, nationalism, protectionism, corporatism, anti-Semitism, goose steps, a proposed Secretariat for Moral and Physical Education, green shirts and black armbands with the Greek letter *sigma* (the symbol of integralism), to form an authentically homegrown overtly fascist movement. Integralismo peaked in 1934 with 180,000 members, some of them prominent in the professions, business, and the military.[52]

It was not the Integralistas who ruled Brazil, however, but a canny though uncharismatic dictator, Getulio Vargas. Vargas became president through a military coup in 1930 and was elected president more normally in 1934. When that term approached its end, Vargas took full power in 1937 and set up the Estado Novo, whose name and authoritarian political system were borrowed from Portugal. He ruled as a dictator until 1945, when the military removed him from power.[53] Vargas's Estado Novo of 1937–45 was a modernizing dictatorship with some progressive features (it curtailed the local powers of the old oligarchy and promoted centralized authority, social services, education, and industrialization). Its protectionism and state-authorized cartels for such products as coffee (whose world price had collapsed in the Depression) resembled the Depression remedies of many 1930s governments, not necessarily fascist. Like Salazar in Portugal, far from governing through a fascist party, Vargas closed down the Integralistas and the pro-Nazi and pro-Fascist movements along with all other parties. Vargas, a slight man who disliked public speaking and admitted that riding a horse hurt his backside,[54] failed to rise even to the *gaucho* image of his home state of Rio Grande do Sul, much less to that of a fascist *jefe.*

Colonel Juan Perón matched that image far more closely, both in his personal charisma and in his political predilections. On the eve of World War II, as assistant Argentine military attaché in Rome, he had admired the order, the discipline, the unity, and the enthusiasm, as he perceived them, of Fascist Italy. Indeed Perón claimed Italian ancestry, like many Argentines (Italy and Spain had furnished most European immigrants to Argentina).[55]

Argentina's adoption of manhood suffrage in 1912 allowed the cautiously reformist Radical Hipólito Yrigoyen to govern after 1916 in what looked like the establishment of constitutional democracy. Yrigoyen's uninspiring patronage-based political machine had no answers, however, to the worldwide decline in agricultural prices that threatened Argentina's wealth in the late 1920s.[56] In September 1930 right-wing army officers overthrew Yrigoyen and ended constitutional rule for what turned out to be an unstable half century of mostly right-wing dictatorships.

At first General José Uriburu attempted to cope with the Great Depression through a corporatist economic system copied from Mussolini's

Italy. Uriburu's "fascism from above" failed to win the necessary support among military, party, and economic leaders, however, and gave way to a series of military-conservative dictatorships punctuated by fraudulent elections that Argentines remember as "the infamous decade." When World War II broke out, Argentina remained neutral and its army leaned toward Germany, source of its arms and training.

When the United States entered the war in December 1941, it subjected Argentina to intense pressure to join the Allied camp along with the rest of Latin America. A new military junta took power in June 1943 determined to resist American pressure and remain neutral. At least some of its members, including Colonel Juan Perón, wanted to continue obtaining arms from Germany to counterbalance U.S. arms and bases in Brazil.[57]

An obscure colonel in the military junta that took power in 1943, Juan Perón asked for the apparently trivial post of secretary for labor and social welfare.[58] Once in control of labor organizations, Perón eliminated their socialist, communist, or anarcho-syndicalist leaders, merged multiple unions into a single state-sponsored worker organization for each sector of the economy, and expanded their membership to the previously unorganized. These steps turned the Confederación General de Trabajo (CGT, General Confederation of Labor) into his personal fiefdom. Perón won authentic gratitude by substantially improving working conditions and obtaining favorable settlement of labor disputes. He was greatly assisted in this project by the personal flair and the anti-establishment radicalism of his mistress, Eva Duarte, an illegitimate country girl struggling to make good as an actress in radio soap operas.

Perón came to power quite unlike Mussolini and Hitler, not at the head of a militant party striving to show that democracy was unworkable (democracy had already been stifled), but by the pressure of a mass demonstration of his worker following. In October 1945 Perón's fellow officers in the junta, alarmed by the young colonel's ambition and demagoguery, influenced by the American ambassador's hostility to him, and offended by the openness of his liaison with the lower-class Eva, stripped him of office and arrested him. On October 17, 1945, a date later celebrated as the national holiday of Peronism, hundreds of thousands of striking workers—mobilized by Eva, according to Peronist legend, but more likely by other aides—occupied downtown Buenos Aires. In the sweltering heat some of them took off their shirts and, before the appalled citizenry, cooled themselves in the elegant fountains of the Plaza de Mayo.

Los descamisados—the shirtless ones—became the equivalent in Peronist legend of the French Revolution's *sans-culottes*.[59]

In order to appease the peaceable but overwhelming crowd, the junta released the colonel and set up a new government composed mostly of his friends. Perón was on track for election as president in 1946. Perón's dictatorship rested thereafter as much on a manipulated CGT as upon the army. It was openly and explicitly directed against "the oligarchy" that had snubbed Evita. Never mind that the dictatorship never threatened property and did its best to support import-substitution industry, and that Perón's CGT became more the manager of a working-class clientele than an authentic expression of its grievances. Perón's popular base was always more explicitly proletarian than that of Mussolini or Hitler, and its animus against the old families of Argentina more overt. While Fascism and Nazism used dictatorship to smash an independent labor movement and shrink the worker share of the national product, Perón increased workers' share of the national income from 40 percent in 1946 to 49 percent by 1949.[60]

Perón's dictatorship (1946–55) was the regime outside Europe most often called fascist, particularly in the United States. Washington officialdom had labeled neutral Argentina firmly as pro-Axis even before Perón came on the scene.[61] With its charismatic leader, the Conductor Perón, its single Peronista party and its official doctrine of *justicialismo* or "organized community," its mania for parades and ceremonies (often starring Eva, now his wife), its corporatist economy, its controlled press, its repressive police and periodic violence against the Left,[62] its subjugated judiciary and close ties to Franco, it did indeed look fascist to a World War II generation accustomed to dividing the world between fascists and democrats.

More recent scholars, however, have preferred to stress Peronism's indigenous roots: a national tradition of salvation by strong leaders; dread of decline, as agricultural exports, the source of Argentina's great wealth, lost value after World War I; a mammoth "red scare" set off by a bloody general strike in January 1919 *(la semana trágica)*; nationalism easily focused upon regaining economic independence from British investors; the political space offered by a tired oligarchy that rested upon the diminished power of the cattle and wheat barons without giving voice to the new urban middle and working classes (the largest in South America); and a widepread conviction that "politicians" were both feckless and corrupt.[63]

Surface appearances aside, Perón's dictatorship worked quite unlike those of Hitler and Mussolini. Whereas these two had come to power against chaotic democracies in the disorder following upon a rapidly broadened suffrage, Perón came to power against a narrowly based military-conservative oligarchy and then broadened the franchise (women could vote after 1947) and increased citizen participation.[64] He won clear electoral majorities in 1946 and 1951, and again in a comeback in 1973, in Argentina's cleanest presidential elections up to that point. Although Perón's dictatorship used police intimidation and controlled the press, it lacked the diabolized internal/external enemy—Jews or others—that seems an essential ingredient of fascism.[65] It expressed no interest in expansion by war.

Finally, Eva Perón filled a role utterly foreign to fascist *machismo*. "Evita" was the first Latin American leader's wife to participate actively in government. This complex and shrewd woman knew how to play on multiple registers: as passionate orator for *los descamisados* and against "the oligarchy"; as organizer of the women's vote at the head of the Peronist Women's Party (though never promoting other women to positions of power); as lady bountiful, distributing favors each day from her desk at the Ministry of Labor and through the mysteriously financed Eva Perón Foundation; and as a glamorous dream object who was said to have donned 306 different lavish outfits in one 270-day period.[66] Outwardly feminine and submissive to the dictator, she was widely perceived as giving her cautious husband backbone. She established a rapport with the Buenos Aires crowd so intense that after her death—by cancer at thirty-three in 1952—she became the object of multiple cults. For a few, she was a revolutionary leader (an image revived by left-wing Peronists in the 1970s); for many others, she was a quasi saint, for whom altars were built and whose carefully embalmed body had to be hidden by subsequent regimes. In the eyes of many upper-class Argentinians, she was a vengeful upstart and sexual manipulator. At her death she was probably the most powerful woman in the world.[67]

Assessing Latin American dictatorships in the optic of fascism is a perilous intellectual enterprise. At worst, it can become an empty labeling exercise. At best, however, it can sharpen our image of the classical fascisms. To compare properly, one must distinguish among various levels of similarity and difference. The similarities are found in the mechanisms of rule, in the techniques of propaganda and image manipulation, and occasionally in specific borrowed policies such as corporatist economic organization. The differences become more apparent when one examines the social and political settings and the relation of these regimes to society. The surgeons' scalpels could look similar, but in Latin America they were operating on different bodies than in Europe.

Both Vargas and Perón took power from oligarchies rather than from failed democracies, and both subsequently broadened political participation. They ruled over only partly formed nations, whose disparate populations and factious local bosses they sought to integrate into unified national states, whereas classical fascist dictators ruled over already established nation-states obsessed by threats to their unity, energy, and rank. Hitler's vision of a perfect Germany sullied by communists and Jews (identical, in his mind) had their parallel in the Brazilian Integralistas and the Argentine Nacionalistas, but Vargas and Perón marginalized them and alarmed them with their populism.[68] Neither Vargas nor Perón felt called to exterminate any group. Their police, though harsh and unchecked, punished individual enemies rather than eliminated whole categories, as Hitler's SS did. Mussolini's less murderous effort to complete the creation of modern Italians worthy of Romanità forms a closer parallel, but he was as dedicated as Hitler to expansive war, a project altogether absent in Vargas and Perón.

In sum, the similarities seem matters of tools or instruments, borrowed during fascism's apogee, while the differences concern more basic matters of structure, function, and relation to society. The Latin American dictatorships are best considered national-populist developmental dictatorships with fascist trappings, perhaps distantly comparable to Mussolini but hardly at all to Hitler (despite wartime sympathy for the Axis).

Once we have established that fully authentic fascism did not exist in even the most advanced Latin American countries during 1930–50, we can pass more rapidly over some of the other Latin American movements and regimes that have been linked to fascism. Aside from small pro-Axis factions in Chile and Peru, the other main example was the "military socialism" of Colonel David Toro in Bolivia in 1936–37 and his successor, Germán Busch, in 1937–39, with its "Legion" of war veterans, its state syndicalism, and its effort to construct a nation-state out of disparate Indian and European components via charismatic dictatorship.[69]

Imperial Japan, the most industrialized country outside the West and the one most powerfully influenced by a selective adoption of things Western, was the other non-European regime most often called fascist. During World War II, Allied propagandists easily lumped imperial Japan with its Axis partners. Nowadays, while most Western scholars consider imperial Japan something other than fascist, Japanese scholars, and not only Marxists, commonly interpret it as "fascism from above."[70]

Fascism in interwar Japan can be approached in two ways. One can focus on the influence "from below" of intellectuals and national regeneration movements that advocated a program closely resembling fascism, only to be crushed by the regime. The other approach focuses upon the actions "from above" of imperial institutions. It asks whether the expansionist militarized dictatorship set up in the 1930s did not constitute a distinctive form of "emperor-system fascism."[71]

Japan had moved several steps toward democracy in the 1920s. In 1926 all adult males received the vote, and even though the appointed upper house and privy council remained powerful and the army escaped parliamentary control, the cabinet was normally headed by the leader of the largest party in the lower house. Among the many opinions heard then were those of Kita Ikki, who has been called an authentic Japanese fascist. Kita's "General Outline of Measures for the Reconstruction of Japan" (1919) advocated state restrictions upon the industrialists and landowners whom he saw as the main barrier to national unification and regeneration. Once free of the division and drag of competitive capitalism, according to Kita, Japan would become the center of a new Asia independent of European domination.[72]

Japan's fledgling democracy did not survive the crises of 1931. The Great Depression had already brought poverty to the countryside, and, starting in September 1931, Japanese military leaders used a pretext to invade Manchuria. Restless junior officers, angered by fruitless attempts by the lower house to limit military expansion and influenced in some cases by the works of Kita Ikki, founded secret societies with names like the Cherry Blossom Association and the Blood Pledge Corps. They tried by assassinations and coup attempts to install a dictatorship under the emperor that would pursue national regeneration by a program of state economic control, social leveling, and expansion. In the most ambitious of these, rebellious young officers occupied downtown Tokyo on February 26, 1936, and killed the finance minister and other officials.[73]

After this insurrection was put down, Kita Ikki was among those executed. The emperor himself thus ended what has been called Japanese "fascism from below." Since 1932 parliamentary party cabinets had given way to "national unity" governments dominated by senior military officers and bureaucrats, and that process accelerated after the repression of the

1936 rebellion. In June 1937, Prince Konoe Fumimaro, an aristocrat who had been president of the Chamber of Peers and who opposed government by parties, became prime minister (1937–39). In July 1937 the Japanese military instigated an incident in China, beginning eight years of total war on the mainland. The Konoe cabinet supported this escalation and mobilized the nation for war. Prime minister again in July 1940, Prince Konoe established an overtly totalitarian domestic "New Order" intended to place a regenerated Japan at the head of what came to be called a "Greater East Asian Co-Prosperity Sphere."

Authentic fascists did appear in Japan in the late 1930s, when Nazi success was dazzling. The Eastern Way Society of the black-shirted Seigo Nakano, "the Japanese Hitler," won 3 percent of the vote in the 1942 election. Nakano, however, was put under house arrest. The Showa Research Assocation was a more scholarly group of intellectuals who drew explicitly upon fascist formulas for popular mobilization and economic organization. Konoe had been advised by the Showa Research Association. In practice, however, Prince Konoe quietly set aside all the solidarist and anticapitalist features of these intellectuals' proposals.[74]

In summary, the Japanese government decided to pick and choose within the fascist menu and adopt a certain number of its measures of corporatist economic organization and popular control in a "selective revolution" by state action, while at the same time suppressing the messy popular activism of authentically (though derivatively) fascist movements.[75]

The militarist expansionist dictatorship that gradually came into being in Japan between 1931 and 1940 is called fascist by some because it consisted of emergency rule by an alliance among the imperial authority, big business, senior functionaries, and the military in defense of threatened class interests.[76] But even if imperial Japan indubitably drew upon fascist models and shared important features with fascism, the Japanese variant of fascism was imposed by rulers in the absence of a single mass party or popular movement, and indeed in disregard of, or even in opposition to, those Japanese intellectuals who were influenced by European fascism. "It was as if fascism had been established in Europe as a result of the crushing of Mussolini and Hitler."[77]

The American sociologist Barrington Moore proposed a longer-term explanation for the emergence of military dictatorship in Japan. Seeking the ultimate roots of dictatorship and democracy in different routes toward the capitalist transformation of agriculture, Moore noted that Britain allowed an independent rural gentry to enclose its estates and expel from the countryside "surplus" labor who were then "free" to work in its precocious industries. British democracy could rest upon a stable, conservative countryside and a large urban middle class fed by upwardly mobile labor. Germany and Japan, by contrast, industrialized rapidly and late while maintaining unchanged a traditional landlord-peasant agriculture. Thereafter they were obliged to hold in check all at once fractious workers, squeezed petty bourgeois, and peasants, either by force or by manipulation. This conflict-ridden social system, moreover, provided only limited markets for its own products. Both Germany and Japan dealt with these challenges by combining internal repression with external expansion, aided by the slogans and rituals of a right-wing ideology that sounded radical without really challenging the social order.[78]

To Barrington Moore's long-term analysis of lopsided modernization, one could add further short-term twentieth-century similarities between the German and Japanese situations: the vividness of the perception of a threat from the Soviet Union (Russia had made territorial claims against Japan since the Japanese victory of 1905), and the necessity to adapt traditional political and social hierarchies rapidly to mass politics. Imperial Japan was even more successful than Nazi Germany in using modern methods of mobilization and propaganda to integrate its population under traditional authority.[79]

Moore's perceived similarities between German and Japanese development patterns and social structures have not been fully convincing to Japan specialists. Agrarian landlords cannot be shown to have played a major role in giving imperial Japan its peculiar mix of expansionism and social control. And if imperial Japanese techniques of integration were very successful, it was mostly because Japanese society was so coherent and its family structure so powerful.[80]

Imperial Japan, finally, despite undoubted influence from European fascism and despite some structural analogies to Germany and Italy, faced less critical problems than those two countries. The Japanese faced no imminent revolutionary threat, and needed to overcome neither external defeat nor internal disintegration (though they feared it, and resented Western obstacles to their expansion in Asia). Though the imperial regime used techniques of mass mobilization, no official party or autonomous grassroots movement competed with the leaders. The Japanese empire of the period 1932–45 is better understood as an expansionist military dictatorship with a high degree of state-sponsored mobilization than as a fascist regime.

Dictatorial regimes in Africa and Latin America that aided American or European interests (resource extraction, investment privileges, strategic support in the cold war) and were, in return, propped up by Western protectors have been called "client fascism," "proxy fascism," or "colonial fascism." One thinks here of Chile under General Pinochet (1974–90) or Western protectorates in Africa like Seko-Seso Mobutu's Congo (1965–97). These client states, however odious, cannot legitimately be called fascist, because they neither rested on popular acclaim nor were free to pursue expansionism. If they permitted the mobilization of public opinion, they risked seeing it turn against their foreign masters and themselves. They are best considered traditional dictatorships or tyrannies supported from outside.

The United States itself has never been exempt from fascism. Indeed, antidemocratic and xenophobic movements have flourished in America since the Native American party of 1845 and the Know-Nothing Party of the 1850s.[81] In the crisis-ridden 1930s, as in other democracies, derivative fascist movements were conspicuous in the United States: the Protestant evangelist Gerald B. Winrod's openly pro-Hitler Defenders of the Christian Faith with their Black Legion; William Dudley Pelley's Silver Shirts (the initials "SS" were intentional);[82] the veteran-based Khaki Shirts (whose leader, one Art J. Smith, vanished after a heckler was killed at one of his rallies); and a host of others. Movements with an exotic foreign look won few followers, however. George Lincoln Rockwell, flamboyant head of the American Nazi Party from 1959 until his assassination by a disgruntled follower in 1967,[83] seemed even more "un-American" after the great anti-Nazi war.

Much more dangerous are movements that employ authentically American themes in ways that resemble fascism functionally. The Klan revived in the 1920s, took on virulent anti-Semitism, and spread to cities and the Middle West. In the 1930s, Father Charles E. Coughlin gathered a radio audience estimated at forty million around an anticommunist, anti–Wall Street, pro–soft money, and—after 1938—anti-Semitic message broadcast from his church in the outskirts of Detroit. For a moment in early 1936 it looked as if his Union Party and its presidential candidate, North Dakota congressman William Lemke, might overwhelm Roosevelt.[84] The plutocrat-baiting governor Huey Long of Louisiana had authentic political momentum until his assassination in 1935, but, though frequently labeled fascist at the time, he was more accurately a share-the-wealth demagogue.[85] The fundamentalist preacher Gerald L. K. Smith, who had worked with both Coughlin and Long, turned the message more directly after World War II to the "Judeo-Communist conspiracy" and had a real impact. Today a "politics of resentment" rooted in authentic American piety and nativism sometimes leads to violence against some of the very same "internal enemies" once targeted by the Nazis, such as homosexuals and defenders of abortion rights.[86]

Of course the United States would have to suffer catastrophic setbacks and polarization for these fringe groups to find powerful allies and enter the mainstream. I half expected to see emerge after 1968 a movement of national reunification, regeneration, and purification directed against hirsute antiwar protesters, black radicals, and "degenerate" artists. I thought that some of the Vietnam veterans might form analogs to the Freikorps of 1919 Germany or the Italian Arditi, and attack the youths whose demonstrations on the steps of the Pentagon had "stabbed them in the back." Fortunately I was wrong (so far). Since September 11, 2001, however, civil liberties have been curtailed to popular acclaim in a patriotic war upon terrorists.

The language and symbols of an authentic American fascism would, of course, have little to do with the original European models. They would have to be as familiar and reassuring to loyal Americans as the language and symbols of the original fascisms were familiar and reassuring to many Italians and Germans, as Orwell suggested. Hitler and Mussolini, after all, had not tried to seem exotic to their fellow citizens. No swastikas in an American fascism, but Stars and Stripes (or Stars and Bars) and Christian crosses. No fascist salute, but mass recitations of the pledge of allegiance. These symbols contain no whiff of fascism in themselves, of course, but an American fascism would transform them into obligatory litmus tests for detecting the internal enemy.

Around such reassuring language and symbols and in the event of some redoubtable setback to national prestige, Americans might support an enterprise of forcible national regeneration, unification, and purification. Its targets would be the First Amendment, separation of Church and State (creches on the lawns, prayers in schools), efforts to place controls on gun ownership,[87] desecrations of the flag, unassimilated minorities, artistic license, dissident and unusual behavior of all sorts that could be labeled antinational or decadent.

Henry Louis Gates, Jr., has detected a "regrettably fascist ring" in the assertion by some African-American nationalists of "the redemptive power of Afrocentricity" against "European decadence" through "the submission of their own wills into the collective will of our people."[88] The classification of peoples advanced by Professor Leonard Jeffries, formerly of the City University of New York, as "sun people" (Africans) and "ice people" (Europeans), and his conspiratorial view that the "ice people" have tried through history to exterminate the "sun people," sound that note even more loudly. If one were to add to this Manichean sense of victimization an exaltation of remedial violence against both external enemies and internal slackers, one would come close to fascism. But such a movement within a historically excluded minority would have so little opportunity to wield genuine power that, in the last analysis, any comparison to authentic fascisms seems far-fetched. A subjugated minority may employ rhetoric that resembles early fascism, but it can hardly embark on its own program of internal dictatorship and purification and territorial expansionism.

I come now to the difficult issue of whether religion may serve as the functional equivalent of fascism to regenerate and unite a humiliated and vengeful people. Was Iran under the Ayatollah Khomeini a fascist regime? What about Hindu fundamentalism in India, al-Qaeda among Muslim fundamentalists, and the Taliban in Afghanistan? Would Protestant fundamentalism play this function for Americans? Payne has argued that fascism requires the space created by secularization, because a religious fascism would inevitably limit its leader not only by the cultural power of the clergy but by "the precepts and values of traditional religion."[89]

This argument applies best to Europe. But conditions there may have been peculiar. The anticlericalism of the first European fascisms was a matter of historical circumstance; both Italian and German nationalism had traditionally been directed against the Catholic Church. Mussolini and Hitler were both nurtured in somewhat different anticlerical traditions: in Mussolini's case revolutionary syndicalism, in Hitler's case anti-Habsburg pan-Germanism. This historical peculiarity of the original fascisms does not mean that future integrist movements could not build upon a religion in place of a nation, or as the expression of national identity. Even in Europe, religion-based fascisms were not unknown: the Falange Española, Belgian Rexism, the Finnish Lapua Movement, and the Romanian Legion of the Archangel Michael are all good examples, even if we exclude the Catholic authoritarian regimes of 1930s Spain, Austria, and Portugal.

Religion may be as powerful an engine of identity as the nation; indeed, in some cultures, religious identity may be far more powerful than national identity. In integrist religious fundamentalisms, the violent promotion of the unity and dynamism of the faith may function very much like the violent promotion of the unity and dynamism of the nation. Some extreme forms of Orthodox Judaism regard the state of Israel as a blasphemy because it was established before Messiah came. Here religious integrism fully replaces national integrism. Fundamentalist Muslims offer little loyalty to the various secular Islamic states, whether presidential or monarchical. Islam is their nation. For Hindu fundamentalists, their religion is the focus of an intense attachment that the secular and pluralist Indian state does not succeed in offering. In such communities, a religious-based fascism is conceivable. After all, no two fascisms need be alike in their symbols and rhetoric, employing, as they do, the local patriotic repertory.

The principal objection to succumbing to the temptation to call Islamic fundamentalist movements like al-Qaeda and the Taliban fascist is that they are not reactions against a malfunctioning democracy. Arising in traditional hierarchical societies, their unity is, in terms of Émile Durkheim's famous distinction, more organic than mechanical. Above all, they have not "given up free institutions," since they never had any.[90]

If religious fascisms are possible, one must address the potential—supreme irony—for fascism in Israel. Israeli reactions to the first and second *intifada* have been mixed. Israeli national identity has been powerfully associated with an affirmation of the human rights that were long denied to Jews in the Diaspora. This democratic tradition forms a barrier against "giving up free institutions" in the fight against Palestinian nationalism. It has been weakened, however, by two trends—the inevitable hardening of attitudes in the face of Palestinian intransigence, and a shift of weight within the Israeli population away from European Jews, the principal bearers of the democratic tradition, in favor of Jews from North Africa and elsewhere in the Near East who are indifferent to it. The suicide bombings of the second *intifada* after 2001 radicalized even many Israeli democrats to the right. By 2002, it was possible to hear language within the right wing of the Likud Party and some of the small religious parties that comes close to a functional equivalent to fascism. The chosen people begins to sound like a Master Race that claims a unique "mission in the world," demands its "vital space," demonizes an enemy that obstructs the realization of the people's destiny, and accepts the necessity of force to obtain these ends.[91]

In conclusion, if one accepts an interpretation of fascism that is not limited to European fin de siècle culture, the possibilities for a non-European fascism are no less great than in the 1930s, and indeed probably greater because of the great increase since 1945 of failed experiments with democracy and representative government.

Now I can refine the question with which we began this chapter. Can fascism still exist? Clearly Stage One movements can still be found in all major democracies. More crucially, can they reach Stage Two again by becoming rooted and influential? We need not look for exact replicas, in which fascist veterans dust off their swastikas. Collectors of Nazi paraphernalia and hard-core neo-Nazi sects are capable of provoking destructive violence and polarization. As long as they remain excluded from the alliances with the establishment necessary to join the political mainstream or share power, however, they remain more a law and order problem than a political threat. Much more likely to exert an influence are extreme Right movements that have learned to moderate their language, abandon classical fascist symbolism, and appear "normal."

It is by understanding how past fascisms worked, and not by checking the color of shirts, or seeking echoes of the rhetoric of the national-syndicalist dissidents of the opening of the twentieth century, that we may be able to recognize it. The well-known warning signals—extreme nationalist propaganda and hate crimes—are important but insufficient. Knowing what we do about the fascist cycle, we can find more ominous warning signals in situations of political deadlock in the face of crisis, threatened conservatives looking for tougher allies, ready to give up due process and the rule of law, seeking mass support by nationalist and racialist demagoguery. Fascists are close to power when conservatives begin to borrow their techniques, appeal to their "mobilizing passions," and try to co-opt the fascist following.

Armed by historical knowledge, we may be able to distinguish today's ugly but isolated imitations, with their shaved heads and swastika tattoos, from authentic functional equivalents in the form of a mature fascist-conservative alliance. Forewarned, we may be able to detect the real thing when it comes along.

CHAPTER 8

What Is Fascism?

At this book's opening, I ducked the task of offering the reader a neat definition of fascism. I wanted to set aside—for heuristic purposes, at least—the traditional but straitjacketing search for the famous but elusive "fascist minimum." I thought it more promising to observe historical examples of fascist successes and failures in action, through a whole cycle of development. Exposing the processes by which fascisms appeared, grew, gained power (or not), and, once in power, radicalized into a "fascist maximum" seemed a more promising strategy than to search for some static and limiting "essence."

Now that we have reached the end of this historical journey, the imperative of definition can no longer be evaded. Otherwise we risk escaping from the nominalism of the "bestiary" only to fall into another nominalism of stages and processes. Generic fascism might disappear in our efforts to pick it apart. But first some other issues need to be considered.

Following fascism through five stages, in each of which it acts differently, raises an awkward question: Which is the real fascism? For some authors, usually those most concerned with fascism's intellectual expressions, the early movements are "pure" fascism while the regimes are corruptions, deformed by the compromises necessary for achieving and wielding power.[1] The regimes, however, for all their pragmatic choices and compromising alliances, had more impact than the movements because they possessed the power of war and death. A definition that does full justice to the phenomenon of fascism must apply to the later stages as effectively as it does to the earlier ones.

Focusing on those later stages requires us to give as much attention to settings and to allies as to the fascists themselves. A usable definition of fascism must also, therefore, find a way to avoid treating fascism in isolation, cut off from its environment and its accomplices. Fascism in power is a *power* compound, a powerful amalgam of different but marriageable conservative, national-socialist and radical Right ingredients, bonded together by common enemies and common passions for a regenerated, energized, and purified nation at whatever cost to free institutions and the rule of law. The precise proportions of the mixture are the result of processes: choices, alliances, compromises, rivalries. Fascism in action looks much more like a network of relationships than a fixed essence.[2]

Conflicting Interpretations

Now that we have watched fascism in action through its entire cycle, we are better prepared to evaluate the many interpretations proposed over the years. The "first takes" I noted in chapter 1—thugs in power and agents of capitalism[3]—have never lost their grip. The German playwright Bertolt Brecht even managed to combine them in his Chicago gangster Arturo Ui, who gets power through a protection racket for vegetable sellers.[4]

Both "first takes," however, had serious flaws. If fascism and its aggressions are simply the evil actions of hoodlums reaching power in an era of moral decline, we have no explanation for why this happened at one place and time rather than another, or how these events might relate to an earlier history. It was difficult for classical liberals like Croce and Meinecke to perceive that part of fascism's opportunity lay in the dessication and narrowness of liberalism itself, or that some frightened liberals had helped it into power. Their version leaves us with chance and the individual exploits of thugs as explanations.

Considering fascism simply as a capitalist tool sends us astray in two respects. The narrow and rigid formula that became orthodox in Stalin's Third International[5] denied fascism's autonomous roots and authentic popular appeal.[6] Even worse, it ignored human choice by making fascism the inevitable outcome of the ineluctable crisis of capitalist overproduction. Closer empirical work showed, to the contrary, that real capitalists, even when they rejected democracy, mostly preferred authoritarians to fascists.[7] Whenever fascists reached power, to be sure, capitalists mostly accommodated with them as the best available nonsocialist solution. We had occasion to see that even the giant German chemical combine

NOT JUST CAP.

I. G. Farben, whose ascent to the rank of the biggest company in Europe had been based on global trade, found ways to adapt to rearmament-driven autarky, and prospered mightily again.[8] The relations of accommodation, foot dragging, and mutual advantage that bound the business community to fascist regimes turn out to be another complicated matter that varied over time. That there was some mutual advantage is beyond doubt. Capitalism and fascism made practicable bedfellows (though not inevitable ones, nor always comfortable ones).

As for the opposite interpretation that portrays the business community as fascism's victim,[9] it takes far too seriously the middle-level frictions endemic to this relationship, along with businessmen's postwar efforts at self-exculpation. Here, too, we need a subtler model of explanation that allows for interplays of conflict and accommodation.

Quite early the "first takes" were joined by other interpretations. The obviously obsessive character of some fascists cried out for psychoanalysis. Mussolini seemed only too ordinary, with his vain posturing, his notorious womanizing, his addiction to detailed work, his skill at short-term maneuvering, and his eventual loss of the big picture. Hitler was another matter. Were his *Teppichfresser* ("carpet eater") scenes calculated bluffs or signs of madness?[10] His secretiveness, hypochondria, narcissism, vengefulness, and megalomania were counterbalanced by a quick, retentive mind, a capacity to charm if he wanted to, and outstanding tactical cleverness. All efforts to psychoanalyze him[11] have suffered from the inaccessibility of their subject, as well as from the unanswered question of why, if some fascist leaders were insane, their publics adored them and they functioned effectively for so long. In any event, the latest and most authoritative biographer of Hitler concludes rightly that one must dwell less on the *Führer*'s eccentricities than on the role the German public projected upon him and which he succeeded in filling until nearly the end.[12]

Perhaps it is the fascist publics rather than their leaders who need psychoanalysis. Already in 1933 the dissident Freudian Wilhelm Reich concluded that the violent masculine fraternity characteristic of early fascism was the product of sexual repression.[13] This theory is easy to undermine, however, by observing that sexual repression was probably no more severe in Germany and in Italy than in, say, Great Britain during the generation in which the fascist leaders and their followers came of age.[14] This objection also applies to other psycho-historical explanations for fascism.

Explanations of fascism as psychotic appear in another form in films that cater to a prurient fascination with supposed fascist sexual perversion.[15] These box-office successes make it even harder to grasp that fascist regimes functioned because great numbers of ordinary people accommodated to them in the ordinary business of daily life.[16]

The sociologist Talcott Parsons suggested already in 1942 that fascism emerged out of uprooting and tensions produced by uneven economic and social development—an early form of the fascism/modernization problem. In countries that industrialized rapidly and late, like Germany and Italy, Parsons argued, class tensions were particularly acute and compromise was blocked by surviving pre-industrial elites.[17] This interpretation had the merit of treating fascism as a system and as the product of a history, as did the Marxist interpretation, without Marxism's determinism, narrowness, and shaky empirical foundations.

The philosopher Ernst Bloch, a Marxist made unorthodox by an interest in the irrational and in religion, arrived in his own way at another theory of "noncontemporaneity" *(Ungleichzeitigkeit)*. Contemplating Nazi success with archaic and violent "red dreams" of blood, soil, and a precapitalist paradise, utterly incompatible with what he considered the party's true fealty to big business, he understood that vestigial values flourished long after they had lost any correspondence with economic and social reality. "Not all people exist in the same Now." Orthodox Marxists, he thought, had missed the boat by "cordoning off the soul."[18] Uneven development continues to arouse interest as an ingredient of prefascist crises,[19] but the case for it is weakened by France's notoriously "dual" economy, in which a powerful peasant/artisan sector coexisted with modern industry without fascism reaching power except under Nazi occupation.[20]

Another sociological approach alleged that urban and industrial leveling since the late nineteenth century had produced an atomized mass society in which purveyors of simple hatreds found a ready audience unrestrained by tradition or community.[21] Hannah Arendt worked within this paradigm in her analysis of how the new rootless mob, detached from all social, intellectual, or moral moorings and inebriated by anti-Semitic and imperialistic passions, made possible the emergence of an unprecedented form of limitless mass-based plebiscitary dictatorship.[22]

The best empirical work on the way fascism took root, however, gives little support to this approach. Weimar German society, for example, was richly structured, and Nazism recruited by mobilizing entire organizations through carefully targeted appeals to specific interests.[23] As the saying went, "two Germans, a discussion; three Germans, a club." The fact that German clubs for everything from choral singing to funeral insurance were already segregated into separate socialist and nonsocialist networks facilitated the exclusion of the socialists and the Nazi takeover of the rest when Germany became deeply polarized in the early 1930s.[24]

An influential current considers fascism a developmental dictatorship, established for the purpose of hastening industrial growth through forced savings and a regimented workforce. Proponents of this interpretation have looked primarily at the Italian case.[25] It could well be argued that Germany, too, although already an industrial giant, needed urgently to discipline its people for the immense task of rebuilding after the defeat of 1918. This interpretation goes seriously wrong, however, in supposing that fascism pursued any rational economic goal whatever. Hitler meant to bend the economy to serve political ends. Even in Mussolini's case, prestige counted far more than economic rationality when he overvalued the lira in 1926, and when, after 1935, he chose the risks of expansionist war over sustained economic development. If Italian Fascism was meant to be a developmental dictatorship, it failed at it. Though the Italian economy grew in the 1920s under Mussolini, it grew substantially faster before 1914 and after 1945.[26] In one genuinely aberrant form, the developmental dictatorship theory of fascism serves to label as "fascist" all sorts of Third World autocracies without an iota of popular mobilization and without the prior existence of a democracy in trouble.[27]

It has also been tempting to interpret fascism by its social composition. The sociologist Seymour Martin Lipset systematized in 1963 the widely held view that fascism is an expression of lower-middle-class resentments. In Lipset's formulation, fascism is an "extremism of the center" based on the rage of once-independent shopkeepers, artisans, peasants, and other members of the "old" middle classes now squeezed between better-organized industrial workers and big businessmen, and losing out in rapid social and economic change.[28] Recent empirical research, however, casts doubt on the localization of fascist recruitment in any one social stratum. It shows the multiplicity of fascism's social supports and its relative success in creating a composite movement that cut across all classes.[29] His eyes glued on the early stages, Lipset also overlooked the establishment's role in the fascist acquisition and exercise of power.

The notorious instability of fascist membership further undermines any simple interpretation by social composition. Party rosters altered rapidly before power, as successive waves of heterogeneous malcontents responded to the parties' changing fortunes and messages.[30] After power, membership "bandwagoned" to include just about everyone who wanted to enjoy the fruits of fascist success[31] — not to forget the problem of where to situate the many fascist recruits who were young, unemployed, socially uprooted, or otherwise "between classes."[32] No coherent social explanation of fascism can be constructed out of such fluctuating material.

A multitude of observers sees fascism as a subspecies of totalitarianism. Giovanni Amendola, a leader of the parliamentary opposition to Fascism and one of its most notable victims (he died in 1926 following a beating by Fascist thugs), coined the adjective *totalitaria* in a May 1923 article denouncing Fascist efforts to monopolize public office. Other opponents of Mussolini quickly broadened the term into a general condemnation of Fascist aspirations to total control. As sometimes happens with epithets, Mussolini took this one up and gloried in it.[33]

Considering how often Mussolini boasted of his *totalitarismo*, it is ironic that some major postwar theorists of totalitarianism exclude Italian Fascism from their typology.[34] One must concede that Mussolini's regime, eager to "normalize" its rapport with a society in which the family, the Church, the monarchy, and the village notable still had entrenched power, fell far short of total control. Even so, Fascism regimented Italians more firmly than any regime before or since.[35] But no regime, not even Hitler's or Stalin's, ever managed to pinch off every last parcel of privacy and personal or group autonomy.[36]

The 1950s theorists of totalitarianism believed that Hitler and Stalin fit their model most closely. Both Nazi Germany and Soviet Russia, according to the criteria developed by Carl J. Friedrich and Zbigniew K. Brzezinski in 1956, were governed by single parties employing an official ideology, terroristic police control, and a monopoly of power over all means of communication, armed force, and economic organization.[37] During the rebellious 1960s, a new generation accused the totalitarianism theorists of serving cold war ends, by transferring the patriotic anti-Nazism of World War II to the new communist enemy.[38]

While its scholarly use declined thereafter for a time in the United States, the totalitarian paradigm remained important to those European scholars, particularly in West Germany, who wanted to affirm, against the Marxists, that what had really mattered about Hitler was his destruction of liberty, not his relation to capitalism.[39] At the end of the twentieth century, after the demise of the Soviet Union had prompted renewed scrutiny of its sins and of many Western intellectuals' blindness to them, the totalitarian model came back into vogue, along with its corollary that Nazism and communism represented a common evil.[40]

Thus the totalitarian interpretation of fascism has been as hotly politicized as the Marxist one.[41] Even so, it should be debated on its merits and not with respect to its enlistment by one camp or another. It purports to explain Nazism (and Stalinism) by focusing on their aspiration to total control, and on the tools by which they sought to exert it. No doubt Nazi and communist mechanisms of control had many similarities. Awaiting the knock in the night and rotting in a camp must have felt very similar to both systems' sufferers (Jews and Gypsies apart, of course).[42] In both regimes, law was subordinated to "higher" imperatives of race or class. Focusing upon the techniques of control, however, obscures important differences.

However similar it might feel, from the victim's point of view, to die of typhus, malnutrition, exhaustion, or harsh questioning in one of Stalin's Siberian camps or in, say, Hitler's Mauthausen stone quarry, Stalin's regime differed profoundly from Hitler's in social dynamics as well as in aims. Stalin ruled a civil society that had been radically simplified by the Bolshevik Revolution, and thus he did not have to concern himself with autonomous concentrations of inherited social and economic power. Hitler (totally unlike Stalin) came into power with the assent and even assistance of traditional elites, and governed in strained but effective association with them. In Nazi Germany the party jostled with the state bureaucracy, industrial and agricultural proprietors, churches, and other traditional elites for power. Totalitarian theory is blind to this fundamental character of the Nazi governing system, and thus tends to fortify the elites' postwar claim that Hitler tried to destroy them (as indeed the final cataclysm of the lost war began to do).

Hitlerism and Stalinism also differed profoundly in their declared ultimate aims—for one, the supremacy of a master race; for the other, universal equality—though Stalin's egregious and barbarous perversions tended to make his regime converge with Hitler's in its murderous instruments. Focusing upon central authority, the totalitarian paradigm overlooks the murderous frenzy that boiled from below in fascism.

Treating Hitler and Stalin together as totalitarians often becomes an exercise in comparative moral judgment: Which monster was more monstrous?[43] Were Stalin's two forms of mass murder—reckless economic experiment and the paranoid persecution of "enemies"—the moral equivalent of Hitler's attempt to purify his nation by exterminating the medically and racially impure?[44]

The strongest case for equating Stalin's terror with Hitler's is the famine of 1931, which, it is alleged, targeted Ukrainians and thus amounted to genocide. This famine, though indeed the result of criminal negligence, affected Russians with equal severity.[45] Opponents would note fundamental differences. Stalin killed in grossly arbitrary fashion whomever his paranoid mind decided were "class enemies" (a condition one can change), in a way that struck mostly at adult males among the dictator's fellow citizens. Hitler, by contrast, killed "race enemies," an irremediable condition that condemns even newborns. He wanted to liquidate entire peoples, including their tombstones and their cultural artifacts. This book acknowleges the repugnance of both terrors, but condemns even more strongly Nazi biologically racialist extermination because it admitted no salvation even for women and children.[46]

A more pragmatic criticism of the totalitarian model complains that its image of an efficient all-encompassing mechanism prevents us from grasping the disorderly character of Hitler's rule, which reduced government to personal fiefdoms unable to discuss policy options and choose among them rationally.[47] Mussolini, assuming multiple cabinet ministries himself but unable to impose orderly priorities on any of them, did no better. The totalitarian image may evoke powerfully the dreams and aspirations of dictators, but it actually obstructs any examination of the vital matter of how effectively fascist regimes managed to embed themselves in the half-compliant, half-recalcitrant societies they ruled.

The older concept of political religion—it dates to the French Revolution—was quickly applied to fascism, as well as to communism, and not only by their enemies.[48] At the level of broad analogy, it points usefully to the way fascism, like religion, mobilized believers around sacred rites and words, excited them to self-denying fervor, and preached a revealed truth that admitted no dissidence. Scrutinized more carefully,[49] the concept of political religion turns out to encompass several quite different issues. The most straightforward one is the many elements that fascism borrows from the religious culture of the society it seeks to penetrate. With its focus upon mechanisms, this subject tells us more about taking root and about exercising power than about achieving power.

A second element of the political religion concept is the more challenging functional argument that fascism fills a void opened by the secularization of society and morality.[50] If this approach is meant to help explain why fascism succeeded in some Christian countries rather than others, it requires us to believe that the "ontological crisis" was more severe in Germany and Italy than in France and Britain in the early twentieth century—a case that might be difficult to make.

It also suggests that established religions and fascism are irreconcilable opponents—a third element of the political religion concept. In Germany and Italy, however, the two had a complex relationship that did not exclude cooperation. They joined forces against communism while competing for the same terrain. While this situation led to a modus vivendi in the Italian case, it generated a "destructive mimesis of Christianity"[51] in the Nazi case. At the opposite extreme, fascism could produce something resembling an unauthorized Christian auxiliary in the Romanian, Croat, and Belgian cases and an Islamic auxiliary, if we accept as fascist some extra-European movements I considered in chapter 7.

The fascist leaders themselves, as we observed in chapter 1, called their movements ideologies, and many interpreters have taken them at their word. It is commonplace to see fascism defined by extracting common threads from party programs, by analogy with the other "isms." This works better for the other "isms," founded in the era of educated elite politics. I tried earlier to suggest that fascism bears a different relation to ideas than the nineteenth-century "isms," and that intellectual positions (not basic mobilizing passions like racial hatreds, of course) were likely to be dropped or added according to the tactical needs of the moment. All the "isms" did this, but only fascism had such contempt for reason and intellect that it never even bothered to justify its shifts.[52]

Nowadays cultural studies are replacing intellectual history as the strategy of choice for elucidating the attraction and efficacity of fascism.[53] As early as World War II, the American ethnographer Gregory Bateson employed "the sort of analysis that an anthropologist applies to the mythology of a primitive or modern people" to pick apart the themes and techniques of the Nazi propaganda film *Hitler Youth Quex*. Bateson believed that "this film . . . must tell us about the psychology of its makers, and tell us perhaps more than they intended to tell."[54] Since the 1970s and increasingly today, decoding the culture of fascist societies by an anthropological or ethnographical gaze has become a fashionable intellectual strategy. It shows vividly how fascist movements and regimes presented themselves. The main problem with cultural studies of fascist imagery and rhetoric is their frequent failure to ask how influential these were. This rule has important exceptions, such as Luisa Passerini's study of the popular memory of Fascism in the Italian city of Turin in the 1980s.[55] Generally, however, the study of fascist culture by itself does not explain how fascists acquired the power to control culture, nor how deeply into popular consciousness fascist culture penetrated in competition with either preexisting religious, familial, or community values or with commercialized popular culture.

In any event, culture differs so profoundly from one national setting and one period to another that it is hard to find any cultural program common to all fascist movements, or to all the stages. The *macho* restoration of a threatened patriarchy, for example, comes close to being a universal fascist value, but Mussolini advocated female suffrage in his first program, and Hitler did not mention gender issues in his 25 Points. Since Mussolini favored the avant-garde, at least until the 1930s, while Hitler preferred conventional postcard art, it is unlikely that we can identify a single immutable fascist style or aesthetic that would apply to all the national cases.[56]

A less-often-mentioned problem with cultural studies of fascism arises from their failure to make comparisons. Comparison is essential, and it reveals that some countries with a powerful cultural preparation (France, for example) became fascist only by conquest (if then). The effect of fascist propaganda also needs to be compared with that of commercial media, which was clearly greater even in fascist countries. Hollywood, Beale Street, and Madison Avenue probably gave more trouble to fascist dreams of cultural control than the whole liberal and socialist opposition put together.[57] The handwriting was on the wall for those dreams one day in 1937 when Mussolini's oldest son, Vittorio, gave his youngest brother Romano a picture of Duke Ellington, and started the boy down the road to a postwar career as a rather good jazz pianist.[58]

All in all, no one interpretation of fascism seems to have carried the day decisively to everyone's satisfaction.

Boundaries

We cannot understand fascism well without tracing clear boundaries with superficially similar forms. The task is difficult because fascism was widely imitated, especially during the 1930s, when Germany and Italy seemed more successful than the democracies. Borrowings from fascism turned up as far away from their European roots as Bolivia and China.[59]

The simplest boundary separates fascism from classical tyranny. The exiled moderate socialist Gaetano Salvemini, having abandoned his chair as professor of history at Florence and moved to London and then to Harvard because he could not bear to teach without saying what he thought, pointed to the essential difference when he wondered why "Italians felt the need to get rid of their free institutions" at the very moment when they should be taking pride in them, and when they "should step forward toward a more advanced democracy."[60] Fascism, for Salvemini, meant setting aside democracy and due process in public life, to the acclamation of the street. It is a phenomenon of failed democracies, and its novelty was that, instead of simply clamping silence upon citizens as classical tyranny had done since earliest times, it found a technique to channel their passions into the construction of an obligatory domestic unity around projects of internal cleansing and external expansion. We should not use the term *fascism* for predemocratic dictatorships. However cruel, they lack the manipulated mass enthusiasm and demonic energy of fascism, along with the mission of "giving up free institutions" for the sake of national unity, purity, and force.

Fascism is easily confused with military dictatorship, for both fascist leaders militarized their societies and placed wars of conquest at the very center of their aims. Guns[61] and uniforms were a fetish with them. In the 1930s, fascist militias were all uniformed (as, indeed, were socialist militias in that colored-shirt era),[62] and fascists have always wanted to turn society into an armed fraternity. Hitler, newly installed as chancellor of Germany, made the mistake of dressing in a civilian trenchcoat and hat when he went to Venice on June 14, 1934, for his first meeting with the more senior Mussolini, "resplendent with uniform and dagger."[63] Thereafter the *Führer* appeared in uniform on public occasions—sometimes a brown party jacket, later often an unadorned military tunic. But while all fascisms are always militaristic, military dictatorships are not always fascist. Most military dictators have acted simply as tyrants, without daring to unleash the popular excitement of fascism. Military dictatorships are far commoner than fascisms, for they have no necessary connection to a failed democracy and have existed since there have been warriors.

The boundary separating fascism from authoritarianism is more subtle, but it is one of the most essential for understanding.[64] I have already used the term, or the similar one of traditional dictatorship, in discussing Spain, Portugal, Austria, and Vichy France. The fascist-authoritarian boundary was particularly hard to trace in the 1930s, when regimes that were, in reality, authoritarian donned some of the decor of that period's successful fascisms. Although authoritarian regimes often trample civil liberties and are capable of murderous brutality, they do not share fascism's urge to reduce the private sphere to nothing. They accept ill-defined though real domains of private space for traditional "intermediary bodies" like local notables, economic cartels and associations, officer corps, families, and churches. These, rather than an official single party, are the main agencies of social control in authoritarian regimes. Authoritarians would rather leave the population demobilized and passive, while fascists want to engage and excite the public.[65] Authoritarians want a strong but limited state. They hesitate to intervene in the economy, as fascism does readily, or to embark on programs of social welfare. They cling to the status quo rather than proclaim a new way.[66]

General Francisco Franco, for example, who led the Spanish army in revolt against the Spanish republic in July 1936 and became the dictator of Spain in 1939, clearly borrowed some aspects of rule from his ally Mussolini. He called himself *Caudillo* (leader) and made the fascist Falange the only party. During World War II and after, the Allies treated Franco as a partner of the Axis. That impression was fortified by the bloodiness of the Franquist repression, which may have killed as many as two hundred thousand people between 1939 and 1945, and by the regime's efforts to close down cultural and economic contact with the outside world.[67] In April 1945 Spanish officials attended a memorial mass for Hitler. A month later, however, the *Caudillo* explained to his followers that "it was necessary to lower some of the [Falange's] sails."[68]

Thereafter Franco's Spain,[69] always more Catholic than fascist, built its authority upon traditional pillars such as the Church, big landowners, and the army, essentially charging them instead of the state or the ever-weaker Falange with social control. Franco's state intervened little in the economy, and made little effort to regulate the daily life of people as long as they were passive.

The Estado Novo of Portugal[70] differed from fascism even more profoundly than Franco's Spain. Salazar was, in effect, the dictator of Portugal, but he preferred a passive public and a limited state where social power remained in the hands of the Church, the army, and the big landowners. In July 1934, Dr. Salazar actually suppressed an indigenous

Portuguese fascist movement, National Syndicalism, accusing it of "exaltation of youth, the cult of force through so-called direct action, the principle of the superiority of state political power in social life, the propensity for organizing the masses behind a political leader"—not a bad description of fascism.[71]

Vichy France, the regime that replaced the parliamentary republic after the defeat of 1940,[72] was certainly not fascist at the outset, for it had neither a single party nor parallel institutions. A governing system in which France's traditional select civil service ran the state, with enhanced roles for the military, the Church, technical experts, and established economic and social elites, falls clearly into the authoritarian category. After the German invasion of the Soviet Union in June 1941 brought the French Communist Party into open resistance and obliged the German occupation to become much harsher in order to support total war, Vichy and its policy of collaboration with Nazi Germany faced mounting opposition. Parallel organizations appeared in the fight against the Resistance: the *Milice* or supplementary police, "special sections" of the law courts for expeditious trials of dissidents, the Police for Jewish Affairs. But even though, as we saw in chapter 4, a few Paris fascists were given important posts at Vichy in the last days of the regime, they served as individuals rather than as chiefs of an official single party.

What Is Fascism?

The moment has come to give fascism a usable short handle, even though we know that it encompasses its subject no better than a snapshot encompasses a person.

Fascism may be defined as a form of political behavior marked by obsessive preoccupation with community decline, humiliation, or victimhood and by compensatory cults of unity, energy, and purity, in which a mass-based party of committed nationalist militants, working in uneasy but effective collaboration with traditional elites, abandons democratic liberties and pursues with redemptive violence and without ethical or legal restraints goals of internal cleansing and external expansion.

To be sure, political behavior requires choices, and choices—as my critics hasten to point out—bring us back to underlying ideas. Hitler and Mussolini, scornful of the "materialism" of socialism and liberalism, insisted on the centrality of ideas to their movements. Not so, retorted many antifascists who refuse to grant them such dignity. "National Social-ism's ideology is constantly shifting," Franz Neumann observed. "It has certain magical beliefs—leadership adoration, supremacy of the master race—but [it] is not laid down in a series of categorical and dogmatic pro-nouncements."[73] On this point, this book is drawn toward Neumann's position, and I examined at some length in chapter 1 the peculiar rela-tionship of fascism to its ideology—simultaneously proclaimed as central, yet amended or violated as expedient.[74] Nevertheless, fascists knew what they wanted. One cannot banish ideas from the study of fascism, but one can situate them accurately among all the factors that influence this com-plex phenomenon. One can steer between two extremes: fascism con-sisted neither of the uncomplicated application of its program, nor of freewheeling opportunism.

I believe that the ideas that underlie fascist actions are best deduced from those actions, for some of them remain unstated and implicit in fas-cist public language. Many of them belong more to the realm of visceral feelings than to the realm of reasoned propositions. In chapter 2 I called them "mobilizing passions":

- a sense of overwhelming crisis beyond the reach of any tradi-tional solutions;
- the primacy of the group, toward which one has duties superior to every right, whether individual or universal, and the subordi-nation of the individual to it;
- the belief that one's group is a victim, a sentiment that justifies any action, without legal or moral limits, against its enemies, both internal and external;
- dread of the group's decline under the corrosive effects of indi-vidualistic liberalism, class conflict, and alien influences;
- the need for closer integration of a purer community, by consent if possible, or by exclusionary violence if necessary;
- the need for authority by natural chiefs (always male), culmi-nating in a national chieftain who alone is capable of incarnat-ing the group's historical destiny;
- the superiority of the leader's instincts over abstract and universal reason;
- the beauty of violence and the efficacy of will, when they are devoted to the group's success;

- the right of the chosen people to dominate others without restraint from any kind of human or divine law, right being decided by the sole criterion of the group's prowess within a Darwinian struggle.

Fascism according to this definition, as well as behavior in keeping with these feelings, is still visible today. Fascism exists at the level of Stage One within all democratic countries—not excluding the United States. "Giving up free institutions," especially the freedoms of unpopular groups, is recurrently attractive to citizens of Western democracies, including some Americans. We know from tracing its path that fascism does not require a spectacular "march" on some capital to take root; seemingly anodyne decisions to tolerate lawless treatment of national "enemies" is enough. Something very close to classical fascism has reached Stage Two in a few deeply troubled societies. Its further progress is not inevitable, however. Further fascist advances toward power depend in part upon the severity of a crisis, but also very largely upon human choices, especially the choices of those holding economic, social, and political power. Determining the appropriate responses to fascist gains is not easy, since its cycle is not likely to repeat itself blindly. We stand a much better chance of responding wisely, however, if we understand how fascism succeeded in the past.

BIBLIOGRAPHICAL ESSAY

Fascism set off a tidal wave of ink. Renzo De Felice included 12,208 books and articles in a bibliography devoted largely to Italian Fascism.[1] Even more has been published about Hitler and Nazism. Another substantial list of works has been devoted to fascism in other countries, plus numerous studies of generic fascism. Obviously, no lone scholar, however diligent, could possibly master all the literature of all the fascisms. This bibliographical chapter is, therefore, necessarily selective. All I can do here is present a personal choice of works that were particularly helpful to me: by marking turning points, defining major interpretations, or covering essential aspects with authority. Many of them contain detailed bibliographies for more specialized reading. I make no claim to completeness.

I. General Works

The most authoritative narrative history of all fascist movements and regimes is Stanley G. Payne's prodigiously learned *A History of Fascism, 1914–1945* (Madison: University of Wisconsin Press, 1995), but it describes better than it explains. Pierre Milza, *Les fascismes* (Paris: Imprimerie Nationale, 1985), is also well informed and wide-ranging. The most influential recent attempt to define fascism comes from Roger Griffin, *The Nature of Fascism* (London: Routledge, 1994), and *International Fascism: Theories, Causes, and the New Consensus* (London: Arnold, 1998), though his zeal to reduce fascism to one pithy sentence seems to me more likely to inhibit than to stimulate analysis of how and with whom it worked.

Short introductions to fascism are legion. Kevin Passmore's *Fascism* (New York: Oxford University Press, 2002) is very brief but lively. Three of the most recent short introductions take sharply contrasting directions. Mark Neocleous, *Fascism* (Minneapolis: University of Minnesota Press, 1997), adopts a cultural-studies approach in which fascism reflects the dark side of modernity and capitalism, driven not by interests but by images of war, nature, and the nation. Philip Morgan, *Fascism in Europe, 1919–1945* (London: Routledge, 2003), presents a careful and thorough historical narrative. He stops in 1945, but Roger Eatwell, *Fascism: A History* (London: Penguin, 1996), devotes half his limited space to the postwar period.

An excellent introduction to the rise of Nazism is Anthony J. Nicholls, *Weimar and the Rise of Hitler*, 4th ed. (New York: St. Martin's Press, 2000). Conan Fischer,

The Rise of the Nazis, 2nd ed. (Manchester: Manchester University Press, 2002), assesses the party's broad appeal.

The classic short introduction to Mussolini's Italy is Alexander De Grand, *Italian Fascism: Its Origins and Development*, 3rd ed. (Lincoln: University of Nebraska Press, 2000). Other useful brief introductions include Philip Morgan, *Italian Fascism 1919–1945* (Basingstoke: Macmillan, 1995); John Whittam, *Fascist Italy* (Manchester: Manchester University Press, 1995); and Pierre Milza, *Le fascisme italien, 1919–45* (Paris: Éditions du Seuil, 1997).

A wide range of countries receive stimulating discussion in Stein U. Larsen, Bernt Hagtvet, Jan P. Myklbust, eds., *Who Were the Fascists: Social Roots of European Fascism* (Oslo: Universitetsforlaget, 1980). Older collective works that remain valuable include Walter Laqueur, ed., *Fascism: A Reader's Guide* (Berkeley and Los Angeles: University of California Press, 1976); Hans Rogger and Eugen Weber, eds., *The European Right: A Historical Profile* (Berkeley and Los Angeles: University of California Press, 1966); and two volumes edited by Stuart J. Woolf, *Fascism in Europe* (London and New York: Methuen, 1981), and *The Nature of Fascism* (New York: Random House, 1968).

Jeremy Noakes and Geoffrey Pridham, *Nazism 1919–45: A Documentary Reader*, rev. ed., 4 vols. (Exeter: University of Exeter Press, 1995–98), offers an outstanding collection of documents, accompanied by illuminating commentary. Documents on Italian fascism are collected in Charles F. Delzell, ed., *Mediterranean Fascism, 1919–1945* (New York: Harper, 1970); Adrian Lyttelton, ed., *Italian Fascisms: From Pareto to Gentile* (New York: Harper, 1975); John Pollard, *The Fascist Experience in Italy* (London: Routledge, 1998); and Jeffrey Schnapp, *A Primer of Italian Fascism* (Lincoln: University of Nebraska Press, 2000). The Delzell volume contains some documents from Franco's Spain and Salazar's Portugal as well. See also Hugh Thomas, ed., *Selected Writings of José Antonio Primo De Rivera* (London: Jonathan Cape, 1972). Eugen Weber, ed., *Varieties of Fascism* (Melbourne, FL: Krieger, 1982), includes an interesting sampling of fascist texts from all the aforementioned countries plus Britain, Norway, Belgium, Hungary, and Romania, chosen to illustrate Weber's thesis of the revolutionary nature of fascism.

II. Interpretations of Fascism

Renzo De Felice found fault with many general approaches in *Interpretions of Fascism* (Cambridge, MA: Harvard University Press, 1977). He finally came to believe that each regime was unique and that no general interpretation works. Pierre Ayçoberry, *The Nazi Question* (New York: Pantheon, 1981), and Wolfgang Wippermann, *Faschismustheorien*, 7th ed. (Darmstadt: Primus/NNO, 1997), discuss various interpretations and their problems. See also Ernst Nolte, ed., *Theorien über den Faschismus*, 6th ed. (Cologne, Berlin: Kiepenheuer and Witsch, 1984).

Carl J. Friedrich and Zbigniew Brzezinski, *Totalitarian Dictatorship and Autocracy*, 2nd ed. (New York: Praeger, 1966), remains the most substantial analysis of the concept of totalitarianism. Abbott Gleason, *Totalitarianism: The Inner History of the Cold War* (New York: Oxford University Press, 1995), expertly reviews the long debate about it. The concept is attacked and defended in Carl J. Friedrich, Benjamin R. Barber, and Michael Curtis, *Totalitarianism in Perspective: Three Views* (New York: Praeger, 1969).

Authoritarianism is best defined and its borders with fascism most clearly traced by Juan J. Linz, "Totalitarian and Authoritarian Regimes," in Fred Greenstein and Nelson Polsby, eds., *Handbook of Political Science*, vol. 3: *Macropolitical Theory* (Reading, MA: Addison-Wesley, 1975), pp. 175–411, reprinted and updated in Linz, *Totalitarian and Authoritarian Regimes* (Boulder, CO: Lynne Rienner, 2000).

III. Biographies

The preeminent biography of Hitler is now Ian Kershaw, *Hitler, 1889–1936: Hubris* (New York: Norton, 1999), and *Hitler, 1936–1945: Nemesis* (New York: Norton, 2000). Kershaw relates the dictator to the society that imagined him, and that "worked toward" its leader without needing to be forced. Among many earlier biographies, Alan Bullock, *Hitler: A Study in Tyranny*, rev. ed. (New York: Harper, 1962), intelligently fits together the man and his circumstances. Joachim C. Fest, *Hitler* (New York: Harcourt, Brace, Jovanovitch, 1974), has vivid detail.

Brigitte Hamann, *Hitler's Vienna: A Dictator's Apprenticeship* (New York: Oxford University Press, 1999), is the fullest account of Hitler's youth. Harold J. Gordon, *Hitler and the Beer Hall Putsch* (Princeton: Princeton University Press, 1972), examines a crucial early step in Hitler's career. The temptation to psychoanalyze Hitler was irresistible. An early example, Walter C. Langer, *The Mind of Adolf Hitler* (New York: Basic Books, 1972), was prepared for U.S. policy-makers during World War II. The 1970s brought Robert G. L. Waite, *The Psychopathic God* (New York: Basic Books, 1977), and Rudolf Binion, *Hitler Among the Germans* (New York, Oxford, Amsterdam: Elsevier, 1976). The most recent study, Fredrick C. Redlich, M.D., *Hitler: Diagnosis of a Destructive Prophet* (New York: Oxford University Press, 1998), is more cautious. Judging a psychoanalysis of Hitler of "little value" because of the scarcity of evidence (p. xiv), Dr. Redlich reviews Hitler's medical history and draws a psychological profile.

Eberhard Jäckel insists in *Hitler's World View: A Blueprint for Power* (Cambridge, MA: Harvard University Press, 1981) that Hitler had a program, despite the inevitable opportunistic adjustments. That his social Darwinism applied to economy and society as well as to international relations is shown by Henry A. Turner, Jr., "Hitlers Einstellung zu Wirtschaft und Gesellschaft," *Geschichte und Gesellschaft* 2:1 (1976), pp. 89–117.

The fullest biography of Mussolini in English is now R. J. B. Bosworth, *Mussolini* (London: Arnold, 2002). It presents the *Duce* as a clever but hollow opportunist. Pierre Milza, *Mussolini* (Paris: Fayard, 1999), now available only in French and Italian, is well informed, balanced, and thoughtful. Denis Mack Smith, *Mussolini* (New York: Knopf, 1982), is condescending, and thin on the broader setting. Also in English is Jasper Ridley, *Mussolini* (London: Constable, 1995), a fluent and reasonably accurate short biography by a nonspecialist. Alessandro Campi, *Mussolini* (Bologna: Il Mulino, 2001), is a suggestive brief assessment. Still valuable for the early years is

Bibliographical Essay

Gaudens Megaro, *Mussolini in the Making* (Boston: Houghton Mifflin, 1938). Luisa Passerini, *Mussolini imaginario: Storia di une biografia, 1915–1939* (Bari: Laterza, 1991), gives a fascinating look at how Mussolini was presented to Italians, but his images were more the result of his power than an explanation for it.

The biography of reference is the uneven and idiosyncratic but exhaustively documented Renzo De Felice, *Mussolini*, 7 vols. (Turin: Einaudi, 1965–97), not quite finished at the author's death in 1996.[2] De Felice's massive work and his fluctuating opinions are usefully assessed by Borden W. Painter, Jr., "Renzo De Felice and the Historiography of Italian Fascism," *American Historical Review* 95:2 (April 1990), pp. 391–405; by Emilio Gentile (De Felice's student) in "Fascism in Italian Historiography: In Search of an Individual Historical Identity," *Journal of Contemporary History* 21 (1986), pp. 179–208; and more critically by MacGregor Knox in "In the Duce's Defense," *Times* (London) *Literary Supplement*, February 26, 1999, pp. 3–4.

IV. Creation of Movements and Taking Root

A thoughtful reflection on the beginnings of fascism is Roberto Vivarelli, "Interpretations of the Origins of Fascism," *Journal of Modern History* 63:1 (March 1991), pp. 29–43.

The dominant approach to fascism's beginnings has been to trace its ideological lineage. Important works in this vein on Italy include Emilio Gentile, *Le origini dell'ideologia fascista: 1918–1925* (Bari: Laterza, 1982), and Zeev Sternhell, with Mario Sznajder and Maia Asheri, *The Origins of Fascist Ideology* (Princeton: Princeton University Press, 1994). The intellectual and cultural roots of Nazism have been studied most influentially by George L. Mosse, *The Crisis of German Ideology* (New York: Howard Fertig, 1998) (orig. pub. 1964), and Fritz R. Stern, *The Politics of Cultural Despair* (Berkeley and Los Angeles: University of California Press, 1974) (orig. pub. 1961).

To understand fascism's later course and following, however, one must also look at the political and social settings and ask how fascism came to represent certain specific interests and engage important allies. Regional differences were also important. The most sophisticated and probing account of how fascism became powerful in one Italian locality is Paul Corner, *Fascism in Ferrara* (Oxford: Oxford University Press, 1976). Other good local studies of how Italian fascism took root include Frank M. Snowden, *Violence and Great Estates in the South of Italy: Apulia 1900–1922* (Cambridge: Cambridge University Press, 1986), and *The Fascist Revolution in Tuscany, 1919–1922* (Cambridge: Cambridge University Press, 1989); Anthony L. Cardoza, *Agrarian Elites and Italian Fascism: The Province of Bologna, 1901–1926* (Princeton: Princeton University Press, 1982); Francis Jay Demers, *Le origini del fascismo a Cremona* (Bari: Laterza, 1979); A. Roveri, *Le origini del fascismo a Ferrara, 1915–25* (Milan: Feltrinelli, 1971); Simona Colarizi, *Dopoguerra e fascismo in Puglia* (Bari: Laterza, 1971); and Alice Kelikian, *Town and Country under Fascism: The Transformation of Brescia, 1915–1926* (Oxford: Oxford University Press, 1985). Jonathan Steinberg, "Fascism in the Italian South," in David Forgacs, ed., *Rethinking Italian Fascism*

(London: Lawrence and Wishart, 1986), pp. 83–109, clarifies the special way Fascism penetrated the clientelism of the *mezzogiorno*.

For the local rooting of Nazism, the reader should not miss the compelling narrative of William Sheridan Allen, *The Nazi Seizure of Power: The Experience of a Single German Town*, rev. ed. (New York: Franklin Watts, 1984). Rudy Koshar has done important work on "the process by which the intermediary structure was taken over by the Nazis." See his "From *Stammtisch* to Party: Nazi Joiners and the Contradictions of Grassroots Fascism in Weimar Germany," *Journal of Modern History* 59:1 (March 1987), pp. 1–24, and his local studies: "Two Nazisms: The Social Context of Nazi Mobilization in Marburg and Tübingen," *Social History* 7:1 (January 1982), and *Social Life, Local Politics, and Nazism: Marburg, 1880–1935* (Chapel Hill: University of North Carolina Press, 1986). See also Anthony McElligott, *Contested City: Municipal Politics and the Rise of Nazism in Altona, 1917–1937* (Ann Arbor: University of Michigan Press, 1998).

Nazism in particular German states is the subject of important works by Jeremy Noakes, *The Nazi Party in Lower Saxony* (London: Oxford University Press, 1971); Geoffrey Pridham, *Hitler's Rise to Power: The Nazi Movement in Bavaria, 1923–1933* (London: Hart-Davis MacGibbon, 1973); Johnpeter Horst Grill, *The Nazi Movement in Baden, 1920–1945* (Chapel Hill: University of North Carolina Press, 1983); and Rudolf Heberle, *From Democracy to Nazism* (New York: Grosset and Dunlap, 1970) (on Schleswig-Holstein).

Conan Fischer evokes the violent, ideologically contradictory subculture of the SA in *Stormtroopers* (London: George Allen and Unwin, 1983). The fullest study now is Peter Longerich, *Die braune Bataillone: Geschichte der SA* (Munich: C. H. Beck, 1989).

Preconditions: Jürgen Kocka thought the persistence of powerful pre-industrial elites was the most important precondition for the growth of fascism. See his "Ursachen des Nationalsozialismus," *Aus Politik und Zeitgeschichte* (Beilage zur Wochenzeitung *Das Parlament*), June 21, 1980, pp. 3–15. Geoff Eley replied with an argument favoring capitalist crisis as the main precondition, in "What Produces Fascism: Preindustrial Traditions or a Crisis of the Capitalist State?" *Politics and Society* 12:2 (1983), pp. 53–82. Gregory M. Luebbert proposed in *Liberalism, Fascism or Social Democracy: Social Class and the Political Origins of Regimes in Interwar Europe* (Oxford: Oxford University Press, 1991), that the most important variable is political coalition building: liberalism prevailed in political systems where labor accepted gradual amelioration and where both labor and family farmers supported liberal reformers, while fascism thrived where labor was militant and where, under crisis conditions, frightened urban liberals and family farmers looked for reinforcements. The political scientists Gisèle de Meur and Dirk Berg-Schlosser set up a system for analyzing multiple political, economic, and social variables to show where fascism was likely in "Conditions of Authoritarianism, Fascism, and Democracy in Interwar Europe," in *Comparative Political Studies* 29:4 (August 1996), pp. 423–68. They point out the difficulties of comparing a very large number of variables for a relatively small number of cases; their approach necessarily leaves out leaders' individual choices.

Bibliographical Essay

Like Luebbert, Barrington Moore, Jr., *The Social Origins of Dictatorship and Democracy: Lord and Peasant in the Making of the Modern World* (Boston: Beacon Press, 1993) (orig. pub. 1966), puts the farm economy at the center of his analysis, but takes a longer-term perspective on the different paths by which agriculture encountered capitalism in Britain, Germany, and Japan.

These studies of preconditions for the implanting of fascism emphasize social and economic forces and grievances. William Brustein, *The Logic of Evil: The Social Origins of the Nazi Party, 1925–33* (New Haven: Yale University Press, 1996), argues back from membership statistics (problematical) to conclude (controversially) that early party members concluded by rational judgment that the Nazi social program would bring them direct benefits, more than because of passions or hatreds.

More authors have stressed fascism's appeal to irrational feelings. The appeal of a masculine fraternity is elaborately illustrated for the Nazi case by Klaus Theweleit, *Male Fantasies* (Minneapolis: University of Minnesota Press, 1987–89), though similar fantasies may have existed in countries that did not go fascist. For Italy, see Barbara Spackman, *Fascist Virilities: Rhetoric, Ideology, and Social Fantasy in Italy* (Minneapolis: University of Minnesota Press, 1997). Between the wars, the sociologists of the Frankfurt School found Freud as useful as Marx for explaining fascism, an interest that produced Theodor Adorno et al., *The Authoritarian Personality* (New York: Norton, 1982) (orig. pub. 1950). Erich Fromm, *Escape from Freedom* (New York: Holt, Rinehart and Winston, 1941), argued influentially that modern freedom is so frightening that many people seek the comfort of submission. Peter Loewenburg's "Psychohistorical Origins of the Nazi Youth Cohort," *American Historical Review* 76 (1971), pp. 1457–1502, based his argument more successfully than most psychohistorians on a specific historical context to show how a whole generation of German children was prepared for Nazism by the "Turnip Winter" of 1917 and the absence of fathers, though the children of all belligerent countries suffered the latter. The problem with all psychological explanations is that it is very difficult to prove that the emotional experiences of Italians and Germans differed decisively from those of, say, the French.

Veterans were a key element in early fascist recruitment (though many were younger). The richest study of any European country's veterans and the roles they played after 1918 is Antoine Prost, *Les Anciens combattants et la société française* (Paris: Presses de la Fondation nationale des Sciences Politiques, 1977). For Germany, one may consult the more narrowly political accounts of Volker R. Berghahn, *Der Stahlhelm* (Düsseldorf: Droste, 1966); Karl Rohe, *Das Reichsbanner Schwarz Rot Gold* (Düsseldorf: Droste, 1966); and, for the Left, Kurt G. P. Schuster, *Der Rote Frontkämpferbund* (Düsseldorf: Droste, 1975). Graham Wootton examines the tactics of British veterans in *The Politics of Influence* (Cambridge, MA: Harvard University Press, 1963). The standard account of Italian veterans, G. Sabatucci, *I combattenti del primo dopoguerra* (Bari: Laterza, 1974), covers only the immediate postwar years.

V. Getting Power

The most penetrating analysis in any language of Mussolini's arrival in power is Adrian Lyttelton, *The Seizure of Power*, 2nd ed. (Princeton: Princeton University

Press, 1987). Angelo Tasca's well-informed and compelling *The Rise of Italian Fascism: 1918–1922* (New York: Howard Fertig, 1966), the work of an ex-socialist exile first published in France in 1938, is still worth reading.

The most authoritative analysis in English of the contingencies, uncertainties, and choices involved in the last steps of Hitler's arrival in power is Henry Ashby Turner, Jr., *Hitler's Thirty Days to Power* (Reading, MA: Addison-Wesley, 1996). The most thorough longer-term historical analysis is Karl Dietrich Bracher, Gerhard Schulz, and Wolfgang Sauer, *Die nationalsozialistische Machtergreifung: Studien zur Errichtung des totalitären Herrschaftssystems in Deutschland, 1933–34,* 3 vols. (Cologne and Opladen: Westdeutscher Verlag, 1960–62). Gerhard Schulz examines in great detail the way constitutional and political systems evolved during the final crisis in *Zwischen Demokratie und Diktatur,* vol. III: *Von Brüning zu Hitler: Der Wandel des politischen systems in Deutschland 1930–33* (Berlin, New York: De Gruyter, 1992). The articles in Peter D. Stachura, ed., *The Nazi Machtergreifung* (London, Boston: Allen Unwin, 1983), are still useful on the reactions of different social groups. Peter Fritzsche, *Germans into Nazis* (Cambridge, MA: Harvard University Press, 1998), gives a lively account of popular enthusiasm.

An essential precondition for the fascist achievement of power is the opening of space brought about by the failure of democracy, a subject too often overlooked because so many assume that the fascist leader did everything himself. A rare and valuable study is Juan J. Linz and Alfred Stepan, ed., *The Breakdown of Democratic Regimes: Europe* (Baltimore: Johns Hopkins University Press, 1978); the article on Italy by Paolo Farneti is particularly helpful. The thoughtful essays in Dirk Berg-Schlosse and Jeremy Mitchell, eds., *Conditions of Democracy in Europe, 1919–1939* (New York: St. Martin's Press, 2000), are also relevant.

On the failure of the Weimar Republic, the classic work is Karl Dietrich Bracher, *Die Auflösung der Weimarer Republik* (Villingen: Ring-Verlag, 1960). Hans Mommsen, *The Rise and Fall of Weimar Germany* (Chapel Hill: University of North Carolina Press, 1996), and Detlev Peukert, *The Weimar Republic: The Crisis of Classical Modernity,* trans. Richard Deveson (New York: Hill and Wang, 1993), are rich and suggestive, while Eberhard Kolb, *The Weimar Republic* (London, Boston: Unwin Hyman, 1988), wears well. Larry Eugene Jones, *German Liberalism and the Dissolution of the Weimar Party System* (Chapel Hill: University of North Carolina Press, 1988), is the most thoughtful account of the collapse of the Weimar political center. Two excellent articles on how another decisive group—farmers—turned to Nazism are Horst Gies, "The NSDAP and Agrarian Organizations in the Final Phase of the Weimar Republic," in Henry Ashby Turner, Jr., ed., *Nazism and the Third Reich* (New York: Franklin Watts, 1972), and Zdenek Zofka, "Between Bauernbund and National Socialism: The Political Orientation of the Peasants in the Final Phases of the Weimar Republic," in Thomas Childers, ed., *The Formation of the Nazi Constituency* (London: Croom Helm, 1986). This work is useful from beginning to end.

Electoral success mattered more for Hitler than for Mussolini. Richard Hamilton, *Who Voted for Hitler* (Princeton: Princeton University Press, 1982), first proved that Hitler's electoral backing included many upper-class as well as lower-middle-class voters. Since then, computer-assisted studies of the Nazi electorate have established firmer knowledge of the Nazi Party's success in drawing votes from all classes, though less so from populations well anchored in another community, such as Catholics or Marxists. Class seems to have mattered less than culture. See Thomas Childers, *The Nazi Voter* (Chapel Hill: University of North Carolina Press, 1983), as well as his aforementioned edited volume, *The Formation of the Nazi Constituency*; and Jürgen Falter, *Hitlers Wähler* (Munich: Beck, 1991). Dick Geary, "Who Voted for the Nazis," *History Today* 48:10 (October 1998), pp. 8–14, summarizes the findings briefly.

Recent studies of party membership, as distinct from voters, have undermined the lower-middle-class interpretation of fascism and have greatly magnified the working-class role, especially if one adds the SA (many of whom were not party members). Major works here include Detlef Mühlberger, *Hitler's Followers* (London: Routledge, 1991), and Conan Fischer, ed., *The Rise of National Socialism and the Working Class* (Providence, RI: Berghahn, 1996). Best in a much smaller field for Italy is Jens Petersen, "Elettorato e base sociale del fascismo negli anni venti," *Studi storici* 3 (1975), pp. 627–69. See in English the article by Marco Revelli on Italy in Detlef Mühlberger, ed., *The Social Basis of European Fascist Movements* (London: Croom Helm, 1987).

Useful social analyses of members and voters in many national cases appear in Larsen et al., *Who Were the Fascists*, and Mühlberger, *Social Basis*, mentioned above. Studies of fascist movements' social composition need to distinguish among different stages, for during the movement stage membership fluctuated, while parties in power enjoyed a bandwagoning effect.

Emilio Gentile, *Storia del Partito Fascista 1919–1922: Movimento e Militia* (Bari: Laterza, 1989), is the first serious history of Mussolini's party. He carries the story further in *Fascismo e antifascismo: I partiti italiani fra le due guerre* (Florence: Le Monnier, 2000), a work that also analyzes the nonfascist and antifascist parties.

The Nazi Party has been much more widely studied. The latest is Michael Kater, *The Nazi Party: A Social Profile of Members and Leaders, 1919–45* (Oxford: Blackwell, 1983), while Dietrich Orlow, *History of the Nazi Party*, 2 vols. (Pittsburgh: University of Pittsburgh Press, 1969–73), is more useful for institutional structures than for membership.

The complicated question of the sources of the Nazis' money has been put on solid ground by Henry Ashby Turner, Jr., who shows, in *German Big Business and the Rise of Hitler* (New York: Oxford University Press, 1985), on the basis of exhaustive studies of business archives, that German industrialists contributed to all non-Marxist parties, that they distrusted Hitler and gave him limited support, and that they preferred that von Papen be chancellor. The Nazis never depended heavily on wealthy contributors, for they drew important sums from rallies and small contributions. The financing of Italian Fascism, less studied, has to be pieced together from De Felice and other biographies. Who paid for Mussolini's new pro-war newspaper in 1915 is definitively settled by William A. Renzi, "Mussolini's Sources of Financial Support, 1914–1915," *History* 56:187 (June 1971), pp. 186–206.

VI. Exercising Power

Ian Kershaw, *The Nazi Dictatorship: Problems and Perspectives of Interpretation*, 4th ed. (London: Arnold, 2000), is a very thoughtful and helpful examination of different intepretations of Nazism in power. A parallel work about Fascist Italy, enlightening despite a testy polemical edge, is R. J. B. Bosworth, *The Italian Dictatorship: Problems and Perspectives in Interpreting Mussolini and Fascism* (London: Arnold, 1998). Bosworth is highly critical of De Felice, his student Emilio Gentile, and cultural studies. A recent brief overview of Hitler's regime is Jost Dülffer, *Nazi Germany: Faith and Annihilation, 1933–1945* (London: Arnold, 1996).

It once seemed natural to view fascist societies as homogeneous emanations of the dictator's will. Today scholars find that how the dictator's will meshed with society is a much more complex and problematical matter than once assumed: Was the fascist project imposed by force, was it applied by the persuasion of propaganda, or was it negotiated around converging interests with powerful elements in society?

Earlier studies of the Nazi regime emphasized dictatorial control from above: for example, Karl Dietrich Bracher, *The German Dictatorship* (New York: Praeger, 1970). See, more briefly, Bracher, "The Stages of Totalitarian Integration," in Hajo Holborn, ed., *Republic to Reich: The Making of the Nazi Revolution* (New York: Pantheon, 1972).

More recently, emphasis has been placed upon the complexity of the Nazi regime, within which many elements of traditional constitutional government and conservative civil society coexisted with capricious party rule, and in which Hitler arbitrated among competing and overlapping agencies. The founding works about this complexity were Ernst Fraenkel, *The Dual State* (New York: Oxford University Press, 1941), with its still-fruitful distinction between the "normative" and "prerogative" states within the Nazi system, and Franz Neumann, *Behemoth* (New York: Oxford University Press, 1942). More recently, Martin Broszat, *The Hitler State* (London and New York: Longman, 1981), and Hans Mommsen in many works, of which a sample is published in English as *From Weimar to Auschwitz* (Oxford: Oxford University Press, 1991), have produced a more sophisticated concept of the complex sharing of power by conservatives and Nazis as "polyocracy." The most complete collection of Hans Mommsen's writings is Hans Mommsen, *Der Nationalsozialismus und die deutsche Gesellschaft: Ausgewählte Aufsätze*, ed. Lutz Niethammer and Bernd Weisbrod (Reinbeck bei Hamburg: Rowohlt, 1991). A recent brief study of the Nazi regime from this perspective is Norbert Frei, *National Socialist Rule in Germany: The Führer State, 1933–1945* (Oxford: Blackwell, 1993; 2nd German ed., 2001). Pierre Ayçoberry revisits these issues in *Social History of the Third Reich* (New York: New Press, 2000).

Similarly, the study of Mussolini's Italy was long dominated by De Felice, who emphasized personal rule and totalitarian aspirations, aided by popular passivity and "consensus." His disciple Emilio Gentile argues in *La via italiana al totalitarismo: Il partito e lo Stato nel regime fascista* (Rome: La Nuova Italia Scientifica, 1995), that the regime made serious progress in this direction in the 1930s. Though he admits that the totalitarian experiment was incomplete, he is less interested in the problem of how the Fascist project was altered and subverted in the process of its integration into Italian society.

Massimo Legnani was developing a polycratic analysis of Fascist Italy at his untimely death. His articles were collected posthumously in Legnani, *L'Italia dal fascismo alla Repubblica: Sistema de potere e alleanze sociali* (Rome: Carocci, 2000), and his approach was taken up by A. de Bernardi, *Une dittatura moderna: Il fascismo come problema storico* (Milan: Bruno Mondadori, 2001)—the word *polycratic* even appears (p. 222). See also Philippe Burrin, "Politique et société: Les structures du pouvoir dans l'Italie fasciste et l'Allemagne nazie," *Annales: Économies, sociétés, civilisations* 43:3 (June 1988).

Several collections of illuminating articles have given welcome emphasis to the complex and selective way Fascism was integrated into Italian society by Mussolini's efforts to "normalize" relations with preexisting social powers, or (less successfully) to dominate them. Outstanding for Italy is Angelo Del Boca, Massimo Legnani, and Mario G. Rossi, eds., *Il Regime Fascista: Storia et storiografia* (Bari: Laterza, 1995). See in English, Roland Sarti, ed., *The Ax Within: Fascism in Action* (New York: Franklin Watts, 1974). Alberto Aquarone and Maurizio Vernassa, *Il regime fascista*, new ed. (Bologna: Il Mulino, 1974); and Guido Quazza, ed., *Fascismo e società italiana* (Turin: Einaudi, 1973), the latter a series of well-informed essays by open-minded Marxists, are still interesting. Edward R. Tannenbaum, *The Fascist Experience: Italian Society and Culture, 1922–1945* (New York: Basic Books, 1972), though dated, has no equivalent in English for life under the dictatorship.

Salvatore Lupo's rich *Il fascismo: La politica in un regime totalitario* (Rome: Donzelli, 2000), takes another innovative look at the complexity of the regime, with its regional variations, personal rivalries, and unfolding radicalization. He is particularly enlightening on the peculiarities of Fascism in the south. Patrizia Dogliani, *L'Italia Fascista, 1922–1940* (Milan: Sansoni, 1999), gives a stimulating new survey of how the regime worked up until entry into World War II, with a very full bibliography. Jens Petersen and Wolfgang Schieder, *Faschismus und Gesellschaft in Italien: Staat, Wirtschaft, Kultur* (Cologne: S. H. Verlag, 1998), contains articles of interest. See also a stimulating discussion among these same scholars and some others in Kolloquien des Instituts für Zeitgeschichte, *Der italienische Faschismus: Probleme und Forschungstendenzen* (Munich: Oldenbourg, 1983).

The willing cooperation of citizens with fascist regimes and the selective nature of these regimes' terror, which did not threaten most ordinary citizens, is the subject of an important new line of research, especially for Nazi Germany. Denunciation, the most common form of citizen cooperation with the fascist regimes, made social control possible with an astonishingly small number of police. See Robert Gellately, *The Gestapo and German Society: Enforcing Racial Policy, 1933–1945* (New York: Oxford University Press, 1990), and *Backing Hitler* (Oxford: Oxford University Press, 2001). A superior synthesis for Germany is Eric A. Johnson, *Nazi Terror: The Gestapo, Jews, and Ordinary Germans* (New York: Basic Books, 1999). Groundbreaking new works on the Italian repressive system are Mimmo Franzinelli's very detailed

Bibliographical Essay

I tentacoli dell'OVRA (Turin: Bollati Boringhieri, 1999); Romano Canosa, *I servizi segreti del Duce: I persecutore e le vittimi* (Milan: Mondadori, 2000); and, for denouncers, Mimmo Franzinelli, *I Delatori!* (Milan: Mondadori, 2001). Paul Corner gives a timely reminder of the harsh side of Mussolini's regime in "Italian Fascism: Whatever Happened to Dictatorship?" in *Journal of Modern History* 74 (June 2002), pp. 325–51.

Education and youth organizations were at the heart of the fascist program of social control. For Italy, see George L. Williams, *Fascist Thought and Totalitarianism in Italy's Secondary Schools: Theory and Practice, 1922–1943* (New York: Peter Lang, 1994); Mario Isnenghi, *L'educazione dell'italiano: Il fascismo e l'organizzazione della cultura* (Bologna: L. Capelli, 1979); Jürgen Charnitsky, *Die Schulpolitik des faschistischen Regimes in Italien (1922–1943)* (Tübingen: Max Niemeyer, 1994), and "Unterricht und Erziehung im faschistischen Italien: Von der Reform Gentile zur Carta della Scuola," in Jens Petersen and Wolfgang Schieder, eds., *Faschismus und Gesellschaft in Italien*, mentioned above, pp. 109–32. Doug Thompson, *State and Control in Fascist Italy: Culture and Conformity, 1925–1943* (Manchester: Manchester University Press, 1991), emphasizes the coercive side.

The fullest accounts of education under Nazism are Michael Grüttner, *Studenten im dritten Reich* (Paderborn: Ferdinand Schöningh, 1995), and Geoffrey G. Giles, *Students and National Socialism in Germany* (Princeton: Princeton University Press, 1985). See also Barbara Schneider, *Die höhere Schule im Nationalsozialismus* (Cologne: Böhlau, 2000), and relevant sections of the Peukert work just below.

Fascist efforts to mobilize youth are treated by Tracy Koon, *Believe, Obey, Fight: Political Socialization of Youth in Fascist Italy* (Chapel Hill: University of North Carolina Press, 1985), and Gerhard Rempel, *Hitler's Children: The Hitler Youth and the SS* (Chapel Hill: University of North Carolina Press, 1989). Detlev Peukert reveals their failure in fascinating chapters on the "Edelweiss Pirates," enthusiasts of swing, and other nonconformist youth in Nazi Germany in *Inside Nazi Germany: Conformity, Opposition, and Racism in Everyday Life* (New Haven: Yale University Press, 1987).

Tom Buchanan and Martin Conway, eds., *Political Catholicism in Europe, 1918–1965* (Oxford: Clarendon, 1996), is a good starting point for the Catholic Church's responses to fascism and to communism (considered the greater threat). See also the more specialized articles in Richard J. Wolff and Jörg K. Hoensch, *Catholics, the State, and the European Radical Right* (Boulder, CO: Social Science Monographs, 1987). The classic works for Italy are Arturo Carlo Jemolo, *Church and State in Italy, 1850–1960*, trans. D. Moore (Oxford: Blackwell, 1960), and Daniel A. Binchy, *Church and State in Fascist Italy* (Oxford: Oxford University Press, 1941). These may now be supplemented by John F. Pollard, *The Vatican and Italian Fascism, 1929–1932* (Cambridge: Cambridge University Press, 1985), and Peter Kent, *The Pope and the Duce* (London: Macmillan, 1981).

For the all-important bureaucracy, the classic work is Hans Mommsen, *Beamtentum im dritten Reich* (Stuttgart: Verlags-Anstalt, 1966). Best in English is Jane Caplan, *Government without Administration: State and Civil Service in Weimar and Nazi Germany* (Oxford: Clarendon Press, 1988). An excellent introduction to the Ital-

Bibliographical Essay

ian civil service under Fascism is Guido Melis, "La burocrazia," in Angelo Del Boca et al., *Il regime fascista*, pp. 244–76. Mariuccia Salvati, *Il regime e gli impiegati: La nazionalizzazione piccolo-borghese nel ventennio fascista* (Bari: Laterza, 1992), places the subject within the social history of modern Italy.

Gordon Craig, *The Politics of the Prussian Army, 1640–1945* (Oxford: Clarendon, 1955), is the classic work on civil-military relations in Germany. The most recent is Klaus-Jürgen Müller, *Army, Politics and Society in Germany, 1933–1945* (Manchester: University of Manchester Press, 1987). The preeminent expert on the Italian army is Giorgio Rochat, in many works, including *Breve storia dell'esercito italiana* (Turin: Einaudi, 1978).

A particularly productive vein of research nowadays explores ways in which fascist regimes established links with the professions and with other organized interests. The close implication of the medical profession in Nazi purification projects has attracted special attention: Robert N. Proctor, *Racial Hygiene: Medicine under the Nazis* (Cambridge, MA: Harvard University Press, 1988); Michael Kater, *Doctors Under Hitler* (Chapel Hill: University of North Carolina Press, 1989); and Robert J. Lifton, *The Nazi Doctors* (New York: Basic Books, 1986). The legal professions, equally crucial, have been less studied. The most authoritative for Germany is Lothar Gruchmann's massive *Justiz im dritten Reich: Anpassung und Unterwerfung der Ära Gürtner* (Munich: Oldenbourg, 1988). In English, see the less complete Ingo Muller, *Hitler's Justice* (Cambridge, MA: Harvard University Press, 1991), and sections of Robert Gellately, *Backing Hitler* (Oxford: Oxford University Press, 2001). The main authority on the Italian judiciary is Guido Neppi Modono, who takes a skeptical view of its independence even before Fascism in *Sciopero, potere politico e magistratura (1870–1922)* (Bari: Laterza, 1969), and addresses the judiciary under fascism more directly in the Del Boca and Quazza volumes mentioned above.

The relationship between business concerns and the Nazi regime is the subject of several exemplary monographs. Peter Hayes shows in *Industry and Ideology: IG Farben in the Nazi Era* (Cambridge: Cambridge University Press, 1987), how the giant chemical consortium, which would have preferred to continue the regime of free trade within which it had become the largest corporation in Europe in the 1920s, adapted itself to Nazi autarky and profited mightily, motivated more by a narrow business success ethic and an eye for opportunity than by ideological enthusiasm for Nazism. Daimler-Benz was more enthusiastic, according to Bernard P. Bellon, *Mercedes in Peace and War: German Automobile Workers, 1903–1945* (New York: Columbia University Press, 1990). The rather successful effort of the insurance business to keep some independence is authoritatively treated by Gerald D. Feldman, *Allianz and the German Insurance Business, 1933–1945* (Cambridge: Cambridge University Press, 2001).

The successful maneuvers by Italian business executives to become the managers of Mussolini's corporatist economic system and retain an area of "private power" within Fascism are explored by Roland Sarti, *Fascism and the Industrial Leadership in Italy, 1919–1940: A Study in the Expansion of Private Power under Fascism* (Berkeley and Los Angeles: University of California Press, 1971). Sarti argues that the industrialists got most of what they wanted. Similar conclusions, with deeper background in earlier Italian history, are found in F. H. Adler, *Italian Industrialists from Liberalism to Fascism: The Political Development of the Industrial Bourgeoisie* (Cambridge: Cambridge University Press, 1995). Among Italian scholars, Piero Melograni, *Gli industriali e Mussolini: Rapporti fra Confindustria e fascismo dal 1919 al 1929* (Milan: Longanesi, 1972), has been criticized for overemphasizing conflicts between supposedly laissez-faire industrialists and Fascism. Franco Castronovo, *Potere economico et fascismo* (Milan: Bompiani, 1974), stresses the advantages enjoyed by business during the Fascist regime. See also his article "Il potere economico e fascismo," in Guido Quazza, ed., *Fascismo e società italiano* (Turin: Einaudi, 1973), pp. 45–88, and his important biography of FIAT chief Agnelli. Rolf Petri, "Wirtschaftliche Führungskräfte und Regime: Interessen, Wertvorstellungen und Erinnerungsprozesse zwischen Konsens und Krise," in Jens Petersen and Wolfgang Schieder, eds., *Faschismus und Gesellschaft in Italien: Staat, Wirtschaft, Kultur* (Cologne: SH-Verlag, 1998), pp. 199–223, analyzes the bases for business leaders' general cooperation with the regime, despite some divergence of interests and values, until defeat became evident in spring 1943.

The best introduction to the relations between fascists and conservatives generally is Martin Blinkhorn, ed., *Fascists and Conservatives: The Radical Right and the Establishment in Twentieth Century Europe* (London: Unwin Hyman, 1990), to which may be added Jeremy Noakes, "Fascism and High Society," in Michael Burleigh, ed., *Confronting the Nazi Past: New Debates on Modern German History* (New York: St. Martin's Press, 1996).

Vera Zamagni, *The Economic History of Italy, 1860–1990* (Oxford: Clarendon, 1993), has an excellent synoptic chapter on Fascist Italy.

For the relationship of the Nazi and Fascist regimes with workers, the most important work is Jane Caplan, ed., *Nazism, Fascism and the Working Class: Essays by Tim Mason* (Cambridge: Cambridge University Press, 1995), pp. 131–211. Also by Mason, the most thoughtful scholar of labor under the Nazis, is *Arbeiterklasse und Volksgemeinschaft: Dokumente und Materialen zu deutscher Arbeiterpolitik, 1936–1939* (Berlin: Freier Universität, 1975). Alf Lüdtke suggests why some workers supported Hitler in "Working Class and Volksgemeinschaft," in Christian Leitz, *The Third Reich: The Essential Readings* (Oxford: Blackwell, 1999), and in "What Happened to the 'Fiery Red Glow'?" in Lüdtke, ed., *History of Everyday Life* (Princeton: Princeton Univeristy Press, 1995), pp. 198–251. Ulrich Herbert explores relations between German workers and foreign slave labor and the resulting satisfactions for the former in *Hitler's Foreign Workers: Enforced Foreign Labor under the Third Reich* (Cambridge: Cambridge University Press, 1997) and other works. The standard of living, including that of women, is examined by Richard J. Overy, "Guns or Butter: Living Standards, Finance and Labour in Germany, 1939–1942," in Overy, *War and the Economy in the Third Reich* (Oxford: Clarendon Press, 1994).

For the Italian case, see Tobias Abse, "Italian Workers and Italian Fascism," in Richard Bessel, ed., *Fascist Italy and Nazi Germany* (Cambridge: Cambridge University Press, 1996), pp. 40–60, and the articles collected in Giulio Sapelli, ed., *La classe operaia durante il fascismo* (Annali Feltrinelli, vol. 20: Milan: Feltrinelli, 1981).

Nazi gender policy is the subject of an enormous literature. Basic works include Jill Stephenson, *Women in Nazi Germany* (New York: Longman's, 2001); Renata

Bibliographical Essay

Bridenthal, Atina Grossmann, and Marion Kaplan, eds., *When Biology Became Destiny: Women in Weimar and Nazi Germany* (New York: Monthly Review Press, 1984); Claudia Koontz, *Mothers in the Fatherland: Women, the Family and Nazi Politics* (New York: St Martin's Press, 1987); Ute Frevert, *Women in German History: From Bourgeoise Emancipation to Sexual Liberation* (Oxford: Oxford University Press, 1989); Tim Mason, "Women in Germany, 1925–1940," *History Workshop*, 1:1 & 2 (1976); Rita Thalmann, *Femmes et fascisme* (Paris: Tierce, 1987); Gisela Bock, "Nazi Gender Policies and Women's History," in Georges Duby and Michelle Perrot, eds., *A History of Women: Toward a Cultural Identity in the Twentieth Century* (Cambridge, MA: Harvard University Press, 1994), pp. 149–77; Helen Boak, "Women in Weimar Germany: The 'Frauenfrage' and the Female Vote," in Richard Bessel and E. J. Feuchtwanger, eds., *Social Change and Political Development in the Weimar Republic* (London: Croom Helm, 1981); Gabriele Czarnowski, "The Value of Marriage for Volksgemeinschaft: Policies towards Women and Marriage under National Socialism," in Richard Bessel, ed., *Fascist Italy and Nazi Germany*, pp. 61–77. For the late resort to women workers, see the article by Richard Overy cited above. Michael Burleigh and Wolfgang Wippermann, *The Racial State: Germany, 1933–1945* (Cambridge: Cambridge University Press, 1991), includes, innovatively, a chapter on men as well as on women.

The indispensable work on women in Fascist Italy is Victoria De Grazia, *How Fascism Ruled Women* (Berkeley and Los Angeles: University of California Press, 1992), a concise version of which appears in Duby and Perrot, eds., *A History of Women*, cited above. Perry R. Willson, "Women in Fascist Italy," in Richard Bessel, ed., *Fascist Italy and Nazi Germany*, pp. 78–93, and the Luisa Passerini and Chiara Saraceno articles in Angelo Del Boca et al., eds., *Il Regime Fascista*, are up-to-date surveys, and one can still consult the earlier articles of Lesley Caldwell, "Reproducers of the Nation: Women and the Family in Fascist Party," in David Forgacs, *Rethinking Fascist Italy* (London: Lawrence and Wishart, 1986), and Alexander De Grand, "Women Under Italian Fascism," *Historical Journal* 19:4 (December 1976), pp. 947–68. Paul Corner, "Women in Fascist Italy: Changing Family Roles in the Transition from an Agricultural to an Industrial Society," *European Studies Quarterly* 23 (1993), pp. 51–68, sets the issue into a longer-term perspective. Luisa Passerini, *Fascism in Popular Memory: The Cultural Experience of the Turin Working Class* (Cambridge: Cambridge University Press, 1987), uses oral history to reconstruct the everyday life of women in Turin under Fascism. Perry R. Willson, *The Clockwork Factory: Women and Work in Fascist Italy* (Oxford: Clarendon Press, 1993), gives a fascinating glimpse of the satisfactions and grievances of women in a Fascist showpiece factory.

Fascism has been provocatively called "a boy's ideology,"[3] though some women supported it eagerly and were assisted by it selectively and in demeaningly paternalistic ways. Richard Evans studied the female vote in "German Women and the Triumph of Hitler," *Journal of Modern History* (March 1976) (supplement). A particularly heated debate over whether German women were victims or collaborators of Nazism is reviewed by Atina Grossmann, "Feminist Debates about Women and National Socialism," in *Gender and History* 3:3 (Autumn 1991), pp. 350–58, and Adelheid von

Saldern, "Women: Victims or Perpetrators?" in David F. Crew, ed., *Nazism and Ger-man Society, 1933–1945* (London: Routledge, 1994), reprinted in Christian Leitz, *The Third Reich: The Essential Readings,* mentioned above.

Peasants and small farmers, important among early supporters of Fascism and Nazism, did not always benefit from these parties' exercise of power. For Nazi agrar-ian policy, see J. E. Farquharson, *The Plough and the Swastika* (Berkeley and Los Angeles: University of California Press, 1976), summarized in Farquharson, "The Agrarian Policy of National Socialist Germany," in Robert G. Moeller, ed., *Peasants and Lords in Modern Germany: Recent Studies in Agricultural History* (Boston: Allen and Unwin, 1986), pp. 233–59; and Anna Bramwell, *Blood and Soil: Richard Walther Darré and Hitler's "Green Party"* (Abbotsbrook: Kensal, 1985).

The large role played by agrarian conflict in the beginnings of fascism is treated in many local studies listed above. The Italian case is reviewed in Mario Bernabei, "La base de masse del fascismo agraria," *Storia contemporanea* 6:1 (1975), pp. 123–53, and Dahlia Sabina Elazar, "Agrarian Relations and Class Hegemony: A Comparative Analysis of Landlord, Social and Political Power in Italy, 1861–1970," in *British Journal of Sociology* 47 (June 1996), pp. 232–54. Fascist Italy's farm policy is discussed by Paul Corner, "Fascist Agrarian Policy and the Italian Economy in the Interwar Years," in John A. Davis, ed., *Gramsci and Italy's Passive Revolution* (London: Croom Helm, 1979), and examined thoroughly in Alexander Nützenadel, *Landwirtschaft, Staat, und Autarkie: Agrarpolitik in faschistischen Italien* (Tübingen: Max Niemayer Verlag, 1997).

Some of the most suggestive works about how fascist rule worked are based on comparison between Nazi Germany and Fascist Italy. There is a tendency to treat this subject by paired articles rather than sustained comparison. Nevertheless the articles are of high quality in Richard Bessel, ed., *Fascist Italy and Nazi Germany: Compari-sons and Contrasts* (Cambridge: Cambridge University Press, 1996), and Wolfgang Schieder, ed., *Faschismus als sozialer Bewegung: Deutschland und Italien im Ver-gleich* (Hamburg: Hoffmann and Campe, 1976). More articles of high quality pair Nazi Germany with Stalinist Russia, in Ian Kershaw and Moshe Lewin, eds., *Stalin-ism and Nazism: Dictatorships in Comparison* (Cambridge: Cambridge University Press, 1997), and Henri Rousso, ed., *Stalinisme et nazisme: Histoire et mémoire com-parées* (Brussels: Complexe, 1999). Authentic sustained comparison between Nazi Germany and Fascist Italy is found in Alexander J. De Grand's succinct *Fascist Italy and Nazi Germany: The "Fascist" Style of Rule* (London: Routledge, 1995), and a very interesting article, Carlo Levy, "Fascism, Nazism, and Conservatism: Issues for Com-parativists," *Contemporary European History* 8:1 (1999).

Articles of enduring value about the way the Nazi regime functioned are col-lected in Peter D. Stachura, ed., *The Shaping of the Nazi State* (London: Croom Helm, 1978); Jeremy Noakes, ed., *Government, Party and People in Nazi Germany* (Exeter: University of Exeter Press, 1980); Thomas Childers and Jane Caplan, eds., *Reevaluating the Third Reich* (New York: Holmes and Meier, 1993); David Crew, ed., *Nazism and German Society* (London: Routledge, 1994); Michael Burleigh, ed., *Con-fronting the Nazi Past* (see above); and Christian Leitz, ed., *The Third Reich: The Essential Readings* (see above).

Bibliographical Essay

Studies of public opinion in the 1980s emphasized the high degree of public acceptance of both the German and Italian dictatorships, despite surprising amounts of grumbling that mostly spared the charismatic leaders. See Ian Kershaw, *"The Hitler Myth": Image and Reality in the Third Reich* (New York: Oxford University Press, 1987), and *Popular Opinion and Political Dissent in the Third Reich, Bavaria 1933–1945* (New York: Oxford University Press, 1983), part of a close scrutiny of Bavaria under the Third Reich organized by Martin Broszat. For Italy, the fullest account is Simona Colarizi, *L'opinione degli italiani sotto il regime, 1929–1943* (Bari: Laterza, 1991). The works already cited on citizens' voluntary cooperation, such as Robert Gellately's works on denunciation in Germany, are relevant here.

Alastair Hamilton explores for the general reader some intellectuals' support for Hitler and Mussolini in *The Appeal of Fascism: A Study of Intellectuals and Fascism, 1919–1945* (London: Anthony Blond, 1971). The best place to start for a general history of political ideas in Italy is Norberto Bobbio, *Ideological Profile of Twentieth Century Italy* (Princeton: Princeton University Press, 1995). The basic works in Italian on intellectuals under Fascism are Luisa Mangoni, *L'interventismo della cultura: Intellettuali e riviste del fascismo* (Bari: Laterza, 1974); Gabriele Turi, *Il fascismo e il consenso degli intellettualli* (Bologna: Il Mulino, 1980); and Michel Ostenc, *Intellectuels italiens et fascisme (1915–1929)* (Paris: Payot, 1983). The collected essays of Mario Isnenghi, *L'Italia del Fascio* (Florence: Giunti, 1996), includes his famous essay on "militant intellectuals and bureaucratic intellectuals." Stimulating short assessments are Norberto Bobbio, "La cultura e il fascismo," in Guido Quazza, ed., *Fascismo e società italiana* (Turin: Einaudi, 1973), pp. 211–46, and Gabriele Turi, "Fascismo e cultura ieri e oggi," in Angelo Del Boca et al., eds., *Il regime fascista*. A lively introduction to Marinetti is James Joll, *Three Intellectuals in Politics* (New York: Pantheon, 1960).

An immense and growing literature is now devoted to a deconstruction of the inner meaning of fascist regimes' cultural projects and rituals. Some examples of this genre that successfully relate culture to institutions and society include Emilio Gentile, *The Sacralization of Politics in Fascist Italy* (Cambridge: Cambridge University Press, 1996); Simonetta Falasca-Zamponi, *Fascist Spectacle: The Aesthetics of Power in Mussolini's Italy* (Berkeley and Los Angeles: University of California Press, 1997); Ruth Ben-Ghiat, *Fascist Modernities* (Berkeley and Los Angeles: University of California Press, 2001); Marla Stone, *The Patron State* (Princeton: Princeton University Press, 1998): a special issue on "The Aesthetics of Fascism" of *The Journal of Contemporary History* 31:2 (April 1996); two special issues on "Fascism and Culture" of *Modernism/Modernity* 2:3 (September 1995) and 3:1 (January 1996); and Richard J. Golsan, ed., *Fascism, Aesthetics and Culture* (Hanover, NH: University Press of New England, 1992). Sometimes works in this genre seem to take the decoding of fascist ritual and art as ends in themselves. David D. Roberts reviews a wide range of cultural studies of fascism with some asperity in "How Not to Think about Fascist Ideology, Intellectual Antecedents, and Historical Meaning," *Journal of Contemporary History* 35:2 (April 2000), pp. 185–211. Roger Griffin does the same with enthusiasm in "The Reclamation of Fascist Culture," *European History Quarterly* 31:4 (October 2001), pp. 609–20.

Bibliographical Essay

Good recent guides to Nazi cultural policy are Alan E. Steinweis, *Ideology and Economy in Nazi Germany: The Reich Chambers of Music, Theater, and the Visual Arts* (Chapel Hill: University of North Carolina Press, 1993), and *National Socialist Cultural Policy* (New York: St. Martin's Press, 1995).

Alan Cassels, *Mussolini's Early Diplomacy* (Princeton: Princeton University Press, 1970), is still valuable, while H. James Burgwyn, *Italian Foreign Policy in the Interwar Period, 1918–1949* (Westport, CT: Praeger, 1997), gives a useful broader survey. A magisterial account of the Third Reich's foreign policy is Gerhard Weinberg, *The Foreign Policy of Hitler's Germany*, 2 vols. (Chicago: University of Chicago Press, 1970, 1980).

VII. Radicalization

Most works about fascist radicalization concern Nazi Germany, of course. Scholars have debated whether the German rush toward war, expansion, and racial purification was imposed by Hitler or germinated within the fascist governing system. Hans Mommsen's theory of "cumulative radicalization" appears in, among other publications, "Cumulative Radicalization and Progressive Self-Destruction as Structural Elements of the Nazi Dictatorship," in Ian Kershaw and Moshe Lewin, eds., *Stalinism and Nazism: Dictatorships in Comparison* (Cambridge: Cambridge University Press, 1997), pp. 75–87.

Italian Fascism was bloodier than Nazism before power, but Mussolini's preference for governing through the state rather than through the party "normalized" the regime after 1929. See for this process Lyttleton, *Seizure*, and Schieder, *Der Faschismus als sozialer Bewegung*, mentioned above. Nevertheless, the rhetoric and self-image of Italian Fascism remained "revolutionary" (in the nationalist and antisocialist meaning the Fascists gave this word), and authentic radicalization came into view with Italian imperial expansion. See the very interesting chapter entitled "Radicalisation" in Pierre Milza, *Mussolini* (Paris: Fayard, 1999). In his colonial campaigns, Mussolini took some steps that Hitler never dared take. For example, he used poison gas in Libya and Ethiopia. Angelo Del Boca, *I gas di Mussolini: Il fascismo e il guerra d'Etiopia* (Rome: Editore Riuniti, 1996). Italian colonial administration was overtly racialist. See Angelo Del Boca, "Le leggi razziali nell'impero di Mussolini" in Del Boca, et al., *Il regime fascista*, pp. 329–51. The war in Ethiopia also helped stimulate radicalization at home in the mid-1930s.

The best works on Mussolini's colonial empire are: Claudio Segrè, *The Fourth Shore: The Italian Colonization of Libya* (Chicago: University of Chicago Press, 1974); Angelo Del Boca, *The Ethiopian War, 1935–1941* (Chicago: University of Chicago Press, 1969), and by the same author, among several works on the Italian empire, *Le guerre coloniale del fascismo* (Bari: Laterza, 1991). Denis Mack Smith in *Mussolini's Roman Empire* (New York: Viking, 1976), makes it seem the *Duce's* personal whim. Luigi Goglia and Fabio Grassi, *Il colonialismo italiano da Adua all'impero* (Bari: Laterza, 1993), reminds us that empire was an Italian nationalist urge even before Fascism.

War played a crucial role in radicalization. War was not accidental but integral to the fascist recipe for national regeneration. But while successful German war making opened the way for radical party rule in the east and for the Final Solution, unsuccessful Italian war making broke Fascism's legitimacy.

The most authoritative account of Germany's war is now Wilhelm Diest et al., *Germany in the Second World War* (Oxford: Clarendon Press, 1990–), planned for ten volumes. Norman Rich gives a comprehensive account of how Nazi ideology was applied through conquest in *Germany's War Aims*, vol. I: *Ideology, the Nazi State and the Course of Expansion* (New York: Norton, 1973), and vol. II: *The Establishment of the New Order* (New York: Norton, 1974). Gerhard Weinberg's collected articles, *Germany, Hitler, and World War II* (Cambridge: Cambridge University Press, 1995), are often illuminating.

The main authority in English on Italy's war is MacGregor Knox, who attributes it to Mussolini's expansionist zeal. See his *Mussolini Unleashed, 1939–1941* (Cambridge: Cambridge University Press, 1982), *Hitler's Italian Allies: Royal Armed Forces, Fascist Regime, and the War, 1940–43* (Cambridge: Cambridge University Press, 2000), and the very interesting comparative study, *Common Destiny: Dictatorship, Foreign Policy and War in Fascist Italy and Nazi Germany* (Cambridge: Cambridge University Press, 2000). Briefer accounts are found in MacGregor Knox, "Conquest, Foreign and Domestic, in Fascist Italy and Nazi Germany," *Journal of Modern History* 56 (1984), pp. 1–57, and "Expansionist Zeal, Fighting Power, and Staying Power in Fascist Italy and Nazi Germany," in Richard Bessel, ed., *Fascist Italy and Nazi Germany: Comparisons and Contrasts* (Cambridge: Cambridge University Press, 1996), pp. 113–33. Aristotle A. Kallis, *Fascist Ideology: Territory and Expansionism in Italy and Germany, 1922–1945* (London: Routledge, 2000), asks why territorial expansion was "the way out" for crisis regimes. John F. Coverdale, *Italian Intervention in the Spanish Civil War* (Princeton: Princeton University Press, 1975), is still valuable.

The most authoritative work on the Italian Social Republic at Salò is now Lutz Klinkhammer, *L'occupazione tedesca in italia 1943–1945* (Turin: Bollati-Boringhieri, 1993), also in German as *Zwischen Bündnis und Besatzung: Das nationalsozialistische Deutschland und die Republik von Salò 1943–1945* (Tübingen: M. Niemeyer, 1993). The classic work in English is F. W. Deakin's powerful *The Six Hundred Days of Mussolini* (New York: Harper & Row, 1966), a revised edition of part III of his authoritative study of the whole German-Italian relationship during World War II, *The Brutal Friendship: Mussolini, Hitler, and the Fall of Italian Fascism* (New York: Harper & Row, 1962, revised 1966).

The heart of internal radicalization was an impulse toward cleansing: first of the mentally ill (begun in Germany when the war began), and then of the ethnically and racially impure and the socially ostracized. See in general Michael Burleigh and Wolfgang Wippermann, *The Racial State 1933–45* (Cambridge: Cambridge University Press, 1992). Robert Gellately and Nathan Stoltzfus, eds., *Social Outsiders in Nazi Germany* (Princeton: Princeton University Press, 2001), treats targets of many kinds. On homosexuals in particular, see Harry Osterhuis, "Medicine, Male Bonding, and Homosexuality in Nazi Germany," *Journal of Contemporary History* 32:2 (April 1997), pp. 187–205; Günter Grau, ed., *Hidden Holocaust? Gay and Lesbian Persecution in*

Bibliographical Essay

Germany, 1933–1945 (London: Cassell, 1995), and Burkhard Jellonek and Rüdiger Lautmann, eds., *Nationalsozialistische Terror gegen Homosexuelle: Verdrängt und Ungesühnt* (Paderborn: Ferdinand Schöningh, 2002).

The Nazi program to kill or sterilize the mentally ill and other kinds of "unfit" persons, long ignored, now seems a key element of the Nazi brand of fascism, and a decisive difference with Italy. Sterilization was by no means a Nazi monopoly. Sweden, Britain, and the United States came closer to Nazism on this matter than did Italy. See generally Maria Sophia Quine, *Population Politics in 20th Century Europe* (London: Routledge, 1996). The Swedish case is evoked in Carl Levy, "Fascism, National Socialism, and Conservatives in Europe, 1914–1945: Issues for Comparativists," *Contemporary European History* 8:1 (1999), p. 120, n. 106. Gisela Bock, *Zwangssterilisation im Dritten Reich: Studien zur Rassenpolitik und Frauenpolitik* (Opladen: Westdeutscher Verlag, 1986), finds a Nazi antinatalism to be a precursor of racial annihilation.

The reverse side of Nazi reverence for the fit body was the impulse for medical cleansing, a subject studied intensely nowadays. See Michael Burleigh, *Death and Deliverance: Euthanasia in Germany, c. 1900–1945* (Cambridge: Cambridge University Press, 1995): His "Between Enthusiasm, Compliance, and Protest: The Churches, Eugenics, and the Nazi Euthanasia Program," *Contemporary European History* 3:3 (November 1994), pp. 253–63, deals with reactions to euthanasia. The dark side of science in Nazi policy is explored in Detlev J. K. Peukert, "The Genesis of the 'Final Solution' from the Spirit of Science," in Thomas Childers and Jane Caplan, eds., *Reevaluating the Third Reich* (New York: Holmes and Meier, 1993), pp. 234–52. Recent scholarly monographs include Hans-Walter Schmuhl, *Rassenhygiene, Nationalsozialismus, Euthanasie: Von der Verhütung zur Vernichtung "lebensunwerten Lebens" 1890–1945* (Göttingen: Vandenhoech and Ruprecht, 1987); Götz Aly, Angelika Ebbinghaus, Matthias Hamann, Freidrich Pfaflin, and Ger Preissler, *Aussonderung und Tod: Die klinische Hinrichtung der Unbrauchbaren* (Berlin: Rotbuch, 1985); Götz Aly, *Cleansing the Fatherland: Nazi Medicine and Racial Hygiene* (Baltimore: Johns Hopkins University Press, 1994); and Benno Müller-Hill, *Murderous Science: Elimination by Scientific Selection of Jews, Gypsies, and Others, Germany 1933–1945* (Oxford: Oxford University Press, 1988). Henry Friedlander, *The Origins of Nazi Genocide: From Euthanasia to the Final Solution* (Chapel Hill: University of North Carolina Press, 1995), explores the links between killing the mentally ill and killing Jews.

Works that consider how intellectuals, including nonfascists, became enlisted in fascist projects include Michael Burleigh, *Germany Turns Eastward: A Study of Ostforschung in the Third Reich* (Cambridge: Cambridge University Press, 1988), and Götz Aly and Suzanne Heim, *Vordenker der Vernichtung: Auschwitz und die deutschen Pläne für eine neue europäische Ordnung* (Hamburg: Hoffman und Campe, 1991).

Fascist Italy was more interested in encouraging maternity than in racial cleansing, but Fascists developed a cultural-historical concept of race *(la razza)* and lineage *(la stirpe)* that could function very much like biological race in the de facto apartheid set up in Italian East Africa. See David G. Horn, *Social Bodies: Science, Reproduction, and Italian Modernity* (Princeton: Princeton University Press, 1994); Carl Ipsen,

Dictating Demography: The Problem of Population in Fascist Italy (Cambridge: Cambridge University Press, 1996); and Angelo Del Boca's own article in his *Il regime fascista*. See also Aaron Gillette, *Racial Theories in Fascist Italy* (London: Routledge, 2002).

The best point of entry into the immense literature on the murder of the Jews is the masterful new synthesis by Saul Friedländer, *Nazi Germany and the Jews*, vol. I: *The Years of Persecution, 1933–1939* (London: Weidenfeld & Nicolson, 1997). Peter Longerith, *Politik der Vernichtung: Eine Gesamtdarstellung der nationalsozialistische Judenverfolgung* (Munich: C. H. Beck, 1998), is an informative recent account. Christopher R. Browning has produced the most convincing current work in English on how the Holocaust was carried out: *Ordinary Germans: Police Battalion 101 and the Final Solution* (New York: HarperCollins, 1992), *The Path to Genocide: Essays on Launching the Final Solution* (Cambridge: Cambridge University Press, 1992), *Nazi Policy: Jewish Workers, German Killers* (Cambridge: Cambridge University Press, 2000), and the forthcoming *Origins of the Final Solution* (Lincoln, NE: University of Nebraska, in press). Examples of the very high quality of current Holocaust research in Germany appear in Ulrich Herbert, ed., *National Socialist Extermination Policy: Contemporary German Perspectives and Controversies* (New York: Berghahn, 2000). The newly discovered importance of the broader Nazi project to redraw the East European ethnic map is reflected there, and in Götz Aly, *Final Solution: Nazi Population Policy and the Murder of the European Jews* (New York: Oxford University Press, 1999). Current knowledge of the Nazi camps is summarized in Ulrich Herbert, Karin Orth, and Christoph Dieckmann, *Die nationalsozialistische Konzentrationslager: Entwicklung und Struktur*, 2 vols. (Göttingen: Wallstein, 1998).

The literature on Italian racial legislation of 1938 is discussed in chapter 6, note 66, p. 293.

VIII. Fascism Elsewhere

European Fascisms For European fascisms outside Germany and Italy, a good place to begin is the collections of excellent articles in the works mentioned in the opening paragraph of this essay by Stein U. Larsen et al., Stuart Woolf, and Hans Rogger/ Eugen Weber. There are short sketches of fascism in various countries and an extensive bibliography in Enzo Collotti, *Fascismo, Fascismi* (Florence: Sansoni, 1989). The succinct comparative essay by Wolfgang Wippermann, *Europäische Faschismus im Vergleich* (Frankfurt-am-Main: Suhrkamp, 1983), is very enlightening.

Works on individual European countries follow:

Austria: Authoritative on the forebears is John W. Boyer, *Political Radicalism in Late Imperial Austria* (Chicago: University of Chicago Press, 1981). See also Andrew G. Whiteside, *The Socialism of Fools: Von Schönerer and Austrian Pan-Germanism* (Berkeley and Los Angeles: University of California Press, 1975). On the Austrian Nazis, see Bruce E. Pauley, *Hitler and the Forgotten Nazis* (Chapel Hill: University of North Carolina Press, 1981); Peter Black, *Ernst Kaltenbrunner: Ideological Soldier in the Third Reich* (Princeton: Princeton University Press, 1984); and Francis L. Carsten,

Fascist Movements in Austria: From Schönerer to Hitler (Los Angeles: Sage, 1977). Lucian O. Meysels, *Der Austrofascismus: Das Ende der ersten Republik und ihr letzter Kanzler* (Vienna: Amalthea, 1992), treats Kurt Schuschnigg.

Baltic States: Andres Kasekamp, *The Radical Right in Interwar Estonia* (New York: St. Martin's Press, 2000).

Belgium: For the period before 1940, see Jean-Michel Étienne, *Le Mouvement Rexiste jusqu'en 1940*, Cahiers de la Fondation Nationale des Sciences Politiques, No. 165 (Paris: Armand Colin, 1968); Martin Conway, "Building the Christian City: Catholics and Politics in Inter-War Francophone Belgium," *Past and Present* 128 (August 1990); the Danièle Wallef article in Larsen et al., *Who Were the Fascists*; and William Brustein, "The Political Geography of Belgian Fascism: The Case of Rexism," *American Sociological Review* 53 (February 1988), pp. 69–80. For the period after 1940, see Martin Conway, *Collaboration in Belgium: Léon Degrelle and the Rexist Movement 1940–1944* (New Haven: Yale University Press, 1993), a work that needs to be combined with John Gillingham's study of more pragmatic collaborators in the business world, *Belgian Business in the Nazi New Order* (Ghent: Jan Dondt Foundation, 1977).

Britain: The essential account is Richard Thurlow, *Fascism in Britain, 1918–1985*, rev. ed. (Oxford: Blackwell, 1998). Thomas Linehan, *British Fascism 1918–1939: Parties, Ideology, Culture* (Manchester: Manchester University Press, 2000), has additional material on attitudes. For the most important movement, Thomas Linehan, *East London for Mosley: The British Union of Fascists in East London and Southwest Essex, 1933–1940* (London: Frank Cass, 1996), is enlightening. Kenneth Lunn and Richard Thurlow, eds., *British Fascism: Essays on the Radical Right in Interwar Britain* (London: Croom Helm, 1980), is still useful. Robert Skidelsky's magisterial *Oswald Mosley*, rev. ed. (London: Macmillan, 1990) (orig. pub. 1975), was empathetic enough to raise hackles. Richard Thurlow, "The Failure of Fascism," in Andrew Thorpe, ed., *The Failure of Political Extremism in Interwar Britain* (University of Exeter Studies in History No. 21, 1989), weighs the various interpretations lucidly.

Croatia: Yeshayahu Jelinek, "Clergy and Fascism: The Hlinka Party in Slovakia and the Croatian Ustasha Movement," in Larsen et al., *Who Were the Fascists*, pp. 367–78.

Czechoslovakia: David D. Kelly, *The Czech Fascist Movement, 1922–1942* (Boulder, CO: Eastern European Monographs, 1995).

Eastern Europe: Peter F. Sugar, *Native Fascism in the Successor States, 1918–1945* (Santa Barbara, CA: ABC-Clio, 1971), is more descriptive than analytical.

France: The most authoritative account in French is Pierre Milza, *Fascisme français: Passé et présent* (Paris: Flammarion, 1987). In English, see Michel Winock, *Nationalism, Anti-Semitism, and Fascism in France*, trans. from the French by Jane Marie Todd (Stanford, CA: Stanford University Press, 1998), and two narrative volumes by Robert Soucy: *French Fascism: The First Wave, 1924–1933* (New Haven: Yale University Press, 1986), and *French Fascism: The Second Wave, 1933–1939* (New Haven: Yale University Press, 1995). Milza, "L'Ultra-Droite dans les années Trente," in Michel Winock, ed., *Histoire de l'extrême droite en France* (Paris: Seuil, 1993), pp. 157–90, and Philippe Burrin, "Le fascisme," in Jean-François Sirinelli, ed., *Histoire des droites en France* (Paris: Gallimard, 1992), vol. I, pp. 603–52, provide stimulating essays. Klaus Jürgen Müller's richly suggestive "Die französische Rechte und der Faschismus in Frankreich 1924–32," in *Industrielle Gesellschaft und politisches System* (Bonn: Verlag Neue Gesellschaft, 1978), pp. 413–30, rejects the usual lists of "symptoms" and analyzes the development of the French Right through time to show that conservatives did not need fascism.

There is finally a biography of Charles Maurras, by Bruno Goyet (Paris: Fondation Nationale des Sciences Politiques, 2000). The English-speaking reader can draw rich detail and perceptive judgments about his movement from Eugen Weber, *Action Française: Royalism and Reaction in Twentieth Century France* (Stanford: Stanford University Press, 1962). A briefer but usable account is Edward Tannenbaum, *Action Française: Die-hard Reactionaries in Third Republic France* (New York: Wiley, 1962). Victor Nguyen, *Aux origines de l'Action française: Intelligence et politique à l'aube du XXe siècle* (Paris: Fayard, 1991), is exhaustive.

Georges Valois has attracted more attention than most French extreme right activists, perhaps because of his genuine ambiguity between Right and Left. See Allen Douglas, *From Fascism to Libertarian Communism: Georges Valois against the French Republic* (Berkeley and Los Angeles: University of California Press, 1992); Yves Guchet, "Georges Valois ou l'illusion fasciste," *Revue française de science politique* 15 (1965) p. 1111–44, and *Georges Valois: L'Action française, le faisceau, la République syndicale* (Paris: L'Harmattan, 2001); Jules Levey, "Georges Valois and the Faisceau," *French Historical Studies* 8 (1973), pp. 279–304; and Zeev Sternhell, "Anatomie d'un mouvement fasciste en France: La Faisceau de Georges Valois," *Revue française de science politique* 26 (1976), pp. 5–40.

Two model regional monographs are Kevin Passmore, *From Liberalism to Fascism: The Right in a French Province, 1928–1939* (Cambridge: Cambridge University Press, 1997), on the Lyon area, and Samuel Huston Goodfellow, *Between the Swastika and the Cross of Lorraine: Fascisms in Interwar Alsace* (DeKalb: Northern Illinois University Press, 1999).

The high point of fascism in France before 1940 was the attack on the Chamber of Deputies of February 6, 1934, which many observers (notably Trotsky in *Whither France* [New York: Pioneer, 1936]) considered the beginning of a fascist "March on Paris." The best-informed account is Serge Berstein, *Le 6 février 1934* (Paris: Gallimard, 1974). In English, the illustrated article of Geoffrey Warner in *History Today* (June 1958) is evocative; see also Max Beloff, "The Sixth of February," in James Joll, ed., *The Decline of the Third Republic*, St. Antony's Papers No. 5 (London: Chatto and Windus, 1959).

The strength of fascism in interwar France has been the subject of an important debate. The classic work of René Rémond, *The Right Wing in France* (Philadelphia: University of Pennsylvania Press, 1969) (most recent version only in French: *Les Droites en France* [Paris: Aubier Montaigne, 1982]), argued that fascism was a foreign import without much impact in France. This view was supported more recently by Serge Berstein in "La France allergique au fascisme," in *Vingtième siècle: revue d'histoire* 2 (April 1984), pp. 84–94, a response to Sternhell.

Bibliographical Essay

On the other side, Soucy (see above) found fascism was highly developed in France. Zeev Sternhell makes the largest claims for the importance of France for the history of fascism: it was in France, he argues, that fascism received its earliest and purest intellectual expression. See *La droite révolutionaire, 1885–1914: Les origines françaises du fascisme* (Paris: Editions du Seuil, 1978); *Maurice Barrès et le nationalisme français* (Brussels: Editions Complexe, 1985); and *Neither Right nor Left: Fascist Ideology in France* (Berkeley and Los Angeles: University of California Press, 1986).

The critical storm stirred up by Sternhell's claim in *Neither Right nor Left* that France was "impregnated"[4] with Fascism in the 1930s, a claim advanced by assigning a broad range of nationalist and conservative authors to the fascist camp, may be reviewed in Antonio Costa Pinto, "Fascist Ideology Revisited: Zeev Sternhell and His Critics," *European History Quarterly* 4 (1986). Philippe Burrin arrives at a subtle analysis of "impregnation différentielle" in "La France dans le champ magnétique des fascismes," *Le Débat* 32 (November 1984), pp. 52–72.

The crucial issue was whether the largest of the interwar militantly nationalist movements, Colonel François de La Rocque's Croix de Feu, transformed after its dissolution by the government in June 1936 into the more moderate electoral Parti Social Français, was fascist or not. The positive case is made for both the league and the party by Soucy and Sternhell (see above) and William D. Irvine, "Fascism in France and the Strange Case of the Croix de Feu," *Journal of Modern History* 63 (1991), pp. 271–95. Kevin Passmore, "Boy Scoutism for Grown-ups? Paramilitarism in the Croix de Feu and the Parti Social Français," *French Historical Studies* 19 (1995), pp. 527–57, sensibly judges the league fascist, more on behavioral than ideological grounds, but not the party. Serge Berstein portrays the ambiguous position of La Rocque's PSF as a conflict between unruly militants and their more cautious leader ("La ligue," in Jean-François Sirinelli, *Histoire des droites en France* [Paris: Gallimard, 1992], vol. II, p. 100). Jacques Nobécourt, *Le Colonel de La Rocque, 1885–1946, ou les pièges du nationalisme chrétien* (Paris: Fayard, 1996), an exhaustive sympathetic biography, portrays La Rocque as a conservative victimized by false accusations and personal rivalries, more accurately understood as a predecessor of Charles de Gaulle's presidential Fifth Republic. The PSF's resort to the ballot box, of course, in no way by itself makes it nonfascist, for elections were essential to the Nazis and Fascists in the stages of taking root and coming to power. For the occupation years, see Sean Kennedy, "Accompanying the Marshal: La Rocque and the Parti Social Français under Vichy," *French History* 15:2 (2001), pp. 186–213.

The most enlightening treatment of other French fascist leaders is Philippe Burrin, *La dérive fasciste: Doriot, Déat, Bergery: 1933–1945* (Paris: Seuil, 1986). One can find additional detail on Doriot and his role in the French Légion des Volontaires Contre le Bolshevisme in Jean-Paul Brunet, *Jacques Doriot du communisme au fascisme* (Paris: Balland, 1986), and in Dieter Wolf, *Die Doriot Bewegung* (Stuttgart: Deutsche Verlags-Anstalt, 1967), also translated into French.

Whether Vichy France (1940–44) should be considered fascist or authoritarian is taken up by Robert O. Paxton, *Vichy France: Old Guard and New Order*, rev. ed. (New York: Columbia University Press, 2001), pp. 251–57; Julian Jackson, *France: The Dark Years, 1940–44* (Oxford: Oxford University Press, 2001), pp. 144, 157–61, 213–14,

261; Michèle Cointet, *Vichy et le fascisme: Les hommes, les structures, et les pouvoirs* (Brussels: Editions Complexe, 1987). An interesting evaluation of Vichy's propaganda efforts as a failed fascist experiment is Denis Peschanski, "Vichy au singulier, Vichy au pluriel: Une tentative avortée d'encadrement de la société (1941–1942)," *Annales: Économies, sociétés, civilisations* 43 (1988), pp. 639–62. One may ask, with Philippe Burrin (*La Dérive fasciste*, p. 414), whether an authentic fascism is compatible with foreign occupation.

Greece: Jon V. Kofas, *Authoritarianism in Greece: The Metaxas Regime* (New York: Columbia University Press, 1983).

Hungary: Basic readings in English are C. A. Macartney, *October Fifteenth: A History of Modern Hungary, 1929–1945*, 2 vols. (Edinburgh: Edinburgh University Press, 1956–57), and the lucid essay by Istvan Deák, "Hungary," in Rogger and Weber, *The European Right*, cited above, pp. 364–407. The fullest work on the Arrow Cross is Margit Szöllösi-Janze, *Die Pfeilkreuzlerbewegung in Ungarn: Historischer Kontext, Entwicklung und Herrschaft* (Munich: Oldenbourg, 1989). See in English Miklós Lackó, *Arrow Cross Men, National Socialists* (Budapest: Studia Historica Academiae Scientiarum Hungaricae No. 61, 1969), and the two articles on Hungary in Larsen et al., *Who Were the Fascists*: Lacko, "The Social Roots of Hungarian Fascism: The Arrow Cross," and György Ranki, "The Fascist Vote in Budapest in 1939." Nicholas M. Nagy-Talavera, *The Green Shirts and the Others: A History of Fascism in Hungary and Romania*, 2nd ed. (Portland, OR: Center for Romanian Studies, 2001), is a lively narrative.

Ireland: Maurice Manning, *The Blueshirts* (Toronto: University of Toronto Press, 1971). For the poet William Butler Yeats's passing interest in Irish fascism, see Elizabeth Cullingford, *Yeats, Ireland, and Fascism* (New York: New York University Press, 1981), and Gratton Fryer, *William Butler Yeats and the Anti-Democratic Tradition* (Totowa, NJ: Barnes and Noble, 1981).

Norway: Oddvar K. Hoidal, *Quisling: A Study in Treason* (Oslo: Norwegian University Press, 1989), is the most detailed biography, but Hans Fredrick Dahl, *Quisling: A Study in Treachery* (Cambridge: Cambridge University Press, 1999), has used some additional personal archives. The most thorough studies in English on Quisling's Nasjonal Samling are the chapters by Larsen, Myklebust, and Hagtvet in Larsen et al., *Who Were the Fascists*, pp. 595–650.

Poland: Edward D. Wynot, *Polish Politics in Transition: The Camp of National Unity and the Struggle for Power, 1935–1939* (Athens, GA: University of Georgia Press, 1974).

Portugal: Stimulating discussions of the special conditions of Portugal are found in A. H. Oliveira Marques, "Revolution and Counter-Revolution in Portugal: Problems of Portuguese History, 1900–1930," in Manfred Kossok, ed., *Studien über die Revolution* (Berlin: Akademie Verlag, 1969); Herminio Martins, "Portugal," in Stuart J. Woolf, ed., *European Fascism* (New York: Random House, 1968), pp. 302–36; and Phillip Schmitter, "The Social Origins, Economic Bases and Political Imperatives of Authoritarian Rule in Portugal," in Larsen et al., *Who Were the Fascists*. For Salazar's dictatorship and Portuguese fascism see Antonio Costa Pinto, *Salazar's Dictatorship* *and European Fascism* (Boulder, CO: Social Science Monographs, 1995), and *The Blue Shirts: Portuguese Fascists and the New State* (Boulder, CO: Social Science Monographs, 2000).

Romania: The most interesting discussion of the Legion of the Archangel Michael in English is Eugen Weber, "The Men of the Archangel," *Journal of Contemporary History* 1:1 (April 1966), pp. 101–26, also published in Walter Laqueur and George L. Mosse, ed., *International Fascism* (New York: Harper, 1966). Weber sees the legion as truly revolutionary, since it introduced popular political mobilization to Romania, where socialism barely existed and the bourgeois parties ruled by oligarchy. The legion aroused peasant solidarity with patriotism, religion, and anti-Semitism, however, and rejected the Western Left's values of individual citizens' rights within a state of law. The most thorough account now is Armin Heinen, *Die Legion "Erzengel Michael" in Rumanien* (Munich: Oldenbourg, 1986).

Accounts of the conflict between fascists and authoritarians in Romania include the brief survey in Stephen Fischer-Galati, *Twentieth Century Rumania* (New York: Columbia University Press, 1974), pp. 46–69; the more analytical Keith Hitchens, *Rumania, 1866–1947* (Oxford: Oxford University Press, 1994), pp. 416–25, 451–71; the dramatic narrative of Nicholas M. Nagy-Talavera, *The Green Shirts and the Others* (listed under Hungary), and the essential article by Eugen Weber: "Romania," in Rogger and Weber, *The European Right* (Berkeley and Los Angeles: University of California Press, 1965), pp. 501–74, first published in the *Journal of Contemporary History* 1:1 (1966).

Scandinavia: Ulf Lindström, *Fascism in Scandinavia* (Stockholm: Almquist and Wiksell International, 1985). Marvin Rintala, *Three Generations: The Extreme Right Wing in Finnish Politics* (Bloomington: Indiana University Press, 1962), explores the Lapua movement and its successor after 1932, the People's Patriotic Movement (IKL). Lena Berggren, "Swedish Fascism: Why Bother?" *Journal of Contemporary History* 37:3 (July 2002), pp. 395–417, is a lively critique of the literature.

Slovakia: The Jelinek article cited under Croatia; and Jörg K. Hoensch, "Slovakia: 'One God, One People, One Party,'" in Richard J. Wolff and Jörg K. Hoensch, eds., *Catholics, the State, and the Radical Right, 1919–1945* (Boulder, CO: Social Science Monographs, 1987), pp. 158–81.

Spain: Shlomo Ben-Ami, *Fascism from Above: The Dictatorship of Primo de Rivera in Spain, 1923–1930* (Oxford: Clarendon Press, 1984), and Carolyn P. Boyd, *Praetorian Politics in Liberal Spain* (Chapel Hill: University of North Carolina Press, 1979), treat the "dictatorship" of the 1920s. For the Falange, see *Selected Writings of José Antonio Primo de Rivera*, ed. Hugh Thomas (London: Jonathan Cape, 1972); Stanley Payne, *Fascism in Spain, 1923–1977* (Madison, WI: University of Wisconsin Press, 1999); Sheelagh M. Ellwood, *Spanish Fascism in the Franco Era: Falange Española de las JONS, 1936–76* (St. Martin's Press, 1988); Paul Preston, *The Politics of Revenge: Fascism and the Military in 20th Century Spain* (London: Routledge, 1995), compares Spain with Germany and Italy and finds it fascist. Paul Preston has written the fullest and most recent biography of Franco, severely critical. The case for Franco's regime as fascist is made powerfully by Michael Richards, *A Time of Silence: Civil War and the*

Culture of Repression in Franco-Spain, 1936–1945 (Cambridge: Cambridge University Press, 1998), at least for the period up to 1945.

Fascism Outside Europe For a skeptical discussion of the applicability (or not) of the fascist concept outside Europe, see Payne, *History*, chap. 10 and pages 512–17. Stein U. Larsen adopts a broad-church approach in his own wide-ranging contribution to Larsen, ed., *Fascism Outside Europe: The European Impulse against Domestic Conditions in the Diffusion of Global Fascism* (Boulder, CO: Social Science Monographs, 2001), with much material on Asia.

    Argentina: The Argentine Right has been most recently examined in Sandra McGee Deutsch and Ronald H. Dolkart, eds., *The Argentine Right: Its History and Intellectual Origins, 1910 to the Present* (Wilmington, DE: Scholarly Resources, 1993), and in Deutsch, *Las Derechas: The Extreme Right in Argentina, Brazil, and Chile* (Stanford, CA: Stanford University Press, 1999). David Rock, *Authoritarian Argentina: The Nationalist Movement, Its History, and Its Impact* (Berkeley and Los Angeles: University of California Press, 1993), finds the Argentine nationalists more reactionary than fascist. Rock explores the "failure of the first [Argentine] experiment in popular democracy" (p. 273) in *Politics in Argentina, 1890–1930: The Rise and Fall of Radicalism* (Cambridge: Cambridge University Press, 1975). Carlos H. Waisman, *Reversal of Development in Argentina: Postwar Counterrevolutionary Policies and Their Structural Consequences* (Princeton: Princeton University Press, 1987), is a stimulating essay assigning blame for the impoverishment of Argentina to the elite's choices of economic and political reaction between 1930 and 1945. Daniel James gives a stimulating account of the ambiguous relationship between the labor movement and Perón in *Resistance and Integration: Peronism and the Argentine Working Class* (Cambridge: Cambridge University Press, 1988). Gino Germani, *Authoritarianism, Fascism and National Populism* (New Brunswick, NJ: Transaction, 1978), treats Peronism as a case of crisis generated within an oligarchy by a "primary mobilization" of masses of new participants in politics. Robert D. Crassweller, *Perón and the Enigmas of Argentina* (New York: Norton, 1987), is a spirited narrative, with much attention to U.S. reactions to Perón. Frederick C. Turner and José Enrique Miguens collect a useful series of articles in *Juan Perón and the Shaping of Argentina* (Pittsburgh: University of Pittsburgh Press, 1983). Joseph R. Barager, ed., *Why Perón Came to Power* (New York: Knopf, 1968), is a classic attempt to place Peronism within Argentine history. One of the most suggestive of many works on Eva Perón is J. M. Taylor, *Eva Perón: The Myths of a Woman* (Chicago: University of Chicago Press, 1979).

    Brazil: The place to begin is Thomas E. Skidmore, *Brazil: Five Centuries of Change* (New York: Oxford University Press, 1999), and *Politics in Brazil, 1930–1964: An Experiment in Democracy* (New York: Oxford University Press, 1967). The most detailed studies of Vargas and the Integralistas are the Deutsch work mentioned under Argentina and Robert M. Levine, *The Vargas Regime: The Critical Years, 1934–1938* (New York: Columbia University Press, 1970). Levine reviews these issues more briefly in *Father of the Poor?: Vargas and His Era* (Cambridge: Cambridge University Press, 1998). Hélgio Trindade, "Fascism and Authoritarianism in Brazil under

Vargas (1930–1945)," in Larsen, ed., *Fascism Outside Europe*, pp. 469–528, assesses *Integralismo*.

China: Fred Wakeman, Jr., "A Revisionist View of the Nanjing Decade: Confucian Fascism," *China Quarterly* 150 (June 1997), pp. 395–430, says that the Blueshirts (1927–37) were not fascist. See Marcia H. Chang, *The Chinese Blue Shirt Society: Fascism and Developmental Nationalism* (Berkeley and Los Angeles: University of California Press, 1985). William C. Kirby, "Images and Realities of Chinese Fascism," in Larsen, ed., *Fascism Outside Europe*, pp. 233–68, ranges more widely.

Japan: An authoritative review of the issue of fascism in Japan is Gregory J. Kasza, "Fascism from Above? Japan's *Kakushin* Right in Comparative Perspective," in Larsen, ed., *Fascism Outside Europe*, pp. 183–232. Maruyama Masao, *Thought and Behavior in Modern Japanese Politics* (New York: Oxford University Press, 1963), is the classic exposition of "emperor-style fascism." William M. Fletcher, *The Search for a New Order: Intellectuals and Fascism in Prewar Japan* (Chapel Hill: University of North Carolina Press, 1982), is a basic English source for intellectuals influenced by fascism. Peter Duus and Daniel I. Okimoto, "Fascism and the History of Prewar Japan: The Failure of a Concept," *Journal of Asian Studies* 39:1 (November 1979), pp. 65–76; George Macklin Wilson, "A New Look at the Problem of Japanese Fascism," *Comparative Studies in Society and History* (1968), pp. 401–12; and Tetsuo Furuya, "Naissance et développement de fascisme japonais," *Revue d'histoire de la 2è guerre mondiale* 86 (April 1972), pp. 1–16, doubt that movements that looked to the army and the emperor for change can be called fascist. Paul Brooker, *The Faces of Fraternalism: Nazi Germany, Fascist Italy, and Imperial Japan* (Oxford: Clarendon Press, 1991), argues that Japan was the most effective of the three in mobilizing mass support for militant nationalism on a traditionalist base.

Latin America: Sandra McGee Deutsch, *Las Derechas* (listed under Argentina), gives an excellent overview of the extreme Right in Argentina, Brazil, and Chile. The essential works for Bolivia are Herbert Klein, *Parties and Political Change in Bolivia* (Cambridge: Cambridge University Press, 1969), and *Bolivia: The Evolution of a Multi-Ethnic Society*, 2nd ed. (New York: Oxford University Press, 1992), pp. 199–216. For a Brazilian point of view, see Hélgio Trindade, "La Question du fascisme en Amérique Latine," *Revue française de Science Politique* 33:2 (April 1983), pp. 281–312.

South Africa: Patrick J. Furlong, *Between Crown and Swastika: The Impact of the Radical Right on the Afrikaner Nationalist Movement in the Fascist Era* (Hanover, NH: University Press of New England, 1991), and Jeff J. Guy, "Fascism, Nazism, Nationalism and the Foundation of Apartheid Ideology," in Larsen, ed., *Fascism Outside Europe*, pp. 427–66.

United States: Seymour Martin Lipset and Earl Raab present a well-informed bestiary of extremist groups on the American Right in *The Politics of Unreason: Right-Wing Extremism in America, 1790–1970* (New York: Harper & Row, 1970). Alan Brinkley scrutinizes some of them elegantly in *Voices of Protest: Huey Long, Father Coughlin, and the Great Depression* (New York: Knopf, 1982), and discusses the appropriateness of the fascist label on pp. 269–83. Nancy MacLean, *Behind the Mask of Chivalry: The Making of the Second Ku Klux Klan* (New York: Oxford University Press,

1994), explores correspondences between the Klan as it was in the early twentieth century and fascism, on pp. 179–88. Leo Ribuffo, *The Old Christian Right: The Protestant Far Right from the Great Depression to the Cold War* (Philadelphia: Temple University Press, 1983), provides the fullest treatment of William Dudley Pelley's Silver Shirts, Gerald L. K. Smith, and other homegrown fascists. Donald I. Warren, "Depression-Era Fascism and Nazism in the United States and Canada: Threat to Democracy or Theater of the Absurd?" in Larsen, ed., *Fascism Outside Europe*, pp. 635–701, surveys the interwar years broadly, while Michael Cox and Martin Durham, "The Politics of Anger: The Extreme Right in the United States," in Paul Hainsworth, ed., *The Politics of the Extreme Right* (London: Pinter, 2000), pp. 287–311, update the postwar period. El Salvador as a case of United States support for something very like fascism overseas is explored by Thomas Sheehan, "Friendly Fascism: Business as Usual in America's Backyard," in Richard J. Golsan, ed., *Fascism's Return* (Lincoln: Univesity of Nebraska Press, 1998), pp. 260–300.

IX. Fascist or Neofascist Movements since 1945

A particularly enlightening article with which one may suitably begin is Diethelm Prowe, " 'Classic' Fascism and the New Radical Right in Western Europe: Comparisons and Contrasts," *Contemporary European History* 3:3 (1994), pp. 289–313. See also a review article surveying recent scholarly work by Roger Karapin, "Radical Right and Neo-Fascist Parties in Western Europe," *Comparative Politics* 30:2 (January 1998), pp. 213–34.

Useful recent descriptions of a broad range of these movements include Paul Hainsworth, ed., *The Extreme Right in Europe and the USA* (New York: St. Martin's Press, 1992), and *The Politics of the Extreme Right: From the Margin to the Mainstream* (London: Pinter, 2000); Peter H. Merkl and Leonard Weinberg, eds., *Encounters with the Contemporary Radical Right* (Boulder, CO: Westview Press, 1993); Jeffrey Kaplan and Leonard Weinberg, *The Emergence of a Euro-American Radical Right* (New Brunswick, NJ: Rutgers University Press, 1998); Luciano Cheles, Ronnie Ferguson, and Michalina Vaughan, eds., *The Far Right in Western and Eastern Europe* (London: Longman, 1995); Hans-Georg Betz, *Radical Right-Wing Populism in Western Europe* (Basingstoke: Macmillan, 1994); Hans-Georg Betz and Stefan Immerfall, eds., *The New Politics of the Right: Neo-Populist Parties and Movements in Established Democracies* (New York: St. Martin's Press, 1998); and Herbert Kitschelt, in collaboration with Andrew J. McGann, *The Radical Right in Western Europe: A Comparative Analysis* (Ann Arbor: University of Michigan Press, 1995); Sabrina P. Ramet, ed., *The Radical Right in Central and Eastern Europe since 1989* (University Park, PA: Pennsylvania State University Press, 1999). Among works in other languages, Piero Ignazi, *L'estrema destra in Europa: Da Le Pen a Haider*, 2nd ed. (Bologna: Il Mulino, 2000), is particularly thoughtful and well informed, though, despite its title, it deals only with western Europe.

For particular countries, one can start with the national articles in the works cited immediately above. For Italy, the most authoritative works now are Franco Ferraresi, "The Radical Right in Postwar Italy," *Politics and Society* 16 (March 1988), pp. 71–119;

and *Threat to Democracy: The Radical Right in Italy after the War* (Princeton: Princeton University Press, 1996), a revision of the 1984 edition; and Piero Ignazi, *Il polo escluso: Profilo del Movimento sociale italiano,* 2nd ed. (Bologna: Il Mulino, 1998).

For Germany, Rand C. Lewis, *A Nazi Legacy: Right-Wing Extremism in Postwar Germany* (New York: Praeger, 1991), provides a quick survey. In addition to good articles on Germany in the collective works already listed, see Richard Stöss, *Politics Against Democracy: Right-Wing Extremism in West Germany* (Oxford, NY: Berg, 1991); Uwe Backes and Patrick Moreau, *Die Extreme Rechte in Deutschland* (Munich: Akademische Verlag, 1993); and Patrick Moreau, *Les héritiers du IIIè Reich: L'extrème droite allemande de 1945 à nos jours* (Paris: Seuil, 1994).

Stephen Shenfield, *Russian Fascism: Tradition, Tendencies, and Movements* (Armonk, NY: M. E. Sharpe, 2001), assesses the post-1989 extreme right in Russia.

The best-informed historical survey of the many fascist and near-fascist groups in France since 1945 is Pierre Milza, *Fascisme français: Passé et présent* (Paris: Flammarion, 1987). Joseph Algazy, *La tentation neo-fasciste en France* (Paris: Fayard, 1984), is thorough for the earlier period. Authoritative recent studies of Front National voters are Pascal Perrineau, *Le symptome Le Pen: Radiographie des électeurs du Front National* (Paris: Fayard, 1997), and Nonna Mayer, *Ces français qui votent Le Pen* (Paris: Flammarion, 1999). English-language studies include Jonathan Marcus, *The National Front and French Politics* (London: Macmillan, 1995), and Harvey G. Simmons, *The French National Front* (Boulder, CO: Westview, 1996).

Neofascism in Austria is examined most recently in Ruth Wodak and Anton Pelinka, *The Haider Phenomenon in Austria* (New Brunswick, NJ: Transaction, 2002).

NOTES

Chapter 1: Introduction

1. Friedrich Engels, 1895 preface to Karl Marx, *The Class Struggles in France (1848–1850)*, in *The Marx–Engels Reader*, ed. Robert C. Tucker, 2nd ed. (New York: W. W. Norton, 1978), p. 571.

2. Alexis de Tocqueville, *Democracy in America*, trans., ed., and with an introduction by Harvey C. Mansfield and Delba Winthrop (Chicago: University of Chicago Press, 2000), p. 662 (vol. II, part 4, chap. 6).

3. Georges Sorel, *Reflections on Violence* (Cambridge: Cambridge University Press, 1999), pp. 79–80.

4. I capitalize Fascism when I refer to the Italian movement, party, and regime; I leave fascism in the lower case when I refer to the general phenomenon.

5. See Maurice Agulhon, *Marianne au combat: L'imagerie et la symbolique républicaine de 1789 à 1880* (Paris: Flammarion, 1979), pp. 28–29, 108–09, and *Marianne au pouvoir* (Paris: Seuil, 1989), pp. 77, 83.

6. Simonetta Falasca-Zamponi, *Fascist Spectacle: The Aesthetics of Power in Mussolini's Italy* (Berkeley: University of California Press, 1997), pp. 95–99.

7. Mussolini had been a leading figure in the revolutionary wing of the Italian Socialist Party, hostile to reformism and suspicious of the compromises of the party's parliamentary wing. In 1912, aged only twenty-nine, he was made editor of the party's newspaper, *Avanti*. He was expelled from the party in fall 1914 by its pacifist majority for advocating Italian entry into World War I.

8. Pierre Milza, *Mussolini* (Paris: Fayard, 1999), pp. 174, 176, 189. As early as 1911, Mussolini was calling the local socialist group he led in Forlì a *fascio*. R. J. B. Bosworth, *Mussolini* (London: Arnold, 2002), p. 52.

9. This term is explained on pp. 5–6.

10. After the defeat of Italian armies at Caporetto in November 1917, a large group of liberal and conservative deputies and senators formed a *fascio parlamentare di difesa nazionale* to rally opinion in support of the war effort.

11. The list swelled later with opportunistic additions when belonging among the founders—the *sansepolcristi*—became advantageous. Renzo De Felice, *Mussolini il rivoluzionario, 1883–1920* (Turin: Einaudi, 1965), p. 504.

12. This term is explained on p. 6.

13. An English version of Mussolini's speeches of that day is published in Charles F. Delzell, *Mediterranean Fascism, 1919–1945* (New York: Harper & Row,

1970), pp. 7–11. The fullest accounts are De Felice, *Mussolini il rivoluzionario*, pp. 504–09, and Milza, *Mussolini*, pp. 236–40.

14. Text of June 6, 1919, in De Felice, *Mussolini il rivoluzionario*, pp. 744–45. English versions in Jeffrey T. Schnapp, ed., *A Primer of Italian Fascism* (Lincoln, NE: University of Nebraska Press, 2000), pp. 3–6, and Delzell, pp. 12–13.

15. Mussolini arrived at this self-dramatizing number by counting all the fragments, large and small, that injured him in February 1917 during a training exercise with a grenade launcher.

16. A helpful introduction to syndicalism is Jeremy Jennings, *Syndicalism in France: A Study of Ideas* (London: Macmillan, 1990). Revolutionary syndicalism appealed more to the fragmented and poorly organized workers of Spain and Italy than to the numerous and well-organized workers of northern Europe, who had something to gain by reformist legislation and tactical strikes in support of specific workplace demands. Indeed it may have attracted more intellectuals than workers. See Peter N. Stearns, *Revolutionary Syndicalism and French Labor: Cause without Rebels* (New Brunswick, NJ: Rutgers University Press, 1971).

17. Zeev Sternhell et al., *The Birth of Fascist Ideology* (Princeton: Princeton University Press, 1994), pp. 16off; David Roberts, *The Syndicalist Tradition and Italian Fascism* (Chapel Hill: University of North Carolina Press, 1979); Emilio Gentile, *Le origini dell'ideologia fascista* (Bari: Laterza, 1975), pp. 134–52.

18. Published in the Paris daily *Le Figaro* on March 15, 1909. Quoted here from Adrian Lyttelton, ed., *Italian Fascisms: From Pareto to Gentile* (New York: Harper Torchbooks, 1973), p. 211.

19. The first Risorgimento, or revival, inspired by the humanist nationalism of Giuseppe Mazzini, had united Italy during 1859–70.

20. Emilio Gentile, *Il mito dello stato nuovo dall'antigiolittismo al fascismo* (Bari: Laterza, 1982); Walter Adamson, *Avant-garde Florence: From Modernism to Fascism* (Cambridge, MA: Harvard University Press, 1993).

21. De Felice, *Mussolini il rivoluzionario*, p. 521.

22. Whether the Nazi party was "fascist" or something sui generis is intensely debated. We will explain in due course why we consider Nazism a form of fascism. For the moment we note simply that Hitler kept a monumental bust of the *Duce* in his office at Nazi Party headquarters in the Brown House in Munich (Ian Kershaw, *Hitler 1889–1936: Hubris* [New York: Norton, 1999], p. 343). Even at the peak of Nazi power, when most Nazis preferred not to lend Italy priority by labeling Germany "fascist," Hitler still called himself Mussolini's "sincere admirer and disciple." A letter in these terms to the *Duce* on October 21, 1942, the twentieth anniversary of the March on Rome, is published in Meir Michaelis, "I rapporti fra fascismo e nazismo prima dell'avvento di Hitler al potere (1922–1933)," *Rivista storica italiana*, 85:3 (1973), p. 545. The most recent examination of Hitler's ties to Mussolini is Wolfgang Schieder, "The German Right and Italian Fascism," in Hans Mommsen, ed., *The Third Reich Between Vision and Reality: New Perspectives on German History* (Oxford, NY: Berg, 2001), pp. 39–57.

23. Mussolini's own words, mocking his enemies' failure to understand "the noble passion of Italian youth." Speech of January 3, 1925, in Eduardo and Duilio

Susmel, eds., *Opera Omnia di Benito Mussolini*, vol. XXI (Florence: La Fenice, 1956), pp. 238ff.

24. Thomas Mann, *Diaries 1918–1939*, selection and foreword by Herman Kesten, trans. from the German by Richard and Clara Winston (New York: H. N. Abrams, 1982), p. 136 and *passim*. Mann's repugnance for Nazi "barbarism" did not prevent him from confessing on April 20, 1933, to "a certain amount of understanding for the rebellion against the Jewish element" (p. 153).

25. Quoted in Alberto Aquarone and Maurizio Vernassa, eds., *Il regime fascista* (Bologna: Il Mulino, 1974), p. 48.

26. Friedrich Meinecke, *Die deutsche Katastrophe* (Wiesbaden: Brockhaus, 1946), trans. as *The German Catastrophe* (Cambridge, MA: Harvard University Press, 1950).

27. Resolution of the Communist International, July 1924, quoted in David Beetham, ed., *Marxists in Face of Fascism: Writings by Marxists on Fascism from the Interwar Period* (Manchester: University of Manchester Press, 1983), pp. 152–53.

28. Roger Griffin, ed., *Fascism* (Oxford: Oxford University Press, 1995), p. 262.

29. The most thorough skeptic is Gilbert Allardyce, "What Fascism Is Not: Thoughts on the Deflation of a Concept," *American Historical Review* 84:2 (April 1979), pp. 367–88.

30. Some 1940s works, colored by wartime propaganda, saw Nazism as the logical fulfillment of German national culture. See, among others, W. M. McGovern, *From Luther to Hitler: The History of Fascist-Nazi Political Philosophy* (Boston: Houghton Mifflin, 1941), and Rohan d'Olier Butler, *The Roots of National Socialism* (New York: E. P. Dutton, 1942). The principal French example is Edmond-Joachim Vermeil, *L'Allemagne: Essai d'explication* (Paris: Gallimard, 1940). The most depressing contemporary example is Daniel Jonah Goldhagen, *Hitler's Willing Executioners* (New York: Knopf, 1996), depressing because the author diverted a valuable study of sadism among the rank-and-file perpetrators of the Holocaust into a primitive demonization of all German people, thereby obscuring both numerous non-German accomplices and some humane Germans.

31. Alexander Stille, *Benevolence and Betrayal: Five Italian Jewish Families Under Fascism* (New York: Penguin, 1993), provides interesting examples of wealthy Jewish backers from Turin and Ferrara, though Jews also figured in the anti-Fascism resistance, notably in the movement Giustizia e Libertà. When the Italian racial laws were enacted in 1938, one Italian Jewish adult in three was a Fascist Party member (p. 22).

32. Philip V. Canistraro and Brian R. Sullivan, *Il Duce's Other Woman* (New York: Morrow, 1993).

33. Susan Zuccotti, *The Italians and the Holocaust: Persecution, Rescue, Survival* (New York: Basic Books, 1987), p. 24.

34. Authoritarian dictatorships govern through preexisting conservative forces (churches, armies, organized economic interests) and seek to demobilize public opinion, while fascists govern through a single party and try to generate public enthusiasm. We discuss this distinction more fully in chapter 8, pp. 216–18.

35. Some authors consider anti-Semitism the heart of the matter; I see it as instrumental. Hannah Arendt, *Origins of Totalitarianism*, rev. ed. (New York: Harcourt, Brace and World, 1966), roots totalitarianism in a fermenting brew of anti-Semitism,

imperialism, and atomized mass society. She did not think Mussolini's Italy was totalitarian (pp. 257–59, 308).

36. Otto Wagener, chief of staff of the SA and head of the economic policy office of the NSDAP before 1933, quoted in Henry A. Turner, ed., *Hitler aus nächster Nähe* (Frankfurt am Main: Ullstein, 1978), p. 374. Wagener nearly became economics minister in June 1933. See chapter 5, p. 146.

37. The Nazis promised land redistribution in Point 17 of their 25 Points of February 24, 1920 (Jeremy Noakes and Geoffrey Pridham, *Nazism 1919–1945*, vol. I: *The Rise to Power, 1919–1934* [Exeter: University of Exeter Press, 1998], p. 15). This was the only one of the "unalterable" 25 Points that Hitler explicitly revised later when, after 1928, he turned his attention to trying to recruit family farmers to his movement. The order of March 6, 1930, "completing" Point 17 and affirming the inviolability of private farm property (except that of Jews) is in *Hitler Reden, Schriften, Anordnungen, Februar 1925 bis Januar 1933*, edited by the Institut für Zeitgeschichte (Munich: K. G. Saur, 1995), vol. III, part 3, pp. 115–20. An English version appears in Norman Baynes, ed., *The Speeches of Adolf Hitler* (Oxford: Oxford University Press, 1942), vol. I, p. 105.

38. Eve Rosenhaft, *Beating the Fascists? The German Communists and Political Violence, 1929–1933* (Cambridge: Cambridge University Press, 1983). The Nazi anthem, the "Horst Wessel Lied" (Horst Wessel Song), memorialized a young Nazi ruffian killed in such a brawl, omitting that the issue was a quarrel with his landlady. See Peter Longerich, *Die braune Bataillonen: Geschichte der SA* (Munich: C. H. Beck, 1989), p. 138.

39. "If there was one thing all Fascists and National Socialists agreed on, it was their hostility to capitalism." Eugen Weber, *Varieties of Fascism* (New York: Van Nostrand, 1964), p. 47. Weber noted, of course, that opportunism limited the practical effect of this hostility. See also Eugen Weber, "Revolution? Counter-Revolution? What Revolution?" *Journal of Contemporary History* 9:2 (April 1974), pp. 3–47, republished in Walter Laqueur, ed., *Fascism: A Reader's Guide* (Berkeley and Los Angeles: University of California Press, 1976), pp. 435–67.

40. For Mussolini's early switch from the proletariat to "productive forces" as the basis of a renewed nation, see Sternhell et al., *Birth*, pp. 12, 106, 160, 167, 175, 179, 182, 219.

41. Authors who lump together these two very different ways of being antibourgeois are simply not reading closely. A recent example is the assertion by the great French historian of the French Revolution François Furet, in repudiation of his own communist youth, that both fascism and communism spring from a common self-hatred by young bourgeois. See *The Passing of an Illusion: The Idea of Communism in the Twentieth Century* (Chicago: University of Chicago Press, 1999), pp. 4, 14.

42. T. W. Mason, "The Primacy of Politics—Politics and Economics in National Socialist Germany," in Jane Caplan, ed., *Nazism, Fascism and the Working Class: Essays by Tim Mason* (Cambridge: Cambridge University Press, 1995), pp. 53–76. (First published in German in *Das Argument* 41 [Dec. 1966].)

43. The issue of "fascist revolution" is dealt with more fully in chapter 5, pp. 141–47.

44. When Mussolini abandoned socialism is a matter of dispute. His principal Italian biographer, Renzo De Felice, thinks Mussolini still considered himself a socialist in 1919 (*Mussolini il rivoluzionario*, pp. 485, 498, 519). Milza, *Mussolini*, thinks he ceased to consider himself a socialist in early 1918 when he changed the subtitle of his newspaper *Il Popolo d'Italia* from "socialist daily" to "daily for warriors and producers," but that even in 1919 he had not yet clearly opted for counterrevolution (pp. 210, 228). Sternhell et al., *Birth*, p. 212, thinks the failure of Red Week (June 1914) in northern Italian industrial cities "put an end to Mussolini's socialism." Emilio Gentile says that Mussolini's expulsion from the PSI in September 1914 started a long ideological evolution, but that Mussolini had always been a "heretical" socialist, more Nietzschean than Marxist (*Le origini dell'ideologia fascista (1918–1925)*, 2nd ed., [Bologna: Il Mulino, 1996], pp. 61–93). Bosworth, *Mussolini*, p. 107, agrees on the timing but suspects that Mussolini was an opportunist for whom socialism was merely the conventional means of ascent for a provincial arriviste. The heart of the matter is how to interpret his lingering verbal commitment to "revolution," a subject to which we will return.

45. This current was stronger among the Nazis (e.g., Walther Darré) and central European fascists than in Italy, but Mussolini exalted peasant life and tried to keep Italians on the land. Paul Corner, in "Fascist Agrarian Policy and the Italian Economy in the Interwar Years," in J. A. Davis, ed., *Gramsci and Italy's Passive Revolution* (London: Croom Helm, 1979), pp. 239–74, suspects this was mainly to keep the unemployed out of the cities, and in no way hindered an economic policy that favored large landowners. Alexander Nützenadel, *Landwirtschaft, Staat, und Autarkie: Agrarpolitik im faschistischen Italien*, Bibliothek des Deutschen Historischen Instituts in Rom, Band 86 (Tübingen: Max Niemeyer Verlag, 1997), p. 45ff, thinks Mussolini wanted even before power to finish the Risorgimento by integrating the peasants.

46. The *Duce* drove his own red Alfa Romeo sports car (Milza, *Mussolini*, pp. 227, 318), sometimes accompanied by his lion cub. Hitler loved to be driven fast in a powerful Mercedes, which the company sold him at half price as advertisement. See Bernard Bellon, *Mercedes in Peace and War* (New York: Columbia University Press, 1990), p. 232.

47. Hitler dazzled electoral meetings by arriving dramatically by plane. Mussolini was an active pilot. During a state visit to Germany he frightened Hitler by insisting on taking the controls of the *Führer*'s official Condor (Milza, *Mussolini*, pp. 794–95). Fascist Italy invested heavily in aviation for prestige, and won world records for speed and distance in the 1930s. See Claudio G. Segrè, *Italo Balbo: A Fascist Life* (Berkeley: University of California Press, 1987), part II, "The Aviator." For the British fascist leader Mosley, another pilot, see Colin Cook, "A Fascist Memory: Oswald Mosley and the Myth of the Airman," *European Review of History* 4:2 (1997), pp. 147–62.

48. In the older literature, two kinds of approach tended to put a revolt against modernity at the heart of Nazism: studies of cultural preparations, such as George L. Mosse, *The Crisis of German Ideology: Intellectual Origins of the Third Reich* (New York: Grosset and Dunlap, 1964), and Fritz Stern, *The Politics of Cultural Despair* (Berkeley and Los Angeles: University of California Press, 1961); and studies of lower-

middle-class resentment, such as Talcott Parsons, "Democracy and Social Structure in Pre-Nazi Germany," in Parsons, *Essays in Sociological Theory* (Glencoe, IL: Free Press, 1954), pp. 104–23 (orig. pub. 1942), and Heinrich A. Winkler, *Mittelstand, Demokratie und Nationalsozialismus* (Cologne: Kiepenheuer & Witsch, 1972). Italy has no equivalent literature — an important difference.

49. A. James Gregor, *Italian Fascism and Developmental Dictatorship* (Princeton: Princeton University Press, 1979); Rainer Zitelmann, *Hitler: Selbstverständnis eines Revolutionärs*, expanded new ed. (Munich: F. A. Habig, 1998). Zitelmann admits that he presents a Hitler who might have been, had he won the war, and not the "current economic and social reality" of the regime when the *Führer* had to "take the views of his conservative alliance partners into account" (pp. 47–48, 502). Articles in the same perspective are collected in Michael Prinz and Rainer Zitelmann, eds., *Nationalsozialismus und Modernizierung* (Darmstadt: Wissenschaftliche Buchgesellschaft, 1991).

50. A. F. K. Organski, "Fascism and Modernization," in Stuart J. Woolf, ed., *Nature of Fascism* (New York: Random House, 1968), pp. 19–41, believes that fascism is likeliest at the vulnerable middle point of a transition to industrial society, when the numerous victims of industrialization can make common cause with a remaining pre-industrial elite.

51. A partial list would include Ezra Pound, T. S. Eliot, W. B. Yeats, Wyndham Lewis, and Gertrude Stein, all of whom employed experimental literary techniques to criticize modern society.

52. Mussolini had his *autostrade*, Hitler his *Autobahnen*, which served job creation as well as symbolic ends. See James D. Shand, "The Reichsautobahn: Symbol of the Third Reich," *Journal of Contemporary History* 19:2 (April 1984), pp. 189–200.

53. The classic study of this process for Germany is David Schoenbaum, *Hitler's Social Revolution: Class and Status in Nazi Germany, 1933–1939* (New York: Doubleday, 1966). For Italy, see the wide-ranging analysis of Tim Mason, "Italy and Modernization," *History Workshop* 25 (Spring 1988), pp. 127–47.

54. Albert Speer, *Inside the Third Reich: Memoirs* (New York: Macmillan, 1970), pp. 11, 14–17.

55. Jeffrey Herf, *Reactionary Modernism: Technology, Culture, and Politics in Weimar and the Third Reich* (Cambridge: Cambridge University Press, 1984), finds the two reconciled in a German cultural tradition of using technology to manage the stresses of modernization. According to Henry A. Turner, Jr., "Fascism and Modernization," in *World Politics* 24:4 (July 1972), pp. 547–64, reprinted in Turner, ed., *Reappraisals of Fascism* (New York: Watts, 1975), pp. 117–39, Nazism instrumentalized modernity in order to achieve an antimodern agrarian utopia in the conquered east.

56. Hans Mommsen sees Nazism as "simulated modernization," the application of modern techniques to irrational destruction and the willful dismantling of the modern state. See Mommsen, "Nationalsozialismus als Vorgetäuschte Modernisierung," in Mommsen, *Der Nationalsozialismus und die Deutsche Gesellschaft: Ausgewählte Aufsätze*, ed. Lutz Niethammer and Bernd Weisbrod (Reinbeck bei Hamburg: Rowohlt Taschenbuch Verlag, 1991), pp. 405ff; "Noch einmal: Nationalsozialismus und Modernisierung," *Geschichte und Gesellschaft* 21:3 (July–September 1995), pp. 391–402;

and "Modernität und Barbarei: Anmerkungen aus zeithistorische Sicht," in Max Miller and Hans-Georg Soeffner, eds., *Modernität und Barbarei: Soziologische Zeitdiagnose am Ende des 20. Jahrhunderts* (Frankfurt am Main: Suhrkamp, 1996), pp. 137–55.

57. The Americans, the British, and even the Swedes were important pioneers in forced sterilization, followed closely by the Germans. See Daniel Kevles, *In the Name of Eugenics: Genetics and the Uses of Human Heredity* (New York: Knopf, 1985). Biological racism was much weaker in Catholic southern Europe, but Mussolini announced a policy of "social hygiene and national purification *[profilassi]*" in his most important policy statement after the establishment of the dictatorship, the Ascension Day Speech of May 16, 1927. For Nazi Germany's medical "purification" policies and Fascist Italy's promotion of *la razza* and *la stirpe* (lineage), understood culturally and historically, see bibliographical essay, pp. 238–40.

58. This thesis was argued provocatively by the late Detlev Peukert, "The Genesis of the 'Final Solution' from the Spirit of Science," in Thomas Childers and Jane Caplan, eds., *Reevaluating the Third Reich* (New York: Holmes and Meier, 1993), pp. 234–52. See also Zygmunt Bauman, *Modernity and the Holocaust* (Ithaca, NY: Cornell University Press, 1989), p. 149: "Considered as a complex, purposeful operation, the Holocaust may be seen as a paradigm of modern bureaucratic rationalism. Almost everything was done to achieve maximum results with minimum cost and effort."

59. P. Sabini and Mary Silvers, "Destroying the Innocent with a Clear Conscience: A Sociopsychology of the Holocaust," in Joel E. Dimsdale, ed., *Survivors, Victims, and Perpetrators: Essays in the Nazi Holocaust* (Washington: Hemisphere Publishing Corp., 1980), pp. 329–30, quoted in Bauman, *Modernity and the Holocaust*, pp. 89–90.

60. The issue is critically reviewed by Carl Levy, "From Fascism to 'post-Fascists': Italian Roads to Modernity," and Mark Roseman, "National Socialism and Modernization," in Richard Bessel, ed., *Fascist Italy and Nazi Germany* (Cambridge: Cambridge University Press, 1996), pp. 165–96 and 197–229. Detlev K. Peukert wove these themes fruitfully into his fine work *The Weimar Republic: The Crisis of Classical Modernity*, translated from the German by Richard Deveson (New York: Hill and Wang, 1991).

61. A brilliant example is Tim Mason, "The Origins of the Law on the Organization of National Labour of 20 January 1934: An Investigation into the Relationship Between 'Archaic' and 'Modern' Elements in Recent Germany History," in Caplan, *Nazism, Fascism and the Working Class*, pp. 77–103.

62. *Kristallnacht* was the Nazis' first and last collective murder of Jews carried out in the streets of German cities—the last pogrom as much as the beginning of the Holocaust (Bauman, *Modernity and the Holocaust*, p. 89). For the public reaction, see William S. Allen, "Die deutsche Öffentlichkeit und die Reichskristallnacht—Konflikte zwischen Wertheirarchie und Propaganda im Dritten Reich," in Detlev Peukert and Jürgen Reulecke, eds., *Die Reihe fast geschlossen: Beiträge zur Geschichte des Alltags unterm Nationalsozialismus* (Wuppertal: Hammer, 1981), pp. 397–412, and public opinion studies cited in chapter 9.

63. Martin Broszat, "A Controversy about the Historicization of National Socialism," in Peter Baldwin, ed., *Reworking the Past: Hitler, the Holocaust, and the Historians' Debate* (Boston: Beacon Press, 1990), p. 127.

64. "Historicizing" fascism sets off alarm bells. When Martin Broszat argued for treating Nazism as part of history instead of abstractly as an emblematic image of evil ("Plädoyer für eine Historisierung des Nationalsozialismus," *Merkur* 39:5 [May 1985], pp. 373–85), the Israeli historian Saul Friedländer warned that tracing continuities and perceiving normalities amidst the criminal acts risked banalizing the Nazi regime. Both articles, and further illuminating interchanges, are reprinted in Baldwin, ed., *Reworking the Past* (see previous note).

65. "Fascism is a genus of political ideology. . . ." (Roger Griffin, *The Nature of Fascism* [London: Routledge, 1991], p. 26). Behind fascism "lay a coherent body of thought" (Roger Eatwell, *Fascism: A History* [London: Penguin, 1996], p. xvii).

66. E. g., Schnapp, *Primer*, p. 63.

67. A useful introduction to the evolving meanings of ideology, a term created during the French Revolution, is Andrew Vincent, *Modern Political Ideologies*, 2nd ed. (Oxford: Blackwell, 1995).

68. Payne, *History*, p. 472.

69. Hitler's *Mein Kampf* ("My Struggle") served as Nazism's basic text. Elegantly bound copies were presented to newlyweds and displayed in Nazi households. It is a powerful and consistent but turgid and self-indulgent collection of autobiographical fragments and personal reflections about race, history, and human nature. For Mussolini's doctrinal writing, see chapter 1, p. 17 and note 76 below.

70. A. Bertelè, *Aspetti ideologici del fascismo* (Turin, 1930) quoted in Emilio Gentile, "Alcuni considerazioni sull'ideologia del fascismo," *Storia contemporanea* 5:1 (March 1974), p. 117. I thank Carlo Moos for help in translating this difficult passage.

71. Isaiah Berlin linked fascism and romanticism explicitly in "The Essence of European Romanticism," in Henry Hardy, ed., *The Power of Ideas* (Princeton: Princeton University Press, 2000), p. 204.

72. Walter Benjamin, "The Work of Art in the Age of Mechanical Reproduction," first published in *Zeitschrift für Sozialforschung* 5:1 (1936), reprinted in Benjamin, *Illuminations* (New York: Schocken, 1969). See especially pp. 241–42, where Benjamin quotes Marinetti on the beauty of the just-completed Ethiopian War: ". . . [war] enriches a flowering meadow with the fiery orchids of machine guns. . . ."

73. Delzell, *Mediterranean Fascism*, p. 14.

74. Quoted in R. J. B. Bosworth, *The Italian Dictatorship: Problems and Perspectives in the Interpretation of Mussolini and Fascism* (London: Arnold, 1998), p. 39.

75. Emilio Gentile, *Storia del partito fascista 1919–1922: Movimento e milizia* (Bari: Laterza, 1989), p. 498.

76. "La dottrina del fascismo," *Enciclopedia italiana* (1932), vol. XIV, pp. 847–51. An English version was given wide dissemination: Benito Mussolini, *The Doctrine of Fascism* (Florence: Vallecchi, 1935, and later editions). A recent English version is in Jeffrey T. Schnapp, ed., *Primer*, pp. 46–61.

77. Arendt, *Origins*, p. 325, n. 39. Cf. Salvatore Lupo, *Il fascismo: La politica in*

un regime totalitario (Rome: Donzelli, 2000): "What determined the Fascist compound was more the hard facts of current politics than the incoherent magma of past ideology" (p. 18).

78. Max Domarus, *Hitler Speeches and Proclamations, 1932–1945* (London: I. B. Taurus, 1990), vol. I, p. 246 (February 10, 1933).

79. Leszek Kolakowski perceived with exemplary clarity the way a closed, totalizing ideology serves to stifle critical questions in "Why an Ideology Is Always Right," in Kolakowski, *Modernity on Endless Trial* (Chicago: University of Chicago Press, 1990).

80. Roger Chartier, *The Cultural Origins of the French Revolution*, translated from the French by Lydia G. Cochrane (Durham, NC: Duke University Press, 1991), p. 2.

81. This combination may surprise, but the brutality of Mussolini's African campaigns, underlined by recent scholarship, needs to be seen as central to his regime. Mussolini used camps and ethnic cleansing, like Hitler, and he used poison gas, which Hitler never dared do. See chapter 6, pp. 165–66, and notes 63 and 68.

82. "The fascist conception of life . . . affirms the value of the individual only insofar as his interests coincide with those of the state." Mussolini, "Doctrine," in Schnapp, *Primer*, p. 48.

83. Michael A. Ledeen, *Universal Fascism* (New York: Howard Fertig, 1972).

84. Marc Bloch, "Towards a Comparative History of European Society," in Bloch, *Land and Work in Medieval Europe: Selected Papers*, trans. J. E. Anderson (Berkeley and Los Angeles: University of California Press, 1967), p. 58 (orig. pub. 1928).

85. See note 29. Several important scholars, notably Sternhell and Bracher, believe that "a general theory that seeks to combine fascism and Nazism . . . is not possible" (Sternhell, *Birth*, p. 5). Their principal reason is the centrality of biological racism to National Socialism and its weakness in Fascism. This book argues that all fascisms mobilize against some enemy, internal as well as external, but that the national culture provides the identity of that enemy.

86. The most impressively erudite survey is Payne, *History*.

87. Griffith, *Nature*, p. 26.

88. "The fascist state is not a night watchman. . . . [It] is a spiritual and moral entity whose purpose is that of securing the political, juridical, and economic organization of the nation. . . . Transcending the individual's brief existence, the state stands for the immanent conscience of the nation." Mussolini, "Doctrine," in Schnapp, *Primer*, 58.

89. An articulate example was Friedrich Percyval Reck-Malleczewen, whose *Diary of a Man in Despair*, trans. from the German by Paul Rubens (London: Macmillan, 1970) (orig. pub. 1947), laments the transformation of Germany since Bismarck into an "industrially overdeveloped ant-heap" (p. 119). Reck-Malleczewen reserved his sharpest invective for Hitler: "forelocked gypsy" (p. 18), "raw-vegetable Genghis Khan, teetotalling Alexander, womanless Napoleon" (p. 27). The Nazis executed him in early 1945. See also the journal of the pacifist arts patron Harry Kessler, *The Diaries of a Cosmopolitan* (London: Weidenfeld and Nicolson, 1971).

90. Giuseppe di Lampedusa, *The Leopard*, trans. from the Italian by Archibald Colquhoun (New York: Pantheon, 1950), p. 40.

Chapter 2: Creating Fascist Movements

1. Joseph Rothschild, *East Central Europe Between the Two World Wars* (Seattle and London: University of Washington Press, 1974), p. 148.

2. For further reading on this and other countries discussed in this chapter, see the bibliographical essay.

3. See chapter 2, p. 47.

4. Brigitta Hamann, *Hitler's Vienna: A Dictator's Apprenticeship*, trans. from the German by Thomas Thornton (New York: Oxford University Press, 1999) (orig. pub. 1996), is the most detailed treatment. William A. Jenks, *Vienna and the Young Hitler* (New York: Columbia University Press, 1960), evokes the setting.

5. The swastika, a symbol based on the sun that represented energy or eternity, among other things, was widely used in early Middle Eastern, Christian, Hindu, Buddhist, and Amerindian cultures. Introduced into Europe in the late nineteenth century by spiritualists and mediums such as the celebrated Madame Blavatsky and by apostles of Nordic religion such as the Austrian Guido von List, it was first used in 1899 to express German nationalism and anti-Semitism in the New Templars Order of Jörg Lanz von Liebenfels (1874–1954). The graphic artist Steven Heller explores its wide-ranging uses in *The Swastika: Symbol Beyond Redemption?* (New York: Allworth, 2001), and its links to Nazism are traced by Nicholas Goodrick-Clarke, *The Occult Roots of Nazism: Secret Aryan Cults and Their Influence on Nazi Ideology: The Ariosophists of Austria and Germany* (New York: New York University Press, 1996).

6. William Sheridan Allen, *The Nazi Seizure of Power: The Experience of a Single Town, 1922–1945*, rev. ed. (New York: Franklin Watts, 1984), p. 32. Spannaus had already become a fan of the Nazi precursor Houston Stewart Chamberlain while living abroad.

7. For the Freikorps see Robert G. L. Waite, *Vanguard of Nazism* (Cambridge, MA: Harvard University Press, 1954).

8. Adolf Hitler, an Austrian citizen, moved to Munich in May 1913 to escape Austrian military service. When World War I began, he volunteered in the German army. For Hitler, Germanness was always more important than loyalty to any particular state; he became a German citizen only in 1932 (Ian Kershaw, *Hitler 1889–1936: Hubris* [New York: Norton, 1998], p. 362). Hitler found his first personal fulfillment as a soldier. He faced danger as a message runner, was promoted to corporal, and was decorated for bravery with the Iron Cross, Second Class and then First Class, the highest possible award for an enlisted man (pp. 92, 96, 216).

9. It was Röhm's commanding officer, Freiherr Ritter von Epp, who later, at the end of 1920, put up half the money from army secret funds to buy the party a newspaper, the *Völkischer Beobachter*, the other half being assembled by the Munich journalist and bon vivant Dietrich Eckhart. Kershaw, *Hitler*, vol. I, p. 156.

10. Hitler adopted the title *"Führer,"* along with the greeting *"Heil,"* from the pan-German leader Georg von Schönerer, so influential in pre-war Vienna. Kershaw, *Hitler*, vol. I, p. 34.

11. See chapter 3, pp. 68–73.

12. Juan J. Linz in "Political Space and Fascism as a Latecomer," in Stein U.

Larsen, Bernt Hagtvet, and Jan Petter Myklebust, *Who Were the Fascists: Social Roots of European Fascism* (Bergen: Universitetsforlaget, 1980), pp. 153–89, and "Some Notes Toward a Comparative Study of Fascism in Sociological Historical Perspective," in Walter Laqueur, ed., *Fascism: A Reader's Guide* (Berkeley and Los Angeles: University of California Press, 1976), pp. 3–121.

13. Those whose adolescence was marked by the war but who missed actual combat because of youth or physical inaptitude could make particularly fanatical fascists. Joseph Goebbels, Hitler's propaganda minister, had missed the war because of his clubfoot. Ralf Georg Reuth, *Goebbels*, trans. from the German by Krishna Winston (New York: Harcourt Brace, 1990), pp. 14, 24.

14. Charles F. Delzell, ed., *Mediterranean Fascism* (New York: Harper & Row, 1970), p. 10.

15. For example, François Furet, *The Passing of an Illusion: The Idea of Communism in the Twentieth Century* (Chicago: University of Chicago Press, 1999), pp. 19, 163, 168. Linz observes in "Political Space," pp. 158–59, that countries neutral in World War I had low levels of fascism, as did most victorious countries. Spain had endured defeat in 1898, however.

16. Elie Halévy, *L'Ere des tyrannies* (Paris: Gallimard, 1938), translated into English as *The Era of Tyrannies: Essays on Socialism and War*, trans. Robert K. Webb (Garden City, NY: Anchor Books, 1965), first noted modern states' discovery during World War I of their potential for controlling life and thought.

17. Gregory M. Luebbert, *Liberalism, Fascism, or Social Democracy* (New York: Oxford University Press, 1991), offers the most sustained comparative analysis of some of these different outcomes, which depend, in Luebbert's view, on whether family farmers allied with the middle class (producing liberalism or fascism) or with socialists (producing social democracy).

18. Mussolini wanted Italy ruled after the war by a *trincerocrazia*, or "trenchocracy," a government of front-line veterans. *Il Popolo d'Italia*, December 15, 1917, quoted in Emilio Gentile, *Storia del partito fascista, 1919–1922: Movimento e milizia* (Bari: Laterza, 1989), p. 19. See also Gentile, *The Sacralization of Politics in Fascist Italy* (Cambridge, MA: Harvard University Press, 1996), pp. 16–17. Angry veterans turned Left as well as Right, of course. See bibliographical essay for bibliography.

19. Giorgio Rochat, *Italo Balbo* (Turin: UTET, 1986), p. 23.

20. Claudio Segrè, *Italo Balbo: A Fascist Life* (Berkeley and Los Angeles: University of California Press, 1987), pp. 28–34, 41–47.

21. Arno J. Mayer underscored that contest in *The Political Origins of the New Diplomacy, 1917–1918* (New Haven: Yale University Press, 1959), and *The Politics and Diplomacy of Peacemaking: Containment and Counterrevolution at Versailles, 1918–1919* (New York: Knopf, 1967).

22. Ernst Nolte, *Der Faschismus in seiner Epoch* (Munich: Piper Verlag, 1963), trans. into English as *Three Faces of Fascism*, trans. Leila Vennewitz (New York: Holt, Rinehart and Winston, 1966).

23. For this British-born apostle of a racially purer, less-materialist Germany, Wagner's son-in-law, see Geoffrey G. Field, *Evangelist of Race: The Germanic Vision of Houston Stewart Chamberlain* (New York: Columbia University Press, 1981).

24. Friedrich Nietzsche, *Thus Spoke Zarathustra*, trans. R. J. Hollingdale (Baltimore: Penguin, 1961), p. 126.

25. Steven E. Aschheim, "Nietzsche, Anti-Semitism, and Mass Murder," in Aschheim, *Culture and Catastrophe* (New York: New York University Press, 1996), p. 71. This lucid account of the successive Nietzsches, from the proto-Nazi of 1945 to Walter Kaufmann's free-spirited Nietzsche of the 1960s to the deconstructionist Nietzsche of today, is expanded in Aschheim, *The Nietzsche Legacy in Germany* (Berkeley and Los Angeles: University of California Press, 1992).

26. Georges Sorel, *Reflections on Violence* (Cambridge: Cambridge University Press, 1999), p. 159.

27. Zeev Sternhell with Mario Sznayder and Maia Asheri, *The Birth of Fascist Ideology* (Princeton: Princeton University Press, 1994), is thorough on Mussolini's use of Sorel. Sorel's favorable comments on Fascism have been reduced by recent scholarship to fleeting references in 1920–21. See J. R. Jennings, *Georges Sorel: The Character and Development of His Thought* (London: Macmillan, 1985); Jacques Julliard and Shlomo Sand, eds., *Georges Sorel en son temps* (Paris: Seuil, 1985); Marco Gervasoni, *Georges Sorel: Una biografia intellettuale* (Milan: Unicopli, 1997).

28. Suzanna Barrows, *Distorting Mirrors: Visions of the Crowd in Late Nineteenth-Century France* (New Haven: Yale University Press, 1981).

29. The classic account of this shift is H. Stuart Hughes, *Consciousness and Society: The Reconstruction of European Social Thought, 1890–1930* (New York: Random House, 1961).

30. Biological struggle as the key to human history, central to Hitler's worldview, was weaker in Italy, though some Italian nationalists arrived at a parallel culturally based ideal of competing national wills via Hegel and Nietzsche. See Mike Hawkins, *Social Darwinism in European and American Thought* (Cambridge: Cambridge University Press, 1997), pp. 285–89.

31. Daniel Kevles, *In the Name of Eugenics: Genetics and the Uses of Human Heredity* (New York: Knopf, 1985). Galton did not himself advocate preventing the "inferior" from reproducing.

32. Léon Poliakov, *The Aryan Myth: A History of Racist and Nationalist Ideas in Europe*, trans. from the French by Edmund Howard (New York: Basic Books, 1974). The cultural-historical *razza* of Italian nationalist rhetoric was no less aggressively competitive.

33. The Italian poet-aesthete Gabriele D'Annunzio strove to "exalt and glorify above all things Beauty, and the power of the pugnacious, dominating male." Anthony Rhodes, *The Poet as Superman: A Life of Gabriele D'Annunzio* (London: Weidenfeld and Nicholson, 1959), pp. 62–63. See also the Marquis de Morès, cited on p. 48. On the Left, anarchist proponents of propaganda of the deed also valued action for itself. The anarchist poet Laurent Tailhade responded to the bombing of the French Chamber of Deputies in December 1893 by saying, "What do these vague beings [the wounded] matter, if the gesture is beautiful?" Teilhade later lost an eye in the anarchist bombing of a Parisian café. James Joll, *The Anarchists* (Boston: Little, Brown, 1964), p. 169.

34. Ernst Jünger, *In Stahlgewittern* (Berlin: E. S. Mittler, 1929), trans. into English as *Storm of Steel* (London: Chatto and Windus, 1929), famously exalted the ennobling effects of combat following World War I. Pro-war literature was far less common than its opposite, such as Erich Maria Remarque's evocation of the horror of trench combat in *All Quiet on the Western Front* (1927). Nazi gangs broke up showings of the film made from Remarque's novel. Jünger (1895–1998) had a strained relationship with Nazism, but he was never in serious opposition to it—a not uncommon position for intellectual fellow travelers.

35. According to Jacob Talmon, *The Origins of Totalitarian Democracy* (London: Secker and Warburg, 1952), Rousseau's foundation of popular sovereignty upon the "general will," rather than upon a majority of individual wills, makes him an ancestor of fascism.

36. J. Salwyn Schapiro, "Thomas Carlyle, Prophet of Fascism," *Journal of Modern History* 17:2 (June 1945), p. 103. See more generally Chris R. Vanden Bossche, *Carlyle and the Search for Authority* (Columbus: Ohio State University Press, 1992).

37. Theodore Deimel, *Carlyle und der Nationalsozialismus* (Würzburg, 1937), cited in Karl Dietrich Bracher, Wolfgang Sauer, and Gerhard Schulz, *Die nationalsozialistische Machtergreifung* (Cologne and Opladen: Westdeutscher Verlag, 1960), p. 264 and note 9.

38. See chapter 2, pp. 37, 39. Stephen P. Turner and Dirk Käsler, eds., *Sociology Responds to Fascism* (London: Routledge, 1992), pp. 6, 9, reflect on sociology's links to fascism.

39. It was the census of 1891 that revealed to the French that their population was not reproducing itself, making this issue central for the first time in a major European state. It was later a staple fascist concern.

40. H. Stuart Hughes, *Oswald Spengler: A Critical Estimate* (New York: Scribner, 1952), republished by Greenwood Press, 1975.

41. Michael R. Marrus, *The Unwanted: European Refugees in the Twentieth Century* (New York: Oxford University Press, 1985), explores the emerging awareness since the 1880s of refugee issues.

42. *Goebbels-Reden*, vol. I (1933–39), ed. Helmut Heiber (Düsseldorf: Droste Verlag, 1971), p. 108.

43. Michael Burleigh, *Death and Deliverance: Euthanasia in Germany, c. 1900–1945* (Cambridge: Cambridge University Press, 1995).

44. See the bibliographical essay, p. 239.

45. George L. Mosse, *The Crisis of German Ideology: Intellectual Origins of the Third Reich* (New York: Grosset and Dunlap, 1964); Fritz Stern, *The Politics of Cultural Despair* (New York: Doubleday, 1961).

46. See chapter 1, note 20.

47. Isaiah Berlin, "Joseph de Maistre and the Origins of Fascism," in Henry Hardy, ed., *The Crooked Timber of Humanity: Chapters in the History of Ideas* (New York: Knopf, 1991), pp. 91–174 (quotations from pp. 112 and 174). A short preliminary sketch for this essay appears in Berlin, *Freedom and Its Betrayal: Six Enemies of Human Liberty*, ed. Henry Hardy (Princeton: Princeton University Press, 2002), pp. 131–54.

48. Sternhell, *Birth*.

49. Sternhell, *Birth*, p. 3. Sternhell is speaking here of Italian Fascism only; he explicitly excludes Nazism from his analysis. In a different register, Mark Mazower's brilliant *Dark Continent* (New York: Knopf, 1999) argues that nondemocratic values were "no more foreign to [European] tradition" than democratic ones (pp. 4–5, 396).

50. Hannah Arendt, "Approaches to the German Problem," in *Essays in Understanding* (New York: Harcourt Brace, 1994 [orig. pub. 1945]), p. 109. I thank Michael Burleigh for this citation.

51. Hughes, *Spengler*, p. 156.

52. Herman Lebovics, *Social Conservatism and the Middle Classes in Germany, 1914–1933* (Princeton, NJ: Princeton University Press, 1969), pp. 86, 107.

53. Ibid., 136.

54. Chapter 1, p. 6.

55. Sternhell, *Birth*, p. 231: "Mussolini came to terms with the existing social forces"; Emilio Gentile, *Le origini, dell' ideologia fascista (1918–1925)*, 2nd ed. (Bologna: Il Mulino, 1996), p. 323.

56. Romke Visser, "Fascist Doctrine and the Cult of Romanità," *Journal of Contemporary History* 27:1 (1992), pp. 5–22. The two thousandth anniversary of the Emperor Augustus was Mussolini's riposte to the Thousand-Year Reich. See Friedemann Scriba, *Augustus im Schwarzhemd? Die Mostra Augustea della Romanità in Rom 1937/38* (Frankfurt am Main: Lang, 1995), summarized in Scriba, "Die Mostra Augustea della Romanità in Rom 1937/38," in Jens Petersen and Wolfgang Schieder, eds., *Faschismus und Gesellschaft in Italien: Staat, Wirtschaft, Kultur* (Cologne: SH-Verlag, 1998), pp. 133–57.

57. Fredric Jameson, *Fables of Aggression: Wyndham Lewis, The Modernist as Fascist* (Berkeley and Los Angeles: University of California Press, 1979).

58. Letter to Ernest Collings, January 17, 1913, in *The Portable D. H. Lawrence* (New York: Viking, 1947), p. 563.

59. Mosse, *Crisis*, p. 6. Cf. Emilio Gentile, *Storia del partito fascista, 1919–1921: Movimento e milizia* (Bari: Laterza, 1989), p. 518: "More than an idea or a doctrine," Fascism represents "a new state of mind" *(stato d'animo)*.

60. A rare study of the way the "victim trope" may generate a desire to exterminate enemies is Omer Bartov, "Defining Enemies, Making Victims: Germans, Jews and the Holocaust," *American Historical Review* 103:3 (June 1998), pp. 771–816, with replies in 103:4 (October 1998). Victimhood may be authentic, of course.

61. Linz, "Political Space and Fascism."

62. During the French Revolution of 1789–1815, all males had the right to vote in only one election: that for the Convention, on August 26, 1792. Even then the citizens chose primary assemblies that, in a second stage, actually chose the deputies. The Constitution of 1793 provided for direct manhood suffrage, but it was never applied. Manhood suffrage really begins in 1848 in Europe, though earlier in most of the American states.

63. A recent reexamination of the emperor's self-dramatization is David Baguley, *Napoleon III and His Regime: An Extravaganza* (Baton Rouge, LA: Louisiana State University Press, 2001).

64. During the high era of fascism, several authors detected fascist elements in Napoleon III's Second Empire, e.g., J. Salwyn Shapiro, in *Liberalism and the Challenge of Fascism* (New York: McGraw-Hill, 1949), pp. 308–31. That spreads the definition too wide, although Louis Napoleon's political strategies following the revolutions of 1848 — mass electoral propaganda, state-sponsored economic growth, foreign adventure — form a significant precursor to later forms of popularly based dictatorship. Louis Napoleon's triumphant election as French president in December 1848 caused problems for Karl Marx, who had expected a different result from the economic development and class polarization of 1840s France. In *The Eighteenth Brumaire of Louis Napoleon* (1850), Marx came up with the explanation that a momentary deadlock between two evenly balanced classes — bourgeoisie and proletariat — gave exceptional leeway to an individual leader, even one of mediocre personal qualities (Marx used some of his richest invective on the despised Louis Napoleon, the "farce" who followed "tragedy"), to govern independently of class interests. This analysis was taken up in the 1920s by the Austrian August Thalheimer and other Marxist thinkers to explain the unexpected success of popular dictatorships after World War I. See Jost Düllfer, "Bonapartism, Fascism, and National Socialism," *Journal of Contemporary History* 11:4 (October 1976), pp. 109–28.

65. Jill Stephenson, *Women in Nazi Society* (London: Croom Helm, 1975), republished 2001; Victoria De Grazia, *How Fascism Ruled Women* (Berkeley and Los Angeles: University of California Press, 1992), pp. 30, 36–38. For other works, see the bibliographical essay.

66. In the French government formed by the moderate democrat Waldeck-Rousseau in September 1899 to undo the legal wrong done to Dreyfus and to defend the Republic against enraged nationalists, the moderate socialist Alexandre Millerand accepted the Ministry of Trade, Industry and Postal Services. He found himself seated in the cabinet's official photograph next to the minister of war, General Gallifet, who had crushed the Parisian revolutionaries in 1871. Some socialists, already reluctant to defend Dreyfus because he was a rich man and a Jew, thought that the purity of the socialist movement came first, while others, around Jean Jaurès, put the defense of human rights first.

67. See chapter 2, pp. 28–30.

68. Carl Schorske's term for the German nationalist movement of Georg von Schönerer in the borderlands of Bohemia during the 1880s. Schorske, *Fin-de-siècle Vienna* (New York: Knopf, 1980), chap. 3.

69. The classic analysis of this development is Max Weber's "Politik als Beruf" (1918). Parliamentarians began to be paid in France in 1848, in Germany in 1906, and, latest among European Great Powers, in Great Britain in 1910. The U.S. Constitution of 1787 established pay for senators and congressmen (Article 1, Section 6).

70. An excellent account of this generational shift in the German Liberal Party in the 1880s is Dan White, *A Splintered Party: National Liberalism in Hessen and the Reich, 1867–1918* (Cambridge, MA: Harvard University Press, 1976). For France, see Michel Winock, *Nationalism, Antisemitism, and Fascism in France* (Stanford, CA: Stanford University Press, 1998), and Raoul Girardet, *Mythes et mythologies politiques* (Paris: Seuil, 1990).

71. Odile Rudelle, *La République absolue, 1870–1889* (Paris: Publications de la Sorbonne, 1982), pp. 164–75, 182–90, 196–223, 228–34, 247–56, 262–78; Christophe Prochasson, "Les années 1880: Au temps du boulangisme," in Michel Winock, ed., *Histoire de l'extrême droite en France* (Paris: Seuil, 1993), pp. 51–82; and William D. Irvine, *The Boulanger Affair Reconsidered* (New York: Oxford University Press, 1989).

72. Ernst Nolte considers the Action Française the "first face" in his *The Three Faces of Fascism* (New York: Holt, Rinehart, and Winston, 1966). Supporting his case are the nationalism, anti-Semitism, antiparliamentarism, and occasional anticapitalism of the movement, together with its cults of youth and action. Weakening the case for fascism is Maurras's advocacy of a restored monarchy and Catholic Church as the solution to French "decline."

73. In addition to the Schorske work referred to in note 68, see John W. Boyer, *Political Radicalism in Late Imperial Vienna: Origins of the Christian Social Movement, 1849–1897* (Chicago: University of Chicago Press, 1981).

74. John W. Boyer, *Culture and Political Crisis in Vienna: Christian Socialism in Power, 1897–1918* (Chicago: University of Chicago Press, 1995).

75. White, *Splintered Party*.

76. Richard S. Levy, *The Downfall of the Anti-Semitic Political Parties in Imperial Germany* (New Haven: Yale University Press, 1975).

77. Zeev Sternhell, *La Droite révolutionnaire, 1885–1914: Les origines françaises du fascisme* (Paris: Seuil, 1978), pp. 391–98. See also Sternhell, *Birth*, pp. 86, 96, 123–27.

78. Valois, quoted in Sternhell, *La Droite révolutionnaire*, p. 394.

79. Maurice Barrès's funeral oration for the Marquis de Morès, in Barrès, *Scènes et doctrines du nationalisme* (Paris: F. Juven, 1902), pp. 324–28.

80. For Morès's outlandish adventures, see Robert F. Byrnes, *Antisemitism in Modern France* (New Brunswick, NJ: Rutgers University Press, 1950), pp. 225–50, and Sternhell, *La Droite révolutionnaire*, pp. 67, 69, 178, 180–84, 197–220.

81. Sternhell, *La Droite*, p. 218.

82. Byrnes, *Antisemitism*, p. 249.

83. Sternhell, *Birth*, pp. 131–59. David D. Roberts, "How Not to Think about Fascism and Ideology, Intellectual Antecedents, and Historical Meaning," *Journal of Contemporary History* 35:2 (April 2002), gives the Italians more intellectual autonomy than Sternhell.

84. Sternhell shows that Mussolini, drawing on both nationalist and syndicalist authors, had arrived at a pro-productivist position by January 1914. *Birth*, pp. 12, 160, 167, 175, 179, 182, 193, 219, 221.

85. See chapter 3, note 46.

86. Hans Rogger, *Jewish Policies and Right-Wing Politics in Imperial Russia* (Berkeley and Los Angeles: University of California Press, 1986), p. 213, calls the Union of the Russian People that emerged in reaction to the revolution of 1905 "the first European fascism."

87. George L. Mosse points to "particularly German values and ideas" and "uniquely German developments" "prepared long beforehand" in his study of Nazism's cultural precursors *The Crisis of German Ideology*, pp. 2, 6, 8, but he does not claim priority for them.

88. David M. Chalmers, *Hooded Americanism: The First Century of the Ku Klux Klan, 1865–1965*, 3rd ed. (Durham, NC: Duke Univerity Press, 1987), chap. 1. Similarities between the rabidly anti-Semitic revived Klan of the 1920s and fascism are explored by Nancy Maclean, *Behind the Mask of Chivalry: The Making of the Second Klan* (New York: Oxford University Press, 1994), pp. 179–88.

89. In fact, many veterans turned to the Left, and veterans formed only a quarter of SA membership. Peter H. Merkl, "Approaches to Political Violence: The Stormtroopers, 1925–1933," in Wolfgang J. Mommsen and Gerhard Hirschfeld, eds., *Social Protest, Violence and Terror in Nineteenth and Twentieth Century Europe* (New York: St. Martin's Press, for the German Historical Institute of London, 1982), p. 379. Many were younger, as we noted above.

90. Bruno Wanrooij, "The Rise and Fall of Fascism as a Generational Revolt," *Journal of Contemporary History* 22:3 (1987).

91. In a seminal article, "The Transformation of the Western European Party System," in Joseph La Palombara and Myron Weiner, eds., *Political Parties and Political Development* (Princeton: Princeton University Press, 1966), pp. 177–210, Otto Kircheimer invented the useful distinction among "parties of individual representation," which existed only to elect a "notable" deputy; "parties of integration," which enlisted their members in active participation; and "catch-all parties," which recruited across class lines. Socialists created the first parties of integration. Fascist parties were the first to be simultaneously parties of integration and catch-all parties.

92. Melitta Maschman, *Account Rendered: A Dossier on My Former Self* (London: Abelard Schuman, 1965), pp. 4, 10, 12, 18, 35–36, and 175, recalled the joy of escaping from her stifling bourgeois household into the cross-class community of the Bund deutscher Mädel.

93. The classic statement of fascism as "extremism of the middle" is Seymour Martin Lipset, *Political Man* (see chapter 8, p. 210 and note 28).

94. Richard F. Hamilton, *Who Voted for Hitler?* (Princeton: Princeton University Press, 1982), pp. 90, 112, 198, 228, 413–18.

95. Thomas Childers, *The Nazi Voter: The Social Foundations of Fascism in Germany, 1919–1933* (Chapel Hill: University of North Carolina Press, 1983), pp. 108–12, 185–88, 253–57; Jürgen Falter, *Hitlers Wähler* (Munich: C. H. Beck, 1991), pp. 198–230. The SA was composed largely of working-class unemployed (see the bibliographical essay). In 1921 the Fascist Party claimed that 15.4 percent of its members were workers. Salvatore Lupo, *Il fascismo: La politica in un regime totalitario* (Rome: Donzelli, 2000), p. 89.

96. W. D. Burnham, "Political Immunization and Political Confessionalism: The United States and Weimar Germany," *Journal of Interdisciplinary History* 3 (Summer 1972), pp. 1–30; Michaela W. Richter, "Resource Mobilization and Legal Revolution: National Socialist Tactics in Franconia," in Thomas Childers, ed., *The Formation of the Nazi Constituency* (Totowa, NJ: Barnes and Noble, 1986), pp. 104–30.

97. Workers, often unemployed, were the largest social category in the Carrara *fascio*. The local *ras*, Renato Ricci, though close to the quarry owners, supported a forty-day strike in late 1924, not a unique case early in the Fascist regime. Lupo, *Il fas-*

cismo, pp. 89, 201; Adrian Lyttelton, *The Seizure of Power: Fascism in Italy, 1919–1929* (New York: Scribner's, 1973), pp. 70–71, 168, 170; Sandro Setta, *Renato Ricci: Dallo squadrismo all Repubblica Sociale Italiano* (Bologna: Il Mulino, 1986), pp. 28, 81–100.

98. Childers, *The Nazi Voter*, p. 185; R. I. McKibbin, "The Myth of the Unemployed: Who Did Vote for the Nazis?" *Australian Journal of Politics and History* (August 1969).

99. Thomas Linehan, *East London for Mosley: The British Union of Fascists in East London and Southwest Essex, 1933–1940* (London: Frank Cass, 1996), pp. 210, 237–97. The BUF received its biggest influx in a backlash against communist and Jewish counterattacks in the Battle of Cable Street (p. 200) (see chapter 3, p. 75).

100. Miklós Lackó, *Arrow Cross Men, National Socialists* (Budapest: Studia Historica Academiae Scientiarum Hungaricae No. 61, 1969); György Ránki, "The Fascist Vote in Budapest in 1939," in Larsen et al., *Who Were the Fascists*, pp. 401–16.

101. William Brustein, *The Logic of Evil: The Social Origins of the Nazi Party, 1925–1933* (New Haven: Yale University Press, 1996), is the strongest advocate of rational choice among Nazi recruits who joined, Brustein argues, because they believed the Nazis' program offered better solutions to Germany's problems. This work's methods and data have been questioned.

102. Ian Kershaw, *Hitler: Hubris*, p. 46, finds no convincing proof of homosexuality. Frederick C. Redlich, M.D., *Hitler: Diagnosis of a Destructive Prophet* (New York: Oxford, 1998), considers Hitler a victim of strong repressions, possibly based on a genital deformity, and possibly a latent homosexual though he "talked a good [heterosexual] game." Lothar Machtan scoured the records for proof of Hitler's homosexuality and found suggestive traces (but less confirmation than he thought) in *The Hidden Hitler*, trans. from the German by John Brownjohn (Oxford: Perseus Books, 2001).

103. See Michael Kater, *The Nazi Party: A Social Profile of Members and Leaders, 1919–1945* (Cambridge, MA: Harvard University Press, 1983), pp. 194–98. Kater may overestimate the Nazi leaders' social solidity in Depression Germany.

104. The supposed killer of Matteotti.

105. Giovanni Gentile, a prestigious idealist philosopher obsessed by the need for national unity via a strong state, served as Mussolini's first education minister and applied reforms that were simultaneously elitist and statist. He was executed by partisans in 1944. The latest biography is Gabriele Turi, *Giovanni Gentile: Une biografia* (Florence: Giunti, 1995).

106. Toscanini, a candidate on the Fascist list in Milan in 1919, broke quickly with the party. In 1931, after being attacked in a Fascist journal as a "pure aesthete who soars above politics in the name of . . . a decadent aestheticism," he accepted a position in New York. Harvey Sachs, *Music in Fascist Italy* (London: Weidenfeld and Nicolson, 1987), p. 216.

107. See chapter 3, pp. 56–57.

108. Speech of October 29, 1933, in Hugh Thomas, ed., *José Antonio Primo de Rivera: Selected Writings* (London: Jonathan Cape, 1972), pp. 56, 57.

109. See chapter 3, note 82. Alice Kaplan notes in *The Collaborator* (Chicago:

University of Chicago Press, 2000), p. 13, that Brasillach's fascism "relied on the reference points and vocabulary of a literary critic—images, poetry, myths—with barely a reference to politics, economics, or ethics."

110. See chapter 3, notes 46 and 47.

111. Gentile, *Storia del partito fascista*, p. 57.

Chapter 3: Taking Root

1. A. Gudmundsson, "Nazism in Iceland," in Stein U. Larsen, Bernt Hagtvet, and Jan Petter Myklebust, eds., *Who Were the Fascists: Social Roots of European Fascism* (Bergen: Universitetsforlaget, 1980), pp. 743–51. Its membership peaked at three hundred in 1936.

2. Keith Amos, *The New Guard Movement, 1931–1935* (Melbourne: Melbourne University Press, 1976).

3. See chapter 2, note 12.

4. Speech of June 10, 1940, in Renzo De Felice, *Mussolini il duce*, vol. II: *Lo stato totalitario, 1936–1940* (Turin: Einaudi, 1981), pp. 841–42. An English version is in Charles F. Delzell, *Mediterranean Fascism* (New York: Harper & Row, 1970), pp. 213–15.

5. See chapter 1, p. 10.

6. Sternhell considers the distinction between producers and social parasites "an essential element in the emergence of the Fascist synthesis." Zeev Sternhell et al., *The Birth of the Fascist Ideology: From Cultural Rebellion to Political Revolution* (Princeton: Princeton University Press, 1994), p. 106.

7. See chapter 2, p. 54.

8. "Socialism . . . was a legitimate reaction against liberal enslavement," José Antonio said in the founding speech of the Falange on October 29, 1933. But socialism was flawed by materialism, the spirit of revenge, and class war, and must be replaced by a higher idealism "neither of the Right nor of the Left," around the nation and the Church. English text in Delzell, *Mediterranean Fascism*, pp. 259–66.

9. The energetic electoral activity of Hitler and Mussolini disproves the contention of some that this suffices to make La Rocque nonfascist. See the bibliographical essay, p. 243.

10. The proclamation that Fascism had become a party, contained in the New Program of the Partito Nazionale Fascista, November 7–10, 1921, is published in Delzell, *Mediterranean Fascism*, pp. 26–27. For internal opposition, see Adrian Lyttelton, *The Seizure of Power* (New York: Scribner's, 1973), pp. 44, 72–75, and Emilio Gentile, "The Problem of the Party in Italian Fascism," *Journal of Contemporary History* 19:2 (April 1984), pp. 251–74.

11. Emilio Gentile, *Le origine dell'ideologia fascista (1918–1925)*, 2nd ed. (Bologna: Il Mulino, 1996), pp. 128–33: "L'antipartito."

12. Delzell, *Mediterranean Fascism*, p. 263.

13. E.g., Adrian Anton Mussert's National Socialist Movement (Nationaal Socialistische Beweging) in the Netherlands.

14. E.g., the Polish Camp of National Unity.

15. E.g., the Vlaamsch Nationaal Verbond of Flemish-speaking Belgium and the Verband van Dietsche Nationaal-Solidaristen (Verdinaso) of the Netherlands.

16. E.g., Marcel Déat's Rassemblement National Populaire, in Nazi-occupied Paris in 1941–44, and Vidkun Quisling's Nasjonal Samling in Norway. General de Gaulle raised eyebrows in 1947 by calling his new movement the Rassemblement du peuple français.

17. See chapter 2, note 91.

18. See chapter 1, pp. 6–7.

19. For D'Annunzio's comic-opera but deadly serious "Republic of Carnaro," see Michael A. Ledeen, *The First Duce* (Baltimore and London: Johns Hopkins University Press, 1977), and John Woodhouse, *Gabriele D'Annunzio: Defiant Archangel* (Oxford: Clarendon, 1998). Pierre Milza, *Mussolini* (Paris: Fayard, 1999), pp. 242–50, and Michel Ostenc, *Intellectuels italiens et fascisme* (Paris: Payot, 1983), p. 122, among others, show how D'Annunzio's fame outshone Mussolini in late 1919 and early 1920.

20. After World War II, defeated Italy was powerless to prevent Yugoslavia from reclaiming Fiume. Renamed Rijeka, it is today the principal port of the post-Yugoslav Republic of Slovenia.

21. Monte Nevoso, a mountain near Fiume which went to Italy by the 1920 settlement, could be claimed as D'Annunzio's conquest. His castle, Il Vittoriale, is today a nationalist pilgrimage site.

22. The principal authorities are listed in the bibliographical essay.

23. A. Rossi [Angelo Tasca], *The Rise of Italian Fascism*, trans. Peter and Dorothy Waite (New York: Howard Fertig, 1966), pp. 119–20 (orig. pub. 1938), figures taken from Fascist Party sources.

24. Christopher Seton-Watson, *Italy from Liberalism to Fascism* (London: Methuen, 1967), p. 572, n. 2.

25. Paul Corner, *Fascism in Ferrara* (Oxford: Clarendon, 1976), pp. 123, 223.

26. Seton-Watson, *Italy from Liberalism to Fascism*, p. 616.

27. See chapter 3, p. 57.

28. See chapter 4, p. 88.

29. English translations of these texts are available in Delzell, *Mediterranean Fascism*, pp. 7–40.

30. Ibid., p. 39.

31. Many contemporary observers expressed such doubts. Renzo De Felice, ed., *Il fascismo: Le interpretazioni dei contemporanei et degli storici*, rev. ed. (Bari: Laterza, 1998).

32. Frank Snowden, *The Fascist Revolution in Tuscany* (Cambridge: Cambridge University Press, 1989), and *Fascism and Great Estates in the South of Italy: Apulia 1900–1922* (Cambridge: Cambridge University Press, 1986); Simona Colarizi, *Dopoguerra e fascismo in Puglia (1919–1926)* (Bari: Laterza, 1971).

33. See works cited in the bibliographical essay.

34. The classic study of Schleswig-Holstein's turn to Nazism was done for a doctorate in political science by Rudolf Heberle just as the Nazis were coming to power. Soon forced into exile, Heberle published his thesis in abbreviated form as *From Democracy to Nazism: A Regional Case Study on Political Parties in Germany* (Baton

Rouge: Louisiana State University Press, 1945). The full text was finally published in Germany as *Landbevölkerung und Nationalsozialismus: Eine soziologische Untersuchung der politischen Willensbildung in Schleswig-Holstein, 1918 bis 1932* (Stuttgart: Deutsche Verlags-Anstalt, 1963).

35. For works on Nazi voters and party members, see the bibliographical essay.

36. Philippe Burrin, "Poings levés et bras tendus," in *Fascisme, nazisme, autoritarisme* (Paris: Seuil, 2000), pp. 183–209, shows that the German Left was first in this domain.

37. Thomas Childers, "The Social Language of Politics," *American Historical Review* 95:2 (April 1990), p. 342.

38. Henry A. Turner, Jr., *German Big Business and the Rise of Hitler* (New York: Oxford University Press, 1985), pp. 54, 339, 350. Turner's work is authoritative not only because of his unmatched command of German business archives but because he understood that the Nazi share of business contributions can be accurately assessed only in comparison with other political groups.

39. Turner, *German Big Business*, pp. 95, 312.

40. Reinhard Kühnl, *Die nationalsozialistische Linke 1925 bis 1930*, Marburger Abhandlungen zur Politischen Wissenschaft, Band 6 (Meisenheim am Glan: Verlag Anton Hain, 1966); Peter D. Stachura, *Gregor Strasser and the Rise of Nazism* (London: Allen and Unwin, 1983). For Otto Wagener, see chapter 1, p. 10, chapter 5, pp. 146–47, and corresponding notes.

41. Peter Hayes, *Industry and Ideology: I. G. Farben in the Nazi Era* (Cambridge: Cambridge University Press, 1987), pp. 61–68. Daimler, by contrast, was a major backer. Bernard Bellon, *Mercedes in Peace and War* (New York: Columbia University Press, 1990), pp. 218, 219, 264. Both profited handsomely from the Nazi regime.

42. Horst Matzerath and Henry A. Turner, "Die Selbstfinanzierung der NSDAP 1930–1932," *Geschichte und Gesellschaft* 3:1 (1977), pp. 59–92.

43. See chapter 2, pp. 47–48.

44. The most authoritative works are listed and discussed in the bibliographical essay, pp. 241–44.

45. René Rémond, *Les Droites en France*, 4th ed. (Paris: Aubier, 1982), pp. 168, 195–230, is the classic statement of this position. The term "Roman whitewash" appears on p. 206. Jean Plumyène and Raymond Lasierra, *Les fascismes français* (Paris: Seuil, 1963), asserted even more bluntly that "fascism was at first a phenonemon foreign to France" (p. 15), and developed there only a "feeble presence" (*réalité dérisoire*) (p. 7).

46. Zeev Sternhell et al., *Birth*, p. 4. See also Sternhell, *La Droite révolutionnaire: Les origines françaises du fascisme* (Paris: Seuil, 1984). Ernst Nolte made Charles Maurras's Action Française one of his *Three Faces of Fascism* (chapter 2, note 66). George Mosse argued in *Masses and Man: Nationalist Perceptions of Reality* (New York: Howard Fertig, 1980), pp. 119ff, 164, and in *Toward the Final Solution: A History of European Racism* (New York: Howard Fertig, 1975), p. 157, that by 1900 racism had developed furthest in France and Vienna. Bernard-Henri Lévy, *L'Idéologie française* (Paris: Grasset, 1981), is polemical.

47. Zeev Sternhell, *Neither Left nor Right: Fascist Ideology in France* (Berkeley: University of California Press, 1988).

48. See the bibliographical essay, p. 242. One of the 1930s writers cited by Stern-hell successfully sued him in a French court for defamation.

49. The PPF could be considered rooted in the Paris working-class suburb of Saint-Denis, where the popularity Jacques Doriot had acquired as a young Communist leader survived his shift to the far Right in 1936. It had other local strongholds in Marseille, where the PPF militant Simon Sabiani became mayor (see Paul Jankowski, *Communism and Collaboration: Simon Sabiani and Politics in Marseille, 1919–1944* [New Haven: Yale University Press, 1989]), and in French Algeria.

50. The Croix de Feu did not wear colored shirts but paraded in berets and medals. I thank Professor Sean Kennedy for help on this point. This debate is considered more fully in the bibliographical essay, pp. 242–43.

51. See the bibliographical essay, p. 243. Colonel de La Rocque backed Marshal Pétain's "National Revolution" and neutral collaboration within Hitler's Europe in 1940–42, without playing the role in the Vichy regime that he thought he merited; some PSF members went immediately to join the Free French in London, and La Rocque was passing information to London after 1942. He was arrested and deported by the Nazis in 1943 and died soon after his liberation in 1945.

52. Serge Berstein, "La France allergique au fascisme," *Vingtième siècle: Revue d'histoire* 2 (April 1984), pp. 84–94.

53. Robert O. Paxton, *Peasant Fascism in France* (New York: Oxford University Press, 1997).

54. Richard Cobb, *The Peoples' Armies: The Armées Révolutionnaires, Instrument of the Terror in the Departments, April 1793 to Floréal Year II* (New Haven: Yale University Press, 1987).

55. Laird Boswell, *Rural Communism in France, 1920–1939* (Ithaca, NY: Cornell University Press, 1998); Gérard Belloin, *Renaud Jean: Le tribun des paysans* (Paris: Editions de l'Atelier, 1993).

56. This produced only 31 parliamentary seats, however, out of 259. Istvan Deák, "Hungary," in Rogger and Weber, *European Right*, p. 392.

57. Eugen Weber, "The Men of the Archangel," *Journal of Contemporary History* 1:1 (1966), pp. 101–26. See chapter 4, p. 97.

58. J.-M. Etienne, *Le mouvement rexiste jusqu'en 1940* (Paris, 1968), pp. 53–58; Danièle Wallef, "The Composition of Christus Rex," in Larsen et al., eds., *Who Were the Fascists*. p. 517.

59. Herman Van der Wusten and Ronald E. Smit, "Dynamics of the Dutch National Socialist Movement (the NSB), 1931–35," in Larsen et al., *Who Were the Fascists*, p. 531.

60. Sten Sparre Nilson, "Who Voted for Quisling?" in Larsen et al., *Who Were the Fascists*, p. 657.

61. Gerry Webber, "Patterns of Membership and Support for the British Union of Fascists," *Journal of Contemporary History* 19 (1984), pp. 575–600. See the bibliographical essay for other readings.

62. See notes 45–47 above.

63. See chapter 3, pp. 68–73.

64. The fullest account is Pierre Birnbaum, *The Anti-Semitic Moment: A Tour of*

France in 1898 (New York: Hill and Wang, 2002). See also Stephen Wilson, *Ideology and Experience: Antisemitism in France at the Time of the Dreyfus Affair* (Rutherford, NJ: Fairleigh Dickinson University Press, 1982).

65. Panikos Panayi, ed., *Racial Violence in Britain, 1840–1950*, rev. ed. (London and New York: Leicester University Press, 1996), pp. 10–11.

66. Albert S. Lindemann, *The Jew Accused: Three Antisemitic Affairs — Dreyfus, Beilis, Frank* (Cambridge: Cambridge University Press, 1991).

67. Richard S. Levy, *The Downfall of the Antisemitic Political Parties in Imperial Germany* (New Haven: Yale University Press, 1975).

68. This case has usually been fortified by the notorious civil-military clash in 1913 in Zabern (or Saverne), Alsace, though David Schoenbaum, *Zabern 1913* (Boston: Allen and Unwin, 1982), finds that the final outcome, where the civilians eventually got some measure of justice, did not make Germany really exceptional.

69. Scholars have paid curiously little attention to the crucial issue of how liberal regimes failed (perhaps because students of fascism tend to make the fascist leader's actions explain everything). The basic work here is Juan Linz and Alfred Stepan, eds., *The Breakdown of Democratic Regimes* (Baltimore and London: Johns Hopkins University Press, 1978).

70. George L. Mosse, *The Nationalization of the Masses: Political Symbolism and Mass Movements in Germany from the Napoleonic Wars through the Third Reich* (New York: Howard Fertig, 1975).

71. Kevin Passmore, *From Liberalism to Fascism: The Right in a French Province, 1928–1939* (Cambridge: Cambridge University Press, 1997), pp. 120, 152. This book relates fascist growth in France directly to the inefficacy of French conservative parties, whose rank and file rebelled against the old leadership and went over to the new antiparliamentary "ligues" in the 1930s. Kérillis was one of the rare French nationalist conservatives to resist that trend; he rejected Vichy and took refuge in New York in 1940.

72. The plebiscite, the Roman republic's term for a decision taken by popular vote, was introduced into modern political life by the French Revolution. An appeal to the entire public was proposed, but not used, when Louis XVI was tried and executed in 1792, and this kind of vote appears in the stillborn Constitution of 1793. General Napoleon Bonaparte gave it its modern form in 1800 by asking the whole male population to vote yes or no on his assumption of dictatorial powers as first consul. The plebiscite contrasts with the classical liberal preference of a vote by a minority of educated men for representatives who will share power with the ruler. Napoleon used it again to legitimate his assumption of the title of Emperor Napoleon I, as did his nephew Napoleon III. Hitler and Mussolini adopted the Napoleonic plebiscite unchanged.

73. See views of Jürgen Kocha, opposed by Geoff Ely, in the bibliographical essay, p. 225. See also the theories of "noncontemporaneity" discussed in chapter 8, p. 209.

74. José Ortega y Gasset, *The Revolt of the Masses* (New York: Norton, 1957) (orig. pub. 1932).

75. R. J. B. Bosworth, *Italy: The Least of the Great Powers: Italian Foreign Policy*

Before the First World War (Cambridge: Cambridge University Press, 1979). For the relation between Italian economic catching-up and politics, see Richard A. Webster, *Industrial Imperialism in Italy, 1908–1915* (Berkeley and Los Angeles: The University of California Press, 1975).

76. Arno Mayer, *The Persistence of the Old Regime: Europe to the Great War* (New York: Pantheon, 1981).

77. Many provincial Germans were offended by the freedom that Weimar German cities offered foreigners, artistic rebels, and homosexuals. Peter Gay, *Weimar Culture: The Outsider as Insider* (New York: Harper & Row, 1968), is the richest account of the overturn in German cultural life after 1919, and the backlash it produced.

78. For the volunteer units around General Kornilov, see Orlando Figes, *A People's Tragedy: A History of the Russian Revolution* (New York: Viking, 1997), pp. 556–62.

79. "History has moved along the line of least resistance. The revolutionary epoch has made its incursion through the least-barricaded gates." Leon Trotsky, "Reflections on the Course of the Proletarian Revolution" (1919), quoted in Isaac Deutscher, *The Prophet Armed: Trotsky, 1879–1921* (New York: Vintage, 1965), p. 455.

80. See chapter 1, note 30, for such works on Germany. The theory that the course of German history was a "special path," or *Sonderweg*, that embodied a particular propensity for fascism has lately been sharply criticized. For a recent review, see Shelley Baranowski, "East Elbian Landed Elites and Germany's turn to Fascism: The Sonderweg Controversy Revisited," *European History Quarterly* 26:2 (1996), pp. 209–40.

81. *The Prelude*, Book XI.

82. In prison, awaiting execution (February 1945), Brasillach wrote nostalgically of "the magnificent radiance of the universal fascism of my youth . . . this exaltation of millions of men, cathedrals of light, heros struck down in combat, the friendship among the young people of the awakened nations." René Rémond, *Les droites en France* (Paris: Aubier Montaigne, 1982), pp. 458–59.

83. Eve Rosenhaft, *Beating the Fascists? The German Communists and Political Violence, 1929–1933* (Cambridge: Cambridge University Press, 1983).

84. It was the attempt by Ernst Nolte in June 1986 to revive this very idea, that the violence of Soviet communism (the "Asiatic deed") was the initial provocation to which Nazi violence was only a response, that ignited the furious "historians' controversy" in Germany. See Charles S. Maier, *The Unmasterable Past: History, Holocaust, and German National Identity* (Cambridge, MA: Harvard University Press, 1988), pp. 29–30, and Peter Baldwin, *Reworking the Past: Hitler, the Holocaust, and the Historians' Debate* (Boston: Beacon Press, 1990).

85. This question has been most carefully examined for the Nazi case by Eric A. Johnson, *Nazi Terror: The Gestapo, Jews, and Ordinary Germans* (New York: Basic Books, 1999). Cf. p. 262: "[T]he ordinary German population . . . did not perceive the Gestapo . . . as terribly threatening to them personally." See also Robert Gellately, *Backing Hitler: Consent and Coercion in Nazi Germany* (New York: Oxford University Press, 2001).

86. Quoted in Ian Kershaw, *Hitler 1889–1936: Hubris* (New York: Norton, 1999), p. 383. The Potempa murderers were released as soon as Hitler took office. See Paul Kluke, "Der Fall Potempa," *Vierteljahrshefte für Zeitgeschichte* 5 (1957), pp. 279–97, and Richard Bessel, "The Potempa Murder," *Central European History* 10 (1977), pp. 241–54.

87. Denise Detragiache, "Il fascismo feminile da San Sepolcro all'affare Matteotti (1919–1925)," *Storia contemporanea* 14:2 (April 1983), pp. 211–50. According to Julie V. Gottlieb, *Feminist Fascism: Women in Britain's Fascist Movement, 1923–1945* (London: Tauris, 2001), 10 percent of candidates for the British Union of Fascists were women, and British fascist women stewards particularly relished beating up Communist women.

88. *Trasformismo* (the word was first used by Prime Minister Depretis in 1876) was the political domestication of antisystem parties by bringing them into the system. Applied to the socialists by Giolitti, *trasformismo* split the reformist parliamentary socialists from the intransigents, such as the revolutionary syndicalists (like the young Mussolini). Having succeeded with the socialists, Giolitti was tempted to try *trasformismo* on the Fascists.

Chapter 4: Getting Power

1. While some fascist writers claim that fifty to seventy thousand Blackshirts were converging on Rome on October 28, and while King Victor Emanuel III later mentioned a figure of one hundred thousand to justify his reluctance to block the march, careful estimates suggest that only about nine thousand Blackshirts were actually in place at the gates of Rome on the morning of October 28. General Emanuele Pugliese, in command of the 16th Infantry Division based in Rome, had available ninety-five hundred seasoned infantrymen, three hundred cavalrymen, plus about eleven thousand police. He had the further advantages of well-fed and well-armed forces and inner lines of communication and defense. Antonino Répaci, *La Marcia su Roma*, new ed. (Milan: Rizzoli, 1972), pp. 441, 461–64.

2. Martin Broszat in Kolloquien des Instituts für Zeitgeschichte, *Der italienische Faschismus: Probleme und Forschungstendenzen* (Munich: Oldenbourg, 1983), pp. 8–9. There is a well-informed brief account in English in Christopher Seton-Watson, *Italy from Liberalism to Fascism* (London: Methuen, 1967), pp. 617–29.

3. This parade is the subject of many photographs purporting to show the "March on Rome." See chapter 4, p. 109 for the incidents.

4. The year V of the Fascist era thus began on October 28, 1927. Emilio Gentile, *The Sacralization of Politics in Fascist Italy* (Cambridge, MA: Harvard University Press, 1996), pp. 90–98.

5. Mabel Berezin, *Making the Fascist Self: The Political Culture of Interwar Italy* (Ithaca, NY: Cornell University Press, 1997), pp. 80, 109, 111–12, 150; this exhibition was repeated in 1942 for the twentieth anniversary (p. 197). See also Roberta Sazzivalli, "The Myth of Squadrismo in the Fascist Regime," *Journal of Contemporary History* 35:2 (April 2000), pp. 131–50.

6. European restabilization after World War I has been most lucidly examined by

Charles S. Maier, *Recasting Bourgeois Europe* (Princeton: Princeton University Press, 1975).

7. Harold J. Gordon, Jr., *Hitler and the Beer Hall Putsch* (Princeton: Princeton University Press, 1972).

8. It was while serving the ensuing year in Landsberg Prison that Hitler wrote *Mein Kampf* ("My Struggle") and began creating his own mythical image.

9. "We want to take power legally. But what we once do with this power when we have it, that's our business." Goering, in the *Reichstag*, February 5, 1931, quoted in Ian Kershaw, *Hitler, 1883–1936: Hubris* (New York: Norton, 1998), p. 704, n. 201. Hitler threatened during a trial in Leipzig on September 25, 1930, that once in power he would "let . . . heads roll." Max Domarus, *Hitler's Speeches and Proclamations, 1932–1945* (London: I. B. Tauris, 1990), p. 244.

10. The average was only eight and a half months. Karl Dietrich Bracher, Gerhard Schulz, and Wolfgang Sauer, *Die nationalsozialistische Machtergreifung* (Frankfurt am Mein/Berlin/Vienna: Ullstein, 1962), vol. I, p. 32.

11. While the Nazis and the communists were the youngest parties in 1932, the SPD had the oldest leadership. Richard N. Hunt, *German Social Democracy, 1918–1933* (Chicago: Quadrangle, 1970), pp. 71–72, 86, 89–91, 246.

12. Erich Mathias and Rudolf Morsey, eds., *Das Ende der Parteien* (Düsseldorf: Droste, 1960), is still authoritative for the reactions of the political parties to Hitler's arrival in power. In English, Donna Harsch, *German Social Democracy and the Rise of Nazism* (Chapel Hill: University of North Carolina Press, 1993).

13. Conan Fischer, *The German Communists and the Rise of Nazism* (New York: St. Martin's Press, 1991). See p. 177 for the transport strike.

14. Kershaw, *Hitler: Hubris*, p. 368.

15. Emilio Gentile, *Storia del partito fascista, 1919–1922: Movimento e milizia* (Bari: Laterza, 1989), p. 202.

16. Jens Petersen estimates that about ten thousand were killed and one hundred thousand injured in all forms of civil conflict in Italy in the early 1920s. Kolloquien des Instituts für Zeitgeschichte, *Der italienische Faschismus*, p. 32. Adrian Lyttelton estimates that five to six hundred persons died in Italy from Fascist violence in 1921 alone. See Lyttelton, "Fascism and Violence in Post-War Italy: Political Strategy and Social Conflict," in Wolfgang J. Mommsen and Gerhard Hirschfeld, eds., *Social Protest, Violence and Terror in Nineteenth and Twentieth Century Europe* (London: Macmillan with Berg Publishers for the German Historical Institute, 1982), p. 262; see also Jens Petersen, "Violence in Italian Fascism, 1919–1925," pp. 275–99 (esp. pp. 286–94).

17. The latest and most convincing account of the choices, in no way inevitable, by which Hitler was made chancellor is Henry A. Turner, Jr., *Hitler's Thirty Days to Power* (Boston: Addison-Wesley, 1996).

18. Bullock, *Hitler*, pp. 253, 277.

19. Bracher et al., *Die nationalsozialistische Machtergreifung*, p. 93.

20. Luigi Salvatorelli and Giovanni Mira, *Storia d'Italia nel periodo Fascista* (Turin: Einaudi, 1964), pp. 137–38. The subsequent election of April 6, 1924, with the Fascists in power, was not run under normal procedures, as we will see.

21. Adrian Lyttelton, *The Seizure of Power: Fascism in Italy, 1919–1929*, 2nd ed. (Princeton: Princeton University Press, 1987), is still the most illuminating analysis. The phrase appears also in the title of the classic work of Bracher et al., *Die national-sozialistische Machtergreifung.*

22. Stanley Payne, *A History of Fascism, 1914–1945* (Madison: University of Wisconsin Press, 1995), considers that authoritarian regimes "served more as a barrier against, rather than an inducement for, fascism" (p. 312), which "paradoxically . . . required political freedom to have a chance to win power" (p. 252). See also pp. 250, 326, 395–6, 492.

23. Works concerning this and other movements discussed in this chapter are listed, and often commented upon, in the bibliographical essay.

24. Payne, *History*, p. 395.

25. A thin veneer of fascist trappings included Antonescu's title of *"conducator,"* leader.

26. Not long before, a general strike by German labor unions had frustrated the Kapp Putsch in 1920.

27. The most celebrated example was Cesari Mori, the strict and ascetic prefect of Bologna who tolerated disorder from neither socialists nor Fascists. Given emergency powers over the whole troubled Po Valley in November 1921, Mori tried to impose order, but his own police fraternized with the Fascists and he was transferred and then dismissed. Later Mussolini sent him to Sicily to repress the Mafia. Christopher Duggan, *Fascism and the Mafia* (New Haven: Yale University Press, 1989), pp. 122–24 and *passim.*

28. Juan J. Linz, "Crisis, Breakdown, and Reequilibration," in Juan J. Linz and Alfred Stepan, eds., *The Breakdown of Democratic Regimes* (Baltimore: Johns Hopkins University Press, 1978), pp. 66, 70, 78.

29. William A. Renzi, "Mussolini's Sources of Financial Support, 1914–1915," *History* 56:187 (June 1971), pp. 186–206.

30. Kolloquien des Instituts für Zeitgeschichte, *Der italienische Faschismus*, p. 62. Cf. the comparable term *"compromesso autoritario"* for Mussolini's choices in the important article of the late Massimo Legnani, "Systema di potere fascista, blocco dominante, alleanze sociali," in Angelo Del Boca et al., *Il regime fascista*, pp. 418–26.

31. Chapter 2, p. 48.

32. Hannah Arendt, *Origins of Totalitarianism*, second enlarged edition (New York: Meridian Books, 1958), p. 375.

33. Henry A. Turner, *Big Business and the Rise of Hitler* (New York: Oxford University Press, 1985), pp. 95–99, 113–15, 133–42, 188, 245, 279–81, 287, shows that most businessmen's worries about Nazi economic radicalism increased in 1932.

34. Federico Chabod, *A History of Italian Fascism* (New York: Howard Fertig, 1975), p. 43 (orig. pub. 1950). "Fear can also be retrospective."

35. The KPD was the only German party whose vote grew without interruption from December 1924 (9 percent) to November 1932 (17 percent), by which time the SPD vote had dropped from a peak of about 30 percent in 1928 to about 21 percent.

36. Roberto Vivarelli, in Kolloquien des Instituts für Zeitgeschichte, *Der italienische Faschismus*, p. 49. Vivarelli pondered these two processes at greater length

in *Il fallimento del Liberalismo* (Bologna: Il Mulino, 1981). The relationship between Fascism and Liberal Italy is reviewed most recently by Paul Corner, "The Road to Fascism: An Italian *Sonderweg?*" *Contemporary European History* 2:2 (2002), pp. 273–95.

37. The Hitler cabinet of January 30, 1933, contained only two other Nazis: Economics Minister Walter Funk and Interior Minister Hermann Goering (a vital post, since it controlled the police; Goering was also minister-president of the largest state in Germany, Prussia). Mussolini's cabinet of October 30, 1922, contained only three other Fascists, alongside seven ministers from other parties (one Liberal, one Nationalist, three Democrats, and two Popolari [Christian Democrats], two military men, and the philosopher Giovanni Gentile). Mussolini, in personal charge of the vital Ministries of the Interior and Foreign Affairs, had more power within his government at the beginning than Hitler. See Lyttelton, *Seizure*, 96, 457.

38. Fritz Tobias, *Der Reichstagsbrand: Legende und Wirklichkeit* (Rastatt-Baden: Grote, 1962), and Hans Mommsen, "The Reichstag Fire and Its Political Consequences," in Hajo Holborn, ed., *Republic to Reich: The Making of the Nazi Revolution* (New York: Pantheon, 1972), pp. 129–222, and in Henry A. Turner, Jr., *Nazism and the Third Reich* (New York: Franklin Watts, 1972), pp. 109–50 (orig. pub., 1964).

39. Sebastian Haffner, *Defying Hitler: A Memoir*, trans. from the German by Oliver Pretzel (New York: Farrar, Straus and Giroux, 2002), gives a chilling description of such scenes as witnessed by a young magistrate who later emigrated.

40. A professor of French in Dresden, Victor Klemperer, took regular notes of the degradation of Nazi language and called it LTI, *Lingua tertii imperii*, "language of the Third Empire," the inflated but empty grandiloquence beloved of Nazi propagandists and no longer specific to fascism: Klemperer, *The Language of the Third Reich: LTI, Lingua tertii imperii: A Philologist's Notebook* (New Brunswick, NJ: Athlone, 2000). Klemperer is best known for his moving diary of enduring in Germany as a Jew married to a non-Jewish woman.

41. The official death toll was eighty-five, fifty of them SA members, but no exact accounting will ever be possible. Kershaw, *Hitler: Hubris*, p. 517.

42. See chapter 6, p. 151.

43. Adrian Lyttelton, "Fascism: The Second Wave," in Walter Laqueur and George L. Mosse, eds., *International Fascism: 1920–1945* (New York: Harper, 1966), pp. 75–100, reprinted from *Journal of Contemporary History* 1:1 (1966).

44. Pierre Milza, *Mussolini* (Paris: Fayard, 1999), p. 307.

45. Ibid., p. 331.

46. They included Salandra, Giolitti, and the powerful Milan *Corriere della Sera*, but the Vatican and some industrialists warned that removing Mussolini would increase disorder. Seton-Watson, *Italy*, pp. 653–57.

47. They called this fruitless gesture the "Aventine Secession," in reference to representatives of the Roman *plebs* who took refuge from patrician oppression on the Aventine Hill in 494 B.C. Divided among Socialists, Popolari, and some liberals, they appealed for a return to legality but could not agree on any action.

48. See chapter 4, p. 97.

49. See chapter 7, p. 193.

50. An interesting proposal to create an additional category, midway between con-

servatism and fascism, of conservative regimes that crush grassroots fascist movements but borrow some of their devices, is Gregory J. Kasza, "Fascism from Above? Japan's *Kakushin* Right in Comparative Perspective," in Stein Ugelvik Larsen, ed., *Fascism Outside Europe* (Boulder, CO: Social Science Monographs, 2001), pp. 183–232. See also note 22 above.

51. "I am fully opposed to any attempt to export National Socialism." *Hitler's Table Talk*, trans. Norman Cameron and R. H. Stevens (London: Weidenfeld and Nicolson, 1953), p. 490 (entry for May 20, 1942).

52. Robert O. Paxton, *Vichy France: Old Guard and New Order*, 2nd ed. (New York: Columbia University Press, 2001), pp. 267, 325.

53. Approximately twenty-five hundred Belgian men served with Degrelle's Légion Wallonie in Russia in 1943 and 1944; about eleven hundred of the two thousand sent to the front in November 1943 died, including its commander, Lucien Lippert. Martin Conway, *Collaboration in Belgium: Léon Degrelle and the Rexist Movement* (New Haven: Yale University Press, 1993), pp. 220, 244.

54. The only European fascist leader to fight in person on the eastern front was Jacques Doriot, who accompanied some six thousand other Frenchmen in the semi-official Légion des Volontaires Contre le Bolshevisme. Philippe Burrin, *La dérive fasciste: Doriot, Déat, Bergery: 1933–1945* (Paris: Seuil, 1986), p. 431.

55. See chapter 4, p. 97.

56. John R. Lampe, *Yugoslavia as History: Twice There Was a Country*, 2nd ed. (Cambridge: Cambridge University Press, 2000), p. 440.

57. Burrin, *La Dérive fasciste*, pp. 451–54, calls the French ultracollaborators like Déat and Doriot "secondary or derived" fascists because they lacked the urge for expansion by war common to Mussolini and Hitler.

58. See chapter 3, pp. 68–73.

59. Peter Baldwin, *The Politics of Social Solidarity: Class Bases of the European Welfare State* (Cambridge: Cambridge University Press, 1990).

60. See chapter 4, p. 101.

61. A penetrating account of the conservatives' actions in Italy in 1920–22 in terms of the narrowing of alternatives is Paolo Farneti, "Social Conflict, Parliamentary Fragmentation, Institutional Shift, and the Rise of Fascism: Italy," in Juan J. Linz and Alfred Stepan, eds., *The Breakdown of Democratic Regimes: Europe* (Baltimore: Johns Hopkins University Press, 1978), pp. 3–33.

62. "These were the conditions that made Fascist victory possible," writes Adrian Lyttelton, "but they did not make it inevitable" (*Seizure*, p. 77). See also Turner, *Hitler's Thirty Days*.

Chapter 5: Exercising Power

1. Franz Neumann, *Behemoth: The Structure and Practice of National Socialism, 1933–1944*, 2nd ed. (New York: Oxford University Press, 1944), pp. 291, 396–97.

2. Karl Dietrich Bracher, *The German Dictatorship: The Origins, Structure, and Effects of National Socialism*, trans. from the German by Jean Steinberg (New York: Praeger, 1970) (orig. pub. 1969), p. 492.

3. Martin Broszat, *The Hitler State: The Foundation and Development of the Internal Structure of the Third Reich*, trans. from the German by John W. Hiden (London: Longman, 1981) (orig. pub. 1969), p. 57.

4. Hans Mommsen, "Zur Verschränkung traditionellen und faschistischen Führungsgruppe in Deutschland beim Übergang von der Bewegungs zur Systemphase," in *Der Nationalsozialismus und die deutsche Gesellschaft*, ed. Lutz Niethammer and Bernd Weisbrod for Mommsen's sixtieth birthday (Reinbeck bei Hamburg: Rowohlt, 1991), pp. 39–66 (quotations from pp. 39, 40, 50).

5. "Sulle origini del movimento fascista," *Occidente* 3 (1954), p. 306, reprinted in *Opere di Gaetano Salvemini*, vol. VI: *Scritti sul fascismo*, vol. III (Turin: Giulio Einaudi, 1974), p. 439. Salvemini here emphasized the multiple roots and successive stages of fascism.

6. Alberto Aquarone, *L'organizzazione dello Stato totalitario* (Turin: Einaudi, 1965), pp. 271, 302. It was, said Curzio Malaparte with scorn, "a Liberal government administered by Fascists" (p. 247).

7. Wolfgang Schieder, "Der Strukturwandel der faschistischen Partei Italiens in der Phase der Herrschaftsstabilisierung," in Schieder, ed., *Faschismus als soziale Bewegung: Deutschland und Italien im Vergleich*, 2nd ed. (Göttingen: Vandenhoeck und Ruprecht, 1983), esp. pp. 71, 90. These points are taken up again by Jens Petersen and Wolfgang Schieder in Kolloquien des Instituts für Zeitgeschichte, *Der italienische Fascismus: Probleme und Forschungstendenzen* (Munich: Oldenbourg, 1983).

8. Massimo Legnani, "Sistema di potere fascista, blocco dominante, alleanze sociali: Contributo a una discussione," in Angelo Del Boca, Massimo Legnani, and Mario G. Rossi, eds., *Il regime fascista: Storia e storiografia* (Bari: Laterza, 1995), pp. 414–45 (quotation from p. 415).

9. Emilio Gentile, *La via italiana al totalitarismo: Il partito e lo stato nel regime fascista* (Rome: La Nuova Italia Scientifica, 1995), pp. 83, 136, 180.

10. A conclusion abetted by some cultural studies that examine the pageantry without weighing its influence. See a fuller discussion in chapter 8, pp. 214–15.

11. Ernst Fraenkel, *The Dual State* (New York: Oxford, 1941).

12. The coexistence within the Nazi regime of legal punctiliousness with blatant lawlessness never ceases to astonish. As late as December 1938 some Jewish victims of individual, unauthorized Nazi violence were able to have their assailants arrested by the German police and punished by German courts at the very moment when authorized violence against Jews was mounting. As one survivor recalled years later, "unofficial crimes were forbidden in the Third Reich." Eric A. Johnson, *Nazi Terror: The Gestapo, Jews, and Ordinary Germans* (New York: Basic Books, 1999), pp. 124–25.

13. Ian Kershaw, *Hitler 1936–1945: Nemesis* (New York: Norton, 2000), p. 253.

14. The persistence in Nazi Germany of a "normative state" should never be construed as exonerating all its officials, who, in practice (and especially after war began), could act as cruelly and as arbitrarily as the "parallel" agencies. See, for example, Nikolaus Wachsmann, " 'Annihilation through Labour': The Killing of State Prisoners in the Third Reich," *Journal of Modern History* 71 (September 1999), pp. 627–28, 659. Many examples are offered as well in Robert Gellately, *Backing Hitler* (New York: Oxford University Press, 2001). The old self-exculpatory distinction between the

"correct" professional army and the criminal SS has also been undermined by Omer Bartov in works cited in chapter 6, note 79.

15. On the usefulness of national emergency for dictators, see Hans Mommsen, "Ausnahmezustand als Herrschaftstechnik des NS-Regimes," in Manfred Funke, ed., *Hitler, Deutschland und die Mächte* (Düsseldorf: Droste, 1976).

16. Emilio Gentile, "The Problem of the Party in Italian Fascism," *Journal of Contemporary History* 19:2 (April 1984), pp. 251–74.

17. It remains uncertain what the initials stood for, if anything. For works on OVRA and the Fascist repressive agencies, see the bibliographical essay, p. 230.

18. The Istituto per la Ricostruzione Industriale, the state holding company set up to rescue failing banks and industries in January 1933. See Marco Maraffi, *Politica ed economica in Italia: Le vicende dell'impresa pubblica dagli anni Trenta agli anni Cinquanta* (Bologna: Il Mulino, 1990).

19. Gentile, *La via italiano*, p. 185: the "acceleration of the totalitarian process." Gentile does not use the "dual state" model, however.

20. Doris L. Bergen, *Twisted Cross: The German Christian Movement in the Third Reich* (Chapel Hill: University of North Carolina Press, 1996); for three "intelligent, well-meaning, reputable [Lutheran] theologians" whose nationalism reconciled them to the regime, see Robert P. Ericksen, *Theologians Under Hitler* (New Haven: Yale University Press, 1985) (quotation on p. 198).

21. Carl J. Friedrich and Zbigniew K. Brzezinski, *Totalitarian Dictatorship and Autocracy,* 2nd ed. (New York: Praeger, 1965), chap. 6.

22. For a vivid local example of how German Catholics rejected some specific Nazi practices that invaded parish "turf" without challenging the regime itself, see Jeremy Noakes, "The Oldenburg Crucifix Conflict," in Peter D. Stachura, *The Shaping of the Nazi State* (London: Croom Helm, 1978), pp. 210–33.

23. Martin Broszat borrowed the German medical term *Resistenz* to express a kind of negative impermeability to Nazi influence (as with the Churches, for example), not to be confused with the more active *Widerstand,* or positive opposition. For this distinction, see Ian Kershaw, *The Nazi Dictatorship: Problems and Perspectives of Interpretation* (London: Edward Arnold, 1989), p. 151.

24. Alf Lüdtke, in *Herrschaft als sozialer Praxis*, Veröffentlichen des Max-Planck-Instituts für Geschichte #91 (Göttingen: Vandenhoeck and Ruprecht, 1991), pp. 12–14, draws "appropriation" from Max Weber, Marx, E. P. Thompson, and Pierre Bourdieu. I draw it from personal experience, having, at the age of thirteen, helped my comrades subvert a well-meant Boy Scout weekend camping program into something closer to *Lord of the Flies.*

25. An important literature on the fascist regimes' encouragement of denunciations, and their worry about false ones, appears in the bibliographical essay, p. 230.

26. Geoffrey G. Giles, "The Rise of the NS Students' Association," in Peter D. Stachura, ed., *Shaping,* pp. 160–85, and *Students and National Socialism* (Princeton: Princeton University Press, 1985), pp. 168, 175–86, 201, 228. There is abundant detail in Helma Brunck, *Die deutsche Burschenschaft in der Weimar Republik und im Nationalsozialismus* (Munich: Universitas, 1999).

27. See more in chapter 5, p. 138 and chapter 6, pp. 152–53.

28. Tracy Koon, *Believe, Obey, Fight: Political Socialization of Youth in Fascist Italy* (Chapel Hill: University of North Carolina Press, 1985), p. 248, gives examples from the war years. I thank Luciano Rebay for personal reminiscences on this point.

29. See chapter 5, p. 124.

30. Michael Burleigh and Wolfgang Wippermann, *The Racial State: Germany 1933–1945* (Cambridge: Cambridge University Press, 1991), p. 353, n. 1, advocate, convincingly, a more anthropologically informed study of how fascist regimes interacted with social and professional groups.

31. Hannah Arendt, *Origins*, pp. 389–90, 395, 398, 402. She credits "shapelessness" to Franz Neumann, *Behemoth*. Broszat revived the term in *The Hitler State*, p. 346. Salvatore Lupo, *Il fascismo: La politica in un regime totalitario* (Rome: Donzelli, 2000), points to Fascist Italy's "frenzy of perpetual motion," citing Arendt (p. 30).

32. This may explain the curious hesitation of the king and conservative and liberal political leaders to remove Mussolini from office after the murder of Matteotti in June 1924. See chapter 4, pp. 109–10.

33. Jens Petersen goes so far as to speak of a de facto system of "checks and balances" in Fascist Italy. Kolloquien des Instituts für Zeitgeschichte, *Der italienische Faschismus*, p. 25. The Nazi system was more clearly dominated by Hitler and party activists, but see Edward N. Peterson, *The Limits of Hitler's Power* (Princeton: Princeton University Press, 1969).

34. Circular of January 5, 1927, quoted in Aquarone, *L'organizzazione*, pp. 485–88.

35. See the illuminating work of Victoria De Grazia, *The Culture of Consent: Mass Organization of Leisure in Fascist Italy* (Cambridge: Cambridge University Press, 1981).

36. Broszat, *The Hitler State*, pp. 218–19.

37. Gentile, *La via italiana*, pp. 177, 179, 183.

38. Martin Clark, *Modern Italy, 1971–1982* (London: Longman, 1984), p. 237.

39. Broszat, *Hitler State*, pp. 199–201.

40. The literature on this controversial point is reviewed in the bibliographical essay, pp. 232–33.

41. R. J. B. Bosworth, *The Italian Dictatorship* (London: Arnold, 1998), pp. 31, 81, notes that no study similar to Peterson, *Limits*, analyzes decision-making in Fascist Italy and limits on Mussolini's claims to total control.

42. The term was invented by Max Weber, who distinguished among bureaucratic, patriarchal, and charismatic authority, the first two stable and based on economic rationality, in their different ways, and the third unstable and outside any formal structure or economic rationality. Charisma rests on a leader's reputation for having extraordinary personal powers that must be constantly reaffirmed by results. Weber derived the term from the Greek word for the Christian concept of grace. See *From Max Weber: Essays in Sociology*, trans., ed., and with an introduction by Hans H. Gerth and C. Wright Mills (New York: Oxford University Press, 1946), pp. 79–80, 235–52, 295–96.

43. Italian Fascist Party officials actually discussed the constitutional issues

involved in the *Duce's* succession. They debated, for example, whether the title passed with the office or belonged personally to Mussolini. Gentile, *La via italiana*, pp. 214–16. Only Hitler could evoke his own succession. See Zitelmann, *Selbstverständnis*, pp. 393, 396.

44. For the many American admirers of Mussolini in the 1920s, see John P. Diggins, *Mussolini and Fascism: The View from America* (Princeton: Princeton University Press, 1972). For British admirers such as George Bernard Shaw and former prime minister David Lloyd George, and many other Europeans, see Renzo De Felice, *Mussolini il Duce*, vol. I: *Gli anni del consenso, 1929–1936* (Turin: Einaudi, 1974), pp. 541–87.

45. See chapter 5, pp. 127–28.

46. The best studies of public opinion in Nazi Germany and Fascist Italy are discussed in the bibliographical essay, pp. 235–36. Joseph Nyomarkay, *Charisma and Factionalism in the Nazi Party* (Minneapolis: University of Minnesota Press, 1967), argued that charismatic rule prevented party factions from joining in an authentic opposition.

47. Kolloquien des Instituts für Zeitgeschichte, *Der italienische Faschismus*, p. 59.

48. The term was first used in 1969 by Broszat, *Hitler State*, p. 294, and more fully developed by Peter Hüttenberger, "Nationalsozialistische Polykratie," *Geschichte und Gesellschaft* 2:4 (1976), pp. 417–72. See further Hans Mommsen in many works, including *From Weimar to Auschwitz* (Cambridge: Cambridge University Press, 1991), and Gerhard Hirschfeld and Lothar Kettenacker, eds., *Der Führerstaat: Mythos und Realität* (Stuttgart: Klett-Cotta, 1981). For interesting comparisons see Philippe Burrin, "Politique et société: Les structures du pouvoir dans l'Italie fasciste et l'Allemagne nazie," *Annales: Économies, sociétés, civilisations*, 43 (1988), pp. 615–37. For the applicability of this concept to Fascist Italy, the debate in Kolloquien des Instituts für Zeitgeschichte, *Der italienische Faschismus*, is enlightening, especially the remarks of Jens Petersen and Wolfgang Schieder.

49. Hans Mommsen first used the term "weak dictator" in *Beamtentum im Dritten Reich* (Stuttgart: Deutsche Verlags-Anstalt, 1966), p. 98, n. 26. In extensive later writings on the Nazi system of rule *(Herrschaftssystem)*, Mommsen made it clear that he considered that Hitler possessed power "unlimited" to a degree "rare in history" but exercised it in a chaotic way that deprived Nazi Germany of the main characteristics of a state, i.e., that capacity to examine options freely and choose among them rationally. See, for example, Mommsen in "Hitler's Position in the Weimar System," *From Weimar to Auschwitz* (Princeton: Princeton University Press, 1991), pp. 67, 75. For the progressive *"Entstaatlichung"* (loss of "state-ness") of the Nazi system, see Mommsen, "Nationalsozialismus als vorgetäuschte Modernisierung," in Lutz Niethammer and Bernd Weisbrod, eds., *Der Nationalsozialismus und die deutsche Gesellschaft: Ausgewählte Aufsätze* (Reinbeck bei Hamburg: Rowohlt, 1991), p. 409.

50. Ian Kershaw, *Hitler 1889–1936: Hubris* (New York: Norton, 1999), chap. 13, "Working Toward the Fuhrer," pp. 527–91.

51. *Rundschau*, the German-language publication of the Communist International, on April 12, 1933, quoted in Julius Braunthal, *History of the International, 1914–1943* (New York: Praeger, 1967), vol. II, p. 394.

52. Karl Dietrich Bracher, Wolfgang Sauer, and Gerhard Schulz, *Die national-sozialistiche Machtergreifung* (Cologne and Opladen: Westdeutcher Verlag, 1960), p. 219.

53. An excellent introduction to conservatives' complex attitudes toward Hitler and their failure to control him is Jeremy Noakes, "German Conservatives and the Third Reich: An Ambiguous Relationship," in Martin Blinkhorn, ed., *Fascists and Conservatives* (London: Allen and Unwin, 1990), pp. 71–97.

54. Albert Speer, just beginning his brilliant career as Hitler's architect with an assignment to transform the vice-chancellor's offices into SA headquarters, remembered averting his eyes from a large pool of dried blood on the floor of the office of Herbert von Bose, an assistant to von Papen. Speer, *Inside the Third Reich*, trans. from the German by Richard and Clara Winston (New York: Macmillan, 1970), p. 53.

55. A recent review of this complex matter is Gerd P. Ueberschär, "General Halder and the Resistance to Hitler in the German High Command, 1938–1940," *European History Quarterly* 18:3 (July 1988), pp. 321–41.

56. Norman Rich, *Hitler's War Aims*, vol. II: *The Establishment of the New Order* (New York: Norton, 1974), pp. 60, 278. By such appointments Ribbentrop was defending his empire against both the diplomatic corps and the agents of his arch-rival Himmler.

57. Arendt, for example (see chapter 8, note 34). Emilio Gentile, by contrast, insists in *La via italiana al totalitarismo*, pp. 67, 136, 180, 254, on the Fascist regime's aspiration to construct a fully totalitarian state, though even he recognizes that, in practice, it remained "incomplete." Totalitarianism is addressed in chapter 8.

58. Adrian Lyttelton, *Seizure*, pp. 127, 273.

59. "Radicals" cited by Clark, *Modern Italy*, p. 259. Clark considers this judgment accurate for the summit political institutions, but that much else in Fascist Italy was new.

60. See chapter 3, p. 66.

61. See chapter 3, p. 68, and chapter 4, p. 101.

62. The seizure of art in conquered territories for the Nazi leaders and for German national museums gave the underemployed mystical prophet Alfred Rosenberg something to do after 1939. The rivalries and place-seeking around Rosenberg were a key example in the development of the "polycratic" interpretation of Nazi rule. See Reinhard Bollmus, *Das Amt Rosenberg und seine Gegner: Zum Machtkampf im nationalsozialistichen Herrschaftssystem* (Stuttgart: Deutsche Verlags-Anstalt, 1979).

63. See chapter 4, p. 110.

64. Emilio Gentile, *Le origini dell'ideologia fascista (1918–1925)*, 2nd ed. (Bologna: Il Mulino, 1996), pp. 335–48 ("Farinacci e l'estremismo intransigente"). In English see Harry Fornari, *Mussolini's Gadfly: Roberto Farinacci* (Nashville, TN: Vanderbilt University Press, 1971).

65. See the bibliographical essay, p. 231.

66. Hans Buchheim, "The SS—Instrument of Domination," in Helmut Krausnick, Hans Buchheim, Martin Broszat, and Hans-Adolf Jacobsen, eds., *Anatomy of the SS State*, trans. from the German by Richard Barry, Marian Jackson, and Dorothy Long (New York: Walker, 1968), pp. 127–301, a study of the Nazi police system pre-

pared for the trial of a group of guards at the Auschwitz extermination camp in 1963, remains the most authoritative account.

67. Gellately, *Backing Hitler*, pp. 34–36, 87–89, 258.

68. Ibid., p. 43.

69. Ibid., p. 31.

70. Only one of 122 judges belonging to various panels of the Supreme Court in Germany was a Social Democrat, and only two were members of the Nazi Party. Most were conservative nationalists. Ingo Müller, *Hitler's Justice: The Courts of the Third Reich*, trans. Deborah Lucas Schneider (Cambridge, MA: Harvard University Press, 1991), p. 37.

71. Lothar Gruchmann, *Justiz im Dritten Reich: Anpassung und Unterwerfung in der Ära Gürtner*, 2nd ed. (Munich: Oldenbourg, 1990).

72. Guido Neppi Modona, "La magistratura e il fascismo," in Guido Quazza, ed., *Fascismo e società italiana* (Turin: Einaudi, 1973), pp. 125–81.

73. Robert N. Proctor, *The Nazi War on Cancer* (Princeton: Princeton University Press, 1999), shows that the Nazi antitobacco campaign could draw upon both Germany's world-class medical research and Hitler's personal hypochondria and dietary crankiness (a vegetarian, he referred to beef broth as "corpse tea").

74. The phrase "medicalized killing" is in Robert Jay Lifton, *The Nazi Doctors: Medical Killing and the Psychology of Genocide* (New York: Basic Books, 1986), p. 14. See also Michael Kater, *Doctors Under Hitler* (Chapel Hill: University of North Carolina Press, 1989).

75. Edward Ross Dickinson, *The Politics of German Child Welfare from the Empire to the Federal Republic* (Cambridge, MA: Harvard University Press, 1996), pp. 204–20 (quotation on p. 211).

76. Gellately, *Backing Hitler*, pp. vii, 51–67, 75, 80–83, 263.

77. See chapter 6, note 77.

78. See chapter 4, note 16.

79. The classic account of this experience is Carlo Levi, *Christ Stopped at Eboli* (New York: Farrar, Straus, 1963).

80. Between 1926 and 1943, the Tribunale Speciale per la Difesa Dello Stato investigated twenty-one thousand cases and sentenced about ten thousand persons to some form of prison sentence (Jens Petersen, Kolloquien des Instituts für Zeitgeschichte, *Der italienische Faschismus*, p. 32). Death sentence figures, mostly involving separatist Croats and Slovenes, are from Petersen, confirmed by Guido Melis in Raffaele Romanelli, ed., *Storia dello stato italiano dall'unità a oggi* (Rome: Donzelli, 1995), p. 390. Italy had more than fifty prison camps in 1940–43, however, of which the largest was Ferramonti di Tarsia in Calabria. See Bosworth, *Dictatorship*, p. 1, and J. Walston, "History and Memory of the Italian Concentration Camp," *Historical Journal* 40 (1997), pp. 169–83.

81. Paolo Ungari, *Alfredo Rocco e l'ideologia giuridica del fascismo* (Brescia: Morcelliano, 1963), p. 64. Rocco, a Nationalist fellow traveler, already took this position before 1914 as a young law professor.

82. Although Hitler refrained from using lethal gas in warfare, Mussolini used it against Libyans and Ethiopians. See Angelo Del Boca, *I Gas di Mussolini: Il fascismo*

e il guerra d'Etiopia (Rome: Editore Riuniti, 1996). Mussolini also herded Senussi tribesmen in Libya into concentration camps. For other works on the Italian colonial empire, see the bibliographical essay.

83. Johnson, *Nazi Terror,* pp. 46–47, and 503–04. Cologne, with three quarters of a million citizens (not counting an additional population of foreign workers) had sixty-nine Gestapo officers in 1942. For the important role played in Nazi enforcement by voluntary denunciations, see the bibliographical essay, pp. 230–31.

84. Tim Mason, "The Containment of the Working Class," in Jane Caplan, ed., *Nazism, Fascism, and the Working Class: Essays by Tim Mason* (Cambridge: Cambridge University Press, 1995), p. 238.

85. Giulio Sapelli, ed., *La classe operaia durante il fascismo* (Milan: Annali della fondazione Giangiacomo Feltrinelli, 20th year, 1979–80), makes this point for Italy.

86. See the bibliographical essay.

87. Sebastian Haffner, *Defying Hitler* (New York: Farrar, Straus, Giroux, 2000), pp. 257ff. Haffner escaped to England in 1937 and wrote this memoir a year later.

88. This was not the general opinion in Italy during the first twenty years after the liberation, when a somewhat inflated view of the Italian resistance prevailed. When Renzo De Felice argued for consensus in *Mussolini il Duce,* vol. I: *Gli anni del consenso* (Turin: Einaudi, 1974), he aroused violent controversy. The mechanisms were worked out by Philip V. Cannistraro, *La fabbricca del consenso: Fascismo e mass media* (Bari: Laterza, 1975), and the results verified by Colarizi, *L'opinione degli italiani.* For the latest synthesis, see Patrizia Dogliani, *Italia fascista 1922–1940* (Milan: Sansoni/RCS, 1999), chap. 3, "L'organizzazione del consenso."

89. Bosworth, *Mussolini,* p. 62.

90. This vote was more nearly a plebiscite than an election: the citizens could vote only "Yes" or "No" to the entire list. Even so, 89.63 percent of those eligible participated, and only 136,198 of them (2 percent) voted "No."

91. See the works of MacGregor Knox discussed in the bibliographical essay, p. 238.

92. Marlis Steinert, *Hitler's War and the Germans* (Athens, OH: Ohio University Press, 1977).

93. The German film *Die Kinder aus Nr. 67* (The Children of No. 67) (1980) shows subtly how the boys and girls of a working-class apartment building in Berlin adapted to the newly obligatory Hitler Youth in spring 1933 under the multiple influences of attraction, peer pressure, parental values, and coercion.

94. Melitta Maschmann's memoir *Account Rendered* (London: Abelard-Schuman, 1965) is eloquent on this point.

95. One German youth admitted, "It's really nice being able to lash out, without being hit back." Michael Burleigh, *The Third Reich: A New History* (New York: Hill and Wang, 2000), p. 237. Jean-Paul Sartre's short fictional essay "L'enfance d'un chef" plausibly evokes an adolescent bully's journey to fascism.

96. For the immense literature on this and other debates about women under fascism, see the bibliographical essay, pp. 233–34.

97. The grinning young woman in a fascist uniform with her cigarette on the

dust jacket of Victoria De Grazia, *How Fascism Ruled Women* (Berkeley and Los Angeles: University of California Press, 1992), displays these ambiguities perfectly.

98. M. Carli, *Fascismo intransigente: Contributo alla fondazione di un regime* (Florence: R. Bemporad e Figlio, 1926), p. 46, quoted in Norberto Bobbio, "La Cultura e il fascismo," in Guido Quazza, ed., *Fascismo e società italiana* (Turin: Einaudi, 1973), p. 240, n. 1.

99. Ibid., p. 240.

100. E.g., the doctor and painter Carlo Levi, whose *Christ Stopped at Eboli*, written during "confinement" in a southern hill town, is one of the masterpieces of modern Italian literature.

101. E.g., the Rosselli brothers, Giovanni Amendola, and Piero Gobetti.

102. See chapter 2, note 105.

103. Sandrine Bertaux, "Démographie, statistique, et fascisme: Corrado Gini et l'ISTAT, entre Science et Idéologie," *Roma Moderna et Contemporanea* 7:3 (September-December 1999), p. 571–98.

104. Gabriele Turi, *Il fascismo e il consenso degli intellettuali* (Bologna: Il Mulino, 1980), pp. 59, 63. Radical fascists protested their presence.

105. Bobbio, "La Cultura," p. 112. Three of these also contributed to the *Enciclopedia* (Turi, *Il fascismo*, p. 63).

106. Monika Renneburg and Mark Walker, eds., *Science, Technology, and National Socialism* (Cambridge: Cambridge University Press, 1994).

107. John L. Heilbron, *The Dilemmas of an Upright Man: Max Planck as Spokesman for German Science* (Berkeley and Los Angeles: University of California Press, 1986).

108. Jerry Z. Muller, *The Other God that Failed: Hans Freyer and the Deradicalization of German Conservatism* (Princeton: Princeton University Press, 1987).

109. Carl Schmitt (1888–1985) argued that complex modern societies required a "total state" capable of efficacious decision-making. A good start in an extensive literature is Richard Wolin, "Carl Schmitt, Political Existentialism, and the Total State," in Wolin, *The Terms of Cultural Criticism: The Frankfurt School, Existentialism, Poststructuralism* (New York: Columbia University Press, 1992), pp. 83–104.

110. Mark Walker, *German National Socialism and the Quest for Nuclear Power, 1939–1949* (Cambridge: Cambridge University Press, 1989), argues the latter case persuasively; Thomas Powers, *Heisenberg's War: The Secret History of the German Bomb* (New York: Knopf, 1993), is more sympathetic to Heisenberg's claims of foot dragging.

111. One of the "Ten Principles of German Music" enunciated when Goebbels established the Reichsmusikkammer on November 15, 1933. Furtwängler rejected, however, the further principles that Judaism and atonalism were incompatible with German music.

112. See Robert Craft, "The Furtwängler Enigma," *New York Review of Books* 40:16 (October 7, 1993), pp. 10–14.

113. See chapter 1, p. 10.

114. See chapter 1, note 53.

115. See Gellately, *Backing Hitler*, on "police justice" (pp. 5, 34–50, 82, 175, 258).

116. The Fascist Party's youth organizations spread nationwide after 1926, when they were united under the Ministry of Education in the Opera Nazionale Balilla (ONB, named after a youth who had died resisting Napoleon). The ONB enrolled boys and girls (separately and less completely) from eight to eighteen; they could start at six as "Wolf Cubs." The ONB was reorganized under Fascist Party control in 1937 as the Gioventù Italiana del Littorio (GIL; the *littorio*, or lictor, was the official who carried the *fasces* before the magistrates in civic processions under the Roman Empire). The GIL was increasingly militarized (for boys) under the motto "Believe, Obey, Fight," and after 1939 it was obligatory. University students belonged to the Gruppi Universitaria Fascista. See the bibliographical essay for relevant works.

117. Jeremy Noakes and Geoffrey Pridham, eds., *Nazism 1919–1945*, vol. 2: *State, Economy, and Society, 1933–1939: A Documentary Reader* (Exeter: University of Exeter Press, 1984), doc. #297, p. 417.

118. Karl-Heinz Jahnke and Michael Buddrus, *Deutsche Jugend 1933–1945: Eine Dokumentation* (Hamburg: VSA-Verlag, 1989), p. 15.

119. Quoted in Arendt, *Origins*, p. 339. She believed him.

120. Mabel Berezin, *Making the Fascist Self* (Ithaca and London: Cornell University Press, 1997).

121. Here is where Rousseau and his fear of faction becomes a possible remote precursor of fascism.

122. See the bibliographical essay, p. 236.

123. Glenn R. Cuomo, ed., *National Socialist Cultural Policy* (New York: St. Martin's Press, 1995), p. 107.

124. Alan E. Steinweis, "The Purge of Artistic Life," in Robert Gellately and Nathan Stoltzfus, eds., *Social Outsiders in Nazi Germany* (Princeton: Princeton University Press, 2001), pp. 108–09.

125. The most illuminating general discussion is Charles S. Maier, "The Economics of Fascism and Nazism," in Maier, *In Search of Stability* (Cambridge: Cambridge University Press, 1988).

126. T. W. Mason, "The Primacy of Politics: Politics and Economics in National Socialist Germany," in Caplan, ed., *Nazism.*

127. Sergio Romano, *Giuseppi Volpi et l'Italie moderne: Finance, industrie et Etat de l'ère giolittienne à la Deuxième Guerre Mondiale* (Rome: École française de Rome, 1982), pp. 141–52; Jon S. Cohen, "The 1927 Revaluation of the Lira: A Study in Political Economy," *Economic History Review* 25 (1972), pp. 642, 654.

128. Peter Hayes, *Industry and Ideology: I. G. Farben in the Third Reich* (Cambridge: Cambridge University Press, 1987), p. 120.

129. This evolution is analyzed masterfully by Hayes, *Industry and Ideology.*

130. Gerhard Th. Mollin, *Montankonzerne und Drittes Reich: Der Gegensatz zwischen Monopolindustrie und Befehlwirtschaft in der deutschen Rüstung und Expansion 1936–1944* (Göttingen: Vandenhoeck and Ruprecht, 1988), pp. 70ff, 102ff, and 198ff.

131. Gerald D. Feldman, *Allianz and the German Insurance Business, 1933–1945* (Cambridge: Cambridge University Press, 2001). For the camps, see pp. 409–15. Otto Wagener is quoted from his diary, *Hitler aus Nächste Nähe*, ed. Henry A. Turner, Jr.

(Frankfurt am Main: Ullstein, 1978), pp. 373–74. The faithful Wagener never ceased to believe, even after 1945, that Hitler's true "national socialist" ideals had been sabotaged by reactionary *Nazisten* around him (p. xi). For Wagener's distaste for "filthy money," see chapter 1, p. 10.

132. John S. Cohen, "Was Italian Fascism a Developmental Dictatorship?" *Economic History Review*, 2nd series, 41:1 (February 1988), pp. 95–113, compares Italian growth rates. For more on the "developmental dictatorship" interpretation of fascism, see chapter 1, note 49, and chapter 8, p. 210.

Chapter 6: The Long Term: Radicalization or Entropy?

1. Adrian Lyttelton, in Kolloquien des Instituts für Zeitgeschichte, *Der italienische Faschismus: Probleme und Forschungstendenzen* (Munich: Oldenbourg, 1983), p. 59.

2. Giuseppe Bottai, "La rivoluzione permanente," in *Critica fascista*, November 1, 1926, quoted in Alexander Nützenadel, "Faschismus als Revolution? Politische Sprache und revolutionärer Stil im Italien Mussolinis," in Christof Dipper, Lutz Klinkhammer, and Alexander Nützenadel, eds., *Europäische Sozialgeschichte: Festschrift für Wolfgang Schieder* (Berlin: Duncker & Humblot, 2000), p. 37. The words recall Trotsky, but Bottai, a former squadrist turned bureaucrat, explained that Fascist "permanent revolution," unlike earlier revolutions, meant long-term change under state direction. Jeremy Noakes surveys this issue elegantly for Germany in "Nazism and Revolution," in Noel O'Sullivan, ed., *Revolutionary Theory and Political Reality* (London: Wheatsheaf, 1983), pp. 73–100. See also Arendt's view in chapter 5, p. 124.

3. This term is defined in chapter 8, pp. 216–18.

4. For a brilliant interpretation of Franco's Spain as fascist (at least until 1945) because of its murderous vengefulness, its quest for cultural purity, and its closed economic system, see Michael Richards, *A Time of Silence: Civil War and the Culture of Repression in Franco's Spain, 1936–1945* (Cambridge: Cambridge University Press, 1998).

5. The latest and fullest biography is Paul Preston, *Franco* (New York: Basic Books, 1994) (quotation on p. 330). More than most biographers, Preston portrays Franco as actively committed to partnership with the Axis up to at least 1942.

6. Ian Kershaw, *Hitler 1936–1945: Nemesis* (New York: Norton, 2000), p. 330.

7. Preston, *Franco*, p. 267.

8. Stanley G. Payne, *Fascism in Spain, 1923–1977* (Madison: University of Wisconsin Press, 1999), pp. 401, 451, and *passim*.

9. Antonio Costa Pinto, *Salazar's Dictatorship and European Fascism* (Boulder, CO: Social Science Monographs, 1995), p. 161.

10. Antonio Costa Pinto, *The Blue Shirts: Portuguese Fascists and the New State* (Boulder, CO: Social Science Monographs, 2000).

11. Costa Pinto, *Salazar's Dictatorship*, p. 204.

12. Roland Sarti, *Fascism and the Industrial Leadership in Italy, 1919–1940: A Study in the Expansion of Private Power under Fascism* (Berkeley: University of California Press, 1971), p. 51.

13. See chapter 4, pp. 109–10.

14. See chapter 5, pp. 132–33. After ten years in the political wilderness, Farinacci returned to prominence in the Ethiopian War, where he distinguished himself by blowing off his own hand while fishing with grenades. He remained on terms of easy familiarity with the *Duce*, always urging greater radicalism, until he encountered German disapproval in 1943.

15. Roland Sarti subtitles his book (note 12 above) "A Study in the Expansion of Private Power Under Fascism." A recent overview of Fascist syndicalism is Adolfo Pepe, "Il sindacato fascista," in Angelo Del Boca Massimo Legnani, and Mario D. Rossi, *Il regime fascista: Storia e storiografia* (Bari: Laterza, 1995), pp. 220–43.

16. See chapter 5, p. 138.

17. Pius XI had already accepted the dissolution of the troublesome Partito Popolare of Dom Luigi Sturzo in 1926. He negotiated a series of concordats with European dictatorships, including Nazi Germany, by which he accepted the dissolution of Catholic parties in return for the continued existence of Catholic Action and parochial schools.

18. Works on Italian church-state relations are in the bibliographical essay.

19. Quoted in Ruth Ben-Ghiat, *Fascist Modernities: Italy, 1922–1945* (Berkeley and Los Angeles: University of California Press, 2001), p. 13.

20. See chapter 6, pp. 156, 164–69.

21. See chapter 5, pp. 127–28.

22. See chapter 6, p. 169.

23. Schwerin von Krosigk remained in office until the very end, but with diminishing authority.

24. Robert Koehl, "Feudal Aspects of National Socialism," *American Political Science Review* 54 (December 1960), pp. 921–33.

25. Jeremy Noakes and Geoffrey Pridham, *Nazism 1919–1945*, vol. 2: *State, Economy and Society, 1933–1939: A Documentary Reader* (Exeter: University of Exeter Press, 1984), pp. 231–32.

26. See chapter 5, note 50.

27. *The Goebbels Diaries*, ed. Louis Lochner (New York: Doubleday, 1948), p. 314 (entry for March 20, 1943). Hitler was speaking of the Jewish issue.

28. A. J. P. Taylor, *Origins of the Second World War* (New York: Atheneum, 1962), pp. 210–12, 216–20, 249–50, 278.

29. Galeazzo Ciano, *Diary 1937–1943* (New York: Enigma, 2002), p. 25 (entry for November 13, 1937).

30. Bruno Biancini, ed., *Dizionario Mussoliniano* (Milan: Ulrico Hoepli, 1939), p. 88 (speech to parliament, May 26, 1934).

31. Edward R. Tannenbaum gives a few examples in *The Fascist Experience: Italian Society and Culture, 1922–1945* (New York: Basic Books, 1972), pp. 306, 329.

32. The standard account, Macgregor Knox, *Mussolini Unleashed* (Cambridge: Cambridge University Press, 1982), attributes the decision solely to Mussolini's bellicosity, though Bosworth, *Mussolini*, dissents, arguing that Mussolini was more cautious in 1939–40 than Liberal Italy in 1911 and 1915, and largely supported by Italian public opinion in his decision to go to war (p. 370).

33. Robert O. Paxton, *Parades and Politics at Vichy* (Princeton: Princeton University Press, 1966), pp. 75–81, 228–37, 321–43.

34. See chapter 8, p. 209.

35. Firmly established a generation ago by Karl A. Schleunes, *The Twisted Road to Auschwitz* (Urbana: University of Illinois Press, 1970), and Uwe Dietrich Adam, *Judenpolitik im dritten Reich* (Düsseldorf: Droste, 1972), the development by stages of Nazi anti-Jewish policy continues to inform the most important syntheses: Saul Freidländer, *Nazi Germany and the Jews*, vol. I: *The Years of Persecution: 1933–1939* (New York: HarperCollins, 1997), and Peter Longerich, *Politik der Vernichtung: Eine Gesamtdarstellung der nationalsozialistische Judenverfolgung* (Munich: Piper, 1998).

36. Hitler chose the "least inclusive" version offered him. Friedländer, *Nazi Germany and the Jews*, vol. I, pp. 148–49.

37. See chapter 1, p. 14.

38. Jeremy Noakes and Geoffrey Pridham, *Nazism: 1919–1945*, vol. II: *State, Economy, and Society, 1933–1939* (Exeter: University of Exeter Press, 1984), p. 559.

39. Götz Aly, "Jewish Resettlement: Reflections on the Prehistory of the Holocaust," p. 64, and Thomas Sandkühler, "Anti-Jewish Policy and the Murder of the Jews in the District of Galicia, 1941–42," pp. 109–11, in Ulrich Herbert, ed., *National Socialist Extermination Policies: Contemporary German Perspectives and Controversies* (New York: Fischer, 1998).

40. The "homecoming" of ethnic Germans from the South Tyrol (or Alto Adige) and a number of eastern European areas, including the Baltic States, Bukovina, Dobrudja, and Bessarabia, had been negotiated with Mussolini and Stalin in 1939. The classic work is Robert L. Koehl, *RKFDV: German Resettlement and Population Policy, 1939–1945* (Cambridge, MA: Harvard University Press, 1957). See also Götz Aly, *"Final Solution": Nazi Population Policy and the Murder of the European Jews*, trans. from the German by Belinda Cooper and Allison Brown (London and New York: Arnold, 1999), esp. chap. 5. A useful synopsis is Aly, "Jewish Resettlement," in Ulrich Herbert, ed., *Extermination Policies*, pp. 53–82.

41. Aly, "Jewish Resettlement," pp. 61, 69, 70, uses the terms "blind alley" and "domino policy." The authoritative work on the Madagascar plan is Magnus Brechtken, *"Madagascar für die Juden": Antisemitische Idee und politische Praxis, 1885–1945* (Munich: Oldenbourg, 1997).

42. See the important new work gathered in Herbert, ed., *Extermination Policies*.

43. Longerich, *Politik der Vernichtung*, pp. 369–410; Christian Dieckmann, "The War and the Killing of the Lithuanian Jews," in Herbert, *Extermination Policies*, p. 231; Sandkühler, "Anti-Jewish Policy," pp. 112–13.

44. David Irving's suggestion in *Hitler's War* (New York: Viking, 1977), pp. 12–13, that Himmler was responsible until 1943 has been discredited. Irving later became a negationist.

45. Gerald Fleming, *Hitler and the Final Solution* (Berkeley and Los Angeles: University of California Press, 1984), assembled overwhelming evidence on this point.

46. Christopher R. Browning, "The Euphoria of Victory and the Final Solution: Summer-Fall 1941," *German Studies Review* 17 (1994), pp. 473–81.

47. Philippe Burrin, *Hitler and the Jews: The Genesis of the Holocaust* (London and New York: Edward Arnold, 1994).

48. Christian Gerlach, *Krieg, Ernährung, Völkermord: Forschungen zur deutschen Vernichtungspolitik im Zweiten Weltkrieg* (Hamburg: Hamburger Edition, 1998), chap. 2: "Die Wannsee Konferenz, das Schicksal der deutschen Juden, und Hitlers politische Grundsatzentscheidung alle Juden Europas zu ermorden."

49. Michael Burleigh, *Death and Deliverance: "Euthanasia" in Germany c. 1900–1945* (Cambridge: Cambridge University Press, 1994) (numbers on p. 160). The decision was actually taken in October 1939 and backdated to September 1, the date the war began. Taking into account local authorities' later deliberate starvation of asylum inmates in Germany and the killing of the insane and incurable in occupied eastern Europe, the total reached about two hundred thousand by 1945.

50. See Helmut Krausnick and H. H. Wilhelm, *Die Truppe des Weltanschauungskrieges: Die Einsatzgruppen der Sicherheitspolizei und des SD, 1938–1942* (Stuttgart: Deutsche Verlags-Anstalt, 1981).

51. Wolfgang Benz, Hermann Graml, and Hermann Weiss, eds., *Enzyklopädie des Nationalsozialismus* (Stuttgart: Klett-Cotta, 1997), p. 815.

52. The phrase "intermediary solution" comes from Götz Aly, "Jewish resettlement," p. 69.

53. Mathias Beer, "Die Entwicklung der Gaswagen beim Mord an den Juden," *Vierteljahrshefte für Zeitgeschichte* 35:3 (July 1987), pp. 403–18.

54. The Nazis divided occupied Poland into three parts in 1939: the western third, officially relabeled the Warthegau, was incorporated into the Reich. The eastern third was occupied by Stalin. The leftover center, ruled as a Nazi Party fiefdom by Governor-General Hans Frank, did not even have a name in the Polish language. The Nazis called it by the vaguely French neologism "*Generalgouvernement.*"

55. Alexander Dallin, *German Rule in Russia: 1941–1945: A Study of Occupation Policies,* 2nd rev. ed. (Boulder, CO: Westview Press, 1981) (orig. pub. 1957), is still essential for the SS administration and exploitation of conquered Soviet territory.

56. Aktion 1005 was a program to cover up the traces of closed killing centers in the eastern occupied areas, as at Chelmno in September 1944. The labor was mostly provided by the last camp inmates, who were shot when the work was done. At times, however, German soldiers, desperately needed at the front, did this work. Walter Manoschek, "The Extermination of Jews in Serbia" in Herbert, *Extermination Policies,* p. 181.

57. Chilling examples are published in Goldhagen, *Hitler's Willing Executioners.*

58. Ian Kershaw, *Popular Opinion and Dissent in the Third Reich: Bavaria 1933–1945* (Oxford: Clarendon Press, 1983), pp. 364–72, 377–78; O. D. Kulka, "The German Population and the Jews," in David Bankier, ed., *Probing the Depth of German Antisemitism* (New York: Berghahn, 2000), p. 276, considers it "general knowledge."

59. See Hans Buchheim's pages on "hardness and camaraderie" in Helmut Krausnick, Hans Buchheim, Martin Broszat, and Hans-Adolf Jacobsen, *Anatomy of the SS-State* (New York: Walker, 1968), pp. 334–48.

60. Speech of October 25, 1932; similar words occur in the "Fascism" entry in the *Enciclopedia italiana*.

61. English excerpts from this speech are published in Charles F. Delzell, ed., *Mediterranean Fascism* (New York: Harper & Row, 1970), pp. 199–200.

62. Luigi Goglia and Fabio Grassi, *Il colonialismo italiano da Adua all'impero* (Bari: Laterza, 1993), p. 221.

63. Goglia and Grassi, *Colonialismo*, pp. 222, 234. See also Nicola Labanca, "L'Amministrazione coloniale fascista: Stato, politica, e società," in Angelo Del Boca, et al., *Il regime fascista*, pp. 352–95.

64. The terms are Renzo De Felice's in *Mussolini: Il Duce: Lo stato totalitario, 1936–1940* (Turin: Einaudi, 1981), p. 100; for controversies surrounding Mussolini's principal biographer, see the bibliographical essay, p. 224.

65. Gabriella Klein, *La Politica linguistica del fascismo* (Bologna: Il Mulino, 1986).

66. The most recent and convincing accounts are by Michele Sarfatti: *Mussolini contro gli ebrei: Cronaca delle leggi del 1938* (Turin: Silvio Zamani Editore, 1994), and *Gli ebrei nell'Italia fascista: Vicende, identità, persecuzione* (Turin: Einaudi, 2000). Sarfatti dwells less upon supposed Nazi influence and more upon Italian roots and support for Mussolini's anti-Jewish measures than earlier standard accounts, Meir Michaelis, *Mussolini and the Jews* (New York: Oxford University Press, 1978), and Renzo De Felice, *The Jews in Fascist Italy: A History* (New York: Enigma Books, 2001) (Italian ed., 1988). Sarfatti presents his conclusions briefly in "The Persecution of the Jews in Fascist Italy," in Bernard D. Cooperman and Barbara Garvin, eds., *The Jews of Italy: Memory and Identity* (Bethesda, MD: University Press of Maryland, 2000), pp. 412–24.

67. John P. Diggins, *Mussolini and Fascism: The View from America* (Princeton: Princeton University Press, 1972), p. 40.

68. For the overt racism with which Fascist colonial wars were waged, including the intent to eliminate whole "inferior" populations, see Angelo Del Boca, "Le leggi razziali nell'impero di Mussolini," in Del Boca et al., *Il regime fascista*, pp. 329–51, and works on Italian colonialism cited in the bibliographical essay, p. 237.

69. David I. Kertzer, *The Popes Against the Jews: The Vatican's Role in the Rise of Modern Anti-Semitism* (New York: Alfred Knopf, 2001), marshals irrefutable evidence from Vatican publications, though he goes too far in including some nonpapal materials.

70. The Vatican explicitly approved Vichy French discrimination against Jews in employment and education. Michael R. Marrus and Robert O. Paxton, *Vichy France and the Jews* (Stanford, CA: Stanford University Press, 1995), pp. 200–02.

71. Jonathan Steinberg, *All or Nothing: The Axis and the Holocaust, 1941–1943* (London: Routledge, 1991).

72. Police chief Bocchini apparently told Mussolini in June 1940 that only anti-Fascists were for war, for they thought it would rid them of the hated regime. Claudio Pavone, *Una guerra civile* (Turin: Bollati Boringhieri, 1991), p. 64.

73. See the bibliographical essay, p. 238.

74. F. W. Deakin, *The Six Hundred Days of Mussolini* (New York: Anchor, 1966), pp. 144–45. Prince Borghese was sentenced to prison in 1949 for his actions against the Italian Resistance, but spent only ten days in jail. After the war he was an official of the Italian neo-Fascist party, the Movimento Sociale Italiano (MSI), for which see chapter 7.

75. Primo Levi, "The Art of Fiction, CXL," *Paris Review* 134 (Spring 1995), p. 202.

76. Sergio Luzzatto, *Il corpo di Mussolini: Un cadavero tra imaginazione, storia, e memoria* (Turin: Einaudi, 1998).

77. Nazi authorities killed anyone trying to surrender, in a policy called "strength through fear." See Antony Beevor, *Berlin: The Downfall, 1945* (London: Viking, 2002), pp. 92–93 and 127; and Robert Gellately, *Backing Hitler*, pp. 236–42.

78. See chapter 6, p. 163.

79. Omer Bartov shows how the harsh conditions and genocidal intentions of the Russian campaign inured the army as well as the SS to brutality in *Hitler's Army: Soldiers, Nazis and War in the Third Reich* (New York: Oxford University Press, 1991), and *The Eastern Front, 1941–1945: German Troops and the Barbarisation of Warfare*, 2nd ed. (New York: Palgrave, 2001).

80. See chapter 5, note 43.

Chapter 7: Other Times, Other Places

1. Ernst Nolte, *Der Fascismus in seiner Epoch* (Munich: Piper, 1963), translated as *Three Faces of Fascism* (New York: Holt, Rinehart and Winston, 1966), p. 4.

2. See chapter 3, note 70.

3. According to Ian Kershaw, *The Hitler Myth: Image and Reality in the Third Reich* (Oxford: Oxford University Press, 1987), pp. 221–22, many Germans blamed Hitler personally by spring 1945 for their suffering.

4. R. J. B. Bosworth, *The Italian Dictatorship* (London: Arnold, 1998), pp. 28, 30, 61, 67–68, 147, 150, 159, 162, 179, and 235, lays more stress than most on an incompatibility between individualistic consumerism and the obligatory community of fascism. Victoria De Grazia, *How Fascism Ruled Women* (Berkeley and Los Angeles: University of California Press, 1992), pp. 10, 15, and *passim*, shows convincingly how consumerist commercial culture helped subvert the Fascist ideal of submissively domesticated womanhood. See also Stanley G. Payne, *A History of Fascism, 1919–1945* (Madison: University of Wisconsin Press, 1995), p. 496.

5. Payne, *History*, concluded that "specific historic fascism can never be recreated" though fascists remain, in reduced numbers, and "new and partially related forms of authoritarian nationalism" might appear (pp. 496, 520).

6. Mirko Tremaglia, who had been a junior official of Mussolini's republic of Salò in 1943–45, was elected at this point chairman of the Foreign Affairs Committee of the Italian parliament. It is true that some officials of the Federal Republic of Germany, including Chancellor Hans-Georg Kiesinger, had been Nazi Party members in their youth, but they had not continued to belong to a neo-Nazi party after the war, and no neo-Nazi party has participated in either local or national government in Germany.

7. See the special issue of *Patterns of Prejudice* 36:3 (July 2002) on radical right *groupuscules*, put together by Roger Griffin.

8. Martin A. Lee, *The Beast Reawakens* (Boston: Little, Brown, 1997).

9. Nolte, *Three Faces*, pp. 421–23.

10. Diethelm Prowe, " 'Classic' Fascism and the New Radical Right in Western Europe: Comparisons and Contrasts," *Contemporary European History* 3:3 (1994); Piero Ignazi, *L'estrema destra in Europa* (Bologna: Il Mulino, 2000).

11. See chapter 7, p. 191, and chapter 8, p. 216.

12. *The Road to Wigan Pier* (New York: Berkeley Books, 1961), p. 176. See also *The Lion and the Unicorn* (1941), quoted in Sonia Orwell and Ian Angus, eds., *The Collected Essays, Journalism, and Letters of George Orwell*, vol. III: *My Country Right or Left, 1940–43* (New York: Harcourt Brace, 1968), p. 93.

13. The Federal Republic of Germany (West Germany) outlawed all overt expressions of Nazism, but permitted party pluralism. Thus radical right parties that were neo-Nazi in all but name and symbolism existed legitimately, plus a more overtly Nazi underground. The German Democratic Republic (East Germany), by contrast, permitted only the Communist Party and the Socialist Unity Party to exist, so no right-wing heirs to Nazism could function overtly in its territory. It claimed that since Nazism derived from capitalism, it could exist only in West Germany. See Jeffrey Herf, *Divided Memory: The Nazi Past in the Two Germanies* (Cambridge, MA: Harvard University Press, 1997).

14. Payne, *History*, p. 500.

15. In the parliamentary elections of 1992, the Lega Nord won almost 19 percent of the northern vote (8.6 percent nationally) by playing on northern small businessmen's resentment of the social burden of the Italian south, expressed in terms approaching racism. See Hans-Georg Betz, "Against Rome: The Lega Nord," in Hans-Georg Betz and Stefan Immerfall, eds., *The New Politics of the Right: Neo-Populist Parties and Movements in Established Democracies* (New York: St. Martin's Press, 1998), pp. 45–57.

16. Tom Gallagher, "Exit from the Ghetto: The Italian Far Right in the 1990s," in Paul Hainsworth, ed., *The Politics of the Extreme Right: From the Margin to the Mainstream* (London: Pinter, 2000), p. 72.

17. Stanley Hoffmann, *Le mouvement Poujade*, Cahiers de la Fondation Nationale des Sciences Politiques #81 (Paris: Armand Colin, 1956).

18. In addition to books on the Front National listed in the bibliographical essay, p. 249, see Nonna Mayer, "The French National Front," in Betz and Immerfall, eds., *New Politics*, pp. 11–25, and Paul Hainsworth, "The *Front National*: From Ascendancy to Fragmentation on the French Extreme Right," in Hainsworth, ed., *Politics of the Extreme Right*, pp. 18–32.

19. A good introduction is Roger Eatwell, "The BNP and the Problem of Legitimacy," in Betz and Immerfall, eds., *New Politics*, pp. 143–55.

20. Stephan and Norbert, *My Father's Keeper: Children of Nazi Leaders* (Boston: Little, Brown, 2001).

21. Piero Ignazi, "The Silent Counter-Revolution: Hypotheses on the Emer-

gence of Extreme Right-Wing Parties in Europe," *European Journal of Political Research* 22 (1992), pp. 3–34, supports most of these points.

22. John M. Cotter, "Sounds of Hate: White Power Rock and Roll and the Neo-Nazi Subculture," *Terrorism and Political Violence* 11:2 (Summer 1999), pp. 111–40. I owe this reference to Jeffrey M. Bale, who points out that "oi" music is not necessarily racist or violent.

23. Susann Backer, "Right-Wing Extremism in United Germany," in Hainsworth, ed., *Politics of the Extreme Right*, p. 102. The most shocking incidents were the firebombing of refugee hostels that killed Turkish women and children: three at Moelln, near Hamburg, in November 1992, and five at Solingen in May 1993.

24. *International Herald Tribune*, June 14, 1994, p. 15.

25. Precedence for the French in employment and exclusion of foreigners from benefits are important elements in the program of the French Front National.

26. The eclipse of the communist enemy permitted some radical Right groups, once grudgingly aligned with the United States through anti-Communism, to give high priority to a previously repressed distaste for "American materialism" and globalized mass culture. See Jeffrey M. Bale, " 'National Revolutionary' Groupuscules and the Resurgence of Left-Wing Fascism: The Case of France's Nouvelle Résistance," *Patterns of Prejudice* 36:3 (July 2002), pp. 24–49.

27. Piero Ignazi, *L'estrema destra in Europe*, p. 12, calls the forms of extreme Right that correspond to these two generations "traditional" and "postindustrial." Pascal Perrineau uses the same distinction.

28. This is the subtitle of Hainsworth, ed., *The Politics of the Extreme Right*.

29. Paul Hainsworth, "The Front National from Ascendancy to Fragmentation on the French Extreme Right," in Hainsworth, ed., *Politics of the Extreme Right*, p. 18.

30. Pascal Perrineau, *Le Symptôme Le Pen: Radiographie des électeurs du Front National* (Paris: Fayard, 1997), identifies five types of FN voters, some coming from the Left, some from the far Right, many from mainstream conservatism. See also Nona Mayer, *Qui vote Le Pen?* (Paris: Flammarion, 1999).

31. While Le Pen talked vaguely of replacing the Fifth French Republic with a "Sixth Republic," he emphasized limited changes like stronger police, economic and cultural protection against "globalization," and "national preference" that would close the welfare state to noncitizens. Hainsworth, "Front National," pp. 24–28.

32. Ibid., p. 20.

33. Berlusconi owned, among many other properties including most of the Italian media, the popular soccer team Milan A.C.

34. Piero Ignazi and Colette Ysmal, "Extreme Right Parties in Europe: Introduction," *European Journal of Political Research* 22 (1992), p. 1.

35. Tom Gallagher, "Exit from the Ghetto: The Italian Far Right in the 1990s," in Hainsworth, ed., *Politics of the Extreme Right*, p. 75.

36. In a poll of delegates to the seventeenth MSI congress in 1990, only 13 percent defined themselves as democrats, while 50 percent considered democracy "a lie"; 25 percent considered themselves anti-Semitic, and 88 percent affirmed that Fascism was for them the key historical reference. Piero Ignazi, *Postfascisti? Dal*

movimento sociale italiano ad Alleanza nazionale (Bologna: Il Mulino, 1994), pp. 88–89.

37. See chapter 3, pp. 69–70.

38. Prowe, " 'Classic' Fascism and the New Radical Right," p. 296. Mussolini, it is true, advocated reduced state economic intervention until 1925.

39. The young man who fired upon French president Jacques Chirac during the July 14, 2002, celebrations in Paris was simultaneously a militant with a neo-Nazi action squad, Unité Radicale, a reader of *Mein Kampf,* and a candidate in local elections for the ostensibly more moderate Mouvement National Républicain of Bruno Mégret, Le Pen's former heir and chief rival. See *Le Monde,* July 30, 2002, p. 7: "Entre mouvements ultras et partis traditionnels, des frontières parfois floues."

40. Marc Swyngedouw, "The Extreme Right in Belgium: Of a Non-Existent Front National and an Omnipresent Vlaams Blok," in Betz and Immerfall, eds., *New Politics,* p. 60.

41. Marc Swyngedouw, "Belgium: Explaining the Relationship between Vlaams Blok and the City of Antwerp," in Betz and Immerfall, eds., *New Politics,* p. 59.

42. Betz, *Radical Right-Wing Populism,* p. 139.

43. Prowe, " 'Classic' Fascism and the New Radical Right," pp. 289–313, finds some resemblance in programs but profound difference in circumstances.

44. Hans Rogger, "Russia," in Rogger and Eugen Weber, eds., *The European Right* (Berkeley and Los Angeles: University of California Press, 1966), p. 491, and *Jewish Politics and Right-Wing Politics in Imperial Russia* (Berkeley and Los Angeles: University of California Press, 1986), pp. 212–32.

45. Walter Laqueur, *Black Hundred* (New York: HarperCollins, 1993), pp 16–28.

46. Michael Cox and Peter Shearman, "After the Fall: Nationalist Extremism in Post-Communist Russia," in Hainsworth, *Politics of the Extreme Right,* pp. 224–46. Stephen D. Shenfield, *Russian Fascism: Traditions, Tendencies, Movements* (Armonk, NY: M. E. Sharpe, 2001); Erwin Oberländer, "The All-Russian Fascist Party," in Walter Laqueur and George L. Mosse, eds., *International Fascism: 1920–1945* (New York: Harper, 1966), pp. 158–73, treats fascism among Russian émigrés in the 1930s.

47. See articles in Cheles et al., *The Far Right in Western and Eastern Europe,* for details.

48. Renzo De Felice writes of fascism's "inseparable link with the crises (moral, economic, social and political) of European society following the First War" in *Il Fascismo: Le interpretazioni dei contemporanei e degli storici,* rev. ed. (Bari: Laterza, 1998), p. 544. See also Payne, *History,* pp. 353–54.

49. See chapter 8, pp. 215–16.

50. Patrick J. Furlong, *Between Crown and Swastika: The Impact of the Radical Right on the Afrikaner Nationalist Movement in the Fascist Era* (Hanover, NH: University Press of New England, 1991).

51. Robert M. Levine, *The Vargas Regime: The Critical Years, 1934–1938* (New York: Columbia University Press, 1970), p. 88.

52. Ibid., pp. 83–85.

53. Vargas returned to power by election in October 1950 and governed as head

of a clientelistic labor party, claiming to be "Father of the Poor," until August 24, 1954, when he committed suicide in the presidential palace while awaiting a military coup. See Robert M. Levine, *Father of the Poor? Vargas and His Era* (Cambridge: Cambridge University Press, 1998).

54. Levine, *Vargas Regime*, p. 36.

55. For this and other countries discussed below, see the bibliographical essay.

56. Argentina was the fifth or sixth wealthiest nation in the world in 1914, based on the export to Europe of beef and wheat from great *pampas* estates.

57. Robert D. Crassweller, *Perón and the Enigmas of Argentina* (New York: Norton, 1987), is particularly informative about U.S. pressures on Argentina during World War II. See also Arthur P. Whitaker, *The United States and Argentina* (Cambridge, MA: Harvard University Press, 1954).

58. His other post, more conventionally powerful, was secretary general of the War Ministry, from which he controlled military appointments. Over the next two years, he also became war minister and vice president.

59. Joseph A. Page, *Perón: A Biography* (New York: Random House, 1983), p. 136n. At first a scornful epithet, the term was taken up proudly by the Peronistas. Daniel James, *Resistance and Integration: Peronism and the Argentine Working Class* (Cambridge: Cambridge University Press, 1988), p. 31.

60. James, *Resistance and Integration*, p. 11; Frederick C. Turner and José Enrique Miguens, *Juan Perón and the Reshaping of Argentina* (Pittsburgh: University of Pittsburgh Press, 1983), p. 4.

61. Crassweller, *Perón and the Enigmas*, pp. 106–09, 124.

62. On April 15, 1953, Peronist action squads burned the Socialist Party's headquarters as well as the oligarchy's exclusive Jockey Club. Page, *Perón*, pp. 271–73. Perón's regime killed far fewer people, however, than the seven thousand or so murdered by the Argentine military dictatorship between 1976 and 1983.

63. A classic in this genre is Joseph R. Barager, ed., *Why Perón Came to Power: The Background to Peronism in Argentina* (New York: Knopf, 1968).

64. The sociologist Gino Germani, in *Authoritarianism, Fascism, and National Populism* (New Brunswick, NJ: Transaction Books, 1978), plausibly distinguishes Perón's "National Populism" from fascism on the basis of the timing of social mobilization. While Perón carried out a "primary mobilization," a first step into mass politics, fascisms, according to Germani, were "secondary mobilizations," an attempt to redirect and discipline an already existing mass politics.

65. Anti-Semitism existed in Peronist Argentina. The right-wing nationalist groups that sacked Socialist headquarters in April 1953 shouted "Jews! Go back to Moscow!" Page, *Perón*, p. 272. One can also find anti-Semitic utterances in Vargas's Brazil, but racism was not central to either regime's propaganda or popular appeal.

66. J. M. Taylor, *Eva Perón: The Myths of a Woman* (Chicago: University of Chicago Press, 1979), p. 81. This is the most sophisticated account of Evita's multiple images from Buenos Aires to Broadway.

67. Ibid., p. 34.

68. Sandra McGee Deutsch, *Las Derechas: The Extreme Right in Argentina, Brazil, and Chile* (Stanford, CA: Stanford University Press, 1999).

69. Herbert S. Klein, *Parties and Political Change in Bolivia* (London: Cambridge University Press, 1969), pp. 235, 243–44, 372–74, and *Bolivia: The Evolution of a Multi-Ethnic Society*, 2nd ed. (New York: Oxford University Press, 1992), pp. 199–216.

70. Gregory J. Kasza, "Fascism from Above? Japan's *Kakushin* Right in Comparative Perspective," in Stein Ugelvik Larsen, ed., *Fascism Outside Europe: The European Impulse against Domestic Conditions in the Diffusion of Global Fascism* (Boulder, CO: Social Science Monographs, 2001), pp. 183–232, reviews Japanese scholarship and analyzes lucidly the appropriateness of the fascist label for imperial Japan. I thank Carol Gluck for this reference.

71. Maruyama Masao, *Thought and Behavior in Modern Japanese Politics*, rev. ed., ed. Ivan Morris (New York: Oxford University Press, 1969), esp. chap. 2, "The Ideology and Dynamics of Japanese Fascism."

72. George M. Wilson, *Revolutionary Nationalist in Japan: Kita Ikki, 1883–1937* (Cambridge, MA: Harvard University Press, 1969).

73. Ben Ami Shillony, *Revolt in Japan: The Young Officers and the February 26, 1936, Incident* (Princeton: Princeton University Press, 1973).

74. Miles Fletcher, *The Search for a New Order: Intellectuals and Fascism in Prewar Japan* (Chapel Hill: University of North Carolina Press, 1982).

75. Kasza, "Fascism from Above?" pp. 198–99, 228.

76. Herbert P. Bix, "Rethinking 'Emperor-System Fascism': Ruptures and Continuities in Modern Japanese History," *Bulletin of Concerned Asian Scholars* 14:2 (April–June 1982), pp. 2–19, restates this thesis, influenced by Marxism, and rejects the contrary opinion of most Western scholars, whom he dismisses as "pluralists." The role of class interests is contested. Kasza, "Fascism from Above?," observes that the great Japanese industrial combines, the *zaibatsu*, "dragged their feet on expansion abroad and militarism at home (though they profited from both" (p. 185).

77. Gavan McCormack, "Nineteen-Thirties Japan: Fascism?" in *Bulletin of Concerned Asian Scholars* 14:2 (April-June 1982), p. 29.

78. Barrington Moore, Jr., *Social Origins of Dictatorship and Democracy* (Boston: Beacon Press, 1966), pp. 228–313.

79. Paul Brooker, *The Faces of Fraternalism: Nazi Germany, Fascist Italy, and Imperial Japan* (Oxford: Clarendon Press, 1991).

80. R. P. Dore and Tsutomo Ouchi, "Rural Origins of Japanese Fascism," in James William Morley, ed., *Dilemmas of Growth in Prewar Japan* (Princeton: Princeton University Press, 1971), pp. 181–209, perform a stringent test of the applicability of the Barrington Moore paradigm to Japan.

81. For bibliography see the bibliographical essay.

82. For Pelley, see Leo P. Ribuffo, *The Old Christian Right: The Protestant Far Right from the Great Depression to the Cold War* (Philadelphia: Temple University Press, 1983).

83. Nicholas Goodrick-Clarke, *Black Sun: Aryan Cults, Esoteric Nazism, and the Politics of Identity* (New York: New York University Press, 2002), pp. 7–15, 37–38.

84. Alan Brinkley, *Voices of Protest: Huey Long, Father Coughlin, and the Great Depression* (New York: Knopf, 1982) (radio figures, pp. 83, 92). Lemke got eight hundred thousand votes.

85. Brinkley, *Voices of Protest*, pp. 273–83, concludes that while the charismatic bond between Long and Coughlin and their publics recalled fascism, their aims—individual liberty from plutocrats more than the triumph of a national *volk*—were quite different. The classic T. Harry Williams, *Huey Long* (New York: Knopf, 1969), pp. 760–62, dismisses the fascist charges.

86. Alan Crawford, *Thunder on the Right: The "New Right" and the Politics of Resentment* (New York: Pantheon, 1980).

87. For the importance of guns in the macho symbolism of both Mussolini and Hitler, see chapter 8, note 61.

88. Henry Louis Gates, Jr., "Blacklash," *The New Yorker*, May 17, 1993, p. 44.

89. Payne, *History*, pp. 16, 490, 516.

90. The Iraqi dictatorship of Saddam Hussein, considered by some to "come closer than any other dictator since 1945" to reproducing the Third Reich (Payne, *History*, pp. 516–17), was based on the secular Ba'ath Party and tried to crush Shi'ite fundamentalism. Samir al-Khalil, *The Monument: Art, Vulgarity, and Responsibility in Iraq* (Berkeley and Los Angeles: University of California Press, 1991), portrays the pair of huge arms, created from casts of Saddam's own arms, holding swords to form triumphal arches over a Baghdad avenue. He does not use the word *fascism*.

91. Quotations from interview with General Effi Eitam, representative of the National Religious Party and minister without portfolio in the government of Ariel Sharon, *Le Monde*, Paris, 7–8 April 2002.

Chapter 8: What Is Fascism?

1. For example, Zeev Sternhell, *Neither Left nor Right: Fascist Ideology in France* (Berkeley and Los Angeles: University of California Press, 1986), p. 270.

2. Wolfgang Schieder characterizes the early Fascist Party as "a loose bundle of person-oriented power groups who scuffle for power," in "Der Strukturwandel der faschistischen Partei italiens in der phase der Herrschaftsstabilisierung," in Schieder, ed., *Der Faschismus als soziale Bewegung* (Hamburg: Hoffman und Campe, 1976), p. 71.

3. See chapter 1, pp. 7–8.

4. Bertolt Brecht, *The Resistable Rise of Arturo Ui* (London: Methuen, 2002, orig. 1941).

5. See chapter 1, p. 8.

6. A few thoughtful Marxists avoided such dogmatisms, among them the Italians Antonio Gramsci, with his reflections on the conditions and limits of Fascist cultural hegemony, and Palmiro Togliatti, *Lectures on Fascism* (New York: International Publishers, 1976) (orig. pub. 1935), who recognized authentic popular appeal on pp. 5–7, 120, though both made fascism more class-specific than most contemporary commentators would. Among Germans there was the philosopher Ernst Bloch (p. 209). After 1968, younger Western Marxists were critical of the Stalinist line. E.g., Nikos Poulantzas, *Fascism and Dictatorship* (London: Verso, 1979) (orig. pub. in France in 1970).

7. See chapter 3, pp. 66–67; chapter 4, p. 100; and chapter 5, pp. 145–46.

8. See chapter 5, p. 146.

9. Carl J. Friedrich and Zbigniew Brzezinski, *Totalitarian Dictatorship and Autocracy* (New York: Praeger, 1965), p. 238, say that Nazi Germany "ceases to be capitalist" when fear replaces confidence. The "fundamental incompatibility" between capitalism and fascism (Alan Milward, quoted approvingly by Payne, *A History of Fascism*, p. 190) might perhaps apply to the final apocalyptic paroxysm of Nazism, but fits poorly the way fascist regimes functioned in more normal times.

10. Ernst von Weizsäcker, the senior official of the German Foreign Office, recalled Hitler treating British ambassador Neville Henderson to a furious tirade on August 23, 1939, only to slap his thigh and laugh as soon as the door closed behind the ambassador: "Chamberlain won't survive that conversation. His cabinet will fall this evening." Alan Bullock, *Hitler: A Study in Tyranny* (London: Odhams, 1952), p. 484. Kershaw, *Hitler 1889–1936: Hubris* (New York: Norton, 1998), p. 281, agrees that such scenes were "often contrived." Richard Nixon is said to have wanted the North Vietnamese to think he was crazy.

11. See examples in the bibliographical essay, p. 223.

12. Kershaw, *Hitler: Hubris*, p. xxvi and *passim*.

13. Wilhelm Reich, *The Mass Psychology of Fascism*, ed. Mary Higgins and Chester M. Raphael (New York: Farrar, Straus, Giroux, 1978) (orig. pub. in 1933).

14. See the bibliographical essay, p. 226, for examples.

15. For example, Luchino Visconti, "The Damned." For Pasolini, see David Forgacs, "Days of Sodom: The Fascist-Perversion Equation in Films of the 1960s and 1970s," in R. J. B. Bosworth and Patrizia Dogliani, eds., *Italian Fascism: History, Memory, and Representation* (New York: St. Martin's Press, 1999), pp. 195–215. In a somewhat different register, Saul Friedländer assailed the treatment of Nazi brutality as spectacle in *Reflections of Nazism: An Essay on Kitsch and Death* (New York: Harper, 1984).

16. Robert Jay Lifton, *The Nazi Doctors: Medical Killing and the Psychology of Genocide* (New York: Basic Books, 1986), probes the astonishing capacity of doctors involved in the selection process at Auschwitz to isolate their normal family lives from their gruesome daytime duties.

17. Talcott Parsons, "Democracy and Social Structure in Pre-Nazi Germany," in Parsons, *Essays in Sociological Theory*, rev. ed. (Glencoe, IL: Free Press, 1954), pp. 104–23 (orig. pub. 1942). In general, see Stephen P. Turner, *Sociology Responds to Fascism* (London: Routledge, 1992).

18. Ernst Bloch, *Heritage of Our Times*, trans. Neville and Stephan Plaice (Cambridge: Polity Press, 1991), part II, "Non-Contemporaneity and Intoxication," pp. 37–185 (quotations from pp. 53, 57, 97).

19. The theory of uneven development and survival of pre-industrial elites was powerfully restated by Jürgen Kocha, "Ursachen des Nationalsozialismus," *Aus Politik und Zeitgeschichte* (Beilage zur Wochenzeitung *Das Parlament*) 21 (June 1980), pp. 3–15. See the reply by Geoff Eley, "What Produces Fascism: Preindustrial Traditions or a Crisis of the Capitalist State?" *Politics and History* 12 (1983), pp. 53–82.

20. See the discussion in chapter 3, pp. 68–73.

21. The classic statement is William Kornhauser, *The Politics of Mass Society*

(Glencoe, IL: Free Press, 1959). A precursor was Peter Drucker, in *The End of Economic Man: A Study of the New Totalitarianism* (London: John Day, 1939), p. 53: "Society ceases to be a community of individuals bound together by a common purpose and becomes a chaotic hubbub of purposeless isolated monads." This approach has been convincingly refuted by Bernt Hagtvet, "The Theory of Mass Society and the Collapse of the Weimar Republic: A Re-Examination," in Stein U. Larsen, Bernt Hagtvet, and Jan Petter Myklebust, eds., *Who Were the Fascists: Social Roots of European Fascism* (Oslo: Universitetsforlaget, 1980), pp. 66–117.

22. Hannah Arendt, *The Origins of Totalitarianism*, rev. ed. (New York: Meridian Books, 1958), esp. pp. 305–40 on "the masses" and "the mob."

23. Horst Gies shows how the Nazis successfully penetrated and used existing agrarian organizations in "The NSDAP and Agrarian Organizations in the Final Phase of the Weimar Republic," in Henry Ashby Turner, Jr., *Nazism and the Third Reich* (New York: Quadrangle, 1972), pp. 45–88. Particularly relevant here are the studies by Rudy Koshar, cited in the bibliographical essay, p. 225, of how the Nazis took over a rich fabric of "apolitical" associations in German towns.

24. William Sheridan Allen, *The Nazi Seizure of Power: The Experience of a Single Town, 1922–1945*, rev. ed. (New York: Franklin Watts, 1984), p. 17. Allen is particularly revealing about the parallel worlds of socialist and nonsocialist organizations and how the Nazis exploited that polarity. See pp. 15ff, 55, 298.

25. See chapter 1, note 49.

26. Jon S. Cohen, "Was Italian Fascism a Developmental Dictatorship?" *Economic History Review*, 2nd series, 41:1 (February 1988), pp. 95–113. Rolf Petri, *Von der Autarkie zum Wirtschaftswunder: Wirtschaftspolitik und industrielle Wandel in Italien, 1935–1963* (Tübingen: Max Niemeyer, 2001), agrees that the Fascist war economy was a "disaster" but finds it impossible to tell whether Italian emergence as an industrial society in the 1960s was impeded or hastened by the Fascist autarky stage.

27. For example, Anthony J. Joes, *Fascism in the Contemporary World: Ideology, Evolution, and Resurgence* (Boulder, CO: Westview Press, 1978); A. James Gregor, *The Fascist Persuasion in Radical Politics* (Princeton: Princeton University Press, 1974).

28. Seymour Martin Lipset, *Political Man* (Garden City, NY: Doubleday, 1963), chap. 5, "Fascism—Left, Right, and Center." Arno Mayer, "The Lower Middle Class as Historical Problem," *Journal of Modern History* 75:3 (October 1975), pp. 409–36, takes class seriously but examines this category critically.

29. For statistical work on the German case, now quite sophisticated, see the bibliographic essay, pp. 227–28. The much shakier Italian data are studied by Jens Petersen, "Ellettorato e base sociale del fascismo negli anni venti," *Studi storici* 3 (1975), pp. 627–69. William Brustein, "The 'Red Menace' and the Rise of Italian Fascism," *American Sociological Review* 56 (October 1991), pp. 652–64, applies rational choice theory to the election of 1921 and finds that Fascist voters chose that party not solely out of fear of socialism but because they preferred the Fascists' defense of private property.

30. Hans Mommsen, in "Zur Verschränkung traditioneller und faschistischer Führungsgruppen in Deutschland beim Übergang von der Bewegung zur Systemphase," in Mommsen, *Der Nationalsozialismus und die Deutsche Gesellschaft: Ausgewählte Aufsätze*, ed. Lutz Niethammer and Bernd Weisbrod (Reinbeck bei

Hamburg: Rowohlt, 1991), p. 47, claims that before September 1930 only about 40 percent of party members were relatively permanent.

31. Philippe C. Schmitter contrasts movements that "vacuum up" discontent from a wide variety of sources with regimes that attract "bandwagoners" in his penetrating article "The Social Origins, Economic Bases, and Political Imperatives of Authoritarian Rule in Portugal," in Stein U. Larsen et al., *Who Were the Fascists*, p. 437.

32. Mathilde Jamin, *Zwischen den Klassen: Zur Sozialstruktur der SA-Führerschaft* (Wuppertal: P. Hammer, 1984); Detlev Peukert, *The Weimar Republic: The Crisis of Classical Modernity*, pp. 238, 255; Christoph Schmidt, "Zu den motiven 'alter Kämpfer' in der NSDAP," in Detlev Peukert and Jürgen Reulecke, eds., *Die Reihe fast geschlossen: Beiträge zur Geschichte des Alltags unterm Nationalsozialismus* (Wuppertal: Peter Hammer, 1981).

33. Jens Petersen has explored the term's origins thoroughly in several works, most recently "Die Geschichte des Totalitarismusbegriffs in Italien," in Hans Meier, ed., *'Totalitarismus' und 'Politische Religionen': Konzepte des Diktaturvergleichs* (Paderborn: Ferdinand Schöningh, 1996), pp. 15–36. In English see Abbott Gleason, *Totalitarianism: The Inner History of the Cold War* (New York: Oxford University Press, 1995), pp. 14–16.

34. E.g., Arendt, *Origins*, p. 257–59, 308.

35. Dante L. Germino, *The Italian Fascist Party in Power: A Study in Totalitarian Rule* (Minneapolis: University of Minnesota Press, 1959), and Emilio Gentile, *La via italiana al totalitarismo: Il partito e lo stato nel regime fascista* (Rome: La Nuova Italia Scientifica, 1995), make the strongest claims for the authentically totalitarian nature of Fascist rule in Italy.

36. Edward N. Peterson, *The Limits of Hitler's Power* (Princeton: Princeton University Press, 1969). For an approach to the Soviet Union that refuses to reduce everything to impulses from above, see Sheila Fitzpatrick, *Everyday Stalinism* (New York: Oxford University Press, 1999), and *Stalin's Peasants* (New York: Oxford University Press, 1994).

37. Friedrich and Brzezinski, *Totalitarian Dictatorship*, p. 22.

38. Benjamin R. Barber, "The Conceptual Foundations of Totalitarianism," in Carl J. Friedrich, Michael Curtis, and Benjamin R. Barber, *Totalitarianism in Perspective: Three Views* (New York: Praeger, 1969).

39. Karl Dietrich Bracher, for example, preferred the totalitarian to the fascist concept because the latter, he thought, obscured the difference between dictatorial and democratic political systems, which, for Marxists, were just alternate forms of "bourgeois hegemony." See Bracher, *Zeitgeschlichtliche Kontroversen: Um Faschismus, Totalitarismus, Demokratie* (Munich: R. Piper, 1976), chaps. 1 and 2, *Schlüsselwörter in der Geschichte: Mit einer Betrachtung zum Totalitarismusproblem* (Düsseldorf: Droste, 1978), pp. 33ff, *Zeit der Ideologien: Eine Geschichte politischen Denkens im 20. Jahrhundert* (Stuttgart: Deutsche Verlags-Anstalt, 1982), pp. 122ff, 155ff. A West German example of the other side is Reinhard Kühnl, *Formen bürgerlicher Herrschaft* (Reinbeck bei Hamburg: Rowohlt, 1971).

40. It informs Michael Burleigh's brilliant indictment of Nazi viciousness, *The*

Third Reich (New York: Hill and Wang, 2000). Martin Malia, *Russia under Western Eyes* (Cambridge, MA: Harvard University Press, 1999), p. 331, dismisses fascism as a category.

41. Gleason, *Totalitarianism*, traces the entire debate lucidly.

42. Margaretta Buber-Neumann experienced both, and wrote a classic memoir about it: *Under Two Dictators* (New York: Doubleday, 1949). We refer here, of course, to concentration camps like Dachau rather than to extermination camps like Auschwitz.

43. Stéphane Courtois et al., *The Black Book of Communism*, trans. from the French by Jonathan Murphy and Mark Kramer (Cambridge, MA: Harvard University Press, 1999), p. 15, argues that Stalin was responsible for four times as many deaths as Hitler, though it denies that it seeks to establish a "hierarchy of cruelty" based on a "macabre comparative system."

44. In addition to Jews, candidates for elimination included Slavs, Gypsies, the insane or chronically ill, and Jehovah's Witnesses. Homosexuals are often included in this list, but although the Nazi regime enforced Article 175 of the German penal code vigorously and jailed thousands of homosexuals, it did not execute them systematically. Hitler himself, though he justified his murder of Ernst Röhm in June 1934 as an action against homosexuality, had, at earlier times, declined to censure Röhm's notorious lifestyle. Kershaw, *Hitler: Hubris*, 348.

45. Even *The Black Book*, p. 168, reviews with skepticism the genocide charge brought by some Ukrainian historians.

46. Alan Bullock refuses to equate the two kinds of killing in *Hitler and Stalin: Parallel Lives* (London: HarperCollins, 1991): "Nowhere was there a [Soviet] counterpart to the Holocaust in which mass murder became not an instrument but an end in itself" (p. 974).

47. Hans Mommsen criticizes totalitarianism theory in these terms, with acerbity in "The Concept of Totalitarianism versus the Comparative Theory of Fascism," in E. A. Menze, ed., *Totalitarianism Reconsidered* (Port Washington, NY: Kennikat Press, 1981), pp. 146–66, and more serenely in "Leistungen und Grenzen des Totalitarismus-Theorems: Die Anwendung auf die nationalsozialistische Diktatur," in Meier, ed., *"Totalitarismus" und "Politische Religionen,"* pp. 291–300. The change reflects the relative calming of German academic conflicts after the extreme tensions of the 1970s.

48. Hitler himself referred as early as 1926 to "our religion." Philippe Burrin, "Political Religion: The Relevance of a Concept," *History and Memory* 9:1 and 2 (Fall 1997), p. 333.

49. Burrin, "Political Religion," provides by far the most complete and thoughtful analysis. Emilio Gentile, "Fascism as a Political Religion," *Journal of Contemporary History* 190 (25), pp. 321–52, and Michael Burleigh, *The Third Reich*, pp. 5, 9–14, and 252–55, defend the concept (Burleigh cites many works on this subject on p. 816, n. 22). See also Meier, *"Totalitarismus."*

50. Nazism, writes Burleigh, *The Third Reich* (p. 255), "sank a drillhead into a deep-seated reservoir of existential anxiety, offering salvation from an ontological crisis."

51. Burrin, "Political Religion," p. 338.

52. See chapter 1, pp. 15–19.

53. Roger Griffin, "The Reclamation of Fascist Culture," *European History Quarterly* 31:4 (October 2001), pp. 609–20, sees it as the "key" to understanding fascism. For some of the many studies of fascist culture see the bibliographical essay, p. 236.

54. Bateson quoted in Eric Rentschler, "Emotional Engineering: Hitler Youth Quex," in *Modernism/Modernity* 2:3 (September 1995), p. 31.

55. Luisa Passerini, *Fascism in Popular Memory: The Cultural Experience of the Turin Working Class* (Cambridge: Cambridge University Press, 1987).

56. Susan Sontag made an interesting effort to extract the elements of a fascist aesthetic from the work of Leni Riefenstahl: "Fascinating Fascism," in Sontag, *Under the Sign of Saturn* (New York: Farrar, Straus and Giroux, 1980), but that mixture of virile heroism, ruralism, and anti-intellectualism may apply best to Germany.

57. R. J. B. Bosworth is one of the rare authors to make this point. See *The Italian Dictatorship: Problems and Perspectives in the Interpretation of Mussolini and Fascism* (London: Arnold, 1998), pp. 159, 162, 179.

58. Murray Kempton, "Mussolini in Concert," *New York Review of Books* 30:6 (April 24, 1983), pp. 33–35. For Nazism's failure to eradicate jazz from Germany, see Michael H. Kater, *Different Drummers: Jazz in the Culture of Nazi Germany* (New York: Oxford University Press, 1992).

59. For Bolivia, see chapter 7, note 69. For China, see Payne, *History*, pp. 337–38; Marcia H. Chang, *The Chinese Blue Shirt Society: Fascism and Developmental Nationalism* (Berkeley and Los Angeles: University of California Press, 1985), and Fred Wakeman, Jr., "A Revisionist View of the Nanjing Decade: Confucian Fascism," *China Quarterly* 150 (June 1997), pp. 395–430. Wakeman does not consider the Blueshirts authentically fascist. I thank him for advice on this point.

60. Gaetano Salvemini's Harvard lectures, published in *Opera de Gaetano Salvemini*, vol. VI, *Scritti sul fascismo*, vol. I, p. 343.

61. For guns as a "love object" of Fascist militants, see Emilio Gentile, *Storia del partito*, p. 498. "As long as I have a pen in my hand and a revolver in my pocket," said Mussolini after breaking with the Socialists in 1914, "I don't fear anyone." In the early 1920s, he kept a revolver and a couple of grenades on his desk. By the 1930s the revolver had migrated into a desk drawer of his grand office in the Palazzo Venezia (Pierre Milza, *Mussolini* [Paris: Fayard, 1999], pp. 183, 232, 252, 442). Hitler preferred dog-whips (Kershaw, *Hitler*, vol. I, p. 188), but he told his lunch guests on April 23, 1942, that "The bearing of arms contributes to a man's pride and bearing." (*Hitler's Table Talk*, trans. Norman Cameron and R. H. Stevens [London: Weidenfeld and Nicolson, 1953], p. 435.)

62. Colored shirts come from the Left, probably from Garibaldi's "Thousand," the red-shirted volunteers who conquered Sicily and Naples for a united, liberal Italy in 1860. The title *Duce* also came from Garibaldi.

63. Alan Bullock, *Hitler: A Study in Tyranny*, rev. ed. (London, Harper & Row 1962), p. 297.

64. Juan J. Linz has made the classic analysis of authoritarianism as a distinct

form of rule: "An Authoritarian Regime: Spain," in Erik Allardt and Stein Rokkan, eds., *Mass Politics: Studies in Political Sociology* (New York: Free Press, 1970), pp. 251–83, "From Falange to Movimiento-Organización: The Spanish Single Party and the Franco Regime, 1936–1968," in Samuel P. Huntington and Clement Moore, eds., *Authoritarian Politics in Modern Societies: The Dynamics of Established One-Party Systems* (New York: Basic Books, 1970), and "Totalitarian and Authoritarian Regimes," in Fred I. Greenstein and Nelson W. Polsby, *Handbook of Political Science* (Reading, MA: Addison-Wesley, 1975), vol. III, esp. pp. 264–350.

65. The authoritarian-fascist border is blurred here, for, in practice, neither gets its wish. Faced with aroused publics, authoritarians as well as fascists may attempt to create a Durkheimian "mechanical solidarity." See Paul Brooker, *The Faces of Fraternalism: Nazi Germany, Fascist Italy, and Imperial Japan* (Oxford: Clarendon, 1991). Even fascists may achieve no more than a "superficial" and "fragile" consent. Victoria De Grazia, *The Culture of Consent: Mass Organization of Leisure in Fascist Italy* (Cambridge: Cambridge University Press, 1981), p. 20, and chap. 8, "The Limits of Consent." The most meticulous study of German public opinion under Nazism, Martin Broszat's "Bavaria program," concluded that it was discontented but atomized, fragmented, and passive. See Ian Kershaw, *Popular Opinion and Dissent in the Third Reich* (Oxford: Clarendon, 1983), pp. 110, 277, 286, 389.

66. See the interesting comparison by Javier Tusell Gomez, "Franchismo et fascismo," in Angelo Del Boca et al., *Il regime fascista*, pp. 57–92.

67. Michael Richards, *A Time of Silence: Civil War and the Culture of Repression in Franco's Spain, 1936–1945* (Cambridge: Cambridge University Press, 1998), shows how economic and cultural autarky fit with internal repression. The estimated number of dead appears on p. 30. Paul Preston, *Franco* (New York: Basic Books, 1994), makes the fascism charge in another way, emphasizing Franco's close relations with the Axis until at least 1942.

68. The indispensable study of the Falange is Stanley G. Payne, *Fascism in Spain, 1923–1977* (Madison: University of Wisconsin Press, 1999) (quotation on p. 401).

69. See chapter 6, pp. 149–50.

70. See chapter 6, p. 150.

71. Quoted in Stanley Payne, *History*, p. 315. Gregory J. Kasza, "Fascism from Above? Japan's *Kakushin* Right in Comparative Perspective," in Stein Ugelvik Larsen, *Fascism Outside Europe* (Boulder, CO: Social Science Monographs, 2001), pp. 223–32, working from the Japanese example, proposes a distinct category of one-party regimes that suppress fascist movements while adopting some fascist devices, such as youth movements and corporatist economies, thus falling between traditional conservatism and fascism. His examples are Japan, Portugal, Poland in 1939, Estonia, and Lithuania. One might add Vargas's Brazil.

72. See above pp. 112–13.

73. Franz Neumann, *Behemoth: The Structure and Practice of National Socialism, 1933–1944*, 2nd ed. (New York: Oxford University Press, 1944), p. 39. Skepticism about fascist ideology is not limited to the Left. Cf. the famous denunciation by the former Nazi president of the Danzig senate, Hermann Rauschning, *Revolution of*

Nihilism (New York: Alliance/Longman's Green, 1939). See also Hannah Arendt's remarks quoted in chapter 2, p. 38.

74. See chapter 1, pp. 15–19.

Bibliographical Essay

1. Renzo De Felice, *Bibliografia orientativa del fascismo* (Rome: Bonacci, 1991). About two thousand of the entries refer to generic fascism and the history of World War II.

2. The final volume, still incomplete, was published posthumously by his students.

3. R. J. B. Bosworth, *The Italian Dictatorship* (London: Arnold, 1998), p. 7.

4. Raoul Girardet, sympathetic himself to the far Right but scrupulously self-effacing in his elegant work, used "impregnation" in almost exactly the same way with impunity in his pioneering "Notes sur l'esprit d'un fascisme français," *Revue française de science politique* 5 (July-September 1955), pp. 529–46.

INDEX

abortion, 202
Açao Integralista Brasileira (AIB), 192–3, 197
Action Française, 47, 48, 56–7, 103, 266n
African-Americans: nationalism, 202–3; prejudice against, 37, 174, 202
agriculture and agrarian policy, 10, 12, 65, 199–200, 235, 254n, 255n; Fascists' ascendancy in Po Valley and, 60–2, 64, 72, 82, 83, 86; *see also* peasants
Algeria, 76, 177–8
Alleanza Nazionale (AN), 173, 183, 184
Almirante, Giorgio, 176, 184
al-Qaeda, 203, 204
Amendola, Giovanni, 211, 287n
American Nazi Party, 201
American popular culture, 180, 188, 215
Amin Dada, Idi, 191
anarchists, 262n
Anti-Bolshevik Committee, 25
Anti-Comintern Pact (1936), 112, 149
antifascists, 38–9, 107, 112, 130, 136, 169, 177, 218. *See also* Giustizia e Libertà
anti-Semitism, 25, 26, 28, 32, 33, 46, 75, 76–7, 209, 298n; discriminatory legislation and, 140, 159, 166; as essence of fascism, 9, 253n–254n; experiments with appeal of, 47–8; in France, 9, 47, 48, 70, 76, 177, 185, 293n; in Germany, 14, 47–8, 70, 76–7, 140, 141, 181 (*see also* Holocaust); in Great Britain, 75, 76; in Italy, 9, 166–7, 169, 293n; in Russia, 76, 188; in United States, 76–7, 201
Antonescu, Ion, 97, 111, 113, 277n
anxiety, in early twentieth century, 35–7, 115
Aquarone, Alberto, 120
Arditi, 5, 7, 202

Arendt, Hannah, 17, 38, 104, 157–8, 170, 209, 253n–254n
Argentina, 193–6, 197, 246, 298n
Arrow Cross, 51, 57, 73, 113
artisans, 10, 12, 26, 27, 45, 79, 83, 142, 179–80, 209, 210
atomization, 157–8, 209, 301n–302n
Australia, 55
Austria, 31, 59, 115, 125, 203, 217; forerunner movement in, 26, 47; interwar, fascism in, 97–8, 240–1; Nazi annexation of, 159; neofascism in, 173, 180, 182, 183, 185, 249
Austrian Nazi Party, 97–8
autarky, 130, 146, 208, 232, 306n
authoritarianism, 9, 22, 43, 68, 70, 78, 98, 112–16, 118, 120, 125, 144, 189, 193, 203, 207, 277n; decay of fascist regimes into, 120–1, 148–50, 153, 171; fascism vs., 216–18, 223, 253n, 305n–306n; fascist junior partners and, 97, 111; military glorified in, 157
automobiles, 6, 66, 255n, 271n
Avanti, 7, 58, 251n
aviation, 66, 154, 255n

Balbo, Italo, 30, 61, 87, 122, 154
Balkans, 5, 116, 173, 186, 188, 189–91
Barrès, Maurice, 33, 48, 266n
Bateson, Gregory, 214
"Beer Hall Putsch" (1923), 91
Belgium: interwar, fascism in, 73–4, 81, 214, 241; neofascism in, 185, 186–7
Benjamin, Walter, 17
Bergson, Henri, 34
Berlin, Isaiah, 37
Berlusconi, Silvio, 173, 183, 184
Bianchi, Michele, 88
Bismarck, Otto von, 43

birth rate, 35, 134, 139, 263n
Black Legion, 201
Blackshirts. *See squadristi* and *squadrismo*
Bloch, Ernst, 209
Bloch, Marc, 20
Blomberg, Werner von, 129
Blueshirts: Ireland, 75; China, 305n
Blum, Léon, 69, 72
Bocchini, Arturo, 134, 152, 293n
Bolivia, 197
Bolshevik Revolution, 27, 31, 44, 78, 80, 81, 85, 88, 105, 106, 116, 172, 212
Bolshevism, 28–9, 36, 39, 44, 81, 85, 187–8; fear of revolution and, 44, 105, 107
Bonomi, Ivanoe, 88
book burning, 36
Borghese, Prince Junio Valerio, 169, 294n
Bormann, Martin, 52
Bosnia, 113–14, 190
Bossi, Umberto, 177, 183, 186
Bottai, Giuseppe, 289n
Boulanger, Georges, 46–7
bourgeois values, 30; enmity towards, 6, 7, 10, 11, 12, 33, 37, 39, 40, 48, 52, 53, 56–8, 62, 84, 97, 131, 139, 141, 148, 166
Bracher, Karl Dietrich, 119–20, 303n
Brasillach, Robert, 53, 83, 269n, 274n
Brazil, 111, 192–3, 197, 246, 297n–298n
Brecht, Bertolt, 207
British National Party (BNP), 185
British Union of Fascists (BUF), 51, 74–5, 114, 268n, 275n
Broszat, Martin, 120, 258n
Brüning, Heinrich, 69, 93, 95, 99
Brzezinski, Zbigniew K., 122, 211
Bullock, Alan, 96
Bush, George W., 21
Busch, Germán, 197
business concerns: fascist regimes' relations with, 13, 145–6, 232–3; financing of Nazis by, 66–7, 100, 228, 271n. *See also* capitalism, capitalists

calendar, 275n
capitalism, capitalists, 6, 7, 19, 79, 115; fascism's relation to, 10–11, 53, 56, 66–7, 145–6, 207–8, 232–3, 254n, 301n
Carlyle, Thomas, 35
Carol, king of Romania, 97
Cartel des Gauches, 68

Catholic Action, 108, 152, 290n
Catholic Church, 50, 71, 73–4, 87, 88, 92, 112, 115, 122–4, 143, 150, 161, 183, 203, 217, 231, 241; anti-Semitism and, 167, 293n; Mussolini's relations with, 63, 125, 131, 138, 152–3, 168, 290n. *See also* Christian Democratic Parties, Partito Popolare Italiano, Zentrum
Cercle Proudhon, 48, 68, 103
Chabod, Federico, 105
Chamberlain, Houston Stewart, 32
Chamberlain, Neville, 155, 301n
charisma, 126, 168, 173, 193, 195, 282n
Chartier, Roger, 18
child welfare professionals, 135
Chile, 197, 201
China, 199, 246–7, 305n
Chirac, Jacques, 182, 297n
Christian Democratic Party (Germany), 176
Christian Democratic Party (Italy), 88, 138, 153, 177, 182–3, 184
Christian Social Party (Germany), 47
Christian X, king of Denmark, 112
Churchill, Winston, 126, 167
Ciano, Galeazzo, 156, 169
citizenship, 11, 142–3, 147
civil service, 85, 100, 119, 125, 129, 130, 133, 134, 152, 153, 155, 158, 162, 166, 170, 218, 231–2
class, 19, 26, 32, 40, 41, 50–1, 57, 58, 74, 79, 88, 103, 137, 143, 144, 150, 188, 199, 209, 210–11, 212–13, 219, 225, 228, 234. *See also* middle class; working class
Clausen, Fritz, 112
Codreanu, Corneliu, 20, 97
cold war, 157, 211
communism, communists, 18, 21, 25, 31, 66–7, 81, 189, 213, 214; collapse of Soviet Union and, 175, 180, 181; fear of, 22–3, 105, 107, 108, 177, 195; totalitarian paradigm and, 211–13; violence against, 10, 84. *See also* Bolshevism; Marxism, Marxists
Communist International, 128, 207
Communist Party (Soviet), 126, 162
community, fear of collapse of, 35, 36, 148, 218
"compromise for rule" (*Herrschafts-kompromiss*), 18, 19, 57, 83, 100, 101–2, 117, 131, 141, 206

concentration camps, 14, 108, 133, 135, 136, 142, 285n, 286n. *See also* Holocaust
conservatism, conservatives, 3, 11, 16, 22–3, 31, 43, 82, 111, 144; cooperation with, in fascist route to power, 57–8, 67–8, 86, 93, 98–104, 107–8, 110, 115–18; emergence of mass politics and, 78–9; power sharing with, in fascist regimes, 119–20, 124, 128–30, 147, 229–30, 233; tug-of-war between fascists and, in exercise of power, 120–1, 124, 125, 128–31
Conservative Party, 114, 185
constitutional systems, 18, 22, 40, 121, 186, 188; deadlocked, fascist route to power and, 88–9, 92–6, 99, 102–3, 105–6, 115–18, 227; post–World War I crisis of liberal state and, 77–81. *See* democracy
consumerism, 173, 215, 294n
Corfu incident (1923), 156
corporatism, 39, 59, 70, 150, 177, 186, 199; in Italy, 137, 145, 152, 192, 193–4, 232–3; in Latin America, 192, 193–4, 196–7
Coughlin, Father Charles E., 201, 202, 300n
coup attempts, failed, 96, 97–8
creating fascist movements (stage one), 23, 24–54, 224–6, 260n–269n; experience of World War I and, 28–32, 261n; intellectual and cultural roots and, 32–40, 76–7, 224, 262n–264n; mobilizing passions and, 40–2, 219–20; preconditions and, 42–4, 225–6; precursor movements and, 44–9, 265n–267n; recruitment in, 49–52, 62, 226, 267n–268n; understanding fascism in light of, 52–4
Croats, Croatia, 113–14, 167, 190, 191, 241, 285n
Croce, Benedetto, 7–8, 39, 140, 207
Croix de Feu, 57, 71, 243, 272n
cultural life, 80, 140, 144–5, 236–7, 274n, 287n; decoding of, 144, 214–15, 236, 305n; defense from degeneracy, 36, 79–80, 82, 144, 148, 149, 180, 182, 186, 187, 215
Currières de Castelnau, Noël, 68
Czechs, Czechoslovakia, 26, 31, 46, 113, 125, 156, 241

Daladier, Édouard, 71
D'Annunzio, Gabriele, 50, 59–60, 62, 85, 89, 101, 262n, 270n
Darré, Walther, 255n

Darwinism, 53. *See also* social Darwinism
Daudet, Léon, 57
De Ambris, Alceste, 59, 60, 147
Déat, Marcel, 113
death penalty, 110, 136, 285n
De Bono, Emilio, 88
decline, fear of, 4, 8, 33, 35–6, 37, 38, 41, 81, 142, 143, 144, 148, 186, 202, 218, 219
De Gaulle, Charles, 126, 270n
Defenders of the Christian Faith, 201
Degrelle, Léon, 73–4, 113, 279n
Del Boca, Angelo, 166
democracy, 3–4; eastern European experiments with, 188, 189; emergence of mass politics and, 42–3, 45–6, 78–9, 80, 82, 172, 187, 265n; fascist assaults on, 33–4, 186, 216; socialist participation in, 43–4; wartime limitations and, 157. *See also* constitutional systems
Democratic Party (Germany), 92
Denmark, occupied, 112
denunciations, 123, 136, 230–1
Depression, Great, 11, 64–5, 67, 68, 71, 74–5, 92, 93, 105, 147, 165, 192, 193–4, 198
De Stefani, Alberto, 109, 151, 154
De Vecchi, Cesare Maria, 88
developmental dictatorship, 12, 147, 193, 197, 210
dictatorship, traditional (tyranny), compared with fascism, 4, 25, 73, 81, 97, 100, 111, 125, 126, 132, 137, 144, 145, 153, 157, 170, 191, 216, 306n
Dollfuss, Engelbert, 97–8, 115
Dopolavoro, 123, 124, 144
Dorgères, Henry, 71–3
Doriot, Jacques, 69, 113, 272n, 279n
Drexler, Anton, 27
Dreyfus Affair, 44, 47, 48, 76, 265n
dual state, 121–2, 124–5, 131, 135, 150, 158, 280n–281n
due process, 86; coexistence of blatant lawlessness and, 121, 280n; suspension of, 20, 122, 129, 142, 147, 169, 205, 216. *See also* rule of law
Dumini, Amerigo, 52
Durkheim, Émile, 35, 143, 204

Eastern Way Society, 199
Ebert, Friedrich, 104
economic crisis of 1880s, 45–8

Index

economic policy: fascist "revolution" and, 145–7. *See also* capitalism, capitalists; corporatism; market economics

education, 44, 103, 108, 123, 143, 152, 231

Eichmann, Adolf, 159

Einsatzgruppen, 159, 161–2

Einstein, Albert, 140

Eliot, T. S., 256n

Enabling Act (1933), 107–8

enemies, 36–7, 84, 174

Engels, Friedrich, 3

Epp, Franz Xaver Ritter von, 260n

Estado Novo (New State), 150, 193, 217

Estonia, 78, 306n

Ethiopian War, 18, 37, 131, 138, 153, 156, 165–6, 170, 237, 285n–286n, 290n

ethnic cleansing, 116, 173, 190. *See also* Holocaust

eugenics, 13, 34, 36–7, 130, 134–5, 161, 238–9, 257n, 292n

European Union, 181, 189

euthanasia, 37, 121, 130, 161

exercising power (stage four), 23, 119–47, 229–37, 279n–289n; conflicts with conservatives and, 120–1, 124, 125, 128–31; dual state and, 121–2, 124–5, 135, 280n–281n; fascist "revolution" and, 141–7; islands of separateness and, 122–3; leader-party conflict and, 131–3; leader's supremacy and, 119, 125–8; party-state conflict and, 121–2, 124–5, 133–5; power sharing with conservatives and, 119–20, 124, 128–30, 147, 229–30, 233; social control and, 135–41, 230–1, 285n–287n; struggles for preeminence and, 120–8, 154–5; voluntary cooperation and, 123, 140–1, 235–6

expansionism, 5, 49, 53, 66, 80, 98, 114, 116, 123, 138, 148, 150, 155–7, 170, 186, 190, 196, 198–200, 201, 203, 210, 216, 218, 238

Facta, Luigi, 88–9, 90

Faisceau, 68

Falange Española, 56, 57, 115, 149–50, 217, 269n

Farben, I. G., 67, 146, 208

Farinacci, Roberto, 61, 131, 132–3, 152, 154, 290n

Fasci di Combattimento, 4, 5, 24, 53–4, 57

fascism: boundaries of, 215–18, 305n–306n;

conventional images of, 9–15; definition of, 14–15, 206–7, 218–20; diversity of national cases of, 8, 20, 21, 39–40; general works on, 221–2; as "ideal type," 21; ideology of, 10–12, 15–19, 64, 141, 214, 218–19, 258n–259n, 306n–307n; interpretations of, 7–8, 207–15, 222–3, 300n–305n; origin of word, 4–5; polemical name-calling and, 8, 173–4; preconditions for, 18, 42–4, 77–80, 81, 225–6, 273n; stages of, 23, 206–7 (*see also* creating fascist movements; exercising power; getting power; radicalization; taking root); supposed death of, in 1945, 172, 173; use of term, 20–1. *See also* leaders, fascist; legacy of fascism; parties, fascist; *specific topics*

"fascist minimum," 14, 20, 206

Fascist Party. *See* Partito Nazionale Fascista

Fatherland Front, 27, 29, 98

Feder, Gottfried, 66

Fédération Nationale Catholique, 68

Federzoni, Luigi, 151

Fermi, Enrico, 166

Fighting League of the Commercial Middle Class, 66, 131

film, 144, 208–9, 214

Fini, Gianfranco, 177, 183, 184, 185

Finland, 203, 245

Finzi, Aldo, 9

Fiume, 59–60, 63

Fortuyn, Pym, 173–4, 183

Forza Italia, 183

Fraenkel, Ernst, 121

France, 30, 31, 42, 44, 78, 82, 104, 149, 156, 209, 215, 264n–265n; anti-Semitism in, 9, 47, 48, 70, 76, 177, 185, 293n; forerunner movements in, 46–7, 48, 49, 53, 56–7, 103, 266n; interwar, fascism in, 53, 68–73, 76, 114, 241–4, 269n, 271n–273n; Nazi defeat of, 69, 112–13, 157, 171; neofascism in, 173, 177–8, 179, 180, 181–2, 185, 249, 296n, 297n; occupied (*see* Vichy France); suffrage in, 42, 43, 45, 264n, 273n

Franco, Francisco, 56, 75, 81, 111, 115, 149–50, 157, 170, 195, 217, 306n

Frank, Hans, 159, 292n

Frank, Leo, 76

fraternities, 123

Index

free institutions, giving up, 191, 204, 216, 218
Freemasonry, 46, 144, 149
Freiheitspartei (Freedom Party), 173, 180, 182, 183
Freikorps, 27, 64, 93, 202
French Communist Party, 73, 218
French Resistance, 218
French Revolution, 18, 22, 73, 213, 264n, 273n
Freud, Sigmund, 34, 226
Freycinet, Charles de, 46
Freyer, Hans, 140
Friedrich, Carl J., 122, 211
Fritsch, Werner von, 129
Front National (FN), 178, 180, 181–2, 187, 296n
Front of National Rebirth, 97
functionalism, 127
Funk, Walter, 278n
Furtwängler, Wilhelm, 141, 287n
Futurism, Futurists, 5, 6, 39, 40, 62

Galton, Francis, 34
Gambetta, Léon, 45, 46, 51
Garibaldi, Giuseppe, 305n
gas warfare, 285n–286n
Gates, Henry Louis, Jr., 202–3
gender policy, 139, 215, 233–5, 286n–287n
Gentile, Emilio, 120
Gentile, Giovanni, 17, 52, 140, 268n, 278n
George, Stefan, 33, 38–9
German Communist Party (KPD), 93, 94, 103, 105, 136–7, 276n, 277n
German National Party (DNVP), 65, 66, 100, 108
German Reich Party (DRP), 176
German Socialist Party (SPD), Social Democrats, 84, 92, 93, 94, 103, 104, 128, 136–7, 176, 276n, 277n
German Workers' Party (DAP), 26, 27–8
Germani, Gino, 298n
Germany: anti-Semitism in, 14, 47–8, 70, 76–7, 140, 141, 181; comparisons between Fascist Italy and, 235; constitutional crisis in, 92–6, 99, 102–3, 105–6; creation of fascist movement in, 26–8, 225, 226; crisis of 1880s in, 45, 46, 47–9; eugenics in, 13, 34, 37, 130, 134–5, 161, 238–9, 257n, 292n (see also Holocaust); forerunner movements in, 47–8; Nazis'

exercise of power in, 119–47, 229–37; Nazis' route to power in, 91–108, 115–18, 227–8, 276n, 278n; neofascism in, 173, 175–6, 179, 181, 248–9, 294n, 295n, 296n; penetration of existing organizations in, 209–10, 302n; racial policies in, 134–5, 158–9, 167 (see also Holocaust); radicalization stage in, 150–1, 153, 158–64, 169–71, 237–40, 291n–292n, 294n; "second revolution" in, 131–2; suffrage in, 43, 45; taking root of fascism in, 56, 57, 64–8, 76–86, 225, 270n–271n. See also Hitler, Adolf; Weimar Republic; specific topics
Gestapo, 123, 125, 136, 274n, 286n
getting power (stage three), 23, 87–118, 226–8, 275n–279n; climate of disorder and, 103–4; comparison to failed attempts at, 110–18; conservative complicities and, 57–8, 67–8, 86, 93, 98–104, 107–8, 110, 115–18; constitutional deadlock and, 88–9, 92–6, 99, 102–3, 105–6, 115–18, 227; coup attempts and, 96, 97–8; electoral successes and, 93, 96, 116–17; financial help from business and, 66–7, 100, 228, 271n; Hitler's "backstairs conspiracy" and, 91–6; Mussolini's "March on Rome" and, 87–91, 275n; negotiation period and, 100–1; occupied or satellite states and, 111–14; prefascist crisis and, 105–6; quasiconstitutional coalition governments and, 96–7, 106; transformation of toehold into outright dictatorship and, 106–10; violence against Left and, 99
Gini, Corrado, 140
Giolitti, Giovanni, 30, 59, 60–1, 64, 86, 88, 89, 100, 101, 102, 275n, 278n
Giulietti, Giuseppe, 50
Giustizia e Libertà, 136, 253n
Gleichschaltung, 123, 128
globalization, 10, 12, 45, 173, 179, 181, 182, 187, 188, 296n
Gobetti, Piero, 287n
Goebbels, Joseph, 14, 36, 52, 159, 261n
Goering, Hermann, 52, 129, 146, 159, 276n, 278n
Goering, Hermann, Werke, 146
Goldhagen, Daniel, 161, 253n
Gömbös, Gyula, 25–6

313

Index

Gramsci, Antonio, 300n
Graziani, Rodolfo, 166
Great Britain, 30, 45, 51, 53, 71, 79, 82, 104, 149, 156, 167, 257n; anti-Semitism in, 75, 76; capitalist transformation of agriculture in, 199–200; interwar, fascism in, 51, 74–5, 114, 241, 268n, 275n; neofascism in, 173, 177, 178–9, 180, 184–5
Greece, 78, 156–7, 244
Greenshirts, 71–3
Griffin, Roger, 21
Gründgens, Gustav, 145
guns, fascist love of, 305n
Gypsies, 37, 135, 162, 212

Habsburg empire, 24, 26, 30, 46, 47, 203
Haffner, Sebastian, 137
Haider, Jörg, 173, 180, 183, 185
Hayes, Peter, 145
Hedilla, Manuel, 149
Heidegger, Martin, 140
Heines, Edmund, 51
Heisenberg, Werner, 140, 287n
Heydrich, Reinhard, 160
Himmler, Heinrich, 51, 52, 125, 133, 160
Hindenburg, Oskar, 94, 96
Hindenburg, Paul, 93, 94, 96, 97, 107, 122, 129
Hindu fundamentalism, 203, 204
Hirihito, emperor of Japan, 198
historicization, 12, 14–15, 118, 258n
Hitler, Adolf, 7, 8, 12, 14, 38, 39, 52, 56, 69, 149, 186, 197, 202, 203, 210, 215; biographies of, 223; creation of fascist movement and, 26–8; downfall of, 172, 173; early years of, 26, 27–8, 260n; exportation of fascism and, 111–14; Holocaust and, 158–61, 163; ideology of, 15, 17, 18, 218, 258n; indolence of, 126, 127–8, 153, 155, 283n; intellectual influences on, 32; military paraphernalia of, 216, 305n; modernist accoutrements of, 12, 255n, 256n; Mussolini's relations with, 167, 168, 252n; nature of rule of, 119–47, 213, 229–37; party conflicts with, 101–2, 108, 131–2, 154; personality of, 51, 208, 268n; postwar admirers of, 174; radicalizing impulses and, 153, 154–6, 170, 171; rule of law and, 121; seizure of power by,

67–8, 91–108, 115–18, 128–30, 227–8, 276n, 278n; suicide of, 164; taking root of Nazis and, 57, 64–8, 85; totalitarian paradigm and, 211–13; war sought by, 155–6; youth organizations and, 143–4. *See also* Germany; *specific topics*
Hlinka, Father Andreas, 113
Holocaust, 7, 13, 37, 127, 132, 158–64, 171, 185, 240, 257n, 291n–292n, 304n; as expression of extreme radicalization, 150–1; hidden from German people and foreign observers, 163–4, 292n; progression from lesser acts to more heinous ones in, 158–62, 291n; Stalinist terror compared to, 212–13, 304n; subordinates' role in, 158, 160, 161, 163, 164; technology for, 162–3
homosexuality, 51, 135, 145, 181, 183, 202, 238–9, 268n, 274n, 304n
Horthy, Miklós, 25, 26, 73, 113
Hugenberg, Alfred, 100, 108
Hungary, 24–6, 32, 51, 57, 73, 81, 97, 113, 244
Hussein, Saddam, 300n

Iceland, 55
ideological approaches, 15–18, 214, 219
ideology, fascist, 10–12, 15–19, 64, 141, 214, 218–19, 258n–259n, 306n–307n
immigration, neofascism and, 173, 175, 178–83, 186, 187
India, 203, 204
individualism, 10, 11, 21, 32, 35, 40, 41, 77, 186, 188, 219
individual rights, 11, 20, 22, 142–3, 147, 259n
Indochina War, 177
industrialization, 12, 79, 80, 200, 256n
inevitability, 79, 80, 81, 86, 104, 118, 123, 148, 207, 220
insurance companies, 146, 232
intellectuals: in early days of fascism, 12, 18, 40, 53, 77; under fascist regimes, 139–40, 236, 239
intentionalism, 127, 128, 153, 160
Interlandi, Telesio, 167
intifada, 204
Iran, 203
Iraq, 300n
Ireland, 75, 244
Irving, David, 291n
Islamic fundamentalism, 203, 204, 214

Index

Islamic immigrants, 180, 181, 183
islands of separateness, 122–3
Israel, 204
Istituto per la Ricostruzione Industriale (IRI), 122
Italian Communist Party, 105
Italy: civil war in, 168; colonial wars and, 37, 122, 131, 136, 138, 153, 156, 165–6, 170, 237, 259n, 285n–286n; constitutional crisis in, 88–9, 99, 105–6; creation of fascist movement in, 4–7, 11, 24, 28, 53–4, 224–5, 226, 251n–253n, 255n; Fascist, comparisons between Nazi Germany and, 95, 101, 108, 130–1, 134, 136, 147, 154, 235, 237; Fascists' exercise of power in, 120–8, 130–40, 143, 145, 229–37, 285n; Fascists' route to power in, 87–91, 93, 95, 96–106, 108–11, 115–18, 136, 226–7, 228, 275n–279n; forerunner movements in, 48–9; Jews of, 9, 160, 166–7, 169, 253n, 293n; neofascism in, 173, 176–7, 181, 182–3, 184, 185, 186, 248, 294n, 295n, 296n–297n; race policy in, 166–7, 239–40, 257n, 293n; radicalization stage in, 151–3, 164–9, 170, 171, 237–40, 293n–294n; Salò republic and, 153, 168–9, 238; taking root of fascism in, 56–64, 76–86, 224–5, 270n, 275n; World War I and, 4, 5, 6, 28, 30, 32, 60, 80; World War II entered by, 167–8, 171. See also Mussolini, Benito; Partito Nazionale Fascista; *specific topics*

Japan, 197–200, 247, 299n, 306n
jazz, 139, 215, 305n
Jeffries, Leonard, 203
Jehovah's Witnesses, 304n
Jeune Nation (JN), 177–8
Jeunesses Patriotes, 68
Jews, 10, 37, 45, 97, 107, 108, 113, 133, 135, 145, 180, 280n; diabolization of, 174; discriminatory legislation against, 140, 159, 166; of Italy, 9, 160, 166–7, 169, 253n, 293n; *Kristallnacht* and, 14, 159, 164, 257n. See also anti-Semitism; Holocaust
Jordan, Colin, 184
Judaism, Orthodox, 204
judiciary, 14, 84, 86, 107, 119, 121, 134, 195, 232, 285n

Jung, Edgar, 129
Jünger, Ernst, 84, 262n–263n

Kahr, Gustav von, 91, 108
Károlyi, Count Michael, 24–5
Kerensky, Alexander, 116
Kérillis, Henri de, 78, 273n
Kessler, Harry, 259n
Khaki Shirts, 201
Khomeini, Ayatollah, 203
Kipling, Rudyard, 34
Kirdorf, Emil, 66
Kita Ikki, 198
Klemperer, Victor, 278n
Konoe Fumimaro, Prince, 199
Kornilov, Lavr Georgyevich, 81, 116
Kristallnacht, 13, 14, 159, 164, 257n
Ku Klux Klan, 49, 201, 267n
Kun, Béla, 25

Labor Exchanges Front (Germany), 137, 144
labor movement, 10, 137, 144; nationalism and, 46; Perón and, 194–5. *See also* syndicalism
language, fascist effect on, 107, 166, 278n
Lanz von Liebenfels, Jörg, 260n
Lapua (Finland), 203, 245
La Rocque, François de, 57, 69–71, 185, 269n, 272n
Lateran Pact (1929), 138, 152
Latin America, 192–7, 201, 246, 247, 297n–298n
Lawrence, D. H., 40
leaders, fascist, 9, 17, 19, 83; *charisma* of, 126, 282n; dramatic promises of, 126, 148, 164; monolithic power ascribed to, 119, 125–7, 229; outsider status of, 51–2; party dominated by, 131–3; radicalizing impulses from below and, 126, 171, 153–4; succession of, 126, 282n–283n. *See also specific leaders*
leadership principle, 127, 141
League of Nations, 59, 63
Le Bon, Gustave, 32, 33–4
legacy of fascism, 172–205, 248–9; outside Europe, 191–205; in post-Soviet eastern Europe, 173, 174, 188–91; in western Europe, 173, 175–88. *See also specific countries*

315

Index

Legion of the Archangel Michael, 73, 97, 111, 113, 245

Légion Wallonie (Belgium), 279n

Legnani, Massimo, 120

leisure-time organizations, 123, 124, 137, 139, 144. *See also* Dopolavoro, Strength Through Joy

Lemke, William, 201, 299n

Lenin, V. I., 18, 25, 31, 33, 44

Le Pen, Jean-Marie, 173, 180, 181–2, 185, 186, 296n

Le Roy Ladurie, Jacques, 72

Levi, Carlo, 287n

Levi, Primo, 169

Lewis, Wyndham, 40, 256n

Ley, Robert, 144

Liberal Democratic Party (LDP), 188–9

liberalism, liberals, 3, 16, 21, 28, 31, 38, 39, 67, 82, 207; crisis of, as precondition for fascism, 19, 77–80, 81, 273n; revolt against, 19, 32, 77, 147; use of term, 21, 22

Libya, 18, 37, 49, 166

Lipset, Seymour Martin, 210, 267n

List, Guido von, 260n

Lithuania, 78, 306n

living space (*Lebensraum*), 155, 157, 204

Long, Huey, 201, 202, 300n

Ludendorff, Erich, 91

Lueger, Karl, 26, 32, 47

Lyttelton, Adrian, 126

Mafia, 277n

Maistre, Joseph de, 37

Mann, Thomas, 7, 140, 253n

"March on Rome," 9, 87–91, 275n

Marinetti, Filippo Tommaso, 6, 7, 40, 58, 84, 258n

market economics, 19, 21, 22, 44, 82, 186, 188, 189. *See also* capitalism, capitalists

Marx, Karl, 3, 4, 16, 18, 265n

Marxism, Marxists, 5–6, 8, 19, 66, 79, 81, 83, 86, 88, 103, 108, 135, 209, 300n; interpretation of fascism, 8, 19, 66, 79, 86, 114–15, 145, 198, 207, 209, 211, 212, 299n, 300n

masculinity, 35, 51, 208, 226, 234

Mason, Tim, 136, 137

mass politics, emergence of, 42–3, 45–6, 78–9, 80, 82, 172, 187, 265n. *See also* democracy; suffrage

mass society, 8, 36, 82, 157–8, 209, 301n–302n

Matteotti, Giacomo, 109–10, 132, 136, 151, 154

Maurras, Charles, 47, 48, 56–7

Mazzini, Giuseppe, 30, 34, 252n

medical profession, 134–5, 232, 285n

Mégret, Bruno, 182, 297n

Meinecke, Friedrich, 8, 207

Mein Kampf (Hitler), 258n, 276n, 297n

Meitner, Lise, 140

Mendel, Gregor, 36

Mengele, Josef, 134

mentally ill, 36, 161, 163, 238, 239

Michels, Roberto, 35, 37

middle class, 6, 19, 22, 30, 43, 44, 45, 47, 50, 67, 73, 79, 80, 81, 84, 85, 92, 94, 105, 114, 200, 210

Miglioli, Guido, 87

military, relationship with fascists, 13, 27, 62, 63, 86, 90, 91, 98, 99, 108, 118, 119, 124, 125, 126, 129–30, 132, 133, 150, 153, 154, 161–2, 165, 166, 170, 194–5, 198–9, 217, 232

militia: (France), 218; (Italy), 110, 124, 133, 165

Milosevic, Slobodan, 116, 189–91

mobilization, 22, 40, 116, 142, 174, 199, 210, 213, 217; primary and secondary, 298n

Mobutu, Seko-Seso, 201

modernization, modernity, 12–13, 79–80, 199–200, 209, 255n–257n; opposition to, 12–18, 36, 77, 178

Moltke, Helmut von, 130

Moltke, J. S. von, 191

Mommsen, Hans, 120, 127–8, 283n, 304n

Montanelli, Indro, 153

Moore, Barrington, 199–200

Morès, Marquis de, 48

Mori, Cesare, 277n

Mosca, Gaetano, 35, 37, 39

Mosley, Sir Oswald, 53, 74–5, 114

Mosse, George, 41

Movimento Sociale Italiano (MSI), 173, 176–7, 182, 183, 184, 294n, 296n–297n

multiculturalism, 180, 181, 182

Mussert, Anton, 112

Mussolini, Alessandra, 177

Mussolini, Benito, 7–8, 12, 26, 36, 39, 52, 75, 111, 122, 127, 149, 186, 197, 202, 203, 215, 217, 261n; anti-Jewish measures and,

166–7, 169, 293n; biographies of, 223–4; colonial wars and, 138, 153, 156, 165–6, 170, 237, 259n, 285n–286n, 293n; corporatism of, 137, 145, 152, 192, 193–4, 232–3; in creation of fascist movement, 4–7, 11, 24, 28, 53–4, 251n–253n, 255n; downfall of, 125–6, 168, 172–3; economic policy of, 145, 151, 152, 210, 232–3; French admiration for, 68, 69, 70; Hitler's relations with, 167, 168, 252n; ideology of, 15, 17, 18, 62–4, 218, 258n; intellectual influences on, 32–4; Jewish backers of, 9, 166, 253n; military paraphernalia of, 216, 305n; modernist accoutrements of, 12, 255n, 256n; nature of rule of, 120–8, 130–40, 143, 145, 213, 229–37, 285n; party dominated by, 124, 131, 132–3; postwar admirers of, 174, 184; race policy and, 257n; seizure of power by, 87–91, 93, 95, 96–106, 108–11, 115–18, 130–1, 136, 226–7, 228, 275n–279n; taking root of Fascism and, 56–64, 85, 86; tensions between radicalization and normalization impulses of, 151–3, 154, 155, 164–9, 170, 237; totalitarian paradigm and, 211; war sought by, 155, 156–7, 290n; World War II entered by, 167–8, 171. *See also* Italy; *specific topics*
Mussolini, Edda, 139
Mussolini, Rachele Guidi, 138
Mussolini, Romano, 215
Mussolini, Vittorio, 215

Nakano, Seigo, 199
Napoleon III, emperor of France, 42, 264n–265n
Nasjonal Samling (NS), 74, 112, 244
Nationaal Socialistische Beweging (NSB), 74
Nationaldemokratische Partei Deutschlands (NPD), 176, 179
National Front, 178, 179, 180, 184–5
nationalism, 5, 7, 25, 26, 27, 28, 32, 41, 45, 46–7, 103, 173
Nationalist Party, 109, 151
"nationalization of the masses," 78, 79, 172
national revival (regeneration), as fascist mission, 20, 21, 26, 39, 40, 117, 142, 144, 174, 188, 202, 207
national socialism, 56; origin of term, 48
National Socialist Movement, 178, 184

Nazi Party (NSDAP), 57, 83–4, 103, 105, 147, 150–1, 170, 228, 276n; business contributions to, 66–7, 100, 228, 271n; as catch-all party, 58, 65–7; electoral politics and, 64–8, 93, 95, 96, 107, 116, 227; founding of, 27–8; Hitler's conflicts with, 101–2, 108, 131–2, 154; parallel structures of, 85, 125, 129, 130; state functions taken over by, 133–5; street violence and, 95, 99; youth organizations and, 143–4
neofascism. *See* legacy of fascism
Netherlands, 74, 112, 173, 183–4
Neumann, Franz, 119, 219
Neurath, Konstantin von, 130, 154
New Deal, 192
"new man," Fascist, 124, 143, 166
New Party, 75
Niekisch, Ernst, 39
Nietzsche, Friedrich, 32–3, 38, 262n
Night of the Long Knives (1934), 75, 108, 129, 132
Nolte, Ernst, 32, 172, 274n
"normalization" of fascism, 17, 63–4, 101–2, 104, 131–2, 148, 151–2, 153, 175, 184–5, 188, 211, 230, 237
Northern League (Lega Nord), 177, 183, 186, 295n
Norway, 74, 111–12, 244
Nuremberg laws, 159, 166

Occident, 178
occupation fascisms, 111–14
O'Duffy, Eoin, 75
ordinary people, complicity of, 13–14, 123, 140–1, 209, 230–1, 235–6
Ordre Nouveau, 178, 179
Organisation de l'Armée Secrète, L' (OAS), 178
Orwell, George, 174, 202
Ossebrandwag (Ox-Wagon Sentinel), 191–2
OVRA, 122, 134

Palestinian nationalism, 204
Pamyat, 188
pan-Germanism, 26, 47, 203
Papen, Franz von, 66, 94, 95, 96, 99, 100, 102, 108, 118, 128, 129
parallel structures, 85, 124–5, 129, 130, 150, 280n

Index

Pareto, Vilfredo, 34, 35, 37

Parsons, Talcott, 209

parties, fascist, 57, 267n; leader's domination of, 131–3; membership in, 103, 125, 228, 267n; parallel structures of, 85, 124–5, 129, 130; pragmatic choices and, 56–8, 83–4; purges and secessions in, 101–2, 108, 117; recruitment into, 49–52, 62, 226, 267n–268n; state functions taken over by, 121, 133–5; in struggle for supremacy within fascist rule, 120–2, 123–4, 127, 131–5. *See also specific parties*

Parti Populaire Français (PPF), 69, 272n

Parti Social Français (PSF), 57, 69–71, 272n

Partito Nazionale Fascista (PNF), 83, 103, 109, 110, 125, 151, 152, 153, 267n; electoral politics and, 53–4, 56, 64, 96, 116; establishment of one-party rule and, 132; Ethiopian War and, 165–6; founding of, 5, 57; Mussolini's domination of, 124, 131, 132–3; parallel structures of, 124–5; program of, 5–6; purists' disaffection with, 62; rightward drift in positions of, 62–4

Partito Popolare Italiano (PPI), 62, 64, 86, 88, 109, 117

Partito Socialista Italiano (PSI), 11, 88, 89, 105, 251n, 255n

Pasolini, Pier Paolo, 301n

Passerini, Luisa, 215

passions, mobilizing, 40–2, 219–20

Pasteur, Louis, 36

patriarchy, 43, 215

Pavelic, Ante, 113, 191

peasants, 3, 4, 10, 12, 30, 38, 61, 65, 81, 97, 142, 163, 178, 200, 209, 210, 235, 254n, 255n; Greenshirts and, 71–3

Pelley, William Dudley, 201

People's Party (Austria), 183

People's Party (Germany), 92

"permanent revolution," 148, 289n

Perón, Eva Duarte, 194, 195, 196

Perón, Juan, 193, 194–6, 197, 298n

Peru, 197

Petacci, Clara, 169

Pétain, Philippe, 9, 112–13, 157, 272n

Petersen, Jens, 120

Pinochet, Augusto, 201

Pius XI, Pope, 108, 138, 152, 167, 290n

Planck, Max, 140

Poland, 18, 31, 76, 78, 150, 163, 244, 306n; German conquest and occupation of, 122, 155–6, 159, 160, 162, 163, 292n

polarization, climate of, 30, 39, 69, 84, 85, 105, 116, 202, 205, 210

police, 13, 61, 62, 85, 86, 89, 91, 97, 98, 99, 105, 107, 119, 121, 124, 125, 133–4, 136, 144, 151, 152, 153, 168, 178, 195–7, 211, 218, 230, 240. *See also* Gestapo, OVRA

political religion, 213–14, 304n

polyocracy, 127, 229–30, 284n

Popolo d'Italia, Il, 100, 255n

Portugal, 78, 111, 114, 150, 157, 171, 193, 203, 217–18, 244, 306n

postindustrial society, 179–80

Poujade, Pierre, 178

Pound, Ezra, 40, 256n

Po Valley, 60–2, 64, 72, 82, 83, 86

preconditions for fascism, 42–4, 225–6

precursor movements, 44–9, 265n–267n

predisposition to fascism, 9, 76, 81–2, 253n, 274n

Preto, Rolão, 150

Prezzolini, Giovanni, 6, 39

Primo de Rivera, José Antonio, 53, 56, 57, 81, 149, 269n

private vs. public sphere, 11, 120, 144, 211, 217

productivisim, 49, 63, 92, 104, 151, 266n

propaganda, 9, 10, 12, 15, 19, 27, 35, 78–9, 80, 82, 87, 116, 119, 122, 123, 126, 131, 139, 145, 154, 196, 200, 205, 215; cultural studies of, 214–15

public opinion, 126, 135–41, 144, 163, 235–6, 306n

psychohistory, 51, 208–9, 226, 268n

purification, as fascist mission, 13, 36–7, 40, 117, 120, 134–5, 142, 144, 148, 163, 174, 202, 203, 207, 212, 213, 216, 218, 239

Putin, Vladimir, 189

Quisling, Vidkun, 74, 111–12, 114, 244

race, theories of, 16, 17, 32, 34, 38, 134

racial hatreds, 18, 32, 55, 174, 186, 257n; ethnic cleansing and, 116, 173, 190. *See also* anti-Semitism; Holocaust

radicalization (stage five), 18, 23, 148–71, 237–40, 289n–294n; challenges faced in,

148; decay into traditional
authoritarianism in, 148–50, 171; in
Germany, 150–1, 153, 158–64, 169–71,
291n–292n, 294n; Holocaust and, 150–1,
158–64, 171, 291n–292n; impulses of
leader vs. underlings in, 153–5; in Italy,
151–3, 164–9, 170, 171, 293n–294n;
normalization pressures in, 148–50,
151–3; Stalinism contasted with, 169–70;
war in, 155–8, 170–1, 237–8
ras, 61–2, 101, 147, 159, 164
Rauschning, Hermann, 306n–307n
Rauti, Pino, 184
Reagan, Ronald, 21
recruitment, 49–52, 62, 226, 267n–268n
Reich, Wilhelm, 208
Reichstag fire (1933), 107, 121
religion and fascism, 20, 63, 97, 174, 203–4;
political religion concept and, 213–14,
304n. *See also* Catholic Church,
Protestants
Republican Party (Germany), 176
revolution of 1918, 137
revolutions of 1848, 42, 43, 265n
Rex, 73–4, 203, 241
Ribbentrop, Joachim von, 85, 125, 130
Ricci, Renato, 267n
Riefenstahl, Leni, 305n
Risorgimento, 6, 37, 39, 252n
Rocco, Alfredo, 285n
Rockwell, George Lincoln, 201
Röhm, Ernst, 27, 51, 108, 260n, 304n
Romania, 24, 25, 31, 73, 78, 97, 111, 113, 214,
245
romanticism, 17, 258n
Roosevelt, Franklin D., 126, 192, 201
Roosevelt, Theodor, 34, 77, 126
Rosenberg, Alfred, 84, 112, 125, 284n
Rosselli brothers, 136, 154, 287n
Rossoni, Edmondo, 104, 131, 147, 152
Rothermere, Lord, 75
Rousseau, Jean-Jacques, 35, 263n
rule of law, 84, 121–2, 129, 142, 186. *See also*
constitutional systems; due process
Russia, 30, 39, 49, 76; post-Soviet,
neofascism in, 174, 188–9. *See also*
Bolshevik Revolution; Soviet Union

SA (Sturmabteilung, Brownshirts, Storm
Troopers), 107, 125, 130, 133–4, 267n;
Hitler's conflicts with, 101, 108, 129, 132;

violence and intimidation tactics of, 38,
67, 84, 95, 96, 99, 170
Sabiani, Simon, 272n
Salandra, Antonio, 89, 90, 102, 278n
Salazar, Antonio de Oliveira, 111, 150, 157,
193, 217–18
Salgado, Plinio, 192–3
Salò republic, 153, 168–9, 238
Salvemini, Gaetano, 120, 191, 216
Sarfatti, Margherita, 9
Scavenius, Erik, 112
Schieder, Wolfgang, 101, 117, 120
Schleicher, Kurt von, 68, 94, 95, 96, 102,
108, 118
Schleswig-Holstein, 64–6, 270n–271n
Schmitt, Carl, 140, 287n
Schmitt, Kurt, 146
Schönerer, Georg von, 26, 32, 47
Schönhuber, Franz, 185
Schröder, Kurt von, 100
Schuschnigg, Kurt, 97–8
Schwerin von Krosigk, Lutz Graf, 154,
290n
September 11, 2001, attacks, 174, 202
Serbs, Serbia, 25, 113, 116, 186, 189–91
Seyss-Inquart, Arthur, 112
shirts, colored, 9, 48, 66, 69, 72, 75, 90, 97,
150, 191, 192, 199, 201, 205, 216, 305n
Showa Research Association, 199
Silver Shirts (SS), 201
Sima, Horia, 97, 113
skinheads, 173, 175, 180–1, 186
Skorzeny, Otto, 168
Slovakia, 113, 245
Slovenes, Slovenia, 37, 59, 114, 189–90,
285n
Smith, Art J., 201
Smith, Gerald L. K., 201–2
social Darwinism, 16, 20, 34, 41, 104, 121,
155, 220, 262n
socialism, socialists, 3, 16, 25, 37, 39, 48–9,
50, 82–3, 269n; enmity towards, 5, 7, 10,
19, 56, 60–2, 63–4; government
participation of, 43–4, 267n; syndicalism
vs., 5–6; violence against, 27, 60–2, 64,
67
Socialist Reich Party (SRP), 176
sociological approaches, 209–11, 226
Solidarité Française, 69
Sontag, Susan, 305n
Sorel, Georges, 4, 32, 33, 38, 48

South Africa, 191–2, 247

Soviet Union, 39, 76, 85, 150, 200, 725; collapse of, 175, 180, 181; compared with Nazi Germany, 18, 85, 119, 126, 169–70, 171, 212; German campaign against and occupation of, 18, 113, 122, 132, 160–3, 170, 218, 279n; Stalin's radicalization of, 169–70; totalitarian paradigm and, 211–13. *See also* Bolshevik Revolution

space, political, 18, 28, 32, 39, 43, 49, 56, 62, 64, 65, 71, 72, 75, 76, 83–4, 110, 114, 115, 116, 118, 172, 175, 176, 182, 184, 185, 187, 195, 203

Spain, 43, 75, 157, 171, 193, 261n; authoritarian regime in, 78, 81, 111, 114, 115, 118, 149–50, 217, 306n; radical Right in, 53, 56, 57, 80–1, 115, 149–50, 203, 245, 269n

Spanish Civil War, 115, 138, 149

Spann, Othmar, 39

Speer, Albert, 12–13, 127, 284n

Spengler, Oswald, 36, 38

sports, 124, 143, 239

squadristi (Blackshirts) and *squadrismo*, 58–62, 99, 100, 101, 109–10, 131, 132, 147, 151, 156, 164, 170; "March on Rome" and, 87–8, 89–91, 109; in Po Valley, 60–2, 72, 82, 86

SS, 129, 133, 144, 146, 159, 163, 168, 170, 185, 197

Stalin, Joseph, 8, 18, 126, 207, 292n; totalitarian paradigm and, 211–13

Starace, Achille, 166

Stauffenberg, Klaus Schenk von, 39

Stein, Gertrude, 256n

Stennes, Walter, 101, 131

sterilization, 36–7, 134, 239, 257n

Sternhell, Zeev, 37, 38, 39, 69, 269n

Stöcker, Adolf, 47

Storm Troopers. *See* SA

Strasser, Gregor, 66, 68, 95–6, 108, 131, 147

Strasser, Otto, 66, 147

Strength Through Joy, 136, 144

Stresemann, Gustav, 51

structuralism, 127, 128, 153

students, 73, 123, 176, 178, 186, 231

Sturzo, Dom Luigi, 290n

subconscious, 34

suffrage, 3, 5, 35, 42–3, 45, 78, 193, 196, 198, 215, 264n, 273n

swastika, 26, 260n

Sweden, 36–7, 257n

Switzerland, 43

syndicalism, syndicalists, 4, 5–6, 33, 44, 49, 62, 203, 252n; in Italy, 131, 152

Szálasi, Ferenc, 57, 73, 113, 114

Taittinger, Pierre, 68

taking root (stage two), 23, 55–86, 224–6, 269n–275n; alliances with conservatives and, 57–8, 60–2; climate of polarization and, 85; comparative analysis of, 76–86; crisis of liberalism and, 77–80, 81; electoral politics and, 57, 64–8, 269n; emergence of leader and, 83; exhaustion of older political options and, 82–3; failed attempts at Bolshevik revolution and, 81; focusing of words and actions and, 55–6; hereditary predisposition and, 9, 76, 81–2, 253n; intellectual preparation and, 76–7; posing as "antipolitics" and, 58; pragmatic choices and, 56–8, 62–4, 83–4; transformation of movement into party and, 57; unsuccessful fascisms and, 68–75; wartime defeat and, 80–1

Taliban, 203, 204

Tambroni, Fernando, 177

Taylor, A. J. P., 155

Terboven, Joseph, 112

terror, "terrorists," 84, 107, 113, 121, 128, 129, 135–7, 159, 166, 178, 191, 202, 211, 212–13, 230–1, 285n

Thatcher, Margaret, 21, 185

Thyssen, Fritz, 66

Tiso, Father Josef, 113

Tito (Josip Broz), 189

Tocqueville, Alexis de, 3–4, 16

Togliatti, Palmiro, 300n

Tönnies, Ferdinand, 35

Toro, David, 197

Toscanini, Arturo, 52, 268n

totalitarianism, 37, 211–13, 222–3, 253n–254n, 303n–304n; as Fascist regime's aspiration, 151, 152, 284n; islands of separateness in, 122–3

trasformismo, 86, 275n

Trotsky, Leon, 81, 289n

Tudjman, Franjo, 191

Turati, Augusto, 152

Turati, Filippo, 89

25 Points, 17, 28, 215, 254n

Uganda, 191
unemployment, 19, 50, 92–4, 105, 137, 179–80, 181, 182, 211, 267n
Union of Russian People (URP), 188
Union Party, 201
unions under fascism, 10, 59, 123, 137, 144, 152, 195
United States, 36–7, 157, 161, 194, 257n; anti-Semitism in, 76–7, 201; fascist themes in politics of, 49, 174, 201–3, 220, 247–8, 267n, 299n–300n
unity, as fascist mission, 4, 6, 12, 32, 38, 40, 41, 57, 58, 63, 74, 111, 117, 142, 143, 145, 148, 188, 192, 193, 197, 198, 202, 203, 216, 218, 219
Uriburu, José, 193–4
Ustaša, 113–14, 191

Valois, Georges, 48, 68
van der Lubbe, Marinus, 107
Vargas, Getulio, 111, 193, 197, 297n–298n
Vecchi, Ferruccio, 7
veterans, 5, 27, 28, 30, 49, 53, 62, 63, 84, 226, 261n, 267n. *See also* Arditi
Vichy France, 9, 71, 112–13, 157, 177, 217, 218, 243–4, 272n, 293n
victimhood, sense of, 41, 218, 219, 264n
Victor Emmanuel III, king of Italy, 120, 122, 131, 165, 168; in Fascists' route to power, 89, 90, 97, 110, 118, 275n
violence, 5, 7, 49, 67, 77, 99, 274n, 276n; aesthetics of, 32, 34–5, 84–5, 155, 186; pragmatic use of, 84–5. *See also* SA; *squadristi* and *squadrismo*
Visconti, Luchino, 301n
Vivarelli, Roberto, 106
Vlaams Blok, 186, 187
Volpe, Gioacchino, 140
Vorticism, 40

Wagener, Otto, 10, 146, 147, 254n, 288n–289n

Wagner, Richard, 32, 261n,
Wannsee Conference (1942), 160
war, 17, 63, 173, 186; aesthetics of, 34–5, 263n; economic policy and, 145, 147; radicalization and, 155–8, 170–1, 237–8
Weimar Republic, 65, 67, 80, 82, 121, 133, 135, 147, 274n; constitutional crisis in, 92–6, 99, 102–3, 105–6, 227
Weichardt, Louis, 191
welfare programs, 135, 147, 181, 187
White Defence League, 178
Wilhelmina, queen of Netherlands, 112
Wilson, Woodrow, 31
Winrod, Gerald B., 201
women, 85, 275n; in fascist regimes, 139, 143, 165, 233–5, 286n–287n; suffrage for, 5, 43, 196
working class, 32, 43, 47, 66, 79, 103, 115, 194–5; containment of, 10, 136–7, 144, 233; fascist recruits from, 50–1, 84, 103, 228, 233, 267n–268n; nationalism and, 26, 46, 48, 83
World War I, 34, 43, 59, 60, 85, 91, 100, 103, 105, 146, 172, 261n; German reparations for, 67, 92, 93; Italian entry into, 4, 5, 6, 28; political space for fascism opened by, 28–32; turmoil following, 8, 24–8, 30–2, 78–80

Yeats, W. B., 75
Yeltsin, Boris, 189
Young Plan, 67, 92, 93
youth: organizations, 138–9, 143–4, 150, 152, 231, 286n, 288n; appeal of fascism to, 9, 53, 62, 83, 103, 138, 143. *See also* students
Yrigoyen, Hipólito, 193
Yugoslavia, 31, 59, 78, 113–14, 270n; postcommunist, 189–91

Zentrum (Center Party), 92, 94, 102–3, 107–8
Zhirinovsky, Vladimir, 188–9